Cover: *Rock carvings, Sanilac County, Michigan.*

Design by Betty E. Odle.

JAMES E. FITTING

THE ARCHAEOLOGY
OF MICHIGAN

A GUIDE TO THE
PREHISTORY
OF THE GREAT LAKES REGION

CRANBROOK INSTITUTE OF SCIENCE

BLOOMFIELD HILLS, MICHIGAN

1975

BULLETIN 56

First edition (1970) published by Doubleday & Company, Inc. Second and revised edition (1975) published by Cranbrook Institute of Science in agreement with Doubleday & Company, Inc.

PREFACE TO THE SECOND EDITION

When an author prepares a book, it is an individual statement. He anticipates the uses of the book but the final result is often something else. The first edition of this book was well-received and became the text in at least four universities and two colleges in Michigan. Within three years of its publication, it was out-of-print. After some negotiation, reprint rights were released to Cranbrook Institute of Science. Robert Bowen, Director of the Institute, was instrumental in bringing this edition to press. He initially suggested that I might want to rewrite and update the second edition; there had certainly been enough new information coming out of the ground to warrant such a revision. However, although the pace of field work in the state has quickened, the pace of analysis and reporting has slackened.

Virtually all of the published monographic material of the past seven years represents information which was available to me in unpublished form when *The Archaeology of Michigan* was written. This would include Janzen's (1968) study of Naomikong Point, Bigony's (1969) analysis of three Saginaw Valley Late Woodland sites, Brose's (1970a, 1970b) study of Summer Island, the portions of Flanders' doctoral dissertation dealing with the North Mound Group (Griffin, Flanders and Titterington, 1970), the Lasanen site report (Cleland, editor, 1971), the Schultz site report (Fitting, editor, 1972), the Moccasin Bluff site report (Bettral and Smith, 1973), the Monroe County Survey report (Brose and Essenpreis, 1973), and the Kantzler site report (Crum-

ley 1973). Lyle Stone has completed a massive monograph on the 1959 through 1966 excavations at Fort Michilimackinac (Stone 1975) and there are studies of both ceramics (Miller and Stone, 1970) and glass (Brown 1971) but these cover work that was reported in at least preliminary form in the first edition of *The Archaeology of Michigan*.

Four monographs, dealing with either excavations or restudies, were initiated after 1968. Three of these deal with the archaeology of the St. Ignace area. They include the preliminary report on the Marquette Mission site (Stone 1972a), a significant restudy of the Gros Cap Cemetery (Nern and Cleland, 1974), and a study of the archaeology of several smaller sites in the St. Ignace area (Fitting, editor, 1974). The other is Richard Wilkinson's study (1971) of the biological relationships of several skeletal populations in the Great Lakes area.

There are also several unpublished dissertations and theses that deal with Michigan sites and collections. It is my hope that several of these will eventually be made available in a more accessible form. Among the more significant are reports on the Mikado Earthwork (Carruthers 1969), the Winter site (Richner 1973), the O'Neil site and its relation to the Traverse Corridor (Lovis 1973), a regional study of the Muskegon River Valley (Prahl 1970), and an analysis of Fletcher ceramics (Brashler 1973).

This presents a difficult situation for an author attempting to update a book. Most of the published literature was considered in at least a preliminary form in the original volume, but most of the really significant field work which has been carried out in the past seven years has not been reported. While I have been able to make a preliminary study of many of the site collections, this is of little value without the knowledge of context which only the excavator controls.

I fully realize that a quality site report may take years to write and a regional study will take even longer. At this point, a major revision of *The Archaeology of Michigan* without the results of the Traverse Corridor and Inland Waterway projects, without the Fletcher site analysis with its important prehistoric and historic components, and without reports on the important Sand Point, Winter and Zemaitis sites, would be a futile effort.

Also, the focus of much of the research during the past seven years has been different from that of the previous decade. It has become more regionally directed and less centered on specific site interpretation. Many of the major projects have involved little or no excavation and the accumulation of very few artifacts. There is little to describe from these surveys, although treating the sites themselves as artifacts in the regional pattern of settlements is rather exciting. It is also difficult to interpret these surveys at this stage in a summary volume such as this. The Monroe County survey (Brose and Essenpreis, 1973) is the only generally available published example of such a regional survey report. Most professional archaeologists have strong reservations about making their survey data available to the public for fear that, through the thoughtless actions of those individuals who are more interested in artifacts that in site information, their survey reports will lead to the destruction of the very sites that they are trying to protect. For the time being, this survey information must remain in a series of manuscripts and files throughout the state although some time in the future it may be used to give a whole new interpretation to the archaeology of Michigan.

Another factor that would need to be taken into account in making major revisions is the changing research orientation of the author. In the past seven years I have become disillusioned, quite frankly, with the entire concept of a "scientific archaeology." My own patterns of thinking have shifted from positivistic to rationalistic to humanistic. In the first edition, I had the belief that we actually could learn things about the past. As I became disillusioned with this idea, I adopted the position that we could learn things about the patterning of human activity which could be applied to the past. I now view all archaeological interpretations as being essentially subjective. Cloaking them in the guise of "science" and "empirical verifiability" adds an aura of pseudoscience but does not really make them scientific. Several reviewers of the book have noted that the original volume was primarily a statement of my own ideas and interpretations. I can accept this and feel that if I were to rewrite it totally, it would be an even more honestly subjective account of Michigan's past. However, in the same way that the moment is not yet upon us for totally rewriting the volume because of the particular state of data reporting and interpretation, my own thinking on what is important in archaeological interpretation is in flux and I am not yet at the point where I could articulate an entire book with this orientation. Therefore, major revisions must wait until we are again on an intellectual and descriptive plateau.

In discussing the volume, Robert Bowen and I concluded that it would be best, in terms of both the present state of knowledge and interpretation, and the economics of publishing, to reissue the book in essentially its original form. At the same time, we decided to include an extended preface to the second edition which would take into account the new data of the past seven years. That is how this introductory section came to be written.

SINCE THE FIRST EDITION

The original manuscript of *The Archaeology of Michigan* was completed in May of 1968, submitted to the Natural History Press at that time, and published in the fall of 1970. For the preceding eight years, I had worked closely with Michigan archaeology, first as a student and later as a faculty member at Wayne State University and the University of Michigan. In the fall of 1968, I joined the faculty of Case Western Reserve University in Cleveland, Ohio, and for the first time in my life became a resident of another state. Between the summer of 1968 and the summer 1972, I had little time to participate actively in Michigan field programs. I still had a strong interest in Michigan, and during these years I was able to complete some projects that had been postponed for a long time (Fitting and Sassé, 1969; Devissher, Wahla, and Fitting, 1970; Butterfield and Fitting, 1971; Fitting, editor, 1972). I was able to make some studies of museum collections (Fitting 1970, 1971a) and, most important, rethink and redefine many of the ideas which I had started to develop in *The Archaeology of Michigan* (Fitting

1969, 1971b, 1972b, 1972c; Fitting n.d.e, n.d.k, n.d.l; Fitting and Zurel, n.d.).

My field research during this period, however, was in New Mexico and Central America; the task of pursuing the raw data of Michigan archaeology was left to others. The archaeology explosion discussed in this book continued to resound. The most spectacular programs were those carried out by Michigan State University. Charles E. Cleland, later assisted by William Lovis, continued to direct the Traverse Corridor project. They expanded their survey efforts into the inland waterway area between Cheboygan and Petoskey. In addition, they carried out numerous smaller excavations and survey projects throughout the state as well as the study of private collections. James Brown directed several seasons of field work at Fort Michilimackinac and the Fletcher site in Bay City before leaving Michigan. His work made this latter project the second largest excavation ever carried out in Michigan (after Fort Michilimackinac). This additional work added information on Middle and Late Woodland and earlier historic components unknown at the time *The Archaeology of Michigan* was written.

For the past several years, Joseph Chartkoff of the Department of Anthropology at Michigan State University has directed field school excavations at the Clark-Stringham and Root sites and directed extensive surveys along the middle Grand River and its tributaries.

Michigan State University has not been the only institution with an active field program. Western Michigan University spent several seasons at the Sand Point site near Baraga with a field school under the supervision of Winston Moore; a single season at the important Winter site on the Garden Peninsula with a program supervised by Jeffrey Richner; a combined season of survey in the Kalamazoo River Valley and excavation at the Schmidt site in the Saginaw Valley under the supervision of Jerry Fairchild. Grand Valley State College has continued a summer field school program under the supervision of Richard Flanders with excavations of particular significance at the Zemaitis site. Flanders has also supervised a continuing survey of the lower Grand River Valley as well.

Marla Buckmaster has developed a field program through Northern Michigan University over the past few years and has emphasized a site survey and testing program throughout the upper peninsula. In addition to collecting site information on the Marquette area, she has concentrated intensively over the past few years on the Menominee River Valley, a key and heretofore little known region.

Central Michigan Univeristy has attempted to develop a field school in several areas. In the early 1970s, Kenneth Carstens directed survey and excavations at a number of sites including Tobico and Tyra. In 1973, the Central Field School worked at the Mill Creek site under the supervision of Patrick Martin; they also established a cooperative program with the Chippewa Nature Center.

Smaller schools have also developed field programs throughout the state. Michigan Technological University has carried out both college and high school training programs at the Cliff, a 19th century historic mining community, first under the supervision of Elinor Deling and later under Marie Campbell. Richard Clute has initiated a survey and testing program in the Alpena area through Alpena Community College and the Besser Museum. Saginaw Valley College has twice had a field school at the Troggen

site under the supervision of Bernard Spencer.

The Chippewa Nature Center in Midland has initiated an intensive survey of Midland County and carried out excavations in the Oxbow Archaeological District as a part of its summer day camp program. More recently, it has collaborated with the Central Michigan University field school.

The Mackinac Island State Park Commission has continued its exemplary work at Fort Michilimackinac. In addition, they have initiated a major project at the nearby Mill Creek site and sponsored work on Mackinac Island and in St. Ignace.

Early in the 1970s, the Michigan History Division (formerly the Michigan Historical Commission) of the Department of State became interested in Michigan archaeology. In the summer of 1972, while directing field work on Mackinac Island and in St. Ignace for the Mackinac Island State Park Commission, I was invited by the Division to accept the position as the first State Archaeologist of Michigan.

Almost immediately, the Michigan History Division became involved in several small field projects. In 1973 we carried out a number of major projects in St. Ignace and at the Carp River Forge near Negaunee. In 1974, the Division was involved in more than a dozen excavations and survey projects throughout the state in both state and municipal parks and on private lands. From a small beginning, the Michigan History Division has come to play a major role in the pursuit of Michigan archaeology.

The Michigan Archaeological Society has continued to grow and prosper during the past seven years. In 1974 the Society received a certificate from the American Association for State and Local History for its ongoing programs of publication and amateur training as well as for its key role in preserving the Sanilac Petroglyph site and bringing that site into public ownership. In addition to the contributions of its individual members, the Society has participated on a formal basis with the Mackinac Island State Park Commission in a training program in historic sites archaeology at Fort Michilimackinac and at the Mill Creek site. In the summer of 1974, the Society established a short training course in prehistoric sites archaeology as well.

In short, the amount of archaeological investigation which has been carried out in the past seven years in the state is little short of overwhelming, and its diversity is far greater than that of the preceding century. Throughout the preparation of this second edition of *The Archaeology of Michigan*, the scope and diversity presented both a pleasure and a challenge. Particularly gratifying was the emphasis on small projects and on surveys where literally thousands of new sites have been uncovered.

THE PALEO-INDIAN OCCUPATION

The past seven years has not been a good period for the discovery of Paleo-Indian sites in Michigan, and there has been little in the way of new interpretation or information. The Barnes site in Midland County was finally excavated in the summer of 1974 by field crews from the Chippewa Nature Center in Midland working under the supervision of Fel Burnett. Their work was partially supported by the State Historic Preservation Grant administered by the Michigan History Division. Since the report on this work has not yet been prepared, all I can

present is the information that, in actual excavation, this was an extremely low density site and that very few additional artifacts were recovered. A preliminary examination indicates that the 1974 collection essentially supports the interpretations made over a decade ago by Wright and Roosa. Roosa, however, suggested in a letter of January 1975 that the site may have been occupied because it was in an ecotonal situation on an old beach ridge rather than on an active beach ridge.

In the fall of 1972, Donald Peru, formerly of Grand Rapids and now a resident of Phoenix, Arizona, sent me a number of artifacts which he had collected from a site in Harrison Township in Muskegon County. They included several points and bases similar to those from the Holcombe site. In 1973, Ida Yaggie called my attention to several Paleo-Indian projectile points which she had obtained from the same general area in Harrison Township over a period of years. We planned text excavations at the site in 1973, but the press of emergency salvage projects prevented this. However, in the spring of 1974, a small field crew from the Michigan History Division spent one week testing the site (Clarke 1974). It proved to be a highly disturbed blowout area. Artifacts from several time periods were mixed, deposits were disturbed, and no Paleo-Indian material was found, making it unlikely that such material would be uncovered *in situ* in the future.

In recent years, Wahla and Devisscher (1969) have given formal definition to the Holcombe point, and a series of additional sites along the Holcombe beach ridge have been the subject of a written report (DeVisscher, Wahla and Fitting, 1970). Two areas were excavated adjacent to the original University of Michigan excavations, and two new Paleo-Indian localities and a mixed Paleo-Indian/Archaic occupation area were excavated in the neighborhood of the site but at some distance from the main concentration. The two areas near the site served to round out the symmetry of the occupation since they represent additional family areas. The two new locations, Holcombe North and Holcombe South, represent small, low density, short-term occupations. These excavations added 96 artifacts to the Holcombe Beach inventory including 27 additional point bases.

Roosa, in a letter written in 1973, suggested that descriptions which I gave in the first edition of *The Archaeology of Michigan* were confusing and not exactly what he had described for these point types. To correct these errors of interpretation, I cite Roosa's definitions in full from his 1965 article:

"There appear to be at least two basic fluting techniques, i.e., the Folsom technique and the Enterline technique. The Enterline fluting technique is distinguished from the Folsom technique chiefly by the fact that there was little beveling and re-beveling of the base to provide a striking platform on Enterline points. The cross section of the base of an unfluted Enterline point was roughly symmetrical, not beveled as with the Folsom technique. After the first face was fluted, the Enterline point was turned over and the second face fluted with little or no rebeveling of the base. Fluting of the two faces of an Enterline point was done from essentially the same striking platform.

"The Folsom technique involved beveling the base plus careful chipping and grinding of the striking platform prior to fluting the first face. After fluting one face the base was extensively rebeveled, thus removing the remains of the old striking platform. Finally a new striking platform was carefully chipped and ground for fluting the second face. In short, the Folsom technique used two carefully prepared striking platforms, one for fluting each face.

"The Folsom technique utilized a wavy basal outline with a very convex striking platform in the center. The Enterline technique started with a straighter base. The striking platforms in both cases were ground or smoothed prior to fluting, however, the Folsom technique involved more elaborate preparation of the striking platform. Both techniques used two preliminary flutes or "guide flakes" prior to the removal of the central flute. "Guide flakes" on Folsom points were quite small compared to the main central flute which followed and often obliterated them. The preliminary side flutes on Enterline points were often as long as or longer than the central flute. In some cases they were so large as to preclude the need for a central flute, resulting in double fluting. The central flute often failed to obliterate the preliminary side flutes on Enterline Points.

"Several Eastern fluted point types which I have designated as Barnes, Bull Brook and Parrish points often employed a basal thinning technique after removal of the main central flute. In this technique one or two large percussion flakes were removed from the base (usually on the last face fluted) to remove the remains of the striking platform and thin the base for hafting. This technique occurs mainly on the thicker points. These flakes often overlap each other and override the central flute, giving the effect of triple fluting . . .

"Fluting length on Enterline points is usually less than that of points with the Folsom technique. Folsom-type fluting usually runs for at least 30 to 40 mm and is 8 to 10 mm wide. Enterline fluting seldom is this long, and the individual flute scars are rarely this wide. Length of fluting on Enterline points is roughly equal to the basal width of the point. Length of fluting on points with Folsom-type fluting is usually much greater than the basal width of the point. The basal concavity resulting from Folsom-type fluting is usually deeper than those produced by Enterline-type fluting. There is some overlap in size of flute scars, etc., but these simple "rules of thumb" will often help to identify the two kinds of fluting . . .

"Bull Brook, Barnes, and Parrish points all

share the Folsom fluting technique and the Barnes finishing technique. Differences between the three types are largely matters of point size and length of fluting. Using only fluting technique as the criterion for forming the type cluster we must include Folsom points and Cumberland points in the same cluster. Both Folsom and Cumberland points form another type cluster in that they share the Folsom fluting technique and the Folsom finishing technique. Thus we have two small type clusters within the larger type cluster of points with Folsom fluting technique. There are probably several other local types within the Bull Brook, Barnes, and Parrish type clusters. It is of interest to note that Clovis points *sensu strictu* appear to fall into another type cluster which uses a different fluting technique . . .

"Clovis fluted points *sensu strictu* are one of many types of partly fluted points. Maximum width is usually at or slightly below the midpoint; thus many Clovis points have relatively long sharp tips. Clovis points have a non-Folsom fluting technique in which there was some beveling and re-beveling of the base to provide striking platforms for fluting the two faces, but little or no careful chipping and grinding to prepare the striking platforms. In other words, the Clovis technique lacked the carefully prepared striking platform so characteristic of the Folsom technique. Finished Clovis points have very shallow basal concavities (on the order of 1 mm to 4 mm) and never have remnants of a basal nipple. Clovis points usually have short multiple (double or triple) fluting. On triple fluted Clovis points the central flute was removed first, followed by two smaller side flutes or finishing flakes which served to widen the base of the flute. These flakes overlap the edges of the central flute slightly but usually do not overlap each other or obscure the basal portion of the central flute. True Clovis points show little, if any, pressure chipping."

Little additional formal work has been done on distributional studies and correlation with lake levels and Paleo-Indian artifact styles in Michigan over the past few years. Much more has been done

along these lines in Ontario where several major sites, particularly the Brophy site excavated by Roosa, show portents of adding significantly to our knowledge of early Paleo-Indian occupation in the Great Lakes area. I suggested in the first edition that Hi-Lo points were part of an Early Paleo-Indian assemblage. Typologically, I still feel this is true. However, survey and excavation data from the Lake St. Clair basin, carried out by Centela and DeVisscher on the American side and Deller on the Canadian side have all demonstrated that this point type is found consistently below 605 feet above sea level. This would require either dating this point type to the period after the first phase of Lake Algonquin or re-examining the entire lake sequence within the Lake St. Clair basin which would then necessitate a re-interpretation of Holcombe site dating. At present, it would seem best to consider these points as Late Paleo-Indian artifacts.

The correlation of the "Mason-Quimby" line and the distribution of proboscidea remains have continued to fascinate researchers in the area. Weston (n.d.b) has suggested that the distribution of fluted points is related to the distribution of large Late Pleistocene vertebrates. The migration routes of these animals and man were blocked by "1) a geological barrier, that is, the Ubly outlet channel of glacial Lake Whittlesey, once drained, developed an extensive swampland and this still exists today within the former channel at the base of the Port Huron Moraine; and 2) an ecological barrier, that is, the higher, better drained areas along and to the north of the Port Huron Moraine developed a considerably different upland environment." Still, additional fluted points have been found along the high terraces of the Manistee River by Ursum, and there is a fluted point, unfortunately of uncertain provenience, in the collections of the Marquette County Historical Society in the upper peninsula. If the occurrence of fluted points can be documented in the upper peninsula, we most certainly will be required to reevaluate our ideas on Paleo-Indian adaptive patterns in the Great Lakes area.

The distribution of Late Paleo-Indian materials has also been a relatively unproductive area of study in recent years. Many researchers are convinced that sites similar to George Lake and Shequiandah will eventually be found along high beaches in the upper peninsula, but the several intensive searches that have been carried out by institutions in that area have, to date, been unproductive.

In the lower peninsula, results of investigations of the Late Paleo-Indian Satchell complex have been ambiguous. Fairchild, in his analysis of the Kralosky site (1970: 33, 35) dated stemmed points of argillite as prior to 5000 B.C. Wahla (1969) and Fincham (1970) used a range of 2000 to 6000 years ago as the age of such artifacts. The only concrete evidence came from the Pinegrove cemetery site in Genessee County (Simons 1972). At that site, a date of 1060 B.C. ± 110 was obtained on a charcoal sample from a hearth with stemmed Satchell complex points of argillite. This seems to support Roosa's contention that some, if not all, of the stemmed argillite material is Late Archaic.

A final note needs to be made on the cultural material recovered from the Tolles site and related sites by Peru (1969), although the temporal placement of this "X" complex is not certain. This complex is known on the basis of surface collections from several sites in western Michigan. The Tolles site itself, located in Van Buren County, has produced 1200 tools but no projectile points. The tools were blade and flake knives, micro-gravers and burins, which accounted for 25 percent of all the artifacts. Peru suggests that this industry has its closest similarities to assemblages from both the Arctic and the Siberian Paleolithic. It is certainly unusual in Michigan and Peru's suggestion that it might be of Paleo-Indian age, or older, should be considered.

THE ARCHAIC AND EARLY WOODLAND PERIOD

The problem of Early and Middle Archaic materials in Michigan, or the lack of them, continues to be a major concern in Michigan archaeology. The number of surface finds of projectile points similar to those dating to the period of 8000 to 2500 B.C. in the southeastern United States has continued to increase but no specific sites suitable for excavation have been identified.

The majority of sites from the slightly later Late Archaic period are concentrated in the southern part of the state, although several important ones have been excavated in the north as well. Since we can assume that Early and Middle Archaic settlement systems were probably similar to those of the Late Archaic, and the essentially southern distribution of Early and Middle Archaic projectile point styles would support this, then we would expect to find sites of this period along old shorelines in the south. It is in these southern areas that the shorelines from the period of 7000 to 2200 B.C. are now submerged under up to 400 feet of water. In the northern parts of the lower peninsula and in the upper peninsula, there has been enough post-glacial uplift to preserve shorelines dating to this time, but this uplift has taken place in areas that were not open to settlement by peoples with a pattern of winter population concentration and summer population dispersal.

The main winter village sites of Early and Middle Archaic peoples, if they exist, are now under the waters of the Great Lakes. While underwater archaeological survey has been initiated in Michigan in the past few years, the small amount done has been directed toward shipwrecks. Even these large features, most of which are less than a century old, are difficult to deal with because of intensive silting. It appears as if it will be almost impossible to locate and identify the much more fragile prehistoric resources that must exist on the bottom lands of the Great Lakes.

Another theory which has been proposed, primarily by Jerry Fairchild in a paper in *The Michigan Archaeologist* (1970) and which will be the subject of his master's thesis at Western Michigan University, contends that much of the cultural material which has been considered to be Late Archaic in the Saginaw Valley, and by extension in the rest of the state, is actually from the Middle Archaic period. This includes Brewerton-like projectile points and, possibly, the distinctive ground base projectile points identified as a separate type by Butterfield and Stroebel (1960) some time ago.

Apparently, this position is supported by the still unpublished results of excavations carried out by the Western Michigan University field school at the Schmidt site in 1973. The Central Michigan University excavations at the Lalone site (Carstens 1970) also identified a Middle Archaic component although the latter site, located at an elevation of 620 feet above sea level,

would not have been submerged during the late high water stages as the Schmidt site seems to have been.

The 1974 Michigan Archaeological Society—Michigan History Division excavations at the Young site in the Saginaw Valley (Fitting n.d.i) could also be interpreted as supporting this position. However, a more parsimonious explanation for this Feeheley-like Archaic component located at an elevation of 585 feet above sea level might be that the occupation took place at a low water interval between the Lake Nipissing high of 605 feet above sea level (ca. 2200 B.C.) and the 595 feet of the Algoma level (ca. 1000 B.C.). In any event, the evidence for a Middle Archaic component in at least the Saginaw Valley is stronger now than in 1968 although still not overwhelming.

Few Late Archaic sites have been excavated and reported in recent years either. The Young site in the Saginaw Valley (Fitting n.d.i) has an Archaic component which is very similar to that from the Feeheley site which has been radiocarbon dated to approximately 1900 B.C. Since almost all of the cultural material is from the plow zone, it adds little to our understanding of this period. This is also true for most of the other Late Archaic components reported, such as those from the Clark-Stringham site in Jackson County (Joseph Chartkoff: personal communication), 20 BY 31 (Butterfield and Fitting, 1971) and the Lalone site in Arenac County (Carstens 1970).

Griffin (1972) has reported on a socketted copper spear point from the Whitefish Bay region on Lake Superior. A Late Archaic site with a number of copper artifacts, the Nelson site, was briefly tested in the city of St. Ignace by a Michigan History Division field party in the summer of 1973 (Fitting 1974b). The Nelson site contained a number of chipped stone projectile points that were most similar to those from Lake Forest Middle Woodland sites in the area, suggesting a close continuity between Late Archaic and what James V. Wright has referred to as the Initial Woodland of the region.

In the first edition of *The Archaeology of Michigan*, and in a subsequent paper (Fitting n.d.1), it was suggested that the major difference between Late Archaic-Early Woodland settlement systems and Middle Woodland settlement systems was a polar reversal of the seasonal pattern with a shift from winter population concentration to summer population concentration. The Nelson site and a second Late Archaic site tested in St. Ignace, SIS-21 (Fitting and Fisher, n.d.), both appear to be low density summer sites similar to the Feeheley and Young sites in the Saginaw Valley.

If there had been pressure to winter north of the "edge" in the central part of the lower peninsula, (the distribution of copper artifacts testify to the importance of the northern areas), then the greatest pressure on the Late Archaic-Early Woodland seasonal pattern would have been above the "edge" where a new settlement system would have been necessary for the effective use of this region. Therefore, it is possible that the development of the Chippewa type of settlement system did take place in this area. This interpretation is supported by the series of early dates which have emerged in the last five years for the Saugeen Complex of Ontario and the North Bay I component in Wisconsin. Both date to the sixth century B.C. Therefore, there are fully ceramic sites with summer population concentrations in the north in the same period as the Archaic (Butterfield), or Early Woodland sites with an Archaic settle-

ment system (Schultz, Kantzler), in the Saginaw region. The Chippewa system does not spread back to the southern parts of the lower peninsula of Michigan until some time around 100 B.C. or later.

The entire problem of the Early Woodland occupation of Michigan has remained essentially unchanged over the past few years. The report on the Kantzler site has now been published (Crumley 1973) and Doreen Oskar is writing a doctoral dissertation at the University of Michigan on the Early Woodland living floors at the Schultz site but, as of this writing, her analysis is not yet completed. Several Early Woodland sherds were recovered from the Fletcher site (Brashler 1973) but there does not appear to have been a major Early Woodland component at that site.

The problem of Adena in Michigan has been reviewed by Fitting and Brose (1971). An additional Adena site has come to light since then although it was actually excavated in the 1930s. This is the Bicknell site in St. Ignace (Fitting 1974a) which is located on the first terrace above the Halberg site in St. Ignace, a Late Woodland site excavated by Charles Cleland in 1967. The Bicknell site is a small sand mound containing a single burial with several large bifacial blades, including one of flint ridge flint, a copper celt, and a blocked-end tubular pipe. The site appears to be similar to, but less elaborate than, the Adena mound excavated at Killarney Bay approximately 90 miles to the east of St. Ignace.

Another Adena occupation has been identified at the Dunn Farm site (Brose 1974) on the Leelanau Peninsula where Brose found cache blades and a blocked-end tubular pipe. This site has also produced wild rice.

THE MIDDLE WOODLAND PERIOD

The first observation which I would like to make on Middle Woodland is to correct a typographical error which occurred in the last paragraph of page 98 of the 1970 edition of the book. The first and second sentences should have read, "Evidences of trade connections between Hopewell Middle Woodland and Lake Forest Middle Woodland groups are slight. Much of the Hopewell Middle Woodland copper probably came from the Lake Superior region and there is evidence that goods moved back to the North."

Several of the major projects dealing with Hopewell Middle Woodland sites, which were cited from manuscript in 1968 have since been published (Griffin, Flanders and Titterington, 1970 for the Norton Mounds; Fitting, editor, 1972 for the Schultz site; Crumley 1973 for the Kantzler Site; Betteral and Smith, 1973 for the Moccasin Bluff site). In addition, Brose's 1966 survey of Monroe County, demonstrating the absence of Hopewell Middle Woodland sites in that area, has been published (Brose and Essenpreis, 1973) and Prahl has completed his study of the Muskegon Valley as a doctoral dissertation at the University of Michigan (1970) which is available in microfilm form. I was also able to restudy the 1885 Coffinberry collections from the Converse Mound in Grand Rapids and prepare a report on this material (Fitting 1971a).

The most significant Hopewell Middle Woodland excavation to be carried out has probably been the work of Dr. Richard Flanders at the Zemaitis site on the Grand River below Grand Rapids. This is a continuing project and no report has yet appeared. In some respects, it is similar to the Spoonville Village site along the Grand River reported on earlier by Flanders. It contains a mixture of specifically Hopewell Middle Woodland ceramic types along with a generalized Woodland component marked by relatively simple globular cordmarked ceramic vessels. In examining some of the collections, I have noted a great deal of Lake Forest Middle Woodland influence in some of the ceramics. Some sherds are very similar to those of the Saugeen Focus in Ontario which has consistently been dated to the sixth and seventh century B.C. The final report on this site could cause major revision in our thinking on Michigan Middle Woodland.

Two additional Hopewell Middle Woodland Village sites have been located in western Michigan. While both have been tested, neither has been subjected to major excavation. These are the Hacklander site on the Kalamazoo River, initially tested by Dr. Elizabeth Baldwin, and the Ayen Site on the West Maple River north of Lansing, discovered by Dr. Joseph Chartkoff.

In the Saginaw Valley, Hopewell Middle Woodland materials furnish a minor but significant component at the Fletcher site in Bay City (Brashler 1973). I have observed some Hopewell influence in collections from the Tyra Site, excavated by Mr. Arthur Graves and a field school party from Central Michigan University, and at the Bugai site excavated by Graves. The Bugai site has produced a platform pipe, and Graves has also found a broken platform pipe while collecting at the Schultz site at Green Point.

Our knowledge of the extent and range of Lake Forest Middle Woodland manifestations in the state has increased considerably during the past seven years. Fitting and Brose (1971: 35) have suggested that some of the ceramics from the

Leimbach site in northern Ohio may even be a part of this tradition although this has been contested by Prufer and Shane (n.d.). There is little question that Lake Forest Middle Woodland ceramics similar to those from the Goodwin-Gresham site are found in the Port Huron area along the St. Clair River (Fitting 1970: 92; Fitting and Zurel, n.d.). Interestingly enough, one additional component with ceramics similar to those from the Goodwin-Gresham site has been identified at the Saari-Miller site, along the shores of Lake Superior near Marquette, by Professor Marla Buckmaster of Northern Michigan University (Franzen and Weston, 1973).

Many surveys have produced traces of more classic Laurel-like ceramics which are now known from sites near Ossineke in Alpena County (Fitting 1970: 103), Mackinac City (Stone 1972b), and in both Chippewa (Franzen 1975) and Mackinac (Fitting and Fisher, n.d.; Fitting and Weston, 1974) counties. Several small excavated sites in St. Ignace have produced these ceramics, including the Ferrier (Lynott 1974), Sposito (Fitting and Cushman, 1974), and Norge Village (Fitting and Lynott, 1974) sites. The Gyftakis site, a major site of this component, was excavated by the Michigan History Division in 1973 (Fitting n.d.f). This latter site was a beach occupation dating to the third century which contained an ossuary burial similar to that found at the Arrowhead Drive site on nearby Bois Blanc Island.

In her survey of the Menominee Watershed in the western part of the upper peninsula of Michigan, Marla Buckmaster has discovered several Middle Woodland components not related to the North Bay culture in Wisconsin. Perhaps the most fascinating site in the general region,

however, is the Winter site excavated in the summer of 1972 by a field school from Western Michigan University under the supervision of Jeffrey Richner. While the findings concerning the ceramics from this site have not yet been published, a report on the excavations and lithic material has been prepared by Richner (1973). The Winter site is located on the Garden Peninsula; yet, in spite of its relative proximity to both the Summer Island and Eckdahl-Goodneau sites, it is distinct from both the Summer Island and Laurel traditions. At least one sherd has a combination of Lake Forest decorative techniques and Havana-zoned decoration. This may be a trade sherd, as I would interpret those from the Holtz site (Lovis 1971), or it could represent a local reinterpretation of an Illinois motif, as has been suggested by Fischer (1972) for the ceramics at the Schultz site.

The transition from Middle to Late Woodland also presents a number of problems in interpretation. Several sites have been identified as transitional in the northern area, including the Steiner site in St. Ignace (Fitting and Fisher, n.d.), several sites in the Traverse Corridor and inland waterway area (Dr. William Lovis: personal communication) and the Fisher Lake site on the Leelanau Peninsula (Brose 1974). In western Michigan, Dr. Richard Flanders (personal communication) believes that both Spoonville and the Zemaitis sites may represent such a transition. The best documentation for such a transition may be in southeastern Michigan where Prahl, Brose, and Stothers (n.d.) have identified the Western Basin Complex dating to the period of A.D. 500 to A.D. 700. This is contemporary with, and influenced by, the Princess Point Complex in Ontario (Stothers n.d.). An understanding of this transition, however, must be based on broader field evidence and the development of the appropriate interpretive models for explaining such a change.

THE LATE WOODLAND PERIOD

Late Woodland sites in the state are numerous and much work has been done in sites of this period in recent years. Rather than discuss them as a single group, it seems preferable to deal with them by the sub-regions for the state as defined earlier.

In southwestern Michigan, Margaret B. Rogers (1972) has prepared a major report on the 46th Street and Fennville sites which were excavated by the Kalamazoo Chapter of the Michigan Archaeological Society and Western Michigan University. These are early Late Woodland sites with globular cordmarked ceramics similar to the Wayne Ware of southeastern Michigan. However, there are sufficient differences, in Roger's opinion, to warrant the establishment of a new ware category which she has called Allegan Ware.

Western Michigan University has also carried out work at a number of sites in the area. One of the major excavations, still unreported, is the Allegan Dam Site in Allegan County. The site contains a mixture of Woodland and Oneota ceramics and probably dates to around A.D. 1300. Another Western Michigan excavation was carried out at the Brainerd site (Cauble 1971), a site which produced skeletal material in what appeared to be a Late Woodland ossuary. The Darrel Coomer site in St. Joseph County, excavated by Richard Drum of the southwestern chapter of the Michigan Archaeological Society (Drum 1974), produced

no cultural material but contained a lodge outline and fire pit which are probably Late Woodland.

After many years, the report on the University of Michigan excavations at the Moccasin Bluff site in Berrien County has been completed (Bettarel and Smith, 1973). Bettarel and Smith recognize three phases of occupation at this site. The earliest occupation has a suggested date of A.D. 700 to A.D. 800 and has been referred to as the Brems Phase. It is marked by small triangular projectile points and globular, cordmarked ceramics with some collaring. The Moccasin Bluff Ware of this report includes ceramics that might have been called Allegan Ware or Wayne Ware in other Michigan studies.

The occupation of the period between A.D. 1050 and A.D. 1300 is called the Moccasin Bluff Phase. The earlier part of this phase is marked by the appearance of rimsherds from vessels with cordmarked bodies which have decorated lips. There is an increase through this period of shell-tempered cordmarked ceramics as well as evidence of an increased occupational density at the site.

The final occupation takes place in the Berrien Phase. This phase is marked by ceramics which are both shell-tempered and grit-tempered plain surface Oneota-like ceramics and ceramics with a notched applique rim or collar strip.

We have already mentioned the Zemaitis site in the Grand River Valley; this site may contain an early Late Woodland component as well as the Middle Woodland component. An enigmatic site, also near Grand Rapids, is the Haieght Mound which contained a single burial in a flexed position with no grave offerings. It was excavated by members of the Wright L. Coffinberry Chapter of the Michigan Archaeological Society (Prahl 1970: 346).

There was a single burial in a flexed position with no grave offerings in this mound. Despite any firm evidence, I would place Haieght Mound with other early Late Woodland burials in this part of the state.

Archaeological surveys have been conducted in the lower Grand River Valley by Dr. Richard Flanders, in the middle part of the valley by Dr. Joseph Chartkoff, and in the upper part of the valley by Dr. Charles Cleland. These have yielded information on the location of hundreds of sites. Chartkoff has undertaken more extensive excavations at two of these sites: the Clark-Stringham site in Jackson County in 1973 and the Root site in Ingham County in 1974. The former site contained a small, early Late Woodland component but virtually all of the cultural material from the site was recovered from the plow zone. The latter site has been known for some time and has been the subject of several previous excavations. Chartkoff's work has demonstrated that this early Late Woodland site is both extensive and, in some areas, extremely rich. Rather than being an inland hunting camp, which was my earlier interpretation, it now appears to be a major base camp at which a wide range of cultural activities took place.

Michigan State University has studied a burial and burial collection from Muir in Ionia County (Cleland and Clute, 1969). The Newaygo Chapter of the Michigan Archaeological Society has obtained a cache of elbow pipes from the Schooler Mound in Newaygo County (cited in Cleland and Clute, 1969: 83).

Our knowledge of southeastern Michigan has been enhanced by the publication of the Monroe County survey report (Brose and Essenpreis, 1973). Fitting and Zurel (n.d.) have prepared a summary study of the archaeology of the Detroit and Sinclair River areas and Prahl, Brose, and Stothers (n.d.) have done the same for the western Lake Erie basins. Several particularly significant site reports have been prepared over the past few years as well. Prahl has published the reports on the Sissung site (Prahl 1969) and the Morin site (Prahl 1974), both in Monroe. The former was briefly mentioned in the earlier edition of this book, but the complete study of the limited excavations which took place then is now available. The Morin site, where limited excavations have indicated an extraordinarily rich site with 76 ceramic vessels represented by rimsherds from a single ten foot square, is probably contemporary with the Sissung site in spite of a radiocarbon date of A.D. 1050. This is further evidence of a major occupation in southeastern Michigan beginning in the seventh or eighth centuries.

To the north, Wayne State University excavations at 20 MB 155 in Macomb County have been reported on by Richard Strachan (1971). This report, however, is more a study in the methodology of low-density site analysis than a contribution to the culture history of the region.

Michigan History Division field parties, working under the supervision of Donald Weston, excavated several sites in the Thumb area in the summer of 1974. The White Rock River site in Huron County (Weston n.d.c) was marked by extremely dense concentrations of chipped stone and a very small number of ceramics. Weston has interpreted this site as a specialized Late Woodland Chippewa station utilizing a local raw material.

A major excavation was carried out, under Weston's supervision, at the Draper Park site in Port Huron. In an earlier study of the work of Henry Gillman in Michigan

(Fitting 1970), I had noted the existence of collections from the Port Huron area. Draper Park (Weston n.d.a) is the same as Gillman's Black River Mound No. 2. It is a dense, early Late Woodland Wayne Tradition site with many features and includes a rich animal bone assemblage probably dating to the period of A.D. 700 to A.D. 900.

Although it is located across the river in Ontario, at least some mention should be made of the Weiser site (Kroon 1972; Fitting and Zurel, n.d.). This is a palisaded village site of the very late prehistoric, possibly post-Wolf Phase period. It is characterized by a variety of unusual ceramics, including late Younge Tradition and Whittlesey types.

The first edition of *The Archaeology of Michigan* failed to make any mention of the Sanilac Petroglyphs near Greenleaf in Sanilac County. These rock carvings, along with the rock paintings at Burnt Bluff in the upper peninsula, are the only verified aboriginal rock art in Michigan (Weston 1975). Other rock art sites have been reported but, upon examination, the reports have turned out to be unfounded or the sites historic (Weston 1975).

The Sanilac Petroglyphs were known to W. B. Hinsdale in the 1920s. Cranbrook Institute of Science has published a bulletin describing them (Hatt, Richards and Papworth, 1958). In the late 1960s, they were purchased by the Michigan Archaeological Society and in 1970, they were given to the State of Michigan as an historic park area. They represent a preservation problem (Butterfield 1971) but no decision has yet been reached as to the means of protecting them from further weathering while, at the same time, making them available for public viewing.

Archaeological field work has been car-

ried out in that area by at least three field parties (Papworth 1957, Mainfort 1973, Weston 1974). Archaeological materials have been found in the general area but it is an extremely low-density occupation. Traces of a possible Late Archaic occupation exist but most of the material dates to the Late Woodland period of around A.D. 1000 (Wayne Tradition). The petroglyphs may have been carved at the time of this occupation.

Further down the Cass River in Tuscola County, the Saginaw Valley Chapter of the Michigan Archaeological Society has undertaken an intensive survey of the Indianfield township area (Thompson 1975) revealing Late Woodland, as well as Late Archaic, materials. Several Late Woodland sites have been excavated in Saginaw County near the mouth of the Cass. Saginaw Valley College conducted a field school at the Troggan site along the Cass under the supervision of Barnard Spencer in the summers of 1972 and 1973, but no report has been published yet on this work. In 1974, the Michigan Archaeological Society and the Michigan History Division conducted a field school at the Young site (Fitting n.d.i) which contained a Late Woodland component dating to around A.D. 1000.

Several studies which were, in part, available to me while writing the section on Saginaw Valley Late Woodland in the first edition, have since been completed and published. These include the report on the Hodges site (Fitting and Sassé, 1969) and the reports on the Stadelmeyer, Mahoney and Fosters sites (Bigony 1969). The report on the Late Woodland occupation at the Kantzler site has also since been published (Crumley 1973).

Additional information on Late Woodland burial practices has been obtained from the work of Arthur Graves and other members of the Saginaw Valley Chapter of the Michigan Archaeological Society at the Bugai and Tyra site. Central Michigan University has also carried out field school excavations at the Tyra site. No reports have been published on these sites, although they will be included, in part at least, in a doctoral dissertation being prepared by John Halsey for the University of North Carolina.

Another site not mentioned in the first edition of this book was the Hamilton Street Bridge site or Fred Dustin's Wright site located just to the north of the Valley Sweets site in the city of Saginaw. Initial excavations at this site were carried out by members of the Saginaw Valley Chapter of the Michigan Archaeological Society in 1960. In the fall of 1974, Donald Weston, working with members of the Saginaw Valley and Flint Chapters of the Michigan Archaeological Society, engaged in salvage excavations, as a road was being rerouted at the site (Weston and Stobby, n.d.). It is Late Woodland, probably contemporary with the Bussinger site and may post-date the Late Woodland occupation of the Valley Sweets site.

The most intensive living area occupation at the Fletcher site (Brashler 1973) was an early Late Woodland Wayne Ware occupation. Over 10,000 square feet of site area were excavated in three field seasons during this extensive project. Brashler's study of the ceramics of the area is most significant. Using a considerably larger sample than was available to me in my southeastern Michigan study, she has suggested a new typological classification for Wayne Ware. Whether this classification is valid only for the Saginaw Valley, or whether it can be extended to the entire state, is a question to be answered in her doctoral dissertation

at Michigan State University.

In Bay County, a Late Woodland occupation may be included with the surface materials collected from 20 BY 31 on the Kawkawlin River (Butterfield and Fitting, 1971). The Tobico site in Kawkawlin Township (Carstens 1972), excavated by a Central Michigan University field party, is certainly Late Woodland. It was occupied by people making local variants of both Wayne Ware and Riviera Wares. Carstens has interpreted this site as an Ottawa-type central village based on intensive collecting rather than on agriculture.

Further to the north and moving into the northeastern Michigan culture area, Carstens has carried out excavations at the Lalone site in Arenac County as a part of the Central Michigan University field program in archaeology (Carstens 1970). While the site does contain some Archaic material, the primary occupation appears to be from the Early Late Woodland period of A.D. 700 to A.D. 900 (Wayne Tradition again).

The report on the Mikado Earthwork near Harrisville in Alcona County was mentioned in the first edition of the book, but Peter Carruthers has since completed an extensive report on the site which necessitates some revisions in my earlier interpretations (Carruthers 1969). The artifact density is much higher than I had first thought and the ratio of chipped stone tools to ceramic vessels is more nearly balanced than our field impressions had suggested. It still appears to be a 15th century fortified village site with strong cultural ties to the Whittlesey focus sites of northern Ohio, but it would now appear to be more a full range base camp of the Pottawatomi- or Miami-type rather than an Ottawa-type Village.

In 1969, I was able to study the collections obtained by Henry Gillman from the Devil River Mound group near Ossineke (Fitting 1970). This collection contained Late Woodland material from both the early Late Woodland period of A.D. 600 to A.D. 1000 and the middle Late Woodland period of A.D. 1000 to A.D. 1300. Here, as in so many sites along the northeastern shore of Michigan, the ceramics represent a fusion of southeastern Michigan and Straits area elements.

In the spring of 1973, I visited the Besser Museum in Alpena and looked over the Haltiner collections with their Curator of Archaeology, Mr. Robert Haltiner, and with Mr. Richard Clute, a faculty member at Alpena Community College. I had not been to this part of the state before, and I was impressed with the richness of the collections. At least one-half dozen major ceramic sites were represented in the collections which ranged from the early Late Woodland through the proto-historic periods. In a field school offered through the Alpena Community College in 1973, Clute devoted much of the class time toward revisiting and testing the sites from which the Haltiner collections were obtained. Haltiner and Clute are now studying this material, which should shed new light on this part of the state.

Much archaeological work has been conducted in the northwestern part of the state including the Straits area. The Michigan State University Traverse Corridor project and their more recent inland waterway (Burt Lake, Mullet Lake) surveys have revealed approximately 200 sites that include many Late Woodland sites. Major excavations have been carried out at the O'Neil (Lovis 1973) site, which contains some trade goods with the Late Woodland material; the Pine River Channel site has Late Archaic and Middle Woodland, as well as Late Woodland

materials. Dr. William Lovis is also conducting a survey of the Sleeping Bear Lakeshore for the National Park Service.

The Michigan History Division undertook a survey of Beaver Island in 1973 (Fitting 1973) which revealed a large Late Woodland occupation in the St. James area; it included some shell-tempered pottery. In the Burdickville area on the Leelanau Peninsula, Dr. David Brose's field work included excavations at the Fisher Lake site; it has a Late Woodland component with ceramics similar to those from the Heines Creek site, Bois Blanc Island and the Spring Creek site (Brose 1974). A radiocarbon date of A.D. 1080 was obtained from this site.

A 1972 archaeological survey of Mackinac City (Stone 1972b) produced a Late Woodland site with a small pit, probably a hide smoking pit, filled with charred corn cobs (Ford 1974).

The area around Haldeman Bay and the City of Mackinac Island on Mackinac Island has produced evidence in sewer trench excavations of a Late Woodland Mackinac Phase occupation (Fitting n.d.d); however, the area is too developed to carry out the extensive excavations that would probably reveal a major site.

On the north side of the Straits of Mackinac, the Michigan History Division excavations have included work at several Late Woodland sites. Just prior to A.D. 1000, there was an intensive Mackinac Phase occupation in the Straits area, and most of the sites of this period produce predominately Mackinac Wares. However, the Ferrier site (Lynott 1974), just to the west of St. Ignace, is predominately a Spring Creek-like occupation. The site has also produced corn. It has been radiocarbon dated to A.D. 930 and A.D. 1085 and interpreted as a southern Late Woodland enclave in the Straits area.

The Beyer site in St. Ignace (Fitting and Clarke, 1974) has two Late Woodland components although one is represented by only a small amount of cultural material. The lowest level at this stratified site has been radiocarbon dated to A.D. 1270 and has produced an Oneota vessel along with a Juntunen Phase assemblage. The White site, located near the mouth of the Pine River on St. Martin Bay (Fitting and Fisher, n.d.), is also a low-density Juntunen Phase site.

The Sposito site (Fitting and Cushman, 1974) is another site in St. Ignace which produced Late Woodland materials in the course of salvage excavations in 1973. The ceramics from this site show similarities to those from the historic component at the Beyer site although no trade materials were found. The site has been interpreted as a very late, possibly 16th century, prehistoric site.

Numerous small Mackinac and Juntunen Phase sites were located during Franzen's (1975) 1974 survey of Chippewa County. Late Woodland occupations were found at both the Johnson (Fitting n.d.b) and Schoolcraft (Fitting n.d.a) house excavations in Sault Ste. Marie. It is hoped that more extensive excavations will be carried out at several of these Chippewa County sites, for the region appears to be as rich as the Straits area.

Late Woodland materials, with strong resemblances to both Heines Creek ceramics and Wisconsin Madison Wares, have been found at a number of sites located in the Menominee watershed. The survey of this region was carried out by Marla Buckmaster and in the western upper peninsula by Franzen and Weston (1973). It might be noted that there is a mixed Upper Mississippian and Late Woodland Village site associated with the Backlund Mounds in Menominee County.

The results of these surveys, along with a synthesis of the archaeology of the region, will be included in Buckmaster's doctoral dissertation being prepared for Michigan State University.

In 1970 and 1971, Winston Moore directed a Western Michigan University field school at the Sand Point site in Baraga County, a site which had been located in an earlier survey of the south shore of Lake Superior by Bigony (1968). This site, now on the National Register of Historic Places, has both linear burial mounds and an extensive village area. The ceramics are a mixture of Upper Mississippian and Late Woodland types. The Late Woodland forms are unlike those dating to the same period in the Straits and St. Mary's River areas, but they have not yet been formally described.

HISTORIC SITES

There has been special emphasis on sites of the historic period in Michigan during the past several years, and a number of sites have been located which can be referred to Quimby's Early Historic Period and the first part of the Middle Historic Period. Brose (1970b) has published a detailed interpretive report on the Summer Island III occupation and, in his survey of the Burdickville area (Brose 1974), has located another contact period site, the Dunn Plateau site, with shell-tempered Dumaw Creek-like ceramics and 17th century trade goods. The O'Neil site in Charlevoix County contained 17th century trade goods with local ceramic types (Lovis 1973) and I located an iron projectile point and a site with bifacial gunflints of aboriginal manufacture in my survey of Beaver Island (Fitting 1973). The upper level at the Beyer site in St.

Ignace (Fitting and Clarke, 1974) also contained iron projectile points and bifacial gunflints. The typological and historical evidence from this site suggests that it may have been occupied by the Petun and their Algonquin allies between 1651 and 1653 as they were moving west to escape the Seneca raids during the Iroquois Wars.

In the St. Ignace area, Michigan State University has published a major report on its first season's work at the Lasanen site (Cleland, editor, 1971). Nern and Cleland (1974) have undertaken a detailed restudy of the collections from the Gros Cap cemetery. Several individual internments from this period have been uncovered in the course of construction activities as well (Fitting n.d.g, n.d.h). Virtually all of these burials appear to date to the closing decade of the 17th century, the period when the population of St. Ignace was at its greatest (Fitting n.d.j).

In 1971, Lyle Stone (1972a) directed a preliminary test-pitting program at the traditional location of the 1671-1705 Mission of St. Ignace established in St. Ignace by Father Jacques Marquette. The results of this work were so productive that the Michilimackinac Historical Society sponsored a full season of field work at the site in 1972 (Fitting n.d.c). During that season, the cellar and many of the other features of the Mission were uncovered.

Also during the 1972 season, a long house pattern was located in the area just to the north of the mission. This was identified as the 1671-1701 village of the Tionontate Huron, a later name for the Petun. The following year, the Michigan History Division excavated one additional long house and cleared approximately 150 feet of the palisade which surrounded the village. Several independent contemporary accounts suggest a population of

around 400 for this village, so it should contain at least 20 additional houses.

The Gyftakis site (Fitting n.d.f), located to the north of the Tionontate Village, was primarily a Middle Woodland site but several features, which seem to be part of a plowed-down garden bed system, contained cultural material relating to the village. One of the features which mark this field system has been radiocarbon dated to the early 18th century. A small, late 17th century component, possibly the temporary camp of a western Algonquin group, has been identified at the Norge Village site (Fitting and Lynott, 1974). A 17th century Ottawa Village, located in the northern part of St. Ignace (Fitting and Fisher, n.d.), is probably associated with the Richardson ossuary previously reported on by Greenman.

The Mackinac Island State Park Commission program at Fort Mackinac in Mackinac City has continued its field work every year. Major reports have appeared on the glass (Brown 1971) and ceramics (Miller and Stone, 1970). Lyle Stone (1975) has also published a complete account of the excavations and artifacts recovered during the excavations carried out between 1959 and 1966. The report on the 1967 through 1969 field season is presently being prepared by Dr. James Brown and should be available shortly.

Between 1971 and 1973, Stone directed a field project in the French settlement outside of Fort Mackinac; the report on this work should add a new dimension to our understanding of the 18th century occupation of the Straits area.

The French established two Fort St. Josephs in Michigan. The first of these was located somewhere in the area of Port Huron at the head of the St. Clair River and was occupied in the 1680s. Weston undertook a search for this fort site during the summer of 1974 but was unable to locate it. A second Fort St. Joseph was established along the St. Joseph River near Niles in approximately 1689. It was occupied first by the French, later by the British, and subsequently was captured by the Spanish in 1781 during the American Revolution. The collections from this key site have not been intensively studied. They are located in the Fort St. Joseph Museum in Niles where many of the artifacts are on display. A test-pitting program was scheduled for the summer of 1974 for the site, which is now buried under six to ten feet of landfill. However, difficulties in obtaining permission to excavate forced the cancellation of this project several days before it was to have started.

In 1967, 1968 and 1970, Michigan State University worked at the important Fletcher site in Bay City (Brashler 1973, Brown 1974, Robert Mainfort: personal communication). In addition to the prehistoric components mentioned earlier, this site contained an important historic burial component which dates to the middle portion of the 18th century rather than to the latter part of the century as I had reported in the first edition of this book. The historic burial component will be the subject of a doctoral dissertation at Michigan State University being prepared by Robert Mainfort.

Several papers now in press deal with the historical and archaeological evidence for patterns of Indian acculturation in the Michigan area. Stone and Chaput (n.d.) and Cleland (n.d.) have prepared primarily historical studies, while I (Fitting n.d.j) have made comparisons between late prehistoric and early historic economy and social organization. It would appear that under the French, the actual economic base and pattern of social organization and wealth distribution changed very little, although Indian peoples developed a reliance on foreign-made trade goods. In order to continue to obtain these trade goods under the British and Americans, major changes had to take place within the aboriginal societies. The societies were, therefore, so weakened that little resistance was offered when the Americans arrived in large enough numbers to take the land for themselves in the 19th century.

A number of archaeological projects have been concerned with late 18th and 19th century sites having Euro-American occupations, although some attention has been directed to aboriginal sites of this period as well (Cleland 1972). A major project has been undertaken by Michigan State University and the Mackinac Island State Park Commission at the Mill Creek site just outside of Mackinac City in northwestern Cheboygan County. Lyle Stone tested this site in 1972, and Patrick Martin supervised extensive excavations in 1973 and 1974. This mill site, located along the old Mackinac Road, was in operation from at least 1780 until well into the 19th century. Lyle Stone carried out excavations in the privy of the Biddle House on Mackinac Island in 1971. His monograph on the "Biddle Jon" site is currently in press (Stone n.d.). In the summer of 1974, the Michigan History Division sponsored excavations by Alan Hugley and Dennis Basler at the John Johnson and Henry Rowe Schoolcraft Houses in Sault Ste. Marie.

Other historic sites projects in the upper peninsula include the Michigan Technological University excavations at the mid-19th century Clifton Village site in Keweenaw County in 1973 and 1974. The Michigan History Division work at the

1847-1855 Carp River Forge site near Negaunee in Marquette County was carried out in 1973 and 1974. The work at Clifton was directed by Elinor Deling in 1973 and by Marie Campbell in 1974; that at Carp River was directed by Burton Barnard in 1973 (Barnard 1974) and Hugley and Basler in 1974 (Hugley and Basler, 1975).

In the course of our other excavations in the St. Ignace area, we have uncovered very late 19th and early 20th century components at a number of sites (Fitting 1975). The Marquette Mission, Tionontate Village and Norge Village sites all had overlays of 19th century material and have been compared as the Highstone Store, Murray House, Wilson House and railroad docks occupations. A very distinct set of correlations were found between the types and quantities of cultural material found at these sites and the known ethnic and economic occupations.

In the Detroit area, several projects have been carried out in recent years. Charles Martinez and Stephen Demeter have undertaken extensive salvage work at the historic burial locality near the Gibraltar site south of Detroit. Ford and Jones (1974) have described some of the cultural material from this project. Dr. Gordon Grosscup has conducted excavations at the Ross Morass House in Detroit, while Stephen Demeter has supervised salvage excavations at a number of sites being destroyed as a part of the Detroit Renaissance Center project.

The last site to be mentioned in this section is the Walker Tavern site, a mid-19th century tavern in Lenawee County. The work at this site, carried out in 1968 and mentioned as forthcoming in the earlier edition of this book, has since been reported (Grosscup and Miller, 1969). Additional work was carried out at the

site by the Michigan History Division in 1974 (Bienenfeld and Smith, 1974).

SPECIAL PROJECTS

Several special projects that do not fit easily into any of the above chronological categories should be mentioned. Richard G. Wilkinson (1971) has published his study of biological relationships of skeletal populations in the Great Lakes region. He found that there was no clear evidence that the Norton Mound population was biologically related to Illinois Hopewell groups and was, in fact, more similar to the early Late Woodland populations from the Fort Wayne Mound and the Bussinger site. Furthermore, the Younge and Juntunen populations are distinct from these and are possibly descended from the Lake Forest Middle Woodland population represented at the Serpent Mounds in Ontario. He has suggested that prior to A.D. 1000 there was a basic Michigan population in the state which tended to be replaced in later centuries by peoples from the east.

Another project, not yet completed, is Barbara Luedke's neutron activation study of cherts and chert sources in the Great Lakes region. This study, which will be the subject of a doctoral dissertation at the University of Michigan, should add much to our knowledge of prehistoric trade and distribution patterns in the area.

THE FUTURE OF MICHIGAN ARCHAEOLOGY

Making statements about the future of anything can be a risky business. The only thing you can be sure about such predictions is that you will probably be wrong.

Several years ago (Fitting 1972a), I predicted that Michigan would soon have new comprehensive antiquities legislation. Not only was I wrong, but this goal seems further away now than ever before. In the absence of such legislation, structures have developed to get the archaeological job done. Many of the functions which might have been exercised by an Office of Michigan Archaeology are now carried out by the Michigan History Division, the Conference on Michigan Archaeology and the universities and colleges within the state.

I think that we have seen the end of the era of major growth in academic programs in archaeology. The major universities are all facing a slowdown in budget growth and new teaching positions will just not be as readily available as they have been in the past. This is coupled with a reduction in graduate programs since there will not be as many jobs available for people completing such programs. A result of this cutback may be a major shift in the type of literature that is produced, with senior archaeologists writing more of the basic data reports themselves rather than supervising large groups of graduate students in dissertation research, the source of most of the major data reports of the past decade. I also foresee a greater equity in the distribution of archaeological resources among the universities in the state. In the past, there has been a tendency for the major universities to dominate the picture but now there are excellent archaeological programs at half a dozen state-supported institutions, and programs are developing at some private colleges as well.

If there is to be an expansion in new archaeological positions, it will probably be in the areas of government and private industry. The type of training program needed to prepare students for such positions will probably need to be very different from the traditional archaeological programs designed to train people for university teaching. This trend is already evident with the addition of several archaeological positions in state government at both the Mackinac Island State Park Commission and the Michigan History Division. Lyle Stone now heads his own research firm, Archaeological Research Services, and Earl Prahl had developed an archaeological program with Commonwealth Associates. He has since gone into contract research on his own, so several of the major contributors of "pure" knowledge are now continuing their work on a commercial basis.

There seems to be a major shift in emphasis in archaeological research in the state away from single site excavations, which were used as the basis for regional interpretations, to regional surveys with only small-scale sampling of specific sites. Virtually all archaeological programs within the state are now developing in this direction. This trend will be encouraged by the recent passage of the Archaeological and Historical Preservation Act of 1974 (the Moss-Bennett Act) which provides funds for archaeological survey and salvage, and by the establishment of a highway salvage program in the state. The amount of effort expended for survey on these projects, along with the surveys that are being encouraged and carried out by the Michigan History Division with National Historic Preservation Survey and Planning funds, will change the entire scope of Michigan archaeology. This is a type of work different from traditional academic research. It is oriented more to immediate problems; project priorities will be determined more by engineers and urban planners than by archaeologists. It will mean that archaeologists will be required to actually complete their reports for a change if such reports are to have any effect on the preservation of cultural resources. This may lead to a much larger emphasis on the archaeology of historic sites as well.

The role of the non-professional archaeologist is also changing. The quality of non-professional contributions has been upgraded by intensive exposure to professional methods in formal training programs developed by the Michigan Archaeological Society working with the Mackinac Island State Park Commission, the Michigan History Division and the Chippewa Nature Center. The Michigan Archaeological Society has established an education committee whose specific purpose is to communicate information on the availability of university, college and community college course offerings to its membership. The non-professional will only rarely be able to assume the role of senior investigator on a project, but his or her efforts can be invaluable in the area of survey since these individuals know their own territory best. The non-professional with excavation training may also turn out to be the backbone of any large-scale salvage program, and such salvage programs seem inevitable in the next decade.

Above all, Michigan archaeology will be changed radically by the new information which will be generated by the survey and salvage data of the next decade. What is done in the next ten years may surpass all that has ever been done before in the state. Our models, hypotheses, and theories, framed on the basis of a near vacuum of site information, are certain to be swept aside and we should all avoid the temptation of maintaining obsolete interpretive positions simply because we have held them in the past. Ten years from now *The Archaeology of Michigan* will certainly need to be rewritten and its form will certainly differ from that of the present volume.

James E. Fitting
Lansing, Michigan
March, 1975

REFERENCES

BARNARD, BURTON
1974 "Archaeological Investigations at the Carp River Forge in 1973." Unpublished manuscript on file with the Michigan History Division.

BETTAREL, ROBERT L. and HALE G. SMITH
1973 "The Moccasin Bluff Site and the Woodland Cultures of Southwestern Michigan." *Anthropological Papers, Museum of Anthropology, University of Michigan*, No. 49. Ann Arbor.

BIENENFELD, PAULA F. and TIMOTHY C. SMITH
1974 "Archaeological Excavations at Walker Tavern in 1974." Unpublished manuscript on file with the Michigan History Division.

BIGONY, BEATRICE A.
1968 "An Archaeological Survey along the South Shore of Lake Superior." Unpublished manuscript on file at the University of Michigan Museum of Anthropology.

1969 "Late Woodland Occupations of the Saginaw Valley." *The Michigan Archaeologist*, Vol. 16, Nos. 3-4, pp. 115-214. Ann Arbor.

BRASHLER, JANET GAIL
1973 "A Formal Analysis of Prehistoric Ceramics from the Fletcher Site." M.A. thesis, Michigan State University.

BROSE, DAVID S.
1970a "The Archaeology of Summer Island: Changing Settlement Systems in Northern Lake Michigan." *Anthropological Papers, Museum of Anthropology, University of Michigan*, No. 41. Ann Arbor.

1970b "Summer Island III: An Early Historic Site in the Upper Great Lakes." *Historical Archaeology*, Vol. 4, pp. 3-33. Lansing.

1974 "Preliminary Report of the 1974 Archaeological Survey of the Area Around Burdickville, Leelanau County, Michigan." Unpublished manuscript on file with the Michigan History Division.

BROSE, DAVID S. and PATRICIA S. ESSENPREIS
1973 "A Report on a Preliminary Archaeological Survey of Monroe County, Michigan." *The Michigan Archaeologist*, Vol. 19, Nos. 1-2, pp. 1-192. Kalamazoo.

BROWN, JAMES A.
1974 Review of: *The Archaeology of Michigan* by James E. Fitting. *American Antiquity*, Vol. 39, No. 2, p. 395-6. Washington, D.C.

BROWN, MARGARET KIMBALL
1971 "Glass From Fort Michilimackinac: A Classification for Eighteenth Century Glass." *The Michigan Archaeologist*, Vol. 18, Nos. 3-4, pp. 97-215. Kalamazoo.

BUTTERFIELD, IRA F.
1971 "The Sanilac Petroglyphs: An Archaeological Time Study." *The Michigan Archaeologist*, Vol. 17, No. 1, pp. 41-44. Kalamazoo.

BUTTERFIELD, IRA F. and JAMES E. FITTING
1971 "Archaeological Salvage at 20 BY 31, Bay County, Michigan." *The Michigan Archaeologist*, Vol. 17, No. 2, pp. 65-90. Kalamazoo.

BUTTERFIELD, IRA F. and RALPH W. STROEBEL
1960 "Grinding on Projectile Points in Bay and Saginaw Counties, Michigan." *The Totem Pole*, Vol. 43, No. 8, pp. 1-9. Detroit.

CARRUTHERS, PETER J.
1969 "The Mikado Earthwork: 20 AA 5." M.A. thesis, University of Calgary.

CARSTENS, KENNETH C.
1970 "The Lalone Site, 20AR1, Arenac County, Michigan." *The Michigan Archaeologist*, Vol. 16, No. 2, pp. 49-82. Ann Arbor.

1972 "Tobico (20BY32), A Late Woodland Site in Bay County, Michigan." *The Michigan Archaeologist*, Vol. 18, No. 3, pp. 113-168. Kalamazoo.

CAUBLE, RONALD G.
1971 "The Brainerd Site (20AE61); An Ossuary in Allegan County, Michigan." *The Michigan Archaeologist*, Vol. 17, No. 1, pp. 1-26. Kalamazoo.

CLARKE, WESLEY S.
1974 "Investigation of the Yaggie and Kierking Sites, Muskegon County, Michigan." Unpublished manuscript on file with the Michigan History Division.

CLELAND, CHARLES E.
1972 "The Mathews Site (20CL61), Clinton County, Michigan." *The Michigan Archaeologist*, Vol. 18, No. 4, pp. 175-208. Kalamazoo.

n.d. *The Indians of Michigan.* Michigan History Division Munson Fund Publications. In press.

CLELAND, CHARLES E. (editor)
1971 The Lasanen Site: An Historic Burial Locality in Mackinac County, Michigan. *Publications of the Museum, Michigan State University, Anthropological Series,* Vol. 1, No. 1. East Lansing.

CLELAND, CHARLES E. and RICHARD CLUTE
1969 "A Late Woodland Burial from Muir, Ionia County, Michigan." *The Michigan Archaeologist*, Vol. 15, No. 3, pp. 78-85. Kalamazoo.

CRUMLEY, CAROLE S.
1973 "The Kantzler Site (20BY30): A Multi-component Woodland Site in Bay County, Michigan." *The*

Michigan Archaeologist, Vol. 19, Nos. 3-4, pp. 183-291. Kalamazoo.

DEVISSCHER, JERRY, EDWARD J. WAHLA and JAMES E. FITTING
1970 "Additional Paleo-Indian Camp-sites Adjacent to the Holcombe Site." *The Michigan Archaeologist,* Vol. 16, No. 1, pp. 1-24. Ann Arbor.

DRUM, RICHARD
1974 "The Darrel Coomer Site, St. Joseph County, Michigan." *The Michigan Archaeologist,* Vol. 20, No. 2, pp. 113-115. Kalamazoo.

FAIRCHILD, JERRY
1970 "The Kralosky Site." *The Michigan Archaeologist,* Vol. 16, No. 1, pp. 33-42. Ann Arbor.

FINCHAM, GLENVAL
1970 "A Suggested Explanation for the Semi-Unmodified Base which Sometimes Occurs on Eastern Scottsbluff." *The Michigan Archaeologist,* Vol. 16, No. 1, pp. 25-32. Ann Arbor.

FISCHER, FRED W.
1972 "Schultz Site Ceramics." In: *The Schultz Site at Green Point: A Stratified Occupation Area in the Saginaw Valley of Michigan* edited by James E. Fitting. Memoirs of the Museum of Anthropology, University of Michigan. No. 4, pp. 137-190, 272-300. Ann Arbor.

FITTING, JAMES E.
1969 "Settlement Analysis in the Great Lakes Region" *Southwestern Journal of Anthropology,* Vol. 25, No. 4, pp. 360-77. Albuquerque.

1970 "Rediscovering Michigan Archaeology: The Gillman Collections at Harvard." *The Michigan Archaeologist,* Vol. 16, No. 2, pp. 83-114. Ann Arbor.

1971a "Rediscovering Michigan Archaeology: Notes on the 1885 Converse Mound Collection." *The Michigan Archaeologist,* Vol. 17, No. 1, pp. 33-41. Kalamazoo.

1971b "Scheduling in a Shared Environment: Late Period Land Use in the Saginaw Valley of Michigan." *Ontario Archaeology,* No. 17, pp. 35-41. Toronto.

1972a "Archaeology in Michigan: Present Knowledge and Prospects." *Kalamazoo College Review,* Vol. 34, No. 4, pp. 2-5. Kalamazoo.

1972b "The Huron as an Ecotype: The Limits of Maximization in a Western Great Lakes Society." *Anthropologica,* Vol. 14, No. 1, pp. 3-18. Montreal.

1973 "An Archaeological Survey of Beaver Island, Charlevoix County, Michigan." *Michigan Department of State, Michigan History Division, Archaeological Survey Reports,* No. 1. Lansing.

1974a "History and Archaeology in St. Ignace." *Le Temps—St. Ignace,* Vol. 3, No. 1, pp. 1 & 4. St. Ignace.

1974b   "The Nelson Site (SIS-34)." *The Michigan Archaeologist,* Vol. 20, Nos. 3-4, pp. 121-138. Kalamazoo.

1975   "St. Ignace Archaeology in the 19th century: Information from Archaeological Remains." Paper presented at the Annual Meeting of the Society for Historical Archaeology.

n.d.a   "Aboriginal Artifacts from the John Johnson House Excavations." Unpublished manuscript to be included with the Johnson House Report.

n.d.b   "Aboriginal Artifacts from the Henry Rowe Schoolcraft House." Unpublished manuscript to be included with the Schoolcraft House Report.

n.d.c   "Archaeological Excavations at the Marquette Mission Site, St. Ignace, Michigan, in 1972." *Reports in Mackinac History and Archaeology.* Mackinac Island State Park Commission. In press.

n.d.d   "An Archaeological Survey of Mackinac Island." Mackinac Island State Park Commission. In press.

n.d.e   "Climatic Change and Cultural Frontiers in Eastern North America." *The Michigan Archaeologist.* In press.

n.d.f   "The Gyftakis Site: A Lake Forest Middle Woodland Site in St. Ignace, Michigan." Unpublished manuscript on file with the Michigan History Division.

n.d.g   "A Late 17th Century Burial from St. Ignace, Michigan (The Marquette Street Burial)." *The Michigan Archaeologist.* In press.

n.d.h   "A Middle Historic Period Burial from St. Ignace, Michigan (The Church Street Burial)." *The Michigan Archaeologist.* In press.

n.d.i   "The Michigan Archaeological Society Field School at the Young Site, 20SA209, Saginaw County, Michigan." Unpublished manuscript on file with the Michigan History Division.

n.d.j   "Patterns of Acculturation in the Straits of Mackinac." Unpublished manuscript on file with the Michigan History Division.

n.d.k   "Regional Culture History: 100 B.C. to A.D. 1000." *Handbook of North American Indians,* Volume on Northeastern North America. Smithsonian Institution. In press.

n.d.l   "Seasonality in Great Lakes Prehistory." In: *Seasonality in Prehistory* edited by Cynthia Irwin-Williams. The University of New Mexico Press. In press.

FITTING, JAMES E. (editor)

1972   "The Schultz Site at Green Point: A Stratified Occupation

Area in the Saginaw Valley of Michigan." *Memoirs of the Museum of Anthropology, University of Michigan,* No. 4. Ann Arbor.

1974 "Contributions to the Archaeology of the St. Ignace Area." *The Michigan Archaeologist,* Vol. 20, Nos. 3-4, pp. 118-286. Kalamazoo.

FITTING, JAMES E. and DAVID S. BROSE
1971 "The Northern Periphery of Adena." In: *Adena: The Seeking of an Identity* edited by B. K. Swartz, pp. 29-55. Ball State University Press. Muncie.

FITTING, JAMES E. and WESLEY S. CLARKE
1974 "The Byer Site (SIS-20)." *The Michigan Archaeologist.* Vol. 20, Nos. 3-4, pp. 227-278. Kalamazoo.

FITTING, JAMES E. and KATHLEEN A. CUSHMAN
1974 "The Sposito Site (SIS-29)." *The Michigan Archaeologist,* Vol. 20, Nos. 3-4, pp. 171-194. Kalamazoo.

FITTING, JAMES E. and PATRICIA L. FISHER
n.d. *"An Archaeological Survey of the St. Ignace Area."* Mackinac Island State Park Commission. In press.

FITTING, JAMES E. and MARK J. LYNOTT
1974 "The Norge Village Site (SIS 16)." *The Michigan Archaeologist,* Vol. 20, Nos. 3-4, pp. 195-226. Kalamazoo.

FITTING, JAMES E. and SUSAN SASSÉ
1969 "The Hodges Site, 20SA130,

Saginaw County, Michigan." *The Michigan Archaeologist,* Vol. 15, No. 3, pp. 57-77. Ann Arbor.

FITTING, JAMES E. and DONALD E. WESTON
1974 "An Archaeological Evaluation of the Marquette Memorial Area in the Straits State Park." Unpublished manuscript on file with the Michigan History Division.

FITTING, JAMES E. and RICHARD ZUREL
n.d. "The St. Clair and Detroit River Area." In: *The Late Period Prehistory of the Lake Erie Basin* edited by David S. Brose. Cleveland Museum of Natural History. In press.

FORD, RICHARD I.
1974 "Corn From the Straits of Mackinac." *The Michigan Archaeologist,* Vol. 20, No. 2, pp. 97-104. Kalamazoo.

FORD, RICHARD I. and VOLNEY H. JONES
1974 "Job's Tears, *Coix lachrymajobi* L., Beads From the West Ridge-Gibraltar Site, Southeastern Michigan." *The Michigan Archaeologist,* Vol. 20, No. 2, pp. 105-112. Kalamazoo.

FRANZEN, JOHN
1975 "An Archaeological Survey of Chippewa County." *Michigan Department of State, Michigan History Division, Archaeological Survey Reports,* No. 5. Lansing.

FRANZEN, JOHN and DONALD WESTON
1973 "An Evaluation of the Archaeo-

logical Resources of the Western Upper Peninsula." *Michigan Department of State, Michigan History Division, Archaeological Survey Reports,* No. 2. Lansing.

GRIFFIN, JAMES B.
1972   "An Old Copper Point from Chippewa County, Michigan." *The Michigan Archaeologist,* Vol. 18, No. 1, pp. 35-36. Kalamazoo.

GRIFFIN, JAMES B., RICHARD E. FLANDERS and PAUL F. TITTERINGTON
1970   "The Burial Complexes of the Knight and Norton Mounds in Illinois and Michigan." *Memoirs of the Museum of Anthropology, University of Michigan,* No. 2. Ann Arbor.

GROSSCUP, GORDON and GEORGE MILLER
1969   "Excavations at Walker Tavern, Cambridge Historical Park." Manuscript on file at the Wayne State University Museum of Anthropology.

HATT, ROBERT T., DARREL J. RICHARDS and MARK L. PAPWORTH
1958   The Sanilac Petroglyphs. *Cranbrook Institute of Science Bulletin* No. 36. Bloomfield Hills.

HUGLEY, ALAN and DENNIS BASLER
1975   "Carp River Forge: 1974 Excavations." Manuscript on file with the Michigan History Division.

JANZEN, DONALD E.
1968   "The Naomikong Point site and the Dimensions of Laurel in the Lake Superior Region." *Anthropological Papers, Museum of Anthropology, University of Michigan,* No. 36. Ann Arbor.

KROON, LEONARD
1972   "Notes on the Ceramic Technology from the Weiser site, Kent County, Ontario." *The Michigan Archaeologist,* Vol. 18, No. 4, pp. 215-222. Kalamazoo.

LOVIS, WILLIAM A., JR.
1971   "The Holtz Site (20AN26), Antrim County, Michigan: A Preliminary Report." *The Michigan Archaeologist,* Vol. 17, No. 2, pp. 49-64. Kalamazoo.

1973   "Late Woodland Cultural Dynamics in the Northern Lower Peninsula of Michigan." Ph.D. dissertation, Michigan State University.

LYNOTT, MARK J.
1974   "The Ferrier Site (SIS-33)." *The Michigan Archaeologist,* Vol. 20, Nos. 3-4, pp. 139-170. Kalamazoo.

MAINFORT, ROBERT J., JR.
1973   "An Archaeological Survey of the Sanilac State Historic Park." Manuscript on file at the Michigan State University Museum.

MILLER, J. JEFFERSON, II and LYLE M. STONE
1970   "Eighteenth-Century Ceramics from Fort Michilimackinac: A Study in Historical Archaeology." *Smithsonian Studies in*

History and Technology, No. 4. Washington, D.C.

NERN, CRAIG F. and CHARLES E. CLELAND

1974 "The Gros Cap Cemetery Site, St. Ignace, Michigan: A Reconsideration of the Greenlees Collection." *The Michigan Archaeologist*, Vol. 20, No. 1, pp. 1-58. Kalamazoo.

PAPWORTH, MARK L.

1957 "The Sanilac Rock Carvings." *The Michigan Archaeologist*, Vol. 3, No. 4, pp. 83-87. Ann Arbor.

PERU, DONALD V.

1969 "The Tolles Site." *The Michigan Archaeologist*, Vol. 15, No. 4, pp. 101-108. Ann Arbor.

PRAHL, EARL J.

1969 "A Preliminary Comparison of Three Prehistoric Sites in the Vicinity of the Western Shore of Lake Erie." *Toledo Area Aboriginal Research Club Bulletin*, Vol. 2, No. 1. Toledo.

1970 "The Middle Woodland Period of the Lower Muskegon Valley and the Northern Hopewell Frontier." Ph.D. dissertation, University of Michigan.

1974 "The Morin Site (20MO40), Monroe County, Michigan." *The Michigan Archaeologist*, Vol. 20, No. 2, pp. 65-96. Kalamazoo.

PRAHL, EARL J., DAVID S. BROSE and DAVID STOTHERS

n.d. "A Preliminary Synthesis of the Late Prehistoric Phenomenon in the Western Lake Erie Shore." In: *The Late Period Prehistory of the Lake Erie Basin* edited by David S. Brose. Cleveland Museum of Natural History. In press.

PRUFER, OLAF H. and ORRIN C. SHANE II

n.d. "The Portage-Sandusky-Vermilion Region." In: *The Late Period Prehistory of the Lake Erie Basin* edited by David S. Brose. Cleveland Museum of Natural History. In press.

RICHNER, JEFFREY J.

1973 "Depositional History and Stone Tool Industries at the Winter Site: A Lake Forest Middle Woodland Cultural Manifestation." M.A. thesis, Western Michigan University.

ROGERS, MARGARET B.

1972 "The 46th Street Site and the Occurrences of Allegan Ware in Southwestern Michigan." *The Michigan Archaeologist*, Vol. 18, No. 2, pp. 47-108. Kalamazoo.

ROOSA, WILLIAM B.

1965 "Some Great Lakes Fluted Point Sites and Types." *The Michigan Archaeologist*, Vol. 11, Nos. 3-4, pp. 89-102. Ann Arbor.

SIMONS, DONALD B.

1972 "Radiocarbon Date from a Michigan Satchell-Type Site." *The Michigan Archaeologist*, Vol. 18, No. 4, pp. 209-214. Kalamazoo.

STONE, LYLE M.

1972a   "Archaeological Investigation of the Marquette Mission Site, St. Ignace, Michigan, 1971: A Preliminary Report." *Reports in Mackinac History and Archaeology*, No. 1. Mackinac Island State Park Commission. Lansing.

1972b   "A Preliminary Report on the 1972 Straits Area Survey." Unpublished manuscript on file with the Mackinac Island State Park Commission.

1975   "Fort Michilimackinac: 1715–1781: An Archaeological Perspective on the Revolutionary Frontier." *Publications of the Museum, Michigan State University, Anthropological Series*, Vol. 2. East Lansing.

n.d.   *The Biddle Jon Site, Mackinac Island, Michigan*. Mackinac Island State Park Commission. In press.

STONE, LYLE M. and DONALD CHAPUT

n.d.   "The Early Historic Period in the Upper Great Lakes." *Handbook of North American Indians*, Northeastern volume. Smithsonian Institution. In press.

STOTHERS, DAVID M.

n.d.   "The Princess Point Complex: A Regional Representative of an Early Late Woodland Horizon in the Western Great Lakes." In: *The Late Period Prehistory of the Lake Erie Basin* edited by David S. Brose. Cleveland Museum of Natural History. In press.

STRACHAN, RICHARD

1973   "The Kade Site: A Methodological and Statistical Analysis of a Michigan Multi-Component Archaeological Site." Ph.D. dissertation, Wayne State University.

THOMPSON, HAROLD W.

1975   "An Archaeological Survey of the Tuscola State Game Area and Peripheral Public and Private Lands." *Michigan Department of State, Michigan History Division, Archaeological Survey Reports*, No. 4. Lansing.

WAHLA, EDWARD J.

1969   *Michigan Projectile Point Types*. Clinton Valley Chapter of the Michigan Archaeological Society.

WAHLA, EDWARD J. and JERRY DEVISSCHER

1969   "The Holcombe Paleo-Point." *The Michigan Archaeologist*, Vol. 15, No. 4, pp. 109–112. Ann Arbor.

WESTON, DONALD E.

1974   "Archaeological Excavations at the Sanilac Petroglyphs State Historical Park: 1974." Unpublished manuscript on file with the Michigan History Division.

1975   "The Indian Rock Art Tradition in Michigan." *Michigan History Division, Great Lakes Informant*, Series 1, Number 5. Lansing.

REFERENCES

n.d.a   "The Draper Park Site: A Late
         Woodland Village in Port
         Huron, Michigan." Unpub-
         lished manuscript on file with
         the Michigan History Division.

n.d.b   "Observations on the Depo-
         sitional History of Probosci-
         dea Remains in Southeastern
         Michigan." *The Michigan Aca-
         demician.* In press.

n.d.c   "White Rock and the White
         River Site, 20HU39, Huron
         County, Michigan." *The Michi-
         gan Archaeologist.* In press.

WESTON, DONALD E. and RICHARD STOBBY
n.d.   "Archaeological Salvage at the
         Hamilton Street Bridge Site,
         Saginaw County, Michigan."
         Unpublished manuscript on
         file with the Michigan History
         Division.

WILKINSON, RICHARD G.
1971   "Prehistoric Biological Rela-
         tionships in the Great Lakes
         Region." *Anthropological Pa-
         pers, Museum of Anthropology,
         University of Michigan,* No. 43.
         Ann Arbor.

PREFACE TO FIRST EDITION

The past decade has been an exciting time for the archaeologists living and working in Michigan. The earlier work of Greenman and Quimby set the stage for the enthusiastic participation of another generation and between 1963 and 1968 the University of Michigan accepted nearly a dozen doctoral dissertations dealing with Great Lakes archaeology. I was able to witness and participate in this program while a student at Michigan State University and the University of Michigan and as a faculty member at Wayne State University and the University of Michigan. The following volume was written between 1964 and 1968 while I was Curator of Great Lakes Archaeology at the University of Michigan Museum of Anthropology. During that period I learned much from both my colleagues and students and from many dedicated members of the Michigan Archaeological Society.

While I directed the University of Michigan Great Lakes field program between 1964 and 1968, I received financial support from a number of sources. I am particularly indebted to the National Science Foundation for the award of grants GS-666 and GS-1486. Additional funds were obtained from NSF-USEP training program support, a University of Michigan Faculty Research grant, and grants from the National Park Service and the Mackinac Island Park Commission.

A number of individuals either directly or indirectly aided in the preparation of this volume. The influence of Charles E. Cleland will be readily apparent. The excellent field program which he developed as Curator of Anthropology at the Michigan State University Museum during the same years I was a curator at the University of Michigan Museum of Anthropology furnished a challenge to our own efforts and I feel that both institutions benefited from such a "cooperative rivalry." George I. Quimby and James B. Griffin influenced this work in many ways. In several instances I have taken them to task on specific points of interpretation but, like St. Augustine, I advise the reader that it is with the Platonists that I must argue for their position is closest to my own.

William B. Roosa and Henry T. Wright read and commented on earlier drafts of Chapters II and III and Donald R. Janzen did the same with Chapter V. I am most grateful to my colleagues at Case Western Reserve University, David S. Brose and Gary A. Wright, for reading and commenting on the entire manuscript. Their careful evaluation led to a number of revisions.

The illustrations for this volume were obtained from many sources. I thank the Princeton University Press for permission to use Figure 9 and the publishers and editors of the following publications for permission to use figures from their publications: the Indiana Academy of Science (8), the Michigan Academy of Science, Arts and Letters (6), *The American Scientist* (3), the Michigan Geological Survey (4), *The Wisconsin Archeologist* (36), and the *Michigan Archaeologist* (13, 14, 15, 26, 67, 114, 116, 120, 122, and 123).

Individuals who have given permission to utilize illustrations prepared in connection with their own work include Jack L. Hough (3), Robert W. Kelley and William R. Farrand (4), Frank N. Himmler (6), William S. Benninghoff (8), Ronald J. Mason (11 and 67), Don V. Peru (13), William B. Roosa (15), Ira Fogel (36), Richard E. Flanders (41, 43, 44, 45, 46, 47, 48, and 49), Earl J. Prahl (50, 51, 52, 53, 54, and 99), David S. Brose (68, 69, 70, 71, 120, 122, and 123), Donald R. Janzen (73, 74, 75, 76, and 77), John R. Halsey (80, 81, 82, 94, and 95), Alan L. McPherron (104 and 105), Moreau S. Maxwell (114), Charles E. Cleland (115), George I. Quimby (116), and Lyle Stone (119 and 121).

Dr. James B. Griffin, Director of the University of Michigan Museum of Anthropology, allowed the reproduction of illustrations from the *Anthropological Papers, Museum of Anthropology, University of Michigan*, Numbers 11, 17, 24, 27, 31, and 36. He also allowed me to use a number of negatives from the Museum files. The figures from these files are listed below with the Museum negative numbers in parentheses: 16(15504), 19(14728), 23(14920), 24(15520), 25(15223), 27(15239), 29(14-738), 30(15690), 31(16042), 32(14914), 35(13986), 43(15282), 44(15701a), 45(15-612), 46(15276), 47(15279), 48(15605),

49(15277), 50(15907), 51(16126), 52(16-129), 53(16121), 54(16133), 56(15791), 57(15945), 80(15941), 81(15942), 82(19-543), 83(14978), 84(16052), 85(14977), 86(16081), 87(16055), 88(16056), 92(155-77), 93(14906), 99(15289), 101(16004), 102(16000), 103(16006), 105(13884), 106 (13963).

Photographs taken specifically for this volume were also filed with the University of Michigan Museum of Anthropology. These figure numbers and the University of Michigan Museum of Anthropology negative file numbers are as follows: 20(16-400), 22(16403), 33(16404), 34(16405), 37(16403), 42(16407), 55(16408), 58(16-409), 59(16410), 60(16412), 64(16413), 65(16414), 66(16415), 74(16417), 75(16-418), 76(16419), 77(16420), 78(16421), 89(16422), 90(16423), 91(16425), 94(16-426), 95(16427), 96(16429), 97(16431), 98(16432), 106(16434), 107(16436), 108 (16438), 109(16440), 110(16441), 111(16-443), 112(16445), 117(16446), 118(16448).

There are three other individuals who need to be singled out for special recognition for their aid. Mr. George Stuber, who has worked with me as illustrator and draftsman on ten books and monographs, took the photographs prepared specifically for this volume. My wife, Molly, read and reread all drafts of the manuscript and did most of the preliminary editing. The final editing was done by Mrs. Elizabeth Knappman of the Natural History Press.

CONTENTS

LIST OF ILLUSTRATIONS

CHAPTER I

INTRODUCTION

A burst of archaeological activity in the state of Michigan has occurred during the past eight years. This "archaeology explosion" (Fitting 1966b) was first heard at the University of Michigan Museum of Anthropology, but that institution has since been joined by Michigan State University and other universities and institutions within the state in major programs of excavation and interpretation. The results of this activity are little known outside of the immediate area. Not a single site in Michigan is mentioned in the recent summary volume, *An Introduction to American Archaeology* (1966) by Gordon Willey. It would be tempting to say that this volume was written to remedy Willey's neglect but it was actually conceived and outlined far in advance of the publication of Willey's volume.

There have been several past summaries of Michigan archaeology and I acknowledge my debt to these works. W. B. Hinsdale's *Primitive Man in Michigan* (1925) is one such work and, still in print today, it enjoys perennial popularity. More recently, our knowledge of the prehistoric occupation of the state was summarized in Quimby's *Indian Life in the Upper Great Lakes* (1960). This volume served as the reference point for my recent excavations. What is presented in the following pages is an attempt to elaborate on the basic pattern which Quimby suggested, to fill in gaps and to present information not available a dec-

ade ago while he was preparing his book.

My own experience in Michigan has been less than a decade. Most of the field work and laboratory analysis reported in this volume has been done by others. The Michigan sequence is clearly the product of a "group effort." "The Schultz site at Green Point," as an example, will have ten co-authors. Single authored volumes, such as the Juntunen site report, are clearly the work of many individuals. Rather than being a totally original work, the present volume should be viewed as a synthesis; as one person's statement about the results of a group effort. I bring their information together here from my position as Curator of Great Lakes Archaeology at the University of Michigan Museum of Anthropology and as editor of the *Michigan Archaeologist*. This volume is a progress report of what is going on in Michigan archaeology.

Before proceeding with what we think we know about Michigan archaeology it is necessary to say a few things about archaeology in general. The study of archaeology is a very personal thing and it is perhaps wise for the reader to be forewarned about the writers' prejudices. There was a time when archaeologists were judged by what they did. The trend today seems to be more in the line of evaluating what they *say* about what they do. Since World War II several significant books (Taylor 1948, Willey and Phillips 1958, Chang 1967) and articles have appeared dealing with "theoretical archaeology." These have tended to evaluate what has been done by contemporary archaeologists and outline what should be done. I doubt that they have altered what was being done to any great extent but they certainly have altered what people call what they are doing. What respectable archaeologist of the late 1950s would want to be caught doing "cultural-historical integration" when greater men were doing "processual interpretation," an obviously higher and better thing. In fact, what unifies most "theoretical studies" is the placement of whatever the writer is doing, or thinks he is doing—be it a "conjunctive approach" or "processual interpretation"—on top of a graded scale of archaeological types.

With this development of "theoretical archaeology," which much of the time has been little more than a justification after the fact of what the theoretical archaeologist was calling his own work, a gradual archaeological orthogenesis developed. Since each succeeding "generation" of archaeologists could see the "theoretical" mistakes of their predecessors but not of themselves, they could state with certainty that "every day and every way we are getting better and better." The culmination of this thinking is the "new archaeology," an unfortunate term which I trace to Joseph Caldwell (1966) although it was apparently used by Clark Wissler in 1917. I would suspect that even Caldwell's "new archaeology" is as up-to-date as Wissler's and that there is a "newer archaeology" waiting in the wings ready to pounce upon the public.

A recent statement of current theoretical position is to be found in Kent V. Flannery's review in *Scientific American* (1967) of the Willey volume. In this review, Flannery opposes the "normative" framework of those concerned with culture history to

that of the "process school." He suggests that about sixty percent of American archaeologists are members of the first group and ten percent belong to the second with the rest somewhere in between. Flannery tries to make a case for the second group and gives the impression that they will prevail.

I approve of the emphasis of systems evaluation in archaeology. Some exemplary work has been done by some members at the "process school." Theirs is an emphasis on the "overlap between a vast number of systems" with culture change being explained by variations in the integration of one or more of these systems. If, however, this is the main emphasis of the "process school," is it not just another tool for the study of culture history? It is a refined tool but so is radiocarbon dating. Is the study of "culture process" an end in itself? I view it as a technique for understanding culture history in the same way that radiocarbon dating or potsherd counting are techniques for the understanding of culture history. For that matter "cultural process" or counting potsherds could be either the means or the end of a particular study at a particular time.

The systems approach to archaeology has the advantage of integrating, rather than separating, past cultural adaptations. Meighan (1966), for example, has written of adaptation to environment as a natural science study; adaptation to others as a social science study; and adaptation to self, as the study of humanistic values. It is this later concern of archaeology which seems most likely to suffer with a systems approach, particularly with an ecological emphasis. It is certainly the weakest area of the present volume. Adapting to others, however, is really part of adapting to the environment, for social organization is a primary part of this adaptation. By extension, the adaptation to self is essentially a part of the adaptation to others so it too can be encompassed in an ecological systems approach to archaeology.

This volume is an ecological approach to Michigan prehistory. Its ecological emphasis is rooted in the traditions of Michigan archaeology which go back beyond my own participation in this study. In 1932 W. B. Hinsdale, the first curator of Great Lakes Archaeology in the University of Michigan Museum of Anthropology, wrote "Distribution of Aboriginal Population of Michigan." The basic concern with man's relationship to his environment expressed in the present volume can be traced to Hinsdale's earlier work.

The general position in this volume is that man must live within his environment. The place which man finds within this environment is his niche and living within this niche requires adapting to it. In a stable adaptation there is a constant series of exchanges, of balanced interrelationships within the environment. However, no adaptation is ever stable over time because no environment is ever stable over a period of time. The energy exchange that supports the adaptation can lead to a disruption of the environment. Any change in the physical or biological environment alters the relationship of the organism to its environment. It places stress on the organism and dislocates the niche. In effect, it creates a new niche through the stress situation. For the organism to survive it must adapt to the new niche and in doing so disrupts the environment of every other organism. This process leads to changes in the forms of life. As organisms must adapt to new niches there is a continual process of natural selection so that only those organisms which adapt to the new niches survive.

Because of this selection there is continuous change in the range of variation within any population.

This concept of population itself is the key to the ecological approach. That a single organism may or may not survive is of little concern except that its failure to survive leads to a change in the nature of population variation and a change in the total environment. How a group of individuals, or a population, react to a stress situation is my main concern. The concept of the community is also important. In theory, the environment consists of everything which surrounds the organisms. In effect, there are both physical and biological factors which delimit the immediate environment. Plant and animal associations are found within restricted physical environments. These biotic communities are a convenient unit of study although their relationship to each other also must be understood.

If the organism under investigation is man, there is another factor in the adaptive system, that of culture. Whole volumes have been written dealing with the definition of culture. I will simply define culture as those nonbiological devices used by man for living in, or coping with, his environment. They can act as shields against the environment: man puts on a coat, builds a fire, or goes inside a house when he gets cold. Or they can serve as a sword to change the environment; man armed is the predator while unarmed he is the prey.

Culture may be the sword and the shield of man but it is a two-edged sword. Man lives in a cultural as well as a natural environment and he is limited by both. C. Loring Brace has described culture as an ecological niche in itself. One of the main trends of human development has been an increasing reliance on cultural rather than biological adaptation to stress situations. As culture becomes more of a factor in human development it, in turn, exerts selective pressure on man. Most biological change today is in response to culturally induced selective pressures.

By viewing culture as an adaptive device we can study the cultural adaptation itself since it, to some extent, controls the biological adaptation. This is what I have done in this volume; I have given cultural adaptations to the surrounding environments the greatest attention. The biological adaptations to the changing cultural environment are a separate study which R. G. Wilkinson and C. Loring Brace may deal with in the future. The emphasis here will be on the interaction between the cultural systems and the environment rather than on the interrelationships between elements of the culture system at any given time. However, change in response to any external factor will affect the relationship of all the elements within the cultural system.

Cultures must change with stress situations and since natural selection operates on cultures there are different levels of cultural efficiency. The concept of community is particularly appropriate to studies of cultural adaptation. This concept *must* be applicable or we could not talk of "cultures," only of continuous cultural variation.

For the archaeologist, the ecological systems approach is a boon and a challenge. Leslie White (1959: 67) has suggested that culture is composed of technological, societal, and ideological elements. Technology furnishes the "hard-goods" of the culture and also the energy base on which the culture is built. Society and ideology serve to integrate the organisms partici-

pating in the community which the culture represents. Kinship terminologies and religious experiences are rarely fossilized for the archaeologist to study, directly. Instead he is left with the nonperishable "hard-goods" and a fair idea of the energy base on which the culture is built.

The real challenge to the archaeologist is filling in the missing data in his study of cultural adaptation. He must go as far as possible in dealing with the societal and ideological elements of culture based on the items which are preserved plus the spatial relationships of these elements. This is often difficult, very speculative, and always fun. That a cemetery with a few status burials implies a ranked society is fairly clear but sometimes it takes elaborate techniques to infer changes in kinship systems from changes in ceramic styles. Such studies are necessary within our ecological framework for societal and ideological elements are key parts of the entire cultural adaptation.

It is necessary to study the relationships, or the series of exchanges, between the cultural and noncultural parts of the environment. The archaeologist starts this study with the nonartifactual material from sites. This includes the animal bone and charred plant remains from refuse pits which indicate how man was living from his environment and interacting with it.

Changes in the adaptive pattern of a culture take the form of changes in the relationship of items within the cultural system as well as the relationship of these items to the environment. If one item changes, all items change and the entire environment is altered. "Culture change comes about through minor variations in one or more systems, which displace or reinforce others and reach equilibrium on a different plain" (Flannery 1967).

4

If we had control of continuous variation in environment and cultural adaptions over time, we would have control of the patterns of culture change and a complete reconstruction of culture history. This type of control does not exist for any area of the earth at any time horizon, the present included. The best we can hope for is a series of sites within a fairly well-circumscribed region representing a single time horizon (broadly defined) which represent a single adaptive system. The archaeological "moment" may span thousands of years and the systemic variations which we can isolate may be very gross.

The sites for a single time horizon need to be studied, compared, and contrasted. Settlement types can be defined on the basis of economic activities carried out at these sites and settlement systems can be revealed from comparisons of settlement types. At the same time, independent studies of environment provide a background against which we can view culture change. When it is apparent that over time a new cultural adaptation has developed, the best the archaeologist can do is study the new adaptation, the new settlement types and systems, and try to infer the particular elements within the many interacting systems that would cause the particular type of change.

The tools which the archaeologist may use have been explained in detail elsewhere (Heizer 1962 and Deetz 1967 as examples). The field techniques used by the University of Michigan have been described in numerous monographs and have been the subject of an article by Papworth and Binford (1962). The field and laboratory techniques used here for analyzing environment largely follow Butzer (1964) with modifications to the particular situations in which I have worked.

Michigan is an ideal area for studies of prehistory which focus on changes in environment and the effect that these changes have had on our cultural systems. The environmental variations of the historic period can be projected back into prehistory (Fitting and Cleland, 1969). Fortunately, the earlier phases of the Michigan archaeological research program included the analysis of plant and animal remains. Yarnell's (1964) "Aboriginal Relationships between Culture and Plant Life in the Upper Great Lakes" and Cleland's (1966) "The Prehistoric Animal Ecology and Ethnozoology of the Upper Great Lakes Region" have served as guides for the present volume.

Since almost all of the plant and animal associations which presently exist. in the state can be projected far back into the prehistoric period, Chapter II of this volume is devoted to the environmental variation which exists within the state of Michigan today. It also deals with how the present environment developed over time. In this chapter, cultural and natural subdivisions within the state are refined for use in later chapters.

Chapter III concerns the earliest inhabitants of the state, the hunters who entered the area following the retreat of the ice. It also traces the disappearance of the environment in which they prospered. They were followed by the Archaic peoples who came back into Michigan when environmental changes were great enough to support a large population. Their adaptation is described in Chapter IV, "The Return of the People." This chapter also includes a description of the first ceramic-using people of the state who had a settlement pattern and cultural adaptation similar to the nonceramic Late Archaic peoples.

Between the Early and Middle Woodland periods there was a major shift in adaptive

5

pattern in both the southern and northern parts of Michigan. The Archaic trend toward a cultural separateness of these areas, which has an economic basis, is even more evident and in Chapter V, "Burials and Fishermen," the two adaptive trends are treated separately. This same separation continues into the Late Woodland period when agriculture becomes important throughout much of the area. This is covered in Chapter VI, "Crops and Cooperation."

The type of adaptations found in the late prehistoric period are similar to those of the early historic period. Chapter VII, "Those Who Were There," is a brief account of some of the key Indian groups in the area during the historic period. Quimby (1966b) has divided the historic period into Early, Middle, and Late Historic units.

One of the fastest growing specializations in American archaeology concerns the study of historic sites and Chapter VIII, "The Archaeology of History," is devoted to this subject. Michigan has supported some key projects in this area of study.

The last chapter, "Patterns of the Past," is a summary of the data sections of the volume. It is historical in the sense that it deals with what has been done, what is being done, and what should be done to keep the study of Michigan prehistory moving forward along unified lines.

While this is primarily a study of Michigan archaeology, the state is a fairly recent political unit. While I have focused my discussion on recent work within the state, I have not limited it to this area. There are numerous instances where Ohio, Indiana, Illinois, Wisconsin, Minnesota, and Ontario sites have a direct bearing on what is happening in Michigan and, in these instances, I have used what I felt was pertinent data without placing it in context within its own regional sequence.

CHAPTER II

ENVIRONMENTS OF MICHIGAN

THE LAND

The land mass of Michigan, almost 58,000 square miles, took hundreds of millions of years to attain its present form. Michigan began as a part of the "Canadian Shield," that mass of igneous rock that was the basis of the original North American continent. This mass of rock extended southward into what is today the western half of the upper peninsula. To the south was a shallow sea covering much of what is the lower peninsula.

During the following geological period sediments from eroding mountains were deposited on the sea floor becoming mountains themselves with each succeeding period of uplift that moved the shoreline to the south. With each uplift the sediments were changed and folded and new igneous rocks were forced into these formations. Today we can see the remnants of the oldest rocks of Michigan in the Huron Mountains and formations like them in the westernmost parts of the upper peninsula. During this period, thick sediments were laid down in the shallow sea in the area which is now Lake Superior. These sediments consisted of sands, fine muds, and lime. Iron minerals accumulated in the sands to form the rich iron deposits of the upper peninsula.

Again uplift and mountain building took place and these lake sediments, in the form of hardened rock, were lifted to

mountain height. Rocks were again changed by heat and pressure: sandstones into quartzite, shales into slate, and limestone into green and white marbles. In what is today the western end of Lake Superior volcanoes became active and poured out lava along with volcanic cinders and ash. The pure copper and silver of Keweenaw, Houghton, and Ontonagon counties were stored in the cracks of the later lava flows and in conglomerates formed from the earlier lava flows.

The next period of mountain building is known as the Killarney revolution after the town of Killarney in Ontario. Again igneous rock surfaced and the existing rocks were further metamorphosed. The massive mountains which formed from these Killarney granites have long since been worn down but remnants are still present in the Porcupine Mountains and near the tip of the Keweenaw Peninsula.

At the beginning of the Paleozoic era, 550 million years ago, a shallow sea spread over what is today Michigan. It is in these deposits that the first fossils, representing the earliest recorded forms of life in the area are found. The center part of the state was the deepest area of this lake basin, for bowl-shaped rock formations formed one on top of the other. On the outer edge of the lake basin, wells have been drilled to the basic granites through thin layers of sedimentary rock, while in the center of the state wells have gone as

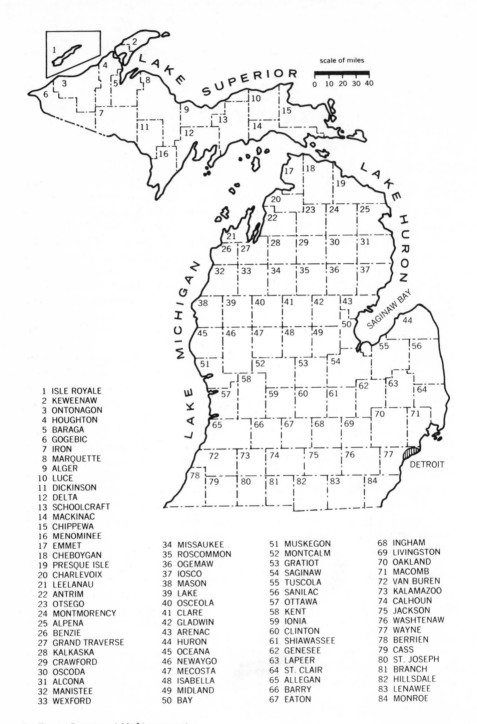

1 ISLE ROYALE	34 MISSAUKEE	51 MUSKEGON	68 INGHAM
2 KEWEENAW	35 ROSCOMMON	52 MONTCALM	69 LIVINGSTON
3 ONTONAGON	36 OGEMAW	53 GRATIOT	70 OAKLAND
4 HOUGHTON	37 IOSCO	54 SAGINAW	71 MACOMB
5 BARAGA	38 MASON	55 TUSCOLA	72 VAN BUREN
6 GOGEBIC	39 LAKE	56 SANILAC	73 KALAMAZOO
7 IRON	40 OSCEOLA	57 OTTAWA	74 CALHOUN
8 MARQUETTE	41 CLARE	58 KENT	75 JACKSON
9 ALGER	42 GLADWIN	59 IONIA	76 WASHTENAW
10 LUCE	43 ARENAC	60 CLINTON	77 WAYNE
11 DICKINSON	44 HURON	61 SHIAWASSEE	78 BERRIEN
12 DELTA	45 OCEANA	62 GENESEE	79 CASS
13 SCHOOLCRAFT	46 NEWAYGO	63 LAPEER	80 ST. JOSEPH
14 MACKINAC	47 MECOSTA	64 ST. CLAIR	81 BRANCH
15 CHIPPEWA	48 ISABELLA	65 ALLEGAN	82 HILLSDALE
16 MENOMINEE	49 MIDLAND	66 BARRY	83 LENAWEE
17 EMMET	50 BAY	67 EATON	84 MONROE
18 CHEBOYGAN			
19 PRESQUE ISLE			
20 CHARLEVOIX			
21 LEELANAU			
22 ANTRIM			
23 OTSEGO			
24 MONTMORENCY			
25 ALPENA			
26 BENZIE			
27 GRAND TRAVERSE			
28 KALKASKA			
29 CRAWFORD			
30 OSCODA			
31 ALCONA			
32 MANISTEE			
33 WEXFORD			

Fig. 1 Location of Michigan counties

Time (in millions of years since beginning of epoch)	Eras	Epochs	Time (as % since origin of life)
1		Pleistocene	99.9
10		Pliocene	
30	Cenozoic	Miocene	
40		Oligocene	
60		Eocene.	
75		Paleocene	96
135		Cretaceous	95
165	Mesozoic	Jurassic	94
205		Triassic	93
230		Permian	92
250		Pennsylvanian	91
280		Mississipian	90
325	Paleozoic	Devonian	89
360		Silurian	88
425		Ordovician	86
500		Cambrian	83
3000	Precambrian	Proterozoic	0
10,000		Archeozoic	—333

Fig. 2 Geological time periods

many as two miles deep without encountering these granites.

The Cambrian deposits, representing the earliest of the Paleozoic seas, were formed 500 million years ago and are marked by coarse sandy sediments which became finer as the sea became shallower near the end of its existence. The sea then deepened as much of the North American continent became submerged. The deposits of the Ordovician period were initially limestones formed from lime muck containing millions of small shells. As the seas were alternately deep and clear, then shallow and muddy, so limestone alternates with shale. The limestones of Menominee County along the Wisconsin-Michigan border represent such formations.

The Ordovician was followed by the Silurian period which was marked by deep seas with clear, warm waters. Great deposits of lime muds and corals, now the Niagara limestones, which are 1600 feet thick in places, were found. Outcroppings of these limestones occur from Manitoulin Island in Lake Huron to the Garden Peninsula in Lake Michigan.

Toward the end of the Silurian, the seas became salty and many forms of life died. Salt beds formed in lake sediments, alternating with shales and limestones. In the center of Michigan 2300 feet of alternating beds have been found, but they are shallower at the edges of the basin of that sea. The Mackinac Island limestone formed on top of these deposits while in the south the Bass Island limestones were formed.

As the Devonian period began, the climate became warm and moist. Michigan was covered by a closed pond, with its north shore across the St. Ignace Peninsula and its south shore in Monroe County. The sand dunes along the south shore became beds of white Sylvania sandstone. The Devonian was an age of fishes and corals; the reefs and lime muds of this period are now recalled in limestones fifty to a thousand feet thick.

As the Devonian seas became shallower, the surrounding rivers brought in sediments, black with vegetation, that marked the beginning of the Carboniferous age. Most of the lower peninsula was covered by a bay of this great sea which alternately expanded and retreated for millions of years. This Mississippian sea was marked by a number of deposits. Toward the base are thick shales covered by the Marshall limestones which in turn are covered by other shale, limestone, and gypsum beds.

The Pennsylvania period, spanning the last 45 million years of the Carboniferous age, is marked by a series of swamp rather than marine deposits. A layer of sand was spread over the Mississippian limestones followed by rich organic levels that have long since become the coal and shale beds of the center part of the lower peninsula.

Once more the seas invaded Michigan during the Permian period during which the seas were shallow and the climate hot and dry. Today it is marked by a layer of red shale with streaks of gypsum covering the last Pennsylvanian limestone.

This sequence takes us up to 220 million years ago. After that time we have no evidence that the salt sea invaded the area again. Michigan shared in the uplift and warping that formed the Appalachian and Rocky mountains; the Lake Superior basin was formed by warping, for example. If any new deposits were formed they have been lost through erosion that has erased the geological record in this area until relatively recent times. Erosion probably cut the river valleys in the softer rocks which later, during glacial times, became the basins of the Great Lakes. It also erased all traces of the dinosaurs, saber-toothed tigers, horses, and other animals that may have roamed the land during the Mesozoic and early Cenozoic eras. We can deal with the formation of the land again only toward the end of the period of continental glaciation which started a mere million years ago.

Michigan, intermittently, lay buried under two to four miles of ice for almost a million years. This advancing mass of ice altered the landscape as it scraped off and incorporated soil and rock from old land surfaces. This debris, imbedded in the glacial mass, scraped, gouged, and scratched the surface over which the ice moved. Areas of hard rock were smoothed and worn down. Less resistant rocks were gouged out by the ice and the preglacial stream beds were widened and deepened to form bowl-shaped basins.

The ice followed the path of least resistance down existing valleys and gorges. Instead of moving uniformly the ice advanced in tongues or lobes down these valleys. Today we can find traces of the Superior lobe with the Keweenaw lobe as an appendage, the Michigan lobe with the Traverse and Green Bay lobes as secondary formations, the Huron lobe with its important Saginaw appendage, and the Erie and Ontario lobes.

The ice moved vast accumulations of debris, but the meltwater from its retreat could carry only the finer sediments. Since the retreat of the last glaciation was rapid, much of this debris was dumped to form the glacial features which mark much of the state today. The glacial drift in these deposits contains many types of rocks, clay, and sand.

The moraines of Michigan mark the stages of this last glacial retreat and stand where each minor readvance took place, pushing up mounds of rubble in front of them. Each lobe left its own set of ice margin features that can be mapped out to tell the tale of its retreat.

The Saginaw lobe, a part of the larger Huron lobe, was thinner than the other lobes and melted faster. The first record we have of a minor readvance is in a moraine near Sturgis, the oldest moraine in Michigan. The retreat across Michigan is further marked by moraines at Tekonsha, Kalamazoo, and Charlotte. In places it is possible to tie in these moraines with the Mississinawa moraine left by the Erie lobe and the Valparaiso moraine left by the retreating Michigan lobe.

The Saginaw lobe left small moraines at Lansing, Grand Ledge, Ionia, Portland,

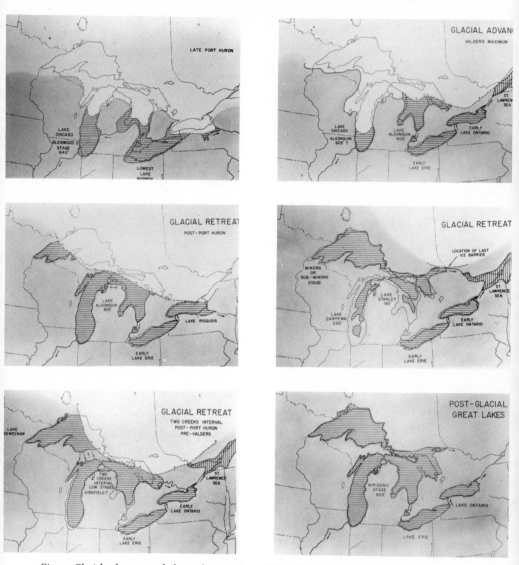

Fig. 3 Glacial advances and the prehistoric Great Lakes (From Hough: 1963)

Lyons, Fowler, St. Johns, Flint, and Owosso. Here the ice retreat stopped and the low and rolling, waterlaid Port Huron moraine was formed. This moraine can be traced from the Genesse Valley in New York to the Lake Michigan shore north of Luding-

ton. The last stand of the ice in the lower peninsula formed the Cheboygan moraine running between Cheboygan and Mackinaw City.

Following the Valparaiso moraine system of the Michigan lobe, the Tinley and Lake

YEARS AGO	DEPLOYMENT OF GLACIER FRONT	BASIN	LAKE	LEVEL (feet above tide)	OUTLETS
16,000	Retreat and halt at Valparaiso	Michigan:	Early Chicago	640?	Illinois
	Charlotte-Ft. Wayne system	Erie:	Highest Maumee	800	Ft. Wayne-Wabash
15,000	Advance and halt at Tinley-Defiance system	Michigan:	Re-occupied by ice		Ft. Wayne-Wabash
		Erie:	Highest Maumee	800	
	Retreat	Michigan:	Chicago	640	Illinois
		Huron:	Early Saginaw	730	Grand
		Erie:	Lowest Maumee	760	Imlay-Grand
14,000	Advance and halt at Lake Border system	Michigan:	Chicago	640	Illinois
		Erie:	Middle Maumee	780	Imlay-Grand (?) and/or Ft. Wayne-Wabash
13,000	Retreat	Michigan:	Chicago	640	Illinois
		Huron:	Arkona	710, 700, 695	Grand
		Erie:			
	Retreat	Conjectural low water interval			East (?)
12,500	Advance and halt at Port Huron system	Michigan:	Chicago	640	Illinois
		Huron:	Saginaw	695	Grand
		Erie:	Whittlesey	738	Ubly
12,500 to 12,000	Retreat	Michigan:	Chicago	620, 605	Illinois
		Huron-	Warren	690, 682	Grand
		Erie:	Wayne	655	Mohawk
			Warren	675	Grand
			Grassmere	640	Grand Traverse ? or Mohawk
			Lundy	620	
12,000	Retreat	Superior:	Keweenaw	(?)	AuTrain-Whitefish
		Michigan-	Two Creeks		(?)
		Huron:	(Kirkfield)		
		Low water interval		below 580	Trent
		Erie:	low water stage	(?)	Niagara
11,800 to 11,500	Advance and halt at Valders system	Superior:	filled with ice		
		Michigan:	Early Algonquin	605	Illinois
		Huron:	Early Algonquin	605	St. Clair
		Erie:	Early Erie	below 572	Niagara

Fig. 4 Principal stages in the evolution of the Great Lakes (After Kelley and Farrand: 1967)

Border moraines formed before the Port Huron moraine. The last deposits of this lobe are the red tills of the Valders substage (Wayne and Zumberg 1965: 72) which postdate the Two Creeks interval of 11,850 years ago.

The Superior lobe formed most of the late glacial features in the upper peninsula where the ice entered from the northeast and covered much of the land area. In the western half of the upper peninsula the areas between the rugged mountains were filled with glacial debris, and moraines blocked the northward flow of many streams. The stands of ice in the eastern half of the upper peninsula are marked by moraines at Munising, Newberry, and Kinross.

At times of major glacial readvance moraines were pushed together. The Irish

YEARS AGO	DEPLOYMENT OF GLACIER FRONT	BASIN	LAKE	LEVEL (feet above tide)	OUTLETS
11,000	Retreat (Trent outlet still blocked by ice?)	Superior:	Duluth	1,085	St. Croix
		Michigan-Huron:	Algonquin	605	Illinois & St. Clair
		Erie:	Early Erie	below 572	Niagara
10,500 to 9,500	Retreat	Superior:	levels lower than Duluth, includes Minong		AuTrain-Whitefish, & others
		Michigan-Huron:	Post-Algonquin series of successively lower levels to	390 (?)	Trent, Fossmill & others
		Erie:	Early Erie, rising levels approaching	572	Niagara
9,500	Final retreat of ice sheet from Great Lakes basins	Superior:	Houghton	360 (?)	St. Marys
		Michigan:	Chippewa (extreme low)	230	Mackinac
		Huron:	Stanley (extreme low)	180 (?)	North Bay
		Erie:	Early Erie, rising levels approaching	572	Niagara
9,000 to 4,500	Ice sheet in Hudson Bay area	Superior:		rising levels	St. Marys
		Michigan:		rising levels	Mackinac
		Huron:		rising levels	North Bay
		Erie:		rising levels	Niagara
4,500 to 3,500	No ice sheet on mainland of North America	Superior:	Nipissing	605	North Bay, Illinois & St. Clair
		Michigan-Huron:	Great Lakes		
		Erie:	Early Erie	570 (approx.)	Niagara
3,500 to 2,000		Superior-Michigan-Huron:	Levels falling slightly with pause at Algoma level	595	St. Clair Illinois (?)
		Erie:	Modern level	571	Niagara
2,000 to Present		Superior:	Modern level	601	St. Marys
		Michigan-Huron:	Modern level	579	St. Clair
		Erie:	Modern level	571	Niagara

Fig. 4 (continued)

Hills in Jackson County are interlobate moraines where the Saginaw and Erie lobes met. The hills in the high central region of the state around Clare, Grayling, and Gaylord were formed by the Huron and Michigan lobes while the hills north and south of Grand Rapids mark where the Saginaw and Michigan lobes met.

There are other features that mark the retreat of the ice. At times, great blocks of ice would break away from the main glacial mass and not melt until long after the main ice body had passed. Its final melting left deep holes, called "kettle holes," in the moraines. Many of these kettle holes filled with water to form lakes which still exist. In addition to these end moraines, the retreating ice left rolling ground moraines, or till plains. These are largely lands of stony clay with irregular depressions marking where small blocks of ice melted.

As the ice retreated, large amounts of water were released carrying the finer glacial debris: silts and gravels. The flat lands of Kalamazoo, Cass, and Roscommon counties represent such stratified gravelly, gently undulating outwash plains. In contrast to till plains formed by the melt in back of moraines, outwash plains are in front of moraines. Hardwood forests grow on till plains and conifers grow on the outwash plains. Farming is more successful on till plains.

Ice trapped under outwash plains melted more slowly because of the sand and gravel cover of the plain, and when it did melt it left basins which filled to form "pit lakes." Houghton, Higgins, Gull, Cadillac, and other inland lakes were formed by this process. Many others have either dried up completely or exist as shallow swamps.

Eskers, which are sand and gravel deposits formed by rivers moving under stagnant ice, are found in many parts of the state where they are known as "hogbacks" and "Indian trails." More than a thousand eskers are known in Michigan but the largest was the Mason esker that has been traced for twenty miles from northeast of Lansing, through Holt, to a point south of Mason. Much of this esker has been removed in sand and gravel operations.

Kames are another type of glacial feature. They are rudely stratified hills of cobbles, gravel, sand, and silt. These deposits were formed by water moving over the ice and falling either through crevices to the base or over the front of the tops of moraines. They are common in the areas between major moraine systems.

In some parts of the state meltwater from the ice was impounded behind the moraines to form large shallow lakes which are now dry lake plains. The large flat areas in central Lapeer County, the northwest corner of Kalamazoo County and in Kalamazoo County south of Kalamazoo were formed in this manner.

The last major land formations in Michigan are former Great Lake beds that are now broad expanses of flat land. They start well south of the Ohio line and are found along the borders of Lakes Erie, St. Clair, and Huron, in scattered areas along Lake Michigan and in many areas in the upper peninsula. Long stretches of sandy gravels, former strand lines, mark the beaches of these lakes. Such beaches, wave-cut notches, and lake terraces have been studied and correlated to tell of the history of the lakes themselves.

THE LAKES

In recent years the history of the Great Lakes has been intensively studied, and several survey publications are available (Hough 1958, 1963; Kelley and Farrand 1967). Four of the five Great Lakes border Michigan and are a key to the understanding of the state. Lake Superior is the northernmost and largest of these lakes. It covers an area of 31,820 square miles and drains an area of 49,180 square miles surrounding the lake. It is 350 miles long, 160 miles wide, and has a maximum depth of over 1300 feet. With a surface elevation of 602 feet above sea level it is the highest of the lakes.

Water from Lake Superior flows down the St. Marys River into Lake Huron, which has a surface elevation of 580 feet above sea level. Lake Huron has a surface area of 23,010 square miles and drains an area of 49,610 square miles. It is 206 miles long, 101 miles wide, and has a maximum depth of 750 feet. The Lake Michigan surface is at the same level as Lake Huron and the two join in the Straits of Mackinac. Lake Michigan has a surface area of 22,400 square miles. It has a maximum depth of 750 feet while it is 307 miles long and 118 miles wide at its widest point.

Lake Erie, which touches the southeastern part of Michigan, has a surface elevation of 572 feet above sea level. Lake Huron drains into Lake Erie by the way of the St. Clair River, Lake St. Clair, and the Detroit River. The drop between Lake Huron and Lake St. Clair is six feet while that from Lake St. Clair to Lake Erie is two feet. Lake Erie is the smallest of the Great Lakes surrounding Michigan, with a surface area of 9930 square miles and a drainage area of 22,560 square miles. It is 241 miles long and 57 miles wide. It is also the shallowest of the lakes with a maximum depth of 210 feet and an average depth of only 58 feet. Its total volume is one thirteenth that of Lake Superior. Lake Erie drains over Niagara Falls into Lake Ontario and out the St. Lawrence River into the Atlantic Ocean.

The history of the Lakes themselves began with the retreat of the ice. During their early history these lakes had glacial ice as their northern shore. Readvances of the dying Wisconsin ice sheet changed drainage patterns by blocking outlets and caused changes in the levels of the lakes. The sequence of Lake stages begins with the early stage of Lake Chicago, in the Michigan basin, which drained out the Illinois River, and highest Lake Maumee in the Erie basin, which drained through the Wabash. We know from old beach levels that this stage of Lake Maumee stood at 800 feet above sea level but the Tinley glacial advance has destroyed the early Lake Chicago beaches.

With the retreat of this ice, the waters from the Lake Erie basin drained around the thumb of Michigan, along the channel of the Grand River, and into the Glenwood stage of Lake Chicago. The Allendale delta at the mouth of the glacial Grand River was formed at this time. The lowest Lake Maumee level in the Erie basin stood at 760 feet above sea level while the Glenwood stage of Lake Chicago was 640 feet above sea level. The next glacial advance, which created the Lake Border moraine, raised the water level in Lake Erie to 780 feet so it must have again drained down the Wabash River since the divide at Fort Wayne, Indiana, is also around 760 feet above sea level.

When the ice again retreated, the lake level in the Erie basin dropped as the waters again drained through the Grand River channel into Lake Chicago, which was held at the 640-foot Glenwood level by a sill of that elevation at Chicago. This stage in the Erie basin is marked by three Arkona beaches at 710, 700, and 695 feet above sea level—a result of alternate downcutting and stabilization of the Grand River channel. The glacial retreat may have been great enough to drain the lakes to an even lower stage with drainage out the St. Lawrence but, if so, later glacial advances and high water stages have destroyed the evidence.

The next glacial advance was the Port Huron which built the prominent moranic system mentioned earlier. It advanced far enough to again isolate the Erie basin, where the water rose to the Lake Whittlesey level of 738 feet above sea level. This lake apparently drained along the ice front into Lake Saginaw in the Huron basin, which had an elevation of 695 feet above sea level.

There may have been two periods of

minor retreat and advance after the main advance of the Port Huron ice. The first of these, "Port Huron 2," built the Bay City moraine in the Saginaw valley and is probably contemporary with the highest Lake Warren level in the Erie basin at 680 feet above sea level. The second minor retreat caused a greater flow of water which cut the Grand River channel deeper, dropping middle Lake Warren to a 670-foot level. This stage probably lasted through the second minor advance, "Port Huron 3," which built the Tawas moraine in the Saginaw Bay area. Another possible advance correlated with a still lower Lake Warren stage has also been postulated.

With the retreat of Port Huron ice, the St. Lawrence drainage was never again completely closed. The succeeding Valders advance stopped north of this outlet. Lake Grassmere at 640 feet, Lake Lundy at 620 feet, and early Lake Algonquin at 605 feet above sea level mark the draining of the Erie basin in pre-Valders times. They correspond with the Glenwood, Calumet, and Toleston stages in the Lake Michigan basin, suggesting an alternative discharge in this direction for the lakes in the Erie basin. This also would have been the period when the sill at the Chicago outlet was cut down to 605 feet.

With the further retreat of the Port Huron ice, the Trent Valley area in Ontario was cleared and water drained rapidly through this outlet during the Kirkfield low stage, which has been correlated with the Two Creeks interval dated to 11,850 years ago. The Lake Superior basin, covered with ice during both the Port Huron and Valders advances, contained a glacial lake—Lake Keweenaw—during the warm interval.

The Valders ice advanced a little before eleven thousand years ago and again closed the Trent waterway as well as the Straits of Mackinac. Water levels in the Lake Huron basin again rose to 605 feet above sea level, the second phase of Lake Algonquin. This lake drained through the St. Clair River, to Lake St. Clair, and out the Detroit River into Lake Erie. Water in the Michigan basin rose to the old Lake Toleston level of 605 feet and again drained into the Illinois River.

After the Valders retreat, lake levels again fell as alternate northern outlets were cleared and new drainage patterns were formed. The main stage of Lake Algonquin had not been present in the Superior basin. Several stages of Lake Duluth, 150 to 225 feet higher than modern Lake Superior, existed in the western area and drained down the St. Croix River and out the Mississippi.

When the Trent and, later, the Ottawa waterways were again uncovered, the waters in the Michigan and Huron basins drained eastward. There are a number of well-marked beaches of these stages preserved by uplift resulting from the postglacial rebound of the land in this area. These lake stages, as represented by beaches and terraces, and their estimated elevations are: Weybridge at 540 feet above sea level, Pentang at 510 feet, Cedar Point at 493 feet, Payette at 465 feet, Sheguiandah at 435 feet, and Korah at 390 feet above sea level.

The Stanley stage in the Huron basin was the lowest of these lakes. It was 390 feet below the present lake level, or 190 feet above sea level. It is correlated with the Chippewa stage in the Michigan basin which drained into Lake Stanley through a deep channel in the Straits of Mackinac. The Houghton stage in Lake Superior, at 340 feet above sea level, also drained into Lake Huron over a sill in the St. Marys

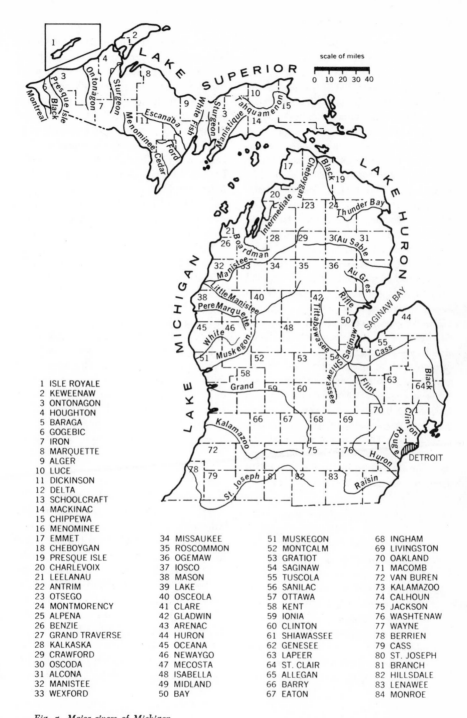

1 ISLE ROYALE
2 KEWEENAW
3 ONTONAGON
4 HOUGHTON
5 BARAGA
6 GOGEBIC
7 IRON
8 MARQUETTE
9 ALGER
10 LUCE
11 DICKINSON
12 DELTA
13 SCHOOLCRAFT
14 MACKINAC
15 CHIPPEWA
16 MENOMINEE
17 EMMET
18 CHEBOYGAN
19 PRESQUE ISLE
20 CHARLEVOIX
21 LEELANAU
22 ANTRIM
23 OTSEGO
24 MONTMORENCY
25 ALPENA
26 BENZIE
27 GRAND TRAVERSE
28 KALKASKA
29 CRAWFORD
30 OSCODA
31 ALCONA
32 MANISTEE
33 WEXFORD

34 MISSAUKEE
35 ROSCOMMON
36 OGEMAW
37 IOSCO
38 MASON
39 LAKE
40 OSCEOLA
41 CLARE
42 GLADWIN
43 ARENAC
44 HURON
45 OCEANA
46 NEWAYGO
47 MECOSTA
48 ISABELLA
49 MIDLAND
50 BAY

51 MUSKEGON
52 MONTCALM
53 GRATIOT
54 SAGINAW
55 TUSCOLA
56 SANILAC
57 OTTAWA
58 KENT
59 IONIA
60 CLINTON
61 SHIAWASSEE
62 GENESEE
63 LAPEER
64 ST. CLAIR
65 ALLEGAN
66 BARRY
67 EATON

68 INGHAM
69 LIVINGSTON
70 OAKLAND
71 MACOMB
72 VAN BUREN
73 KALAMAZOO
74 CALHOUN
75 JACKSON
76 WASHTENAW
77 WAYNE
78 BERRIEN
79 CASS
80 ST. JOSEPH
81 BRANCH
82 HILLSDALE
83 LENAWEE
84 MONROE

Fig. 5   Major rivers of Michigan

River. The age of this low stage has been estimated at 9500 years ago.

Since then, uplift of the land in the northern parts of the lakes has played the key role in their history. Gradual uplift of the Trent and Ottawa outlets caused the lakes in the Michigan and Huron basins to rise to the levels of their old southern outlets of 605 feet above sea level. This Lake Nipissing stage, dated at 4200 years ago, extended into the Lake Superior basin.

The sill at Chicago was on bedrock but the St. Clair River outlet on glacial till was cut down to its present level of 580 feet with at least one brief period of stabilization at 595 feet at some time between 2500 and 3500 years ago. This caused the formation of the Lake Algoma beaches in the Upper Lakes basins.

For the past 2500 years there has been little change in the elevations of Lakes Huron and Michigan with the possible exception of a brief stage between 590 and 595 feet above sea level some time between 1500 and 1800 years ago (Mason 1966, Speth n.d.). Lake Superior has continued to rise because of the great uplift in this area. This process still continues and the north shore is rising faster than the south shore, causing swampy conditions along the southern shore.

THE RIVERS AND SMALL LAKES

In addition to the Great Lakes, Michigan has more than 36,000 miles of rivers and streams. There are over 11,000 small lakes, with a water surface area of more than 1000 square miles, located in all but two of the 83 counties.

The rivers of Michigan are both diverse and uniform. No single system dominates the state and, in comparison to other parts of North America, all have relatively uni-

form rates of flow. In all, there are thirty-four primary river systems in Michigan with watershed areas of 250 square miles or more (McNamee 1930). McNamee rated seven of these as first class rivers with watersheds of 2000 square miles or more. These include, in order of size: the Saginaw, Grand, St. Joseph, Menominee, Muskegon, and Au Sable rivers, although the later drainage is just below 2000 square miles. The Manistee too falls just 80 square miles short of this drainage area and since it is well over twice as long as the next largest river I include it with the first class rivers of Michigan.

Six of these eight rivers drain into Lake Michigan. The largest of these is the Grand, the second largest river in the state. The Grand River is at least 300 miles long, counting all its many bends and curves, and has a watershed of 5572 square miles. It has a pear-shaped basin about 100 miles long and 60 miles wide. The headwaters in Jackson County have an elevation of over 1000 feet above sea level. Important tributaries include the Flat, Maple, Lookingglass, and Red Cedar rivers. Only three lakes in this drainage have an area of over one square mile (Jordan, Reeds, and Crystal) but together with smaller lakes and some marshes about nine percent of the entire area is covered by water.

The St. Joseph River system lies in both Michigan and Indiana. It has a watershed of 4586 square miles, a length of 160 miles, and a basin with a maximum length of 110 miles and a width of 65 miles. It has its source in eastern Hillsdale County at an elevation of over 1100 feet above sea level and falls about 500 feet to its mouth. From its source in Hillsdale County it flows northwesterly to near Homer in Calhoun County, southwesterly across Branch and St. Joseph counties in Michigan, and from there into Elkhart County, Indiana. From South Bend, Indiana, it flows north to its mouth at St. Joseph in Michigan. It has the Paw Paw, Elkhart, Pigeon, Fawn, Prairie, and Portage rivers as tributaries. Twelve lakes with an area over one square mile are located within this watershed: Coldwater, Marble, Austin, Diamond, Klinger, Corey, Paw Paw, Long, Indian, Wawasee, James, and Crooked lakes. These, along with smaller lakes and several large marshes, account for ten percent of the area of the drainage.

North of the Grand is the Muskegon River, the fifth largest in the state. It has a watershed of 2663 square miles and is about 150 miles long. It has a basin about 120 miles long varying from 10 to 30 miles in width. Part of its drainage is well over 1200 feet above sea level but its main source at Higgins Lake is only 1160 feet above sea level. About two thirds of its watershed is over 1000 feet. The Little Muskegon is its largest tributary. There are seven lakes with surface areas over one square mile in this drainage. Houghton Lake, with a surface area of 31 square miles, and Higgins Lake, with a surface area of 15 square miles, are the largest; but Muskegon, Big Clam, Missaukee, Little Clam, and Fremont lakes are also important. These, together with smaller lakes and swamps, account for approximately 16 percent of the drainage area.

The Kalamazoo River, flowing to the south of the Grand and north of the St. Joseph, is the sixth largest river in the state. It has a tributary watershed of 2064 square miles, a length of 125 miles, and a basin 100 miles long varying in width from 10 to 30 miles. It has its origin near the Jackson-Hillsdale county line at an elevation slightly over 1100 feet. It has two branches which join near Albion. There

are four lakes with surface areas over one square mile: Gun, Gull, Crooked, and Pine. These, together with smaller lakes and marshes, account for eleven percent of the surface of this drainage basin.

The Manistee River, eighth largest in the state, is located to the north of the Muskegon. Estimates of its watershed vary between 2120 and 1920 square miles so it is on the border of McNamee's first class river classification. It is 200 miles long and has a basin 110 miles long. The upper half of this basin is less than 15 miles wide while the lower half is almost 40 miles wide at its maximum. The Little Manistee, which McNamee considers as a separate primary river, joins it near its mouth in Manistee County. The Manistee has its origin in a series of lakes along the boundary of Antrim and Otsego counties. It flows across Kalkaska, Missaukee, Wexford, and Manistee counties. Over eighty percent of the watershed is at elevations above 1000 feet, with the highest point over 1600 feet, giving it more than a 1000-foot drop to its mouth. There are four lakes with more than one square mile of water surface: Bear, Portage, Manistee, and Crooked. These, along with smaller lakes and swamps, account for ten percent of the total drainage area.

The last primary Michigan river draining into Lake Michigan is in the upper peninsula and is the only first class river in this part of the state. The Menominee River is the fourth largest river in Michigan. It has a watershed of about 4000 square miles and is 180 miles long. It has its origin in the eastern part of Baraga County where it flows in a small stream to Lake Michigamme. The Michigamme River flows from Lake Michigamme to a point in southwestern Iron County where it joins the Brule River to form the Menominee. It has its source at an elevation over 1600 feet above sea level and falls over 1000 feet to its mouth. Its watershed is in both Wisconsin and Michigan and its important tributaries include the Paint, Michigamme, Brule, Sturgeon, Little Cedar, Pine, and Pemebonwon rivers. In its watershed there are four lakes with surface areas over one square mile: Michigamme, Chicagoan, Antoine, and Ned. These, taken with a number of smaller lakes and a large marsh area, constitute fifteen percent of the total drainage area.

There are eleven other rivers in Michigan draining into Lake Michigan with watersheds of 250 square miles or more. In the lower peninsula there are six which, going from south to north, include the White, Pere Marquette, Little Manistee, Boardman, Intermediate, and Pine. The White River, which empties in Muskegon County, drains 490 square miles, has a basin about 50 miles long, and drops 400 feet. The Pere Marquette, with its mouth in Mason County, has a watershed of 740 square miles, a basin 48 miles long and 30 miles wide and drops 500 feet. The Little Manistee, with its outlet in Manistee County, has a watershed of 267 square miles, a basin about 40 miles long which is only about 5 miles wide for most of its length, and a drop of 500 feet. The Boardman drains into Grand Traverse Bay and has a watershed of 304 square miles. Its basin is about 35 miles long, 10 miles wide, and it drops 625 feet.

The Intermediate also drains into Grand Traverse Bay and has a drainage area of 335 square miles. It has a very irregular basin and drops about 220 feet. It drains through a series of lakes including Torch, with a surface area of 27 square miles, and Elk, with a surface area of 10 square miles. In all, twenty-three percent of the total drainage area is covered by water.

The last major lower peninsula river draining into Lake Michigan is the Pine. The Pine is a relatively short stream draining Lake Charlevoix, which has a surface area of 27 square miles, into Lake Michigan. Lake Charlevoix is fed by the Boyne and Jordan rivers. The system has a drainage area of 315 square miles, twenty-four percent of which is covered by surface water. It has a basin 20 miles long and 5 miles wide and a drop of 650 feet.

From east to west along the south shore of the upper peninsula there are five primary rivers. The Manistique, its mouth in Schoolcraft County, has a watershed of 1450 square miles, a basin 42 miles long and 37 wide and a drop of 350 feet. It drains several lakes and large swamps so forty-seven percent of the surface area of the drainage system is covered with water. The Whitefish River runs into Little Bay de Noc in Delta County. It has a watershed of 340 square miles, a basin 30 miles long and 10 miles wide, and falls 400 feet. Because of extensive marshes thirty-five percent of the surface area of this drainage is covered by water. The Escanaba is also a tributary of Bay de Noc. It has a watershed of 890 square miles, a basin 30 miles long and 25 miles wide at its greatest point and falls 1000 feet. It too is swampy, and twenty-eight percent of the drainage basin is covered with surface water. The Ford and the Cedar rivers both drain into Green Bay. The former has a watershed of 460 square miles, a basin 50 miles long and 10 miles wide, and a drop of 800 feet while the latter has an area of 400 square miles, a drainage basin about 75 miles long, and a drop of 400 feet. The areas covered by surface water account for twenty-six percent of the Ford drainage and fifteen percent of the Cedar drainage.

In the Lake Superior basin there are six

Michigan rivers with significant drainage systems. The westernmost is the Montreal. It has a drainage area of 285 square miles, a basin 30 miles long and 10 miles wide, and drops 1000 feet. Surface water covers fifteen percent of the total drainage area. The Black River also has its origin in Wisconsin. It has a watershed of 320 square miles, nineteen percent of which is covered with surface water, a basin 35 miles long and 10 wide, and a drop of 1000 feet. The Presque Isle River has a watershed of 360 square miles, a basin 40 miles long and 50 miles wide, and drops 1000 feet. The Ontonagon, with its mouth in Ontonagon County, has a drainage area of 1340 square miles, fifteen percent of which is covered by surface water. It has a basin 35 miles long and just about as wide, and a drop of 1000 feet. The Sturgeon River drains into Portage Lake, an arm of Lake Superior. It has a watershed of 730 square miles, a basin 45 miles long and 15 miles wide, and falls about 1100 feet. Surface water covers twenty-one percent of the drainage area. The Tahquamenon, which drains into Whitefish Bay in Chippewa County, has a drainage area of 806 square miles, with forty-seven percent covered by small lakes and marshes, a basin 20 miles long and 50 miles wide, and a total drop of 300 feet. Lake Superior drains into Lake Huron by way of the St. Marys River which passes Sault Ste. Marie.

Only two first class rivers flow into Lake Huron from Michigan. The northernmost is the Au Sable with its source in Otsego County at an elevation of over 1200 feet above sea level. Its mouth is near Oscoda in Iosco County. It has a drainage area of 1932 square miles which puts it, like the Manistee, on the border between first and second class rivers. Its basin is 80 miles long and 30 miles wide. There are five lakes

with surface areas over one square mile: St. Helen, Otsego, Margrethe, East Twin, and West Twin with the surface water covering fourteen percent of the watershed.

The largest river system in the state is the Saginaw with a drainage area of 6260 square miles. The Saginaw itself is only 20 miles long and flows from the city of Saginaw into Saginaw Bay at Bay City. Its tributaries, which flow together near Saginaw, include the Flint, Cass, Shiawassee, and Tittabawassee rivers. The Flint has a valley 120 miles long and drains 1350 square miles while the Cass is 75 miles long and drains a little less than 1000 square miles. These, together with the Shiawassee, with a watershed of 1070 square miles, drain the southern half of the valley. The Tittabawassee, with a watershed of 2620 square miles, drains the northern half of the Saginaw Valley. It is shorter but because of its greater fall, 700 feet as opposed to 425 for the Shiawassee, 320 for the Flint and 220 for the Cass, and a greater velocity, it carries more water than the other three rivers combined. There are only two lakes, Chippewa and Long, with areas over one square mile and only nine percent of the watershed is covered by surface water.

Four smaller rivers flow into Lake Huron from Michigan. The Cheboygan River system has a watershed of 1594 square miles, a basin 50 miles long and 30 miles wide, and a fall of 700 feet. The Sturgeon, Pigeon, Black, and Crooked rivers are important tributaries. Because of several large lakes, particularly Mullett, Burt, and Black, along with several large marshes, twenty-three percent of the drainage area is covered by surface water. The Thunder Bay River flows into Thunder Bay near Alpena. It drains 1275 square miles, twenty-

21

five percent of which is covered by surface water, has a roughly circular basin about 40 miles in diameter and falls 700 feet. The Au Gres River has a watershed of 455 square miles with a basin 30 miles long and 15 miles wide, and a fall of 325 feet. Only ten percent of its drainage is covered with surface water. The Rifle River has a drainage of 390 square miles, five percent covered by lakes and marshes, a basin 40 miles long and 10 miles wide, and a drop of 750 feet.

Lake Huron drains into Lake St. Clair through the St. Clair River which is 37 miles long. The Black River flows into it near Port Huron. The Black River is 60 miles long and has a watershed area of 690 square miles. It falls 200 feet and, because of swamps, twenty-one percent of its drainage is covered by water.

Lake St. Clair is a shallow body of water with a single major tributary, the Clinton River. The Clinton, draining 761 square miles, eight percent of which is covered by water, has a basin about 50 miles long and a fall of 425 feet.

The Detroit River is 27 miles long and connects Lake St. Clair with Lake Erie. Its only tributary is the Rouge River with a watershed of 465 square miles, a length of 32 miles, and a fall of 360 feet. Only four percent of its drainage is covered by surface water.

Only two large rivers flow into Lake Erie from Michigan: the Huron and the Raisin. The former has a watershed of 935 square miles, thirteen percent of which is covered by surface water, is about 80 miles long, and falls 440 feet. The latter has a drainage of 1125 square miles, five percent of which is covered by surface water, and a roughly circular basin about 40 miles in diameter with a drop of 430 feet.

The rivers of Michigan fall into several groups. The Lake Michigan side of the lower peninsula is marked by a series of large, long rivers with a few smaller ones in intervening drainage areas. These rivers are marked by few large marshes, many medium-sized lakes and about ten percent surface water cover. The Lake Huron side of the state is dominated by a single river system, the Saginaw, flowing into Saginaw Bay. The Au Sable and several smaller rivers draining into Lake Huron fall more into the pattern observed on the Lake Michigan side of the state. In the more northern parts of the lower peninsula, roughly from Traverse City to Cheboygan, large lakes and swamps account for a greater percentage of the drainage area. This could be a result of the relative immaturity of the drainage systems. This trend is further magnified in the eastern part of the upper peninsula where large swamps are even more frequent and drainage basins are covered by up to forty-seven percent surface water. This is true of rivers draining into both Lake Michigan and Lake Superior. In the western parts of the upper peninsula swamps are less common but, because of the generally rougher topography, rivers have a greater fall and faster flow. Southeastern Michigan is marked by relatively small rivers, with very few swamps and lakes, which flow into the St. Clair and Detroit rivers as well as Lakes St. Clair and Erie.

CLIMATE

Climate is a key factor in determining the biological associations of the major life zones of the world. Soil types, which determine vegetation and, eventually, animal life, are formed by the action of climate on the basic land forms. Three main

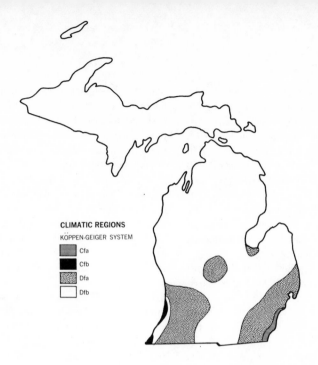

CLIMATIC REGIONS
KÖPPEN-GEIGER SYSTEM
Cfa
Cfb
Dfa
Dfb

Fig. 6   Climatic regions of Michigan (After Himmler and De Long: 1963)

factors seem to affect the climate of Michigan (Eichmeier 1964): the latitude, the surrounding Great Lakes, and the variation in elevation within the state. The area generally falls within a zone of humid, temperate climate (Butzer 1964: 53). The Great Lakes, however, have a stabilizing influence and, because of prevailing western winds, summers are cooler and winters warmer than in Wisconsin and Minnesota. The lakes also cause late fall and early winter cloudiness with attendant snow flurries as the warm air over the lakes comes in contact with the cold winds of the season coming from the west.

The mean January temperature in Michigan in recent years has varied between 13° and 27° Fahrenheit (Himmler and Delong 1963) while the mean July temperature has varied between 64° and 72°. Himmler and Delong recognize four Köppen-Geiger climate regions in Michigan:

Cfa, Cfb, Dfa, and Dfb. The Dfb climate is characteristic of most of the state. It is marked by cold winters, with temperatures averaging below 27° Fahrenheit, and relatively long but cool summers with temperatures averaging below 72° Fahrenheit. There are regions of Dfa climate in southeastern Michigan, with a western boundary along a line running from approximately Port Huron through Ann Arbor to Adrian, and in southwestern Michigan with an eastern boundary following a line running approximately from Grand Haven east toward Lansing and south to Three Rivers. There are Dfa pockets around Alma and in southern Bay County. These areas are marked by relatively cold winters, with January temperatures averaging less than 27° Fahrenheit, and by hot summers with temperatures in July averaging over 72°.

In extreme southeastern Michigan, in a

23

narrow strip between Detroit and Toledo, there is a Cfa climate marked by slightly warmer winters, with average January temperatures over 27°, and hot summers with July temperatures averaging over 72°. In contrast, there are two pockets of Cfb climate in southwestern Michigan, one around New Buffalo, the other around South Haven. These areas are marked by winters with a mean January temperature over 27°, and relatively cool summers, with a July average under 72°.

Eichmeier (1964) noted that the length of the growing season in Michigan, measured by the average number of frost-free days, varies from 60 days in the western part of the upper peninsula to over 170 days in the southwestern part of the lower peninsula. Most of the lower peninsula has a growing season of 130 to 180 days, but in the center of the northern half of the lower peninsula, in the high area that Davis (1936) calls the high plains, the growing season falls under 100 days.

Yarnell (1964: 126–37) has dealt with the importance of the growing season for agriculture at some length. He has concluded that while corn and other cultigens mature in under 100 days, the chance factors of time of planting and harvesting make 120 frost-free days the effective limit of prehistoric agriculture.

Recent studies of temperature in Michigan show a great deal of variation from the patterns we have so far discussed. Himmler and Delong (1963) have demonstrated that major variations in climate occurred between 1951 and 1960. Prahl (1966: 184) has pointed out that the data on length of growing season gathered by Yarnell from a 1941 source may not apply today, with one station reporting an average of ten less frost-free days since 1941

than it did before that time. Such climatic fluctuations certainly have occurred in the past and on a much larger scale, a point of great importance for our interpretation of the aboriginal occupation of the state.

The state had an average rainfall of 31 inches per year for the period of 1931–55 (Eichmeier 1964) with a range running from an average of 28 inches per year for the Lake Huron littoral, an area in the high plains, and the region around Escanaba to an average of 36 inches per year in southwestern Michigan and in the western part of the upper peninsula.

Brunnschweiler (1962) has suggested three types of seasonal rainfall patterns in the lower peninsula. Maximum annual rainfall occurs either in May or in May and June south of a line running from Benton Harbor through Lansing to Port Huron. This pattern also exists on the edges of Saginaw Bay. There is a September or August-September maximum in the northern section of the lower peninsula which extends down the high plains into the south-central part of the state. This rainfall pattern also exists in a small area around Muskegon. The central part of the lower peninsula is generally characterized by two peaks of precipitation, one in the spring and a second in the early fall.

There is a great deal of variation in average snowfall (Eichmeier 1964) resulting from the westerly winds, moisture from the lakes, and existing temperature patterns. There is an annual average of 160 inches of snow per year in the western part of the upper peninsula while southeastern Michigan averages less than 30 inches per year. Even in the lower peninsula the western areas receive a heavier snowfall than the eastern part of the state.

Fig. 7 Soils of Michigan

SOILS

Soil is a zone of weathering, consisting of a mixture of mineral and organic materials, that overlies unweathered parent material. The nature of the soil is dependent on the parent material, the climate, topography, drainage pattern, vegetation, and time. With the complex geological history of Michigan and the complex pattern of lakes and rivers, we would expect a great deal of variation in soil types. Whiteside, Schneider, and Cook (1956) list twenty-six land divisions, forty-one soil associations, and over eighty soil types for the state.

The humid climate of Michigan has led to the removal of the most easily dissolved substances from the upper levels of its soils. In the southern part of the lower peninsula there are gray-brown podzolic soils. Here subsoils have been enriched with clay washed down from the upper horizons. These clay horizons are finer textured than either the upper or lower horizons in the same profile. These soils, which are relatively fertile and amenable to agriculture today, were probably covered by broad-leafed forests in the prehistoric period.

The northern part of the state is marked by podzols formed in well-drained areas from coarse to medium textured materials. They have a humic horizon at the surface while just below this is a bleached horizon consisting of minerals in the sand-size range. The next deeper horizon consists of a light brown zone of redeposited aluminum and iron sesquioxides (Butzer 1964: 85). In Michigan the southern limit of white pine corresponds with the southern limit of podzols.

Soils are shallow in areas where they have been formed from unconsolidated

25

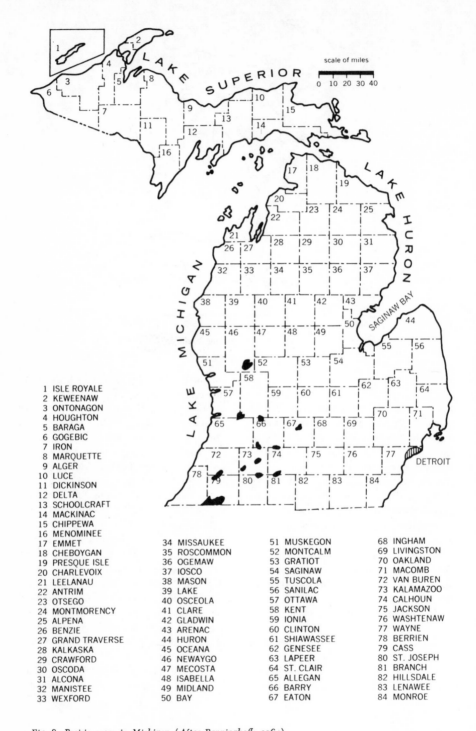

1 ISLE ROYALE	34 MISSAUKEE	51 MUSKEGON	68 INGHAM
2 KEWEENAW	35 ROSCOMMON	52 MONTCALM	69 LIVINGSTON
3 ONTONAGON	36 OGEMAW	53 GRATIOT	70 OAKLAND
4 HOUGHTON	37 IOSCO	54 SAGINAW	71 MACOMB
5 BARAGA	38 MASON	55 TUSCOLA	72 VAN BUREN
6 GOGEBIC	39 LAKE	56 SANILAC	73 KALAMAZOO
7 IRON	40 OSCEOLA	57 OTTAWA	74 CALHOUN
8 MARQUETTE	41 CLARE	58 KENT	75 JACKSON
9 ALGER	42 GLADWIN	59 IONIA	76 WASHTENAW
10 LUCE	43 ARENAC	60 CLINTON	77 WAYNE
11 DICKINSON	44 HURON	61 SHIAWASSEE	78 BERRIEN
12 DELTA	45 OCEANA	62 GENESEE	79 CASS
13 SCHOOLCRAFT	46 NEWAYGO	63 LAPEER	80 ST. JOSEPH
14 MACKINAC	47 MECOSTA	64 BRANCH	81 BRANCH
15 CHIPPEWA	48 ISABELLA	65 ALLEGAN	82 HILLSDALE
16 MENOMINEE	49 MIDLAND	66 BARRY	83 LENAWEE
17 EMMET	50 BAY	67 EATON	84 MONROE
18 CHEBOYGAN			
19 PRESQUE ISLE			
20 CHARLEVOIX			
21 LEELANAU			
22 ANTRIM			
23 OTSEGO			
24 MONTMORENCY			
25 ALPENA			
26 BENZIE			
27 GRAND TRAVERSE			
28 KALKASKA			
29 CRAWFORD			
30 OSCODA			
31 ALCONA			
32 MANISTEE			
33 WEXFORD			

Fig. 8 Prairie areas in Michigan (After Benninghoff: 1964)

rocks since time has not permitted much weathering. Outcrops of bed rock are common in such areas. Such soils are found in the western and southwestern part of the upper peninsula and in a few areas along Lake Huron and in the western part of the lower peninsula. In the western part of the upper peninsula, where older rocks are common, soils contain less free lime and have a different character from those in the rest of the podzol region. The western limit of beech tree growth corresponds with the approximate western limit of limy soils and is marked by a line running roughly from Marquette to Menominee.

In the southwestern part of the state are scattered prairie areas with distinctive soils. They are usually darker and deeper and lack the bleached horizons characteristic of the timbered areas of the state—the gray-brown podzolics of the south and the gray-wooded soils of the northern podzol region. The darker color is caused by the organic material which has been added to the soil by the fine roots of prairie grasses. In wooded areas organic material is contributed by leaf and needle fall which is concentrated in a shallow humus zone.

Organic soils, peats and mucks, have developed in the swamps of both the podzol and podzolic regions. Many poorly drained soils in the lower peninsula, which were not completely covered with water and which did not form organic soils, have proved to be very productive when drained.

PLANTS AND ANIMALS

Michigan contains both boreal coniferous forests and deciduous mixed forests. In the northern peninsula and the north-

ern half of the southern peninsula are mixed conifer-hardwood forests (Cushing 1965: 407). This forest type has been called the Lake Forest formation in contrast to the coniferous forests which predominate to the north and the deciduous forests to the south. White pine, red pine, and hemlock are the most prevalent boreal species while sugar maple, beech, basswood, and yellow birch share dominance with the coniferous species. Different combinations of these species are found in different areas. The occurrence of many broadleaf species in the Lake Michigan shore area between Traverse City and Harbor Springs had a positive influence on aboriginal occupation of this area. Indeed, this Lake Forest, with its continuous vegetation variation in space and time, delineates a dynamic prehistoric cultural unit in northeastern North America.

To the south of this mixed forest formation Cushing describes a band of maple-basswood-beech forest roughly following the Grand and Saginaw river valleys and the south shore of Lakes Huron, St. Clair, and Erie. Farther to the south, covering the lower two tiers of Michigan counties, is an area of oak-hickory climax forest.

There is a significant distinction in the vegetation in the Lake Forest region and the deciduous areas to the south. Many species have their northern limits along this line including black gum, flowering dogwood, rock elm, chinquapin oak, swamp white oak, black oak, sassafras, tulip tree, American sycamore, shagbark hickory, black walnut, and box elder (Zim and Martin 1956).

The prairie areas in the southwestern part of the state were an important factor for human occupation. Here early settlers found areas of grasses mixed with scat-

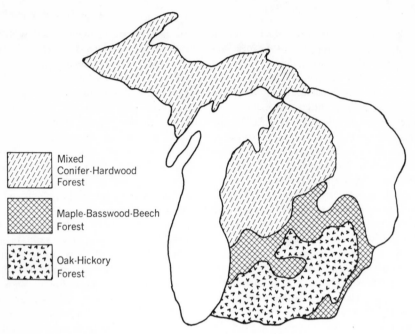

Mixed Conifer-Hardwood Forest

Maple-Basswood-Beech Forest

Oak-Hickory Forest

Fig. 9 Forests of Michigan (After Cushing: 1965)

tered burr oak. These oak openings appear to be a part of a once more extensive prairie peninsula. It is well marked by both plant associations (Benninghoff 1964: 120) and by the distinctive soils which develop in these areas (Whiteside, Schneider, and Cook 1956: 11). Cleland (1966: 75) has called attention to historic sources pointing out the significance of these oak openings for the aboriginal population. Hinsdale (1932: 31–32) felt that the existence of several prairies in central Newaygo County was one of the key reasons for the relatively high density of prehistoric Indian sites there.

Yarnell (1964: 44) has estimated the total number of species of vascular plants in the Great Lakes region to be approximately two thousand. According to the ethnographic literature about twenty percent of this number was used by the aboriginal inhabitants.

The lists of plants include 130 that were used for food, 18 for beverages and flavoring, 68 for medical teas, 207 for other medicines, 31 for charms and ceremonial purposes, 27 for smoking, 25 for dyeing, and 52 for various other utilitarian purposes. In all, there were about 560 uses recorded for 373 different plant species. Hinsdale (1932: 19–29) felt that thorn apples, pawpaws, mandrakes, plums, berries, crab apples, grapes, nuts, and cherries were important, but gave even more emphasis to wild rice and the sugar maple.

The vegetation of the Great Lakes, like the lakes themselves, has varied through time. Yarnell (1964: 8–10) feels that, in general, the vegetation types now present have predominated through time but with some geographical variation. There must have been a period when the landscape was open, following the retreat of the ice. During this cool, moist period fir and spruce became the dominant species. This period lasted until around 8000 B.C. when spruce and fir were replaced by pine and, to a lesser extent, oak, birch, willow, tamarack, and elm. They were followed by maple, beech, basswood, and hemlock. He places the pine maximum at 6000 B.C. with a deciduous forest maximum reached by 2000 B.C. The earliest dated oak specimen from Michigan has a date of 3350 B.C. After 2000 B.C. the vegetation cover may have become more boreal in nature over large parts of the state.

The Great Lakes region is rich in mammals. The larger species include elk, white-tailed deer, moose, woodland caribou, black bear, red and gray foxes, coyote, gray wolf, lynx, and bobcat. There are eleven species of small carnivores, including raccoons, weasels, and skunks, ten species of bats, a dozen species of moles and shrews, over thirty species of rodents, and one marsupial, the opossum (Burt 1957).

Plants and animals are associated with certain vegetation zones. It is not surprising, therefore, that the difference in northern and southern vegetation groups is reflected in the distribution of mammals. Sixteen northern species have their southern limits in the Great Lakes area, while seventeen find their northern limits in the same region. The northern forms are mammals of the coniferous forests, swamps, and bogs while the southern species are mammals associated with deciduous forests and semi-open country. Distinctive northern mammals in Michigan include the northern water shrew, black bear, fisher, shorttail weasel, river otter, gray wolf, bobcat, northern flying squirrel, beaver, boreal redback vole, woodland jumping mouse, porcupine, snowshoe hare, and moose. Distinctive southern species

include the opossum, least shrew, evening bat, southern flying squirrel, white-footed mouse, prairie vole, pine vole, and eastern cottontail rabbit.

Hinsdale (1932: 12–15) felt that all quadruped mammals were fair game for the Indian. He considered the deer to be the perennial stand-by but included elk, moose, bear, and beaver as key food sources. The quantity of some of these mammals must have been great if the recorded hunting records of the late nineteenth century are at all accurate. In 1877, in a sixty-day season, 10,700 deer were killed, totaling 1,070,000 pounds of meat (cited from Hinsdale 1932: 12–15).

Prehistoric mammalian distributions are difficult to deal with because of the lack of data. We know that three species, the mountain lion, wolverine, and bison, have become extinct during the historic period. A number of other species are represented only by fossil specimens. These include the mammoth, mastodon, musk ox, Barren Ground caribou, giant beaver, peccary, and giant moose. Most seem to represent adaptations to the cooler climates which existed between the time of the retreat of the ice and 2000 B.C. The remains of seal, walrus, and whale have also been found in the upper Great Lakes region.

In Michigan 326 species of birds have been positively identified including 215 which are considered common to the area (Zimmerman and Van Tyne 1959). Many of these are migratory birds and are useful in identifying the season of occupation at prehistoric sites where their remains occur. These migratory birds were attracted, in part, by the many lakes and rivers. The almost endless flocks of passenger pigeons which frequented the hardwood forests of the state surely had great importance to the aboriginal inhabitants (Hinsdale 1932: 17–19). Turkey and

29

grouse were important and the eggs of wild birds also served as a food source. Going to late nineteenth-century sources we can note that in 1875 2,000,000 pounds of young "squabs," almost two and one half million birds, were shipped out of Newaygo, Oceana, and Grand Traverse counties alone.

Zim and Smith (1964) include nine turtles, one lizard, eleven snakes, and fourteen amphibians among the wild life of Michigan. The state marks the north-ernmost limit for four species of turtles (musk, soft-shelled, box, and spotted); one species of lizard (the skink); six species of snakes (green, hog-nosed, blue racer, common red snake, fox snake, and king snake); as well as for the cricket toad and four-toed salamander.

Over 230 species of fish, representing 29 families, live in the Great Lakes (Hubbs and Lagler 1947). The most important to man are: the sturgeon, salmon, white-fish, grayling, smelt, pike, bass, and drum families. Hinsdale (1932: 16) thought that fish determined the population dis-tribution of the Indians in the state. In the northern areas, where game was scarce, fishing kept the population near the lakes and rivers.

Molluscs, plentiful in some areas, were a key food source. Some 112 species lived in waters in and around Michigan (Winslow 1925, Goodrich 1932) and at least 13 species have been found in con-text indicating their use as food in pre-historic times.

NATURAL AND CULTURAL AREAS OF MICHIGAN

Each square foot of Michigan is, in its own way, unique. Each river and stream has its own drainage pattern, while the surrounding lands have distinctive soils and vegetation. It is still possible to rec-ognize some regularity and to pick out patterns of topography, climate, and plant and animal associations. Since our pri-mary study is of adaptive patterns of groups over time and not of unique, non-repetitive events, it is necessary to deal with major natural and cultural areas.

Within the past few years a number of archaeologists have attempted to in-terpret Michigan prehistory in light of Lee R. Dice's biotic provinces (Cleland 1966, Fitting 1966a). This is not a new approach. It was followed by Hinsdale (1932: 5-6) over thirty-five years ago who then acknowledged his debt to the in-terpretive format furnished by Dice.

Cleland (1966) has recently dealt with the biotic provinces of Michigan in rela-tion to prehistoric occupations. Four such provinces are present in the Great Lakes Region: the Illinoian, the Hudsonian, the Canadian, and the Carolinian. The Illi-noian biotic province is a prairie and forest area represented in Michigan only in scattered areas in the western and southwestern parts of the lower penin-sula. If we stick strictly to the zonal concept (Butzer 1964), this biotic prov-ince, as a continuous area, does not oc-cur at all within the state.

The true northern boreal forest is as-sociated with the Hudsonian biotic prov-ince that today is found north of the north shore of Lake Superior. While it is not found in the state today, this biotic province must have been well represented in the past and an understanding of its plant and animal associations is important for an understanding of Michigan pre-history.

The southern plant and animal associa-tion in our area is called the Carolinian

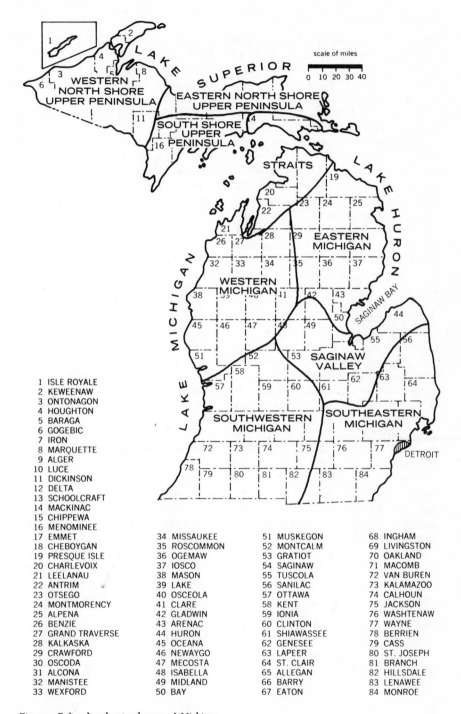

1 ISLE ROYALE
2 KEWEENAW
3 ONTONAGON
4 HOUGHTON
5 BARAGA
6 GOGEBIC
7 IRON
8 MARQUETTE
9 ALGER
10 LUCE
11 DICKINSON
12 DELTA
13 SCHOOLCRAFT
14 MACKINAC
15 CHIPPEWA
16 MENOMINEE
17 EMMET
18 CHEBOYGAN
19 PRESQUE ISLE
20 CHARLEVOIX
21 LEELANAU
22 ANTRIM
23 OTSEGO
24 MONTMORENCY
25 ALPENA
26 BENZIE
27 GRAND TRAVERSE
28 KALKASKA
29 CRAWFORD
30 OSCODA
31 ALCONA
32 MANISTEE
33 WEXFORD

34 MISSAUKEE
35 ROSCOMMON
36 OGEMAW
37 IOSCO
38 MASON
39 LAKE
40 OSCEOLA
41 CLARE
42 GLADWIN
43 ARENAC
44 HURON
45 OCEANA
46 NEWAYGO
47 MECOSTA
48 ISABELLA
49 MIDLAND
50 BAY

51 MUSKEGON
52 MONTCALM
53 GRATIOT
54 SAGINAW
55 TUSCOLA
56 SANILAC
57 OTTAWA
58 KENT
59 IONIA
60 CLINTON
61 SHIAWASSEE
62 GENESEE
63 LAPEER
64 ST. CLAIR
65 ALLEGAN
66 BARRY
67 EATON

68 INGHAM
69 LIVINGSTON
70 OAKLAND
71 MACOMB
72 VAN BUREN
73 KALAMAZOO
74 CALHOUN
75 JACKSON
76 WASHTENAW
77 WAYNE
78 BERRIEN
79 CASS
80 ST. JOSEPH
81 BRANCH
82 HILLSDALE
83 LENAWEE
84 MONROE

Fig. 10 Cultural and natural areas of Michigan

biotic province. This province is characteristic of the lower half of the lower peninsula. The northern half of the lower peninsula along with the upper peninsula fall within the Canadian biotic province. While northern trees, such as the white pine, and many northern animals have their southern limits in this area, it also contains many southern forms. Indeed, the entire Canadian biotic province, which roughly corresponds with the mixed forest Lake Forest formation, is itself a transitional area. Within it are closed stands of pines as well as extensive areas of hardwoods. It contains areas which are rich for man as well as inhospitable areas such as the sandy high pine plains of the lower peninsula and the extensive areas of interior swamps in the upper peninsula.

These biotic provinces can be mapped today although lines on maps can do great injustice to individual situations. We must assume that these plant and animal communities were as dynamic in the past as they are today and that there have been many significant shifts in relative geographical positions of these communities. Since the earliest dated oak is only a little over five thousand years old and the southern oak-hickory forest did not become fully established until around 2000 B.C., the placement of these biotic provinces, as we know them today, has meaning only for recent times.

Our main goal, wherever it is possible, is to interpret the prehistoric occupations of Michigan in light of the particular environment existing at the time of such an occupation. In some instances we have good information derived from fauna associated with prehistoric sites or from fossil pollen recovered on, or near, the sites. Where these are lacking we can still interpolate from what we generally know of environment at the time of site occupation from other areas and by considering the influence of nearby lakes, rivers, and local land forms.

Although the major biotic provinces have shifted in the past, there seem to be a number of geographical areas which have some physical and cultural cohesiveness throughout the prehistoric period. I have found it convenient to use these geographical and cultural areas for describing prehistoric occupations of the state. Today there is some natural basis for these regions and we can probably assume that even in the past they maintained internal environmental consistency and tended to vary *as units* with the major climatic, floral, and faunal shifts of the past fourteen thousand years.

Southwestern Michigan, located in the Carolinian biotic province, is a fairly uniform area today. This is the area where the greatest concentration of prairies are found. It is drained by three major rivers: the Grand, the St. Joseph, and the Kalamazoo. To the north, the Muskegon and Manistee River drainages, along with several small rivers, dominate an area which is primarily within the Canadian biotic province. This area has sometimes in the past looked to the south and sometimes to the north for close cultural contacts. I will refer to it as western Michigan.

From Grand Traverse Bay to Cheboygan in the lower peninsula, and around St. Ignace and eastern Mackinaw County in the upper peninsula is a region which forms a coherent Straits of Mackinac cultural area.

I shall refer to the area around the Au Sable and the several other small rivers in the northeastern part of the lower peninsula as eastern Michigan. This, like the straits, is within the Canadian biotic province. The Saginaw Valley, the largest drainage system in the state, needs to be considered as a separate unit. Both Carolinian and Canadian associations are present within the drainage and it is a key area for the study of the relationship between these biotic provinces.

Southeastern Michigan includes the areas in the Carolinian biotic province southeast of the moraines running between Flint and Ann Arbor, together with the areas drained by the Black, Clinton, Rouge, Huron, and Raisin rivers. It is culturally, as well as geographically, a part of the lower rather than the upper Great Lakes.

The region west of the Straits of Mackinac along the south shore of the upper peninsula, with several small rivers flowing into Lake Michigan and much swampy land, is an additional natural area. The Menominee is a first class river and its drainage includes the mountainous region in the western upper peninsula. Partly for convenience and partly because we know so little about the prehistory of this region, I will include it with the rest of the south shore of the upper peninsula.

In the same way, the eastern part of the north shore of the upper peninsula, up to a point around Marquette, can be viewed as a unit with much swampy land and limy soils. The western part of the upper peninsula along the Lake Superior shore differs from the eastern part in the absence of limy soils and beech cover, with much rougher topography, and it has a number of rivers with a thousand feet or more of fall in a short distance, hence, a very rapid rate of flow. This forms a distinctive physical unit but, again, we know very little about the prehistoric cultural adaptations of the area.

I realize that major physical areas in the state, such as the high plains, have been cut by as many as four of the above-mentioned natural areas. These areas are arbitrary units which have more meaning during some periods of prehistory than during others. The boundary between southeastern and southwestern Michigan, as another example, is a uniform physical area very distinct from the river mouths of either extremity. I do this knowingly because it is the lake shores and lower reaches of these rivers that are most important for the aboriginal inhabitants and the key to an understanding of prehistoric cultural groupings. For future reference, then, I shall divide Michigan into nine natural and cultural units: southwestern, western, southeastern, Saginaw Valley, eastern, Straits, south shore of the upper peninsula, eastern north shore of the upper peninsula, and the western north shore of the upper peninsula including Isle Royale.

CHAPTER III

THE EARLY HUNTERS

MAN IN THE NEW WORLD

Folsom, New Mexico, in 1926 was the area at which Folsom points were first discovered with the extinct *Bison antiqus* thereby contributing to the controversy over the origin of man in the New World. The bison kill site indicated man's occupation of the New World took place in the era when many now-extinct prehistoric animals roamed the plains of North America.

Man did not evolve in the New World. The antecedents of modern man are found in the Old World, where many likely ancestors are found in the fossil deposits of distant ages. The native New World primates are, at best, distant cousins of the higher Old World primates to which man is most akin.

It is from the Old World that we must bring man to the New World but the how and when of the movement are elusive. The antecedents of the earliest inhabitants of the New World, the Paleo-Indians, have been sought in Asia and Europe as well as continents like Atlantis and Mu. It has been suggested that they came on foot across from Asia on dry land or that they navigated small or vast bodies of water in skin-covered boats. Some came 70,000 years ago, others 40,-000 years ago, and many even more recently.

Advocates of an early entry find one of

their most fluent spokesmen in Alex Kreiger (1964) who has documented hundreds of sites in North and South America which may show traces of very early occupation, or occupation suggested to belong to a period before man made projectile points. His arguments are very convincing to many, and some prominent archaeologists seem willing to accept this position. In his general work, *An Introduction to American Archaeology*, Willey (1966: 33) states that "as things stand now, the 'pre-projectile point horizon' will not be demonstrated beyond reasonable doubt until a complex or assemblage of materials attributable to it are found stratigraphically beneath artifacts of the well-known 10,000 to 12,000 a year old, bifacially flaked lanceolate or leaf shaped point class, or lacking this, until the crude, nonprojectile point complexes are found in indisputable association with middle or early Pleistocene deposits and convincing radiocarbon dating." In spite of this, Willey (1966: 37) feels ". . . it is likely that the 'pre-projectile point horizon' is a reality and that man first crossed into America as far back as 40,000 to 20,000 B.C."

Jelinek (1965) has made a case for a later date for the entry of man into the New World. He argues that in light of what we know of the Old World Upper Paleolithic way of life and the glacial and climatic conditions in northeastern Asia and the Bering sea land bridge, the earliest possible entry date into the New World would have been 30,000 B.C. and probably much later. According to radiocarbon dates, this entry may have taken place as late as 15,000 B.C. to 12,000 B.C. (Jelinek n.d.).

The first widespread recognizable archaeological horizon in North America is represented by cultural groups with a Clovis type of projectile point as its most distinctive artifact (Mason 1962, Haynes 1964). Plains sites with these large fluted projectile points have been dated to a period between 11,000 and 11,500 years ago. Haynes (1966) characterizes these people as big game hunters and suggests that the widespread distribution of Clovis artifacts represents similar distribution of the Paleo-Indian hunters.

Haynes's 1966 article is a significant contribution, for in it he goes beyond problems of typology and chronology to deal with the potential for expansion of groups such as the Clovis hunters. Using conservative population increase models plus the richness of the environment for such hunters, he accounts for the spread of this cultural complex throughout North America in as little as five hundred years. This seems realistic for a pioneer hunting group in a new and previously uninhabited territory where the game is not accustomed to a predator such as man (see Jelinek n.d. for a more complete development of this point).

While Haynes's description of a mammoth-hunting economy may be accurate for the plains, it does not do justice to the more complex environmental situation in areas to the east. Here we are dealing with different and more varied environments. Prehistoric cultural remains from these areas must be interpreted in light of the local situation, not according to environments where typologically similar materials have been found.

ENVIRONMENTAL POTENTIAL AND EARLY MAN

The principal environments in eastern North America would have consisted of both boreal and deciduous forest areas similar to those of today. The bio-geographical areas in eastern North America were, however, subject to the influences of continental glaciation. Quimby has pointed out that (1954: 317) the natural and cultural areas of the Paleo-Indian were not the same as those of his ancestors. For example, recently deglaciated areas would be free of vegetation cover and subject to plant colonization. It is possible that a true tundra zone existed for a short time near the retreating glacial fronts. This would have soon given way to an open spruce parkland, then a closed spruce forest, eventually a spruce-pine forest and, in some areas, a deciduous forest climax. The boreal forest border, during periods of glacial advance, would have been far to the south of the present boundaries, and the deciduous forest area would have been more restricted than it is today.

In newly deglaciated areas one might have found treeless tundra or boreal woodland, the latter described as "a Savanna formation of needle-leaved trees scattered in a shrub and lichen mat" (Martin 1958: 379). I have called this spruce parkland (Fitting, DeVisscher, and Wahla 1966: 120). Such a low latitude forest-tundra edge situation is mentioned by Butzer (1964: 145) as an optimal environmental situation for man. It is in this area that the migrating herds of gregarious animals from the open country would seek winter shelter. The available tree cover would lessen winter storms and forest species would also be available as food resources.

Butzer (1964: 137–38) has also dealt with the richness of Pleistocene low latitude forest-tundra in contrast to modern high latitude tundra. Our Paleo-Indian hunters would have had a richer environment than that of modern tundra hunters because of more open-drainage patterns allowing richer vegetation, more direct solar radiation, and shorter periods of hibernal darkness for many animal species which were hunted. As boreal forests became established in deglaciated areas, the hunters of the spruce parkland may have followed the fronts of the retreating ice to the north. If so, the environment would have become less advantageous as the Paleo-Indian entered the more northern latitudes.

The boreal forests themselves, which once existed far to the south of their present-day limits (Whitehead 1965), are included with Butzer's marginal environments (1964: 145). Game is rare with few species available, and plant foods are not abundant. As W. B. Hinsdale (1932: 7) pointed out in his early environmental studies in Michigan "Indians procured very little, if any, kind of food from conifers . . . Animals whose flesh made human food could not subsist upon resinoid kinds of trees; whereas fruits, nuts, berries, sugars, building barks, and browse for some of the animals came from other types of vegetable growth. The gloomy recesses of the pine woods, monotonous and scant in nutritional plants, were not often frequented by animal and bird life in appreciable numbers."

Butzer (1964: 145) included the broad-leaf forests with intermediate environments. I think he is too conservative about their potential for man. He also suggests that the ungulate biomass, the total meat mass of the larger game animals, is the same for this zone as for the temperate grasslands which he includes with the optimal environments. This is a rich situation for man not only because of the abundant game resources but because of the presence of those very food plants whose absence Hinsdale noted for the coniferous forest areas.

Admittedly, this is an oversimplified picture of the environmental conditions in the eastern United States. It fails to take into consideration small, local environmental situations. It does suggest a pattern for the occupation of the eastern parts of North America but only if we assume that our Paleo-Indian peoples were fairly intelligent and interested in their own survival. As Cleland (1966: 49) has pointed out, the idea of these people wandering around in the woods in the eastern United States for several thousand years in an unadapted condition, presumably in a constant state of hunger in a rich environment, is unacceptable. They may have been tundra hunters when they came over from the Old World and big game hunters on the plains in North America before entering the eastern Woodlands, but once they got there it was the local resources to which they turned for survival. In some situations in eastern North America, hunting may have accounted for almost all of the diet of some Paleo-Indian peoples. In other areas vegetable food probably accounted for a large percent of the diet. Service (1966) writes that where environment permits, band groups use up to eighty percent vegetable sources of food.

In the eastern parts of North America there would have been an area of high Paleo-Indian population density near the glacial fronts. Here the forest-tundra edge situation would allow for large groups of specialized hunters. Such sites as the Holcombe site in Michigan (Fitting, DeVisscher, and Wahla 1966) and the Debert site in Nova Scotia (McDonald 1966) are representative of this peri-glacial hunting adaptation.

To the south of the peri-glacial hunters was a zone of boreal forest. Survival here was based on special situations. Such a situation was found in the Great Lakes when land areas drained while the lake levels fell after the Valders retreat. Each year, an area varying from a few feet to many yards in width would have been available for new plant colonization along the receding lake shores. There would be a period of herb and brush colonization of perhaps a hundred years before spruce and pine forests closed in on the land. This allowed a continued high animal and, therefore, human population for perhaps one to two thousand years longer than would have been possible in closed forests alone. Similar situations might have occurred in river valleys, around inland lakes or draining kettle holes, and in areas cleared by burning. All of these, however, would be islands of plenty in an otherwise less hospitable boreal environment. The boreal forest period in the northeastern parts of North America is marked by a relative lack of cultural material when compared with the preceding and following periods. Ritchie (1965) has commented on this in New York but a similar hiatus seems to exist throughout the entire area. It is a real situation and not an archaeological oversight.

At the same time there was an intensive occupation of the deciduous forest areas of the southeast. There are many large sites with tool inventories containing fluted points, but in proportionally fewer numbers to other tools than are found at the peri-glacial sites. This would suggest less emphasis on hunting and more on collecting than in the northeast at the same time. Mason (1962) has noted the diversity and variety of Paleo-Indian projectile point styles, that is, variants of the fluted point types, in this area. The greatest variation that I found in my own metrical studies of some eastern fluted points (Fitting 1965e) was between Virginia and Kentucky. This suggests a higher population density and a series of more restricted hunting territories in the southeast than in the plains. The former situation suggests less cultural contact, with less diffusion of ideas and concepts, between distant areas than is indicated on the plains where the uniformity of artifact styles suggests wide ranges and close contact between distant groups.

In the southeast Williams and Stoltman (1965) find difficulty in distinguishing between the Paleo-Indian and Meso-Indian eras. Guthe (1967) has noted a strong continuity between Paleo-Indian projectile points and later forms in Tennessee. In this area, in contrast to the northeast, there is a real cultural continuity. This explains why such workers in the northeast as Mason and Ritchie can see clear distinctions between Paleo-Indian artifacts and those of later groups while their colleagues to the south see a change which is more gradual. To attempt to apply one scheme of development to the entire eastern part of north America with an arbitrary date of 8000 B.C. for the end of the Paleo-Indian period, as suggested by Griffin (1964: 660), can be misleading. To quote William Blake, "One law for the lion and ox is oppression."

In terms of subsistence, what little data we have available, such as that from Modoc Rock Shelter (Fowler 1959) and Graham Cave (Walter Klippel, personal communication), suggest that small game played a more important part in the diets of these omnivorous gatherers and hunters than it did in later periods in the same area. At this time there is no evidence to suggest that the very large Pleistocene animals, such as the mastodon, were ever hunted by peoples in the southeastern parts of North America. We know that they were present but I suspect that alternate food forms then available were more attractive.

With this overview we can now turn our attention to Michigan and adjacent parts of the Great Lakes area. We have already suggested two phases for the Paleo-Indian occupation of Michigan. The initial occupation seems to have been by peri-glacial hunters. This corresponds to Mason's Early Paleo-Indian stage marked by lanceolate, concave base projectile points, the majority of which are fluted (1962). With the establishment of the boreal forests and the dropping lake levels following 9000 B.C., the Great Lakes areas were inhabited primarily by makers of stemmed, lanceolate projectile points. This occupation falls into Mason's Late Paleo-Indian stage. During this occupation some elements of the southern Archaic cultural pattern may have occupied the lower portion of the state and evidence of their influence has been found on almost all of the Late Paleo-Indian sites to the north.

EARLY PALEO-INDIAN OCCUPATIONS

It was to a new land, newly freed of ice, that the first of the peri-glacial hunters came. Here they hunted and left ample evidence of their activities. Michigan has been the subject state for several distribution studies by Quimby (1958), Mason (1958), and, more recently, Peru (1965, 1967). These studies have all dealt with the meaning of the location of fluted points.

These distribution studies demonstrated several things. First, Paleo-Indian peoples were present in the state of Michigan in appreciable numbers, as Mason's study of over a hundred points alone indicates. (Mason's count was below the number of points which have been found.) Almost every major private collection in the state has at least one fluted point and some have as many as thirty or more. A detailed survey would probably indicate hundreds of such artifacts. Such a study would probably duplicate the distributional results obtained from Mason's sample.

Mason's paper pointed to a concentration of fluted points in southwestern Michigan, that area which contains the greatest number of prairie remnants today. Either this area was occupied by grassland hunters with fluted points long after the rest of the state was covered with boreal forest, or the cold steppe or grassland conditions of the times supported a denser population than the spruce parkland which followed the glacial retreat over much of the state.

At the time of preparation of these studies these writers seemed to have felt the most important result of their

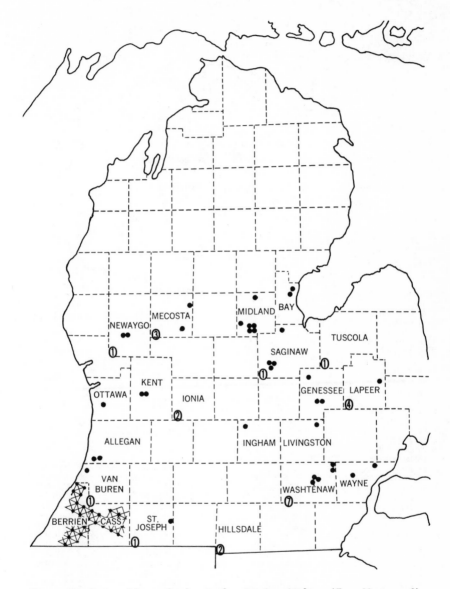

Fig. 11 *Distribution of known fluted projectile points from Michigan* (From Mason: 1958)

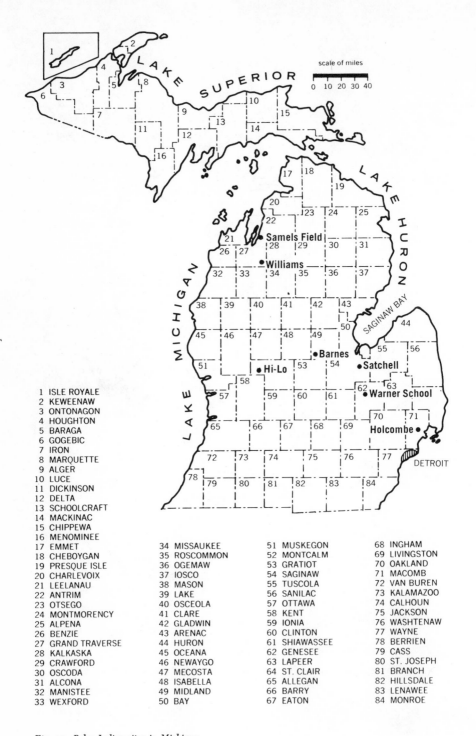

1 ISLE ROYALE	34 MISSAUKEE	51 MUSKEGON	68 INGHAM
2 KEWEENAW	35 ROSCOMMON	52 MONTCALM	69 LIVINGSTON
3 ONTONAGON	36 OGEMAW	53 GRATIOT	70 OAKLAND
4 HOUGHTON	37 IOSCO	54 SAGINAW	71 MACOMB
5 BARAGA	38 MASON	55 TUSCOLA	72 VAN BUREN
6 GOGEBIC	39 LAKE	56 SANILAC	73 KALAMAZOO
7 IRON	40 OSCEOLA	57 OTTAWA	74 CALHOUN
8 MARQUETTE	41 CLARE	58 KENT	75 JACKSON
9 ALGER	42 GLADWIN	59 IONIA	76 WASHTENAW
10 LUCE	43 ARENAC	60 CLINTON	77 WAYNE
11 DICKINSON	44 HURON	61 SHIAWASSEE	78 BERRIEN
12 DELTA	45 OCEANA	62 GENESEE	79 CASS
13 SCHOOLCRAFT	46 NEWAYGO	63 LAPEER	80 ST. JOSEPH
14 MACKINAC	47 MECOSTA	64 ST. CLAIR	81 BRANCH
15 CHIPPEWA	48 ISABELLA	65 ALLEGAN	82 HILLSDALE
16 MENOMINEE	49 MIDLAND	66 BARRY	83 LENAWEE
17 EMMET	50 BAY	67 EATON	84 MONROE
18 CHEBOYGAN			
19 PRESQUE ISLE			
20 CHARLEVOIX			
21 LEELANAU			
22 ANTRIM			
23 OTSEGO			
24 MONTMORENCY			
25 ALPENA			
26 BENZIE			
27 GRAND TRAVERSE			
28 KALKASKA			
29 CRAWFORD			
30 OSCODA			
31 ALCONA			
32 MANISTEE			
33 WEXFORD			

Fig. 12   Paleo-Indian sites in Michigan

work was the temporal placement of these artifacts through a detailed geological study of the places where they were found. Quimby and Mason dealt with gross geomorphology and the relationship of find spots to former lake beds and shore lines. They found that many finds were in areas that had been covered by late Cary glacial ice. This meant that they must have been left there after fourteen thousand years ago. They also noted that all finds were at least 605 feet above sea level. Since this was the

Fig. 13 Some fluted points from western Michigan (From Peru: 1965)

elevation of glacial Lake Algonquin they concluded that these projectile points had reached the place where they were eventually recovered while this lake was still in existence. Using Hough's recent interpretations of the age of this lake it would mean that these artifacts were utilized before 9000 B.C. This estimated age is in quite close agreement with Haynes's radiocarbon dates on similar western material and supports his observations on the potentially rapid pioneer settlement of North America.

Peru (1965) has dealt with the location of fluted points in Kent, Allegan, and Cass counties in relation to glacial channels. His evidence points toward the early end of the time range suggested by Mason and Quimby. More recently (Peru 1967) he has suggested an even greater age for fluted points, more than fourteen thousand years, than earlier work had indicated. He based this conclusion on the occurrence of fluted points from Cass County on the shores of glacial Lake Dowagiac. A high percentage of his fluted points, however, were recovered from within the bed of this glacial lake. Peru has tended to overemphasize the maximum possible age for these artifacts and not given the minimum possible age indicated by his data.

There is other evidence which favors the recent end of the time scale. The northern limit of fluted points in Michigan has been extended in recent reports by Brunett (1966) and Dekin (1966). Brunett has reported a fluted point from the Williams site located at the edge of the Port Huron moraine in Missaukee County. This point was found in 1923. Brunett and I, along with a field crew from Michigan State University, returned to the site in 1967 and collected two addi-

Fig. 14 Hi-Lo projectile points (From Fitting: 1963a)

tional biface fragments. Unfortunately, neither was diagnostic of a Paleo-Indian occupation.

Dekin has reported a fluted point from Grand Traverse County that was recovered from a location on the Valders moraine and may be associated with a lake stage existing after 9000 B.C. This is the youngest suggested placement of a Michigan fluted point.

In western Michigan the Hi-Lo site (Fitting 1963b), located on the property of the Hi-Lo Gun Club overlooking the Flat River in Montcalm County, may also be an early Paleo-Indian site. The collections from this site are small and contain a few obviously non-Paleo-Indian artifacts. When I first studied this material I felt that it belonged to a time period after the fluted point hunters were gone from the Great Lakes. The majority of the small complete concave base projectile points were either unfluted or not as fully fluted as the points outlined and illustrated by Mason and Quimby. In the original report I suggested three variants of Paleo-Indian points from the site: a short triangular concave base form represented by a single example; a short expanding sided variant with basal thinning rather than fluting; a large variant represented only by very large bases. These bases were fluted for what remained of their lengths on one or both faces.

Since preparing the Hi-Lo report I have had the opportunity to hear the views of William B. Roosa on such material. Roosa feels that our picture of Folsom points in the West, to use one example, is biased by the high percentage of short points which have been recovered. He suggests that larger points that were broken were whenever possible, resharpened. This resharpening went on until the point was too short to use at which time it was discarded. Using the unbroken points from a site to estimate the average length of points used by their manufacturers could then be very misleading. With this interpretation we can view the small points from the Hi-Lo site as examples of artifacts resharpened until they were too short to use. The bases of the larger points, broken off too close to the base to allow resharpening, are indicators of the cultural affiliation of the entire group of artifacts.

Included with the Hi-Lo assemblage are several end-scrapers, an ovate quartzite biface, and an object which I did not

Fig. 15 *Projectile points and point fragments from the Barnes site* (*From Roosa: 1963*)

identify at the time I prepared the original report but will now class as a small core used as a wedge for splitting bone. All of these tools are duplicated in other Paleo-Indian assemblages in the state.

Roosa (1963, 1965) has made a detailed study of fluting patterns of Paleo-Indian projectile points, with particular emphasis on Michigan, that is potentially very important for the study of early man. He has used fluting and finishing techniques as the primary attributes for establishing subcategories of these artifacts. He has distinguished two major fluting techniques in use in the Great Lakes area: the Folsom fluting technique with beveling of the base and careful preparation of the striking platform before fluting, and the Enterline fluting technique with little reworking of the base before the removal of the flutes.

Four local variants of points are recognized by Roosa. These include: true Folsom points plus Barnes and Bull Brook points, both with basically the Enterline fluting technique but with the removal of large flakes (two in the case of the former and one with several finishing flakes in the case of the latter); and Enterline points with triple fluting similar to those from the Shoop site in Pennsylvania where Witthoft (1952) defined the Enterline Chert Industry.

What distributional data Roosa presents is significant for it indicates that some of these fluted point types are contemporary. As I have suggested before (Fitting 1965b), this diversity of artifact styles within a fairly circumscribed time horizon, just prior to 9000 B.C., could be interpreted as indicating distinct groups of peoples. If data on exact fluting patterns were available for all of Michigan, we might be able to work out the extent of band hunting territories and patterns of seasonal migration within these territories. Roosa's detailed work on artifact typology has cleared the way for future research on the people who were responsible for the manufacture of the artifacts.

Roosa has also suggested several related point types which appear to be rare in Michigan. These include Parrish points, defined from the Parrish Village site in Kentucky; Cumberland points and Ross County points. He is also very adamant and very convincing about restricting the term "Clovis" to those projectile points similar to those from the Clovis site and closely related sites in the southwestern United States. Using strict definitions, there are few, if any, Clovis points east of the Mississippi River. There is a tendency to call almost all large, partially fluted projectile points "Clovis points" perhaps because of the rather loose definition in the popular survey volume by Wormington (1957). Part of the misunderstanding which surrounds the early industries of eastern and western North America can be traced to such loose artifact definitions and to the attribution of close cultural affiliation to artifacts related only on a broad horizon level—in this case a horizon covering the eastern three quarters of North America.

The Barnes site itself—located in Midland County, Michigan—has been the subject of an intensive analytical report (Wright and Roosa 1966). Its minimum age seems to be 9000 B.C. The artifacts from the site are stained with iron and one has an encrustation of iron-cemented sand. Such stains indicate deposition in the iron-cemented accumulation zone of the Ogemaw sandy loam found on the site. This soil has formed on top of a beach 605 feet above sea level in Saginaw County. The newly formed beach covered a spruce forest which has been radiocarbon

dated to 9850 B.C.±400 years (M-1603). The soil, began to form after the retreat of the main phase of Lake Algonquin, and since the artifacts appear to have been deposited before this time they too must predate 9000 B.C. A maximum age of 11,000 B.C. has been suggested for the site. This is based on the beach sequence in the area and considerations of post-glacial uplift. The site, apparently, would have been covered by the waters of Lake Warren and must postdate this lake stage.

The collection from the site consists of forty artifacts and forty-four waste chips collected over a number of years by Mr. Wallace Hill who lives nearby. Only one of these objects, a notched scraper, is at odds with the rest of the assemblage and may come from a larger site about 150 feet to the north of Barnes containing material of later time periods. The majority of the objects are projectile points and point fragments, most broken during manufacture. These account for twenty-one of the forty artifacts. Wright and Roosa note a chisel- or burin-like appearance on several of the fractured bases but do not suggest use of the bases as burins. A few preforms—blanks of flint for the preparation of points—were found on the site and four additional preforms from the Vibber cache were included in the analysis because Wright and Roosa see a similarity in the chert types at the two sites. There are also nine distinctive channel flakes—the flakes removed in the process of fluting a point—from the site, so material from all stages of point manufacture is present even in this small collection. The rest of the recovered cultural material consisted of flakes of which only some were used as tools.

In reconstructing the industry, Wright and Roosa suggest that irregular flakes were removed from the corners of tabular cores and worked into heavy scrapers, while large symmetrical flakes were removed from the above cores as they became exhausted. This is hypothetical since no cores and only six flakes with any indication of a striking platform were recovered from the site. The flakes were bifacially retouched and served as preforms. If the preform was of a suitable shape, it was fluted and finished as a projectile point. It was noted that sixty percent of these preforms were discarded during the process of working them into artifacts. Since most of the points from the Barnes site were broken during manufacture, only a few had the distinctive double flute of Roosa's Barnes type point.

The Barnes site represents a short-term camp of a small group. Almost all recovered flint debris relates to the preparation of projectile points. The larger numbers of scrapers and other tools which might reflect other types of economic activity are absent. The Barnes site assemblage does not represent a large group or a full family group. I suspect that this site was occupied for an extremely short period of time, perhaps several days, by a small group consisting primarily, of males. It might have served as a spot to refurbish spears on a hunting expedition. Although Wright and Roosa do not mention it, I suspect that the site is close to a source of raw material. Their evidence that sixty percent of the preforms were broken during manufacture contrasts with that of the Holcombe site to the south where flint utilization from necessity was more efficient. Further, since Wright and Roosa (1966: 851) suggest a spruce cover for the site at the time of occupation it is doubtful if much game was present. I think this site, if located near a still

unreported chert source, might have been a workshop area occupied by males away from their family groups.

The only excavated Early Paleo-Indian locality in Michigan is the Holcombe beach ridge in Macomb County just to the north of the city of Detroit. The Holcombe site was excavated by a University of Michigan field crew, and several smaller sites were excavated by members of the Aboriginal Research Club of Detroit. A report on the Holcombe site and three additional sites along this beach ridge has been prepared by Fitting, DeVisscher, and Wahla (1966). Since the publication of that report, four more Paleo-Indian sites have been located and excavated along the Holcombe beach, and an additional report is being prepared on that material. The Holcombe site itself is also important for the identification of the bone of a Barren Ground caribou (Cleland 1965) from a hearth area indicating that this was the animal being hunted by the Holcombe peoples.

The sites along the Holcombe beach present another example of beach dating in the Great Lakes. The sites are all located at elevations slightly more than 605 feet above sea level. They appear to be on a beach or sand spit that was associated with a 605-foot lake level. This is the elevation of Lake Algonquin; the Holcombe beach is connected with this lake stage by way of Lake Clinton, a shallow glacial lake located behind the Mount Clemens moraine during the Lake Algonquin stage. Furthermore, we can place it within the main phase of Lake Algonquin following the Kirkfield low stage, which is associated with the Two Creeks interval. Almost identical artifacts have been found along Lake Erie in areas that would have been flooded by the

Fig. 16 *Feature from the Holcombe site where Barren Ground caribou was recovered (University of Michigan Museum of Anthropology)*

first phase of Lake Algonquin, but not the second phase (Brose and Fitting n.d.). Since hundreds of Paleo-Indian artifacts have been found along this beach and none have been found within the bed of this lake, it appears to be a good association and suggests an occupation just prior to 9000 B.C.

Several criticisms have been made of the dating of this site (Stoltman 1966, MacDonald 1967). It has been suggested that this might have been a high ground occupation within a forested area during a later time period. I might point out that although later artifacts, left by people who lived in the area when the lake was no longer there, are found primarily in high areas, they are also found frequently in low, former lake bed areas nearby below a 605-foot elevation. Hundreds of Paleo-Indian artifacts are, to date, *never* found below this elevation. With the very rapid drop in water level following the main stage of Lake Algonquin, this area would have been a high and well-drained plateau, possibly with a lower water table resulting from the downcutting of the Clinton River through the Mount Clemens moraine, a result of the additional 400 feet the river had to drop to reach the level of Lake Stanley in the Lake Huron basin. Assuming normal patterns of plant succession, this would have been a closed spruce or spruce-pine forest within a century. There would have been little usable game and little to draw occupants, particularly when contrasted to the richer lakeshore environments that must have existed. I see nothing that could have drawn the dense numbers of people at the Holcombe beach site until several thousand years after the second phase of Lake Algonquin. It is only after the establishment of broadleaf forests and modern drainage patterns that people once again could live here in large numbers.

Another reason that many fail to recognize the Holcombe industry as an Early Paleo-Indian occupation is that the very small, thin, concave-base, lanceolate points tend to be basally thinned rather than fully fluted (perhaps a result of their thinness). This does not fit well with the generally accepted evolutionary development suggested for such projectile points (Wormington 1957). One thing I have tried to emphasize is the diversity of Paleo-Indian fluted points. Points similar to those from Holcombe do occur with both Folsom (Roberts 1935) and Clovis (Leonardy 1966) assemblages, so that their appearance as a dominant point type in an area where the flint sources are small and in short supply is not surprising.

At the Holcombe site the sample from the surface collection and 2675 square feet of excavation consisted of 385 Paleo-Indian artifacts, including 110 points and fragments, and over 11,000 fragments of waste chippage showing no signs of retouch or use. The smallest site of the group so far reported was Paleo-II-W-A with only 339 flakes and 41 artifacts.

A detailed examination of artifacts and chippage allowed a tentative reconstruction of the pattern of industrial activity at Holcombe. The vast majority of artifacts and flakes were made from Bayport chert derived from quarries about a hundred miles to the north of the site. It was brought to the site in the form of preforms. Here it was apparently heated in the sand near a central fire that darkened its color and improved its flaking properties. Preforms prepared in this manner broke when too much heat was applied. The majority were finished into projectile points, the most abundant class of artifacts on the site, by pressure flaking. These distinctive small pressure-retouch flakes with an average weight of less than a tenth of a gram account for nearly eighty percent of the flakes from the site by count. It was their distinctive appearance that led to the location and isolation of additional Paleo-Indian sites along the Holcombe beach.

Using the excavated material from the Holcombe site we estimated group size and composition. From the distribution of flake types on the site, we noted that rough flint working activities took place in the central part of the site while finishing activities, as shown by the distinctive retouch flakes, took place on the peripheries of the site. By cross-correlating flake distribution with the distribution of chert types we also found that while all chert variants were found

Fig. 17(a) *Projectile points, point fragments, and preforms from the Holcombe site (From Fitting, DeVisscher, and Wahla: 1966)*

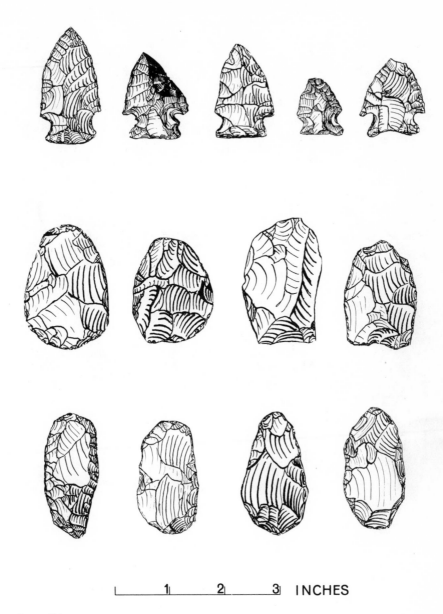

1 2 3 INCHES

Fig. 17(b)

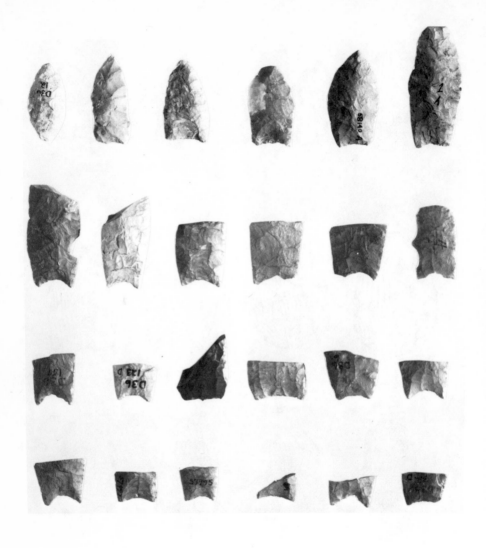

Fig. 17(c)

INCHES
1 2 3

METRIC
1 2 3 4 5 6 7 8

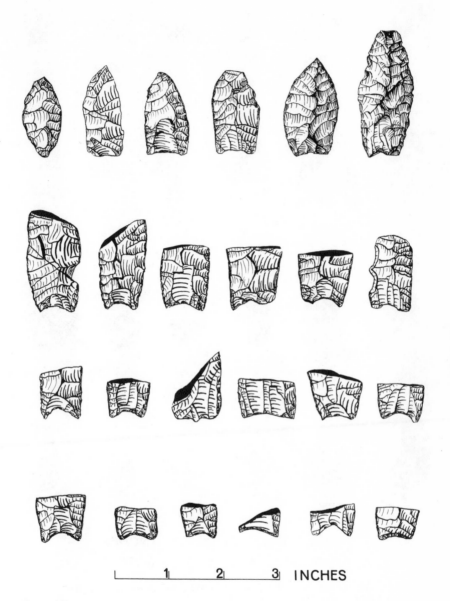

1 2 3 INCHES

Fig. 17(*d*)

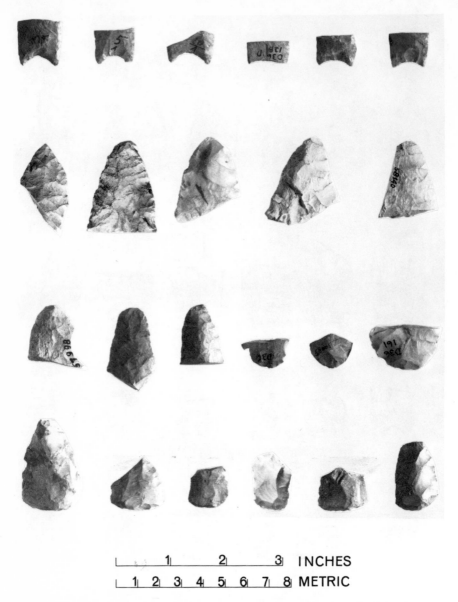

```
          1          2          3   INCHES
    1   2   3   4   5   6   7   8   METRIC
```

Fig. 18(a) Projectile point bases, biface fragments and other artifacts from the Holcombe
site (From Fitting, DeVisscher, and Wahla: 1966)

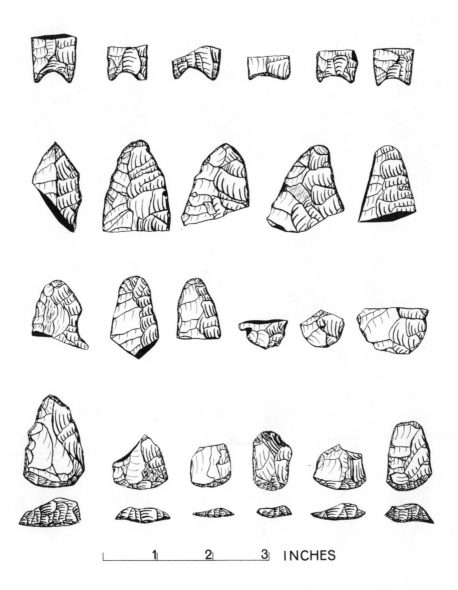

Fig. 18(b)

1 2 3 INCHES

1 2 3 4 5 6 7 8 METRIC

Fig. 18(c)

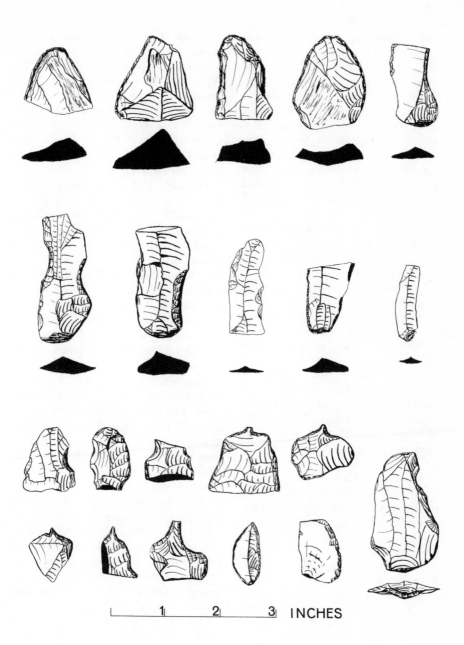

1 2 3 INCHES

Fig. 18(d)

in about equal frequencies in the center of the site, the finishing areas were marked by a series of distinctive chert profiles with distinct preferences for different types of chert. We defined five such areas and suggested at least three more to make the camp symmetrical. This meant five to eight males finishing artifacts and, since there was a balance of non-projectile point artifacts, five to eight families—somewhere between thirty and sixty individuals in the band group at the site.

A comparison of the sites along this beach ridge is also revealing. The Holcombe site was based on a successful kill of one or more Barren Ground caribou. It may have been occupied for several weeks; the extremely high ratio of point bases to complete, unreworked points (about fifty to one) indicates much refurbishing of broken spears. The other sites were occupied for shorter periods of time as shown by the lower actual number of flakes and artifacts. Lower ratios of flakes to artifacts and point bases to complete, unreworked points indicates less industrial activity. At Paleo-II-W-A this ratio is one to one. A number of lithic techniques were known to these knappers; at one site, where the lowest ratio of chips to artifacts was encountered, small, bipolar cores were used to derive flakes for tools and, when spent, were used as tools themselves.

The close dating of the Holcombe site allows a tie-in with nearby pollen profiles, and the occurrence of Barren Ground caribou correlates with the floral assemblage. This part of the state was free from glacial ice for some time and, in well-drained areas, was covered by a closed forest. Along the margins of the lakes, however, soil instability and fluctuating levels of soil moisture allowed a flora similar to that of recently deglaciated landscapes (Cushing 1965: 412). The floral assemblage consisted of a sparse cover of spruce with a ground cover of herb plants including several that are very characteristic of a tundra environment (Andersen 1954). Toward the interior, away from the lakes, there was a greater spruce domination.

An animal such as the Barren Ground caribou could survive and thrive in this situation. These animals, often traveling in herds of tens of thousands, today spend the summer in the tundra and winter in the forest-tundra edge (Burt and Grossenheider 1964). Ethnographic accounts tell of hunting camps and kill sites located at the headwaters of glacial lakes where men harvested this important food resource as the animals returned to the forest in the fall. The Holcombe beach is such a locality.

The distribution of points similar to those from the Holcombe site follow the spruce parkland corridors that were open along the lakes at this time. This distribution is in sharp contrast to the general pattern of fluted point distribution which, although concentrated in southwestern Michigan, covers the entire lower portion of the state (Mason 1958). It suggests that the general fluted-point distribution reflects the distribution of Paleo-Indian people prior to the establishment of closed forests within the center of the state. Such fully fluted points must then be centuries earlier than those from the Holcombe beach.

Projectile points similar to those from the Holcombe beach have been recovered as surface finds in northern Ohio and western Michigan. The morphology is the same but there are distinctive chert differences occur between various areas that provide the bases for establishing hunting territories. Black Upper Mercer Flint defines such a territory in northern Ohio; Bayport chert characterizes the eastern Michigan area; and the majority of such points that I have seen from western Michigan are made of a distinctive banded chert, the source of which I do not recognize. There is some overlap of chert types with some Bayport chert in western Michigan, a minority occurrence of Upper Mercer Flint in eastern Michigan, and a minority occurrence of Bayport chert in northern Ohio. This supports the idea of trade associations and intermarriage between bands.

The Holcombe peoples represent the "last gasp" of the Early Paleo-Indian tradition in lower Michigan. With the dropping of lake levels new artifact styles became dominant. On the north shore of Lake Superior there is a site which was under glacial ice when the Holcombe site was occupied. The Brohm site (MacNeish 1952) looks like it was occupied by the descendants of the Holcombe people, who had been following the ice front north for several generations. This site contains similar artifact styles, including points, preforms, and other tools similar to those recovered from the Holcombe beach. Differences exist because of the local source of raw material, a nearby Taconite quarry. This site is an anomaly at a time period when most of the upper Lakes area was occupied by makers of stemmed, lanceolate projectile points. I can picture the descendants of the Holcombe hunters, following the ice fronts northward while talking about how difficult it was to find caribou anymore.

LATE PALEO-INDIAN OCCUPATIONS

The people who inhabited the upper Great Lakes area as the water level fell after Lake Algonquin, faced a different environment and exploited it in a different way than their predecessors. They lived in a forested land, with the richest ecological niches near the receding lake shores. Shay (1963) has reported that deer, muskrat, wolf, black bear, turtle, bird, and fishbone along with *Bison occidentalis* occurred at the Itasca kill site in Minnesota. Cleland (1966: 49) holds that while these people were certainly hunters, they were specifically hunters of the forests and would have been adapted to a forest way of life.

One of the major problems encountered in our study of the Late Paleo-Indian groups of this time is the location of sites. The richest environment was the shoreline and, since the low water stages in the Great Lakes were as much as four hundred feet below present lake levels, many of the richest sites are far out from the present-day shores and under many feet of water. We are left with scattered surface finds of artifacts and occasional sites in areas of the upper Great Lakes where land rebounded and rose, following the retreat of the ice. These sites are found in northern forests. Their scattered distribution and cultural connections over long distances is what we would expect for the entire area of Late Paleo-Indian occupation in a similar environment.

The distinctive artifacts of these people are stemmed, lanceolate projectile points, although examples of notched points similar to the predominant styles of this time period on sites farther to the south furnish evidence of contact with southern cultures.

Fig. 19 Artifacts of argillite and quartzite from the Warner School site (University of Michigan Museum of Anthropology)

Quimby (1959, 1960) has used the term "Aqua-plano" to describe these artifacts. In doing so he incorporates the western term "Plano," used for a projectile point type cluster including stemmed Eden and Scottsbluff point types as well as non-stemmed lanceolate point types such as Midland, Milnesand, and Plainview (Wormington 1957), with his own obser-vation that they are found in the Great Lakes (Aqua) region.

I find Quimby's term unsatisfactory for two reasons. As Mason (1963) has pointed out, there is no need to separate this material on typological grounds from that found in the western parts of the United States as long as the projectile point type definitions now found in the literature are used on this material. Grouping this material is also unnecessary and tends to obscure important differences. Some of the artifacts illustrated by Quimby and referred to as "Aquaplano" (1960: Figure 14) would be better placed with earlier cultural materials, at least in the southern parts of the upper Great Lakes, than they would with the stemmed lanceolate points, which he would also include in this category (Quimby 1960: Figure 13). Mason (1963) uses specific western point names for these artifacts.

In the lower peninsula of Michigan, Peske, Fitting, and others have been using the term "Satchell complex" for several years to describe this type of cultural material (Griffin 1964: 252). This term is derived from the Satchell site in the Saginaw Valley where Scottsbluff type projectile points manufactured from such diverse materials as quartzite, argillite, and flint were collected on the site surface by Fred Dustin of Saginaw in the early part of this century. Peske's (1963) studies have concentrated more on material alone, particularly argillite, than on projectile point typology. Roosa (1965: 32) unjustly criticizes Peske for including all argillite in the Satchell complex. I think that Roosa's evaluation of the Satchell complex, as a unit, as Late Archaic is invalid. Even if the Warner School site (Roosa 1966) is Late Archaic, there is a Late Paleo-Indian stemmed lanceolate point complex that can be inferred from surface material in the southern Michigan peninsula and from excavated materials in the more northern area.

These peoples were forest hunters who avoided the plains area in southwestern Michigan. Therefore, both "Plano" and "Aqua-Plano" are misleading. Like Mason, I prefer to use specific cultural designa-

tions where possible with the use of the term "Satchell complex" as a generic classification.

The pattern of surface distribution of this type of cultural material throughout the state is interesting. Quimby (1959) has shown that many of these artifacts are of post Lake Algonquin age. Peske (1963: 559) noted the near absence of argillite artifacts in the southwestern parts of the state and suggested that this was caused by a lack of argillite in this area. While argillite artifacts are lacking it is also true that all lanceolate stemmed point variants are very rare in the southwestern part of the state (Fitting 1963a). At one time I correlated this with the high concentrations of fluted points noted by Mason (1958) for the same counties where in Late Paleo-Indian artifacts are rare. Now I believe that these two occupations are on mutually exclusive time horizons or, at best, overlap only slightly in time.

The high frequency of artifact styles similar to those found further to the south during this time period suggests another explanation. If the greater numbers of artifacts indicate a larger number of people, there was a relatively dense population of Early Archaic people in the river valleys of southwestern Michigan following the Early Paleo-Indian occupation of the area, which was also heavy. The Late Paleo-Indian hunters are not found in this area of prairies but are restricted to the more northern boreal forests. The common occurrence of Archaic artifact styles in Late Paleo-Indian sites and the near absence of Late Paleo-Indian artifacts in Early Archaic sites is a result of population density. Artifact styles and concepts diffused more rapidly from the high population density areas

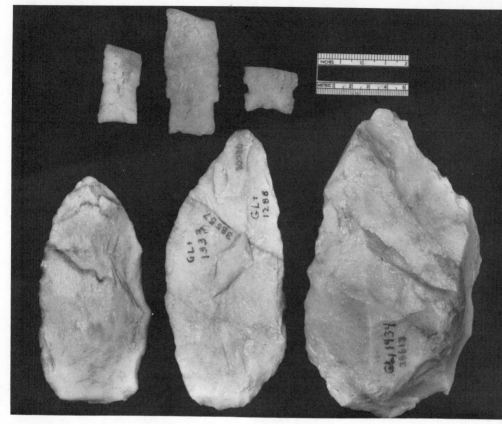

Fig. 20 *Projectile point bases and large bifaces of quartzite from George Lake* (*University of Michigan Museum of Anthropology*)

to low population density areas than they moved back to the centers of population. Even today there are more artifacts of American manufacture or style of manufacture in a Canadian home than there are Canadian artifacts in a home in the United States. This "one-way" spread of artifacts and concepts from high to low population areas characterizes much of Michigan's prehistory.

The first of the Late Paleo-Indian sites to be excavated in the upper Great Lakes was in the Manitoulin district of Ontario. Here Emerson F. Greenman of the University of Michigan Museum of Anthropol-

ogy undertook a series of studies that lasted from the late 1930s into the mid 1950s. An early note on one site (Greenman and Stanley 1940) suggested only that flint and quartzite artifacts, associated with the bones of beaver, deer, moose, and sturgeon, were found in beach deposits of pre-Lake Nipissing age. In later reports (Greenman and Stanley 1943, Greenman 1948) this site and others were tied in with the post-Lake Algonquin beach sequence. Some artifacts, found on an early beach, were waterworn, suggesting that they were deposited there at a time when the beach was still active.

The cultural material from the two earliest sites excavated by Greenman (George Lake 1 and George Lake 2, both located about eight miles to the northwest of Killarney, Ontario) is made up of quartzite. The artifacts include semi-lunar knives, choppers, ovate bifaces, quadrangular bifaces, and retouched flakes. Thousands of unmodified flakes of this distinctive Killarney quartzite were also recovered from the sites. Projectile point fragments were rare. There are a few crude lanceolate objects of quartzite which might have served as projectile points. The diagnostic forms include two Eden Point bases and one small side-notched projectile point.

Greenman interpeted this site as a quarry area as well as a hunting and fishing camp. He was impressed with the great amount of chipping debris and unfinished artifacts in relation to the small numbers of finished items. This fits well, as we shall see, with the widespread distribution of quartzite on sites of this and later time periods in the upper Great Lakes.

The next site of this time horizon and cultural tradition to be excavated was the Sheguiandah site on the eastern end of Manitoulin Island, Ontario. It was worked at various times between 1951 and 1954 by Thomas E. Lee who has prepared a number of short reports on various aspects of its occupation (Lee 1953, 1954, 1955, 1956, 1957, 1964, and others). All of these are of a preliminary nature and most seem to have been prepared within a short period of time (even the 1964 report was prepared in 1955). While, as with Greenman's work, a single comprehensive report on the site has yet to appear, we can make some observations on the recovered material.

The site was utilized as both a quarry and habitation. Lee believes that the environment alone indicates that fishing was an important activity. The site has a rich archaeological assemblage with quartzite again predominating. In addition to large bifacial quartzite ovates, finished scrapers, drills, and ovate bifacial knives were recovered. There is at least one Eden style projectile point from the site as well as a side-notched point similar to the one from George Lake. Lee suggests several occupations of the site, and certainly there is a good Middle Woodland component (Lee 1965). I am hesitant, however, about accepting Lee's multiple earlier occupations without statistical evidence of artifact association and better indications that he is not attributing chronological value to functional differences.

The time of the earlier Sheguiandah occupation has also been open to various interpretations. As Quimby (1959) and others (Griffin 1965b) have pointed out, the elevation and position of this site suggests that it was underwater until sometime after the Lake Algonquin high stage and was first inhabited sometime between that stage and the Lake Stanley low stage in the Lake Huron basin. John Sanford, one of the geologists who worked with Lee (about a hundred visited the site: Lee 1954: 16), noted that some of the artifacts were found in "a heterogeneous mixture of soil, pebbles, and boulders of uncertain origin," which has been interpreted by some as glacial till. If this is the case, then this material *might* have been of preglacial origin.

Archaeologists working in the Great Lakes region have almost universally rejected the idea that this cultural material is of preglacial origin; it would suggest a pattern of cultural development at variance with all other indications so far known in the area and would be based on evidence which is far from conclusive. Sanford himself suggested that the "till" might be redeposited. This position has been accepted by Griffin (1965b: 660) and is the position I present in this volume.

A radiocarbon date of 7180 B.C.±250 years (W-345, Lee 1956) was obtained from the bottom of a peat layer covering clays containing artifacts in a small swampy area near the site. Since the occupation predates the radiocarbon date and postdates Lake Algonquin, the site would have been initially occupied somewhere between 7000 and 9000 B.C.

Michigan State University field parties working under the direction of Dr. Charles E. Cleland and Dr. Elizabeth Baldwin (Cleland 1967) have recently located and excavated a Satchell complex site, the Samels Field site, on Skegemog Point in Grand Traverse County. It too is located on a raised beach that indicates an age of about ten thousand years. Long lanceolate projectile points, preforms, knives, side-scrapers made on long flakes and gravers were recovered. A detailed report on this material is in preparation.

In Brown County, Wisconsin, the Renier site (Mason and Irwin 1960) has also produced Eden and Scottsbluff points and quartzite tools. This site was excavated because it looked like a good place for an early site to be located on top of an old Algonquin beach ridge. Because of stylistic considerations Mason and Irwin feel that the site must have been occupied within the several millennia following the Lake Algonquin high water level.

All of the artifacts from the site have been heat altered. Coupled with the occurrence of cremated human bone this indicates a single cremation burial and that the artifacts from the site were grave offerings accompanying the burial.

The artifacts include twelve Eden and Scottsbluff projectile points of quartzite, one side-notched point of dull black flint, two quartzite scrapers, and many fragments of ovate quartzite bifaces. Mason and Irwin interpret these last objects as preforms and relate them to similar bifaces from Greenman's George Lake site. In age, as well as form, they are also similar to some of the material from the Sheguiandah site.

The sociological implications of quartzite industries in the upper Great Lakes such as the closely related George Lake, Sheguiandah, and Renier industries is interesting. The Brohm site (MacNeish 1952) on Lake Superior, occupied at this same time period, but discussed as a holdover of the Early Paleo-Indian occupation, also includes a few large quartzite objects in an assemblage composed primarily of local taconite. To the south I noted a quartzite biface at the Hi-Lo site in western Michigan and the use of argillite in eastern Michigan. Almost all of the northern quartzite tools have duplicates in argillite from surface collections in lower Michigan. At the Satchell site itself, stemmed lanceolate points have been found made of flint, quartzite, and argillite. This preference for less satisfactory knapping materials is also evident in Ohio where Late Paleo-Indian knappers selected the poorer quality Nellie chert while better quality Upper Mercer flint was available in the same deposits (Prufer 1963).

I can think of several explanations for this and there are probably many others. At Naomikong Point in Whitefish Bay on Lake Superior, which was occupied at a later time period, the primary source of raw material for knapping was small beach pebbles which were worked with a bipolar small core technique. The resulting flakes and tools were very small and the larger implements from this site were all made of nonlocal materials, primarily quartzite. Almost all of Mason and Irwin's points were over four inches long and, in many parts of the upper Great Lakes, quartzite might have been the only material large enough to furnish a source for this type or artifact. The same thing might be true for the Saginaw Valley where the local Bayport chert tends to be found in nodules of four inches or less in diameter (Dustin 1935, 1968). With a scarcity of usable flint, quartzite and argillite may have been the most suitable material available. This, however, would not explain the situation in Ohio where better quality raw material could have been derived from the same quarry as the poorer material selected for actual use.

Another explanation is more speculative. These Lake Paleo-Indian peoples were the last remnants of the cultural tradition responsible for the settlement of the New World. In the Great Lakes, at least, they were dependent on a changing environment, the newly drained shore of the receding glacial lakes. In addition to living in an unstable environmental niche they were able to view, and were influenced by, the Early Archaic cultures in areas to the south. At all of the late Paleo-Indian sites discussed there is evidence of contact with peoples to the south. I imagine that these groups were admiring yet apprehensive about the newcomers who had a more efficient adaptation. The emphasis on less favorable knapping materials could have been one way a dying tradition maintained its cultural integrity.

After the Chippewa-Stanley low stage around 7500 B.C., the lake basins began to fill again. The forests which had colonized the draining lake shores were flooded. The environment that supported the Late Paleo-Indian peoples was gone. People were still there but in numbers so diminished the area looks empty to the archaeologist. Some of these forest hunters may have moved north to the draining lakes of the Manitoba area. Many probably joined the Archaic groups in the southern parts of the state. Perhaps their descendants, after several thousand years and many changes in the lakes and land, moved back to the north and recolonized the lands their forefathers had abandoned.

CHAPTER IV

THE RETURN OF THE PEOPLE

THE CONCEPT OF THE ARCHAIC

The Archaic period is a term that has been widely used in the eastern United States since Ritchie applied it to his New York Lamoka Culture in 1932. Definitions of the Archaic focus on time, subsistence pattern, technology, or combinations of these factors.

Ritchie, and most others who used the term in the 1930s and 1940s, recognized that the cultural materials of these people represented a very different way of life from that of most historic Indians. Stratigraphy, and later radiocarbon dating, confirmed that the Archaic peoples predated the Woodland and Mississippian groups that followed. Today radiocarbon dates of around 7000 B.C. have been obtained for Archaic sites in southern Illinois, West Virginia, North Carolina, Georgia, and Alabama.

Griffin (1964: 225), while also considering the economy and technology, begins the Archaic at 8000 B.C. and includes cultural manifestations after this time, including several that I would call Paleo-Indian, as Archaic. He believes that the Archaic lasts until some time around 1000 B.C. in northeastern North America when the introduction of ceramics serves as an indicator of the Early Woodland period. A second, and very popular, basis for defining the Archaic is the subsistence pattern. Griffin (1964: 252), Ritchie (1965:

31–36), and others emphasize that this is a hunting, gathering, and fishing stage of cultural development. Both Caldwell (1958) and Fowler (1959) emphasize the adaptations to local environments and local resources. There is an implication here that the adaptation of Archaic peoples contrasts with that of their Paleo-Indian predecessors. Rolingson and Schwartz (1966: 2–3) are quite specific about this. They use the term Paleo-Indian ". . . to refer to that cultural stage dependent on big game hunting adapted to late Pleistocene and early recent climatic and physiographic conditions" while the term Archaic is used ". . . to refer to a stage of cultural adaptation which utilized a wide variety of local fauna."

While this is a nice contrast in adaptive patterns, I have trouble associating these adaptive patterns with cultural materials. Caldwell (1959: 8) writes that the southeast is "living country." He points out that some of the European colonists starved while learning to live in the woods but some did not and the children of those who lived would inherit the land. I can picture one generation, at the most, of hungry big game hunters in this area. There is no reason why a person cannot make fluted points while foraging for the main part of his diet. Some fluted point makers were undoubtedly big game hunters, particularly in the plains and peri-glacial environments as discussed in the last chapter. To consider all fluted point makers as big game hunters is to underrate their adaptive capacity.

Cleland (1966: 47) emphasizes that "the nature of the transition from those cultures which we call Paleo-Indian to those which we recognize as Archaic could not have been gradual in those areas where biotic change was rapid." We can note a gradual transition in the southeastern parts of the United States, but not in the Great Lakes area. Rolingson and Schwartz (1966: 157–60) have suggested several alternative patterns of Paleo-Indian Archaic relationships based on their definitions of these as adaptive patterns. Their models are not mutually exclusive and in some areas there is a great deal of continuity between the two while in other areas the contrast is much more marked.

The third type of definition used for the Archaic is technological. To many, myself included, the Archaic is marked by the predominance of notched projectile points; also stemmed and shouldered projectile points dissimilar to the Late Paleo-Indian forms. Since these projectile points appear in some areas at a very early date, long before Paleo-Indian projectile points have been abandoned in other areas, I cannot set an arbitrary date for the beginning of the Archaic. In some areas, like the Great Lakes, Archaic projectile points are found in Paleo-Indian assemblages. This reinforces my view that these traditions may have existed during the same period of time.

I believe that the appearance of Archaic materials in Michigan marks the introduction of a hunting, gathering, fishing economy adapted to a potentially rich deciduous forest-riverine environment which contrasts to the boreal lakeshore environment frequented by the Late Paleo-Indian peoples. When this environment was limited, so were the peoples who lived there. With the establishment of modern biotic areas and the return of the high lake levels, a form of cultural development comparable to that farther to the south was reached.

This chapter deals with these hunting, fishing, and gathering peoples in Michigan after the area had been abandoned by peri-glacial hunters. While we may only be dealing with a decline, followed by an increase, in population, I believe that there are other factors which point to actual movement, to a return, of people into the area following the establishment of environmental conditions similar to those which exist today. It is to this movement that I shall turn my attention.

I mentioned earlier that Griffin used the introduction of pottery to mark the end of the Archaic and the beginning of the Early Woodland period. I will accept this for a cultural definition but, in Michigan at least, the introduction of pottery made little difference in the way of life of its users. Therefore, I am including my discussion of the Early Woodland occupation of Michigan with the Archaic. As during the Early Archaic, Early Woodland groups to the south of Michigan were developing a more efficient cultural adaptation and more spectacular cultural forms than those found in the Great Lakes area.

THE EARLY AND MIDDLE ARCHAIC

After 9000 B.C. there appears to have been first a boreal forest period, lasting from between 8000 and 9000 B.C. to 6000 or 7000 B.C., followed by a pine period, lasting from 6000 or 7000 B.C. up to approximately 3500 B.C. (Cushing 1965). These would correspond roughly to the Early and Middle parts of the Archaic in our area. They are also times when Michigan was marked by a very low population density.

It is during the boreal forest period that we find our Late Paleo-Indian occupations in the newly drained lakeshore areas of the upper Great Lakes during the drop to the low water stages. While this northern area is completely boreal, there were some deciduous forest elements in the southern parts of the state. Cleland (1966: 20) suggests that "it is probable that a few mammals found in deciduous forest situations also inhabited the Great Lakes at this time." This boreal forest cover of spruce and pine gradually evolved into the predominantly pine cover of the following period.

The pine period, which is marked by an ever stronger deciduous forest element in the southern parts of the state, was probably warmer, and possibly drier, than the preceding boreal period. This was the time when lake levels were slowly rising and drowning forests along their shores. It is likely that the most favorable environments would have been in the broadleaf forests near the prairies along the interior river valleys of the southern part of the state. Here, on a limited scale, there would have been environments like that which supported the Modoc Rock Shelter occupation in Illinois (Fowler 1959).

There are only traces of Archaic peoples in Michigan during these times. In the potentially rich areas of southwestern Michigan only a few sites, Sattler, Frantz,

Herick, Graham, and Kersterke, reveal projectile points of an early Archaic cast (Fitting 1963a: 21). These are points similar to the Big Sandy and Cypress points in Tennessee (Lewis and Lewis 1961), the notched and stemmed forms from the lower levels of Modoc Rock Shelter (Fowler 1959: 23), and the bifurcate stemmed forms (Fitting 1964a) which have recently been demonstrated to be very early in the eastern United States (Broyles 1966). These, however, are all surface collections that have been gathered throughout large areas of southwestern Michigan over long periods of time. They all contain Paleo-Indian elements as well as items which are post-Archaic.

The same thing is true of southeastern Michigan; all we have are surface sites. I noted the occurrence of bifurcate stemmed points on many of these sites along with other possible early Archaic points several years ago (Fitting 1964a), and since then Jerry DeVisscher and other members of the Aboriginal Research Club of Detroit have been working at isolating these sites. So far the DeCook site has the greatest potential. Similar "Early Archaic" artifacts have been reported in collections from the Welti site in Monroe County (Fitting 1963c) and the Stone School site in Washtenaw County (Wobst 1965). At the Welti site there was a series of broad-bladed side-notched points with a distinctive bevel on either side as if from resharpening. These are common in surface collections from southern Michigan, one of which was illustrated over forty years ago by Hinsdale (1925: 190). There are indications in the southeastern United States and in Illinois that these are also Early Archaic forms but, again, we have no stratigraphic evidence to prove this from Michigan.

It is possible that the Warner School site in Genesee County contains Early and Middle Archaic elements (Roosa 1966). It is also typical of what is encountered when excavating such possibly early sites. In several weeks' time 375 square feet were excavated and thirty-eight flint artifacts, seventeen argillite artifacts, and nineteen potsherds were recovered. The only features were a Late Woodland fire pit, a Late Woodland burial, and a possible Archaic fire pit which was devoid of cultural material.

The site was selected for excavation because of the argillite materials which had been found there. It was hoped that it would shed light on what later became known as the Satchell complex. While some argillite artifacts have a Paleo-Indian cast (Roosa 1966: 27), several also resemble Archaic stemmed points. Roosa noted that the artifacts with the greatest average depth were the small bifurcate-stemmed points from the site.

The Warner School occupation was not long or intensive at any time. It consists of a series of superimposed hunting camps, although the Late Woodland occupation may have been for a longer duration. It also suggests that most Early and Middle Archaic sites in Michigan, if similar—as surface collections indicate—were also short-term camps. The artifacts which we have discussed may represent the debris of hunting parties from farther to the south moving seasonally into the area. They also could represent, in some areas, small camps of seasonally mobile peoples—the forerunners of the more successful settlements of the Late Archaic—attempting to permanently occupy the area.

We know that Archaic peoples were in the state between 9000 and 3000 B.C. This is demonstrated by radiocarbon dates from cultural levels at sites in surrounding states such as the Raddatz Rock Shelter in Wisconsin (Wittry 1959) and the Rohr Shelter in the upper Ohio Valley (Dragoo 1959). There also is the troublesome feature ⚹11 from the Andrews site, a fragmentary burial with some red ocher and no grave goods, radiocarbon dated to 3350 B.C.±150 years (M-941), that indicates someone was here at the time. To date, however, no large, permanent sites of these people have been found. I doubt this is the result of poor site sampling, since several intensive surveys have been carried out in key areas where one would expect to find sites of this time period—Macomb and Monroe counties being examples. There has been an intensive search for such materials by amateur archaeologists in the state envious of the early sites excavated by their brethren farther to the south. Another possibility is that Early and Middle Archaic sites were in lakeshore areas that have since been covered with water as the lake levels rose from the Chippewa-Stanley low to the Nipissing level. Although this might be true in the south, there is no evidence to validate it. In the north, where sites have been preserved by the rebound of the land, the occupations for the first part of this period are Paleo-Indian, with only traces of Archaic influences.

The explanation I favor is that during the Early and Middle Archaic there were very few people in Michigan because the environments to which Archaic peoples were best adapted either did not exist or existed in more limited areas than they did after 3000 B.C.

THE LATE ARCHAIC

The Late Archaic period in Michigan, as I will use the term, lasts from around 3000 B.C. up through the introduction of pottery making into the state, a trait which marks the beginning of the Early Woodland occupation. The information gathered by both Cleland and Yarnell suggests that the time of 3500 to 2000 B.C. saw the formation of essentially modern environments in Michigan. The deciduous forest may even have had a greater distribution at 2000 B.C. than today. Thus, for the first time in Michigan prehistory, we are dealing with an environmental situation similar to that described in Chapter II.

Another important element of this time period, perhaps a key factor for the Late Archaic settler, was the re-establishment of high water levels in the Great Lakes. During the low water stages the fall of the rivers would have been greater, and they would have run more rapidly. With high lake levels they would again flow more slowly. The fish found in archaeological sites of the Late Archaic (Cleland and Kearney 1966: 82) are species which avoided rapid currents. In contrast, Hinsdale (1932: 4) has pointed out that rapidly flowing streams in the state carry a native fish population insufficient to afford much food. Fish may not have been the primary food source, but they may have furnished the "vital margin" of subsistence. They were a food source which became important after 3000 B.C. as did deer which were dependent on the broadleaf forests that were also more common after this time.

Throughout the northeastern part of North America the Late Archaic is a period of increased occupational intensity; a great deal of cultural similarity is found in the entire area. Terms like "Laurentian Archaic" are applied to the cultural materials from New England to the upper Mississippi Valley. Cleland (1966: 52) observed that the term "Boreal Archaic" as used by Byers (1959) and Quimby (1960) is invalid since the existence of this culture is dependent on deciduous and mixed forest situations.

The comparative framework of prehistoric economies developed by Cleland (1966: 42–45) is also useful for understanding Late Archaic subsistence. Cleland proposes a continuum of subsistence patterns running from a focal economy, specializing in the exploitation of a single food resource, through a diffuse economy making a perfectly balanced use of all available food resources. All groups fall somewhere between these extremes, but it is possible to recognize both focal and diffuse tendencies in prehistoric groups. Paleo-Indian hunters, specializing in hunting certain forms of game, and settled village agriculturists both have more focal economies than people who seasonally hunt, gather wild plants, and fish. Late Archaic peoples clearly have a more diffuse economy than their Paleo-Indian predecessors.

Economies with diffuse adaptations have another characteristic. By not being committed to a single exploitative pattern they are more adaptable to change. By shifting their economic emphasis they can exploit new or old resources in new ways. Cleland calls them "pre-adapted" societies. I suggest that such groups not only have more open economies but also more open societies. They are as ready to accept and incorporate new social patterns as economic patterns.

There are similarities in ideological

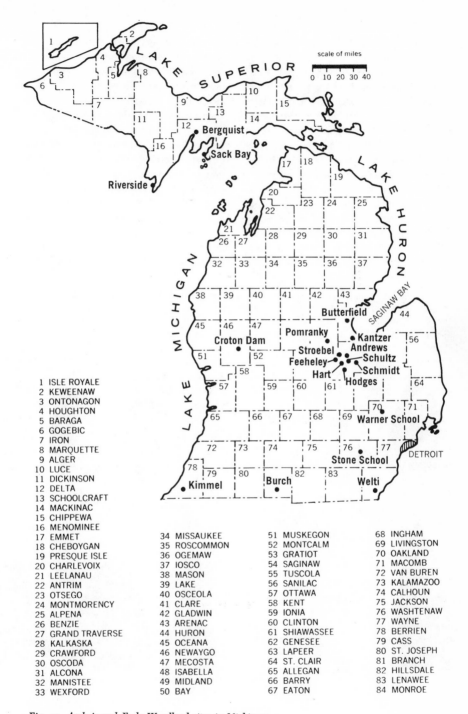

1 ISLE ROYALE
2 KEWEENAW
3 ONTONAGON
4 HOUGHTON
5 BARAGA
6 GOGEBIC
7 IRON
8 MARQUETTE
9 ALGER
10 LUCE
11 DICKINSON
12 DELTA
13 SCHOOLCRAFT
14 MACKINAC
15 CHIPPEWA
16 MENOMINEE
17 EMMET
18 CHEBOYGAN
19 PRESQUE ISLE
20 CHARLEVOIX
21 LEELANAU
22 ANTRIM
23 OTSEGO
24 MONTMORENCY
25 ALPENA
26 BENZIE
27 GRAND TRAVERSE
28 KALKASKA
29 CRAWFORD
30 OSCODA
31 ALCONA
32 MANISTEE
33 WEXFORD

34 MISSAUKEE
35 ROSCOMMON
36 OGEMAW
37 IOSCO
38 MASON
39 LAKE
40 OSCEOLA
41 CLARE
42 GLADWIN
43 ARENAC
44 HURON
45 OCEANA
46 NEWAYGO
47 MECOSTA
48 ISABELLA
49 MIDLAND
50 BAY

51 MUSKEGON
52 MONTCALM
53 GRATIOT
54 SAGINAW
55 TUSCOLA
56 SANILAC
57 OTTAWA
58 KENT
59 IONIA
60 CLINTON
61 SHIAWASSEE
62 GENESEE
63 LAPEER
64 ST. CLAIR
65 ALLEGAN
66 BARRY
67 EATON

68 INGHAM
69 LIVINGSTON
70 OAKLAND
71 MACOMB
72 VAN BUREN
73 KALAMAZOO
74 CALHOUN
75 JACKSON
76 WASHTENAW
77 WAYNE
78 BERRIEN
79 CASS
80 ST. JOSEPH
81 BRANCH
82 HILLSDALE
83 LENAWEE
84 MONROE

Fig. 21 *Archaic and Early Woodland sites in Michigan*

patterns as well as economic adaptations throughout the northeast as illustrated by Ritchie's "Early Woodland Burial Cult" (1955) and its overlap with the "Red Ocher Culture" (Ritzenthaler and Quimby 1962). The fact that minute differences between widely separated grave lots of similar artifacts can be quantitatively studied (Binford 1963c) is indicative of cultural similarity. Again we have a widespread cultural horizon in North America with a degree of stylistic uniformity similar to that of the Paleo-Indian period of occupation. I suggest that the reasons for this are the same. Both populations were pioneer cultures that entered unoccupied or sparsely occupied territories. They passed over existing territorial boundaries and established new frontiers with free movement and communication of ideas along these frontiers. As in more recent frontier situations, there was a great deal of cooperativeness among these people and a lack of clannishness among local groups. There were also widespread kin groups and visiting over great distances, particularly on ceremonial occasions.

Several Late Archaic sites have been excavated in Michigan in recent years which allow us to draw some conclusions about the nature of this occupation in the Saginaw Valley and eastern Michigan.

Fig. 22 Possible Early and Middle Archaic projectile points from Michigan surface collections (University of Michigan Museum of Anthropology)

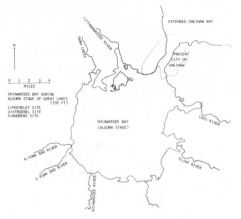

Fig. 23 *Shiawassee Bay during the Algoma stage of the prehistoric Great Lakes (University of Michigan Museum of Anthropology)*

These include the Schmidt, Hart, Feeheley, and Butterfield sites.

The Schmidt site was excavated by a University of Michigan field crew in 1964 (Harrison 1966, Crumley 1966, Allison 1966, Cleland and Kearney 1966). Within several weeks' time 350 square feet were excavated. The site was occupied after the Lake Nipissing maximum or sometime after 2000 B.C., with occupation occurring in a lakeshore-dune situation up to about 1700 B.C. The site is located on the shore of a large shallow lake or embayment, which existed in the low-lying areas of the Saginaw basin during the high water stages. This is called Shiawassee Bay, since it existed in the area which is now referred to as the Shiawassee flats.

The site is stratified as far as the projectile point styles go, but Harrison does not find this true for the other artifact types. This, along with the uniformity of the fauna and flora from all levels of the site, indicates that several projectile point styles were used by peoples with a single economic adapation.

Tools recovered from the site include thumbnail-scrapers, side-scrapers, end-scrapers, composite scrapers, quartzite end-scrapers, adzes and small wedges, possibly used as bone-splitting tools. The projectile points include one stemmed point from the upper levels and a small triangular point from the lowest level on the site. The largest group of projectile points consists of twenty-seven narrow-bladed, expanding-stemmed forms, which Harrison called Dustin points. There were sixteen other non-Dustin projectile points, most of a style which Taggart (1967) would call Feeheley points. Having found both projectile point styles in non-Archaic context, I am hesitant about using these type names. I do so now with the stipulation that the type names apply only to the several sites under consideration here.

The relative stratigraphic position of these styles is confusing. The Dustin point was first described by Binford and Papworth (1963: 105) who associated it with the Lamoka complex in New York, which has been consistently dated to around 2500 B.C. The many published references to "Dustin points" and the "Dustin complex" refer back to this Binford and Papworth report, which consists of a description of a single "Dustin" point from the Eastport site, which may not even be an Archaic site. Ritchie (1961: 29–30) accepted the Dustin point as being somewhat similar to the New York Lamoka forms on the basis of a sample of points selected out of surface collections and sent to him for examination. Harrison, dealing with a more realistic sample of excavated materials, found that the points were about the only part of the complex which resembled New York Lamoka. Furthermore, the Dustin points were stratigraphically above Laurentian-like pro-

Fig. 24 University of Michigan excavations at the Schmidt site in 1964 (University of Michigan Museum of Anthropology)

jectile points, a reverse situation from that of New York. This was predicted by Dragoo (1959: 219), who found Lamoka-like projectile points to be characteristic of the upper levels of the Annis shell mound in Kentucky while Laurentian-like points were found throughout the deposits.

Other narrow-bladed expanding stemmed points have been found in Archaic levels that are post-Lamoka in the Riverton complex of the Wabash Valley (Winters 1963:

33–41) and the Sylvan Lake complex of New York (Funk 1965). What this demonstrates is that Lamoka peoples had no monopoly on this artifact style. Not only is it found in a series of Late Archaic complexes, but it is found in a number of Late Woodland complexes as well.

Cleland and Kearney identified five mammal, nine bird, eleven fish, and two reptile species from the Schmidt site. Their conclusion, based on this faunal

Fig. 25 *Profile of the trench wall at the Schmidt site* (*University of Michigan Museum of Anthropology*)

assemblage, is that these Late Archaic peoples camped near a shallow, weedy pond or lake where they fished and hunted birds during the summer and fall. During the winter they hunted deer, which was the main subsistence element at the site, accounting for over seventy-seven percent of the meat used by these people. Both the fauna and flora, studied by April Allison, reflect an environmental situation similar to that found in the area today with the addition of a large shallow body of water in what is today the center of the valley.

The Hart site (Wright and Morlan 1964) is another Dustin site which was located on the shores of Shiawassee Bay. Excavations here were limited, and all artifacts in the University of Michigan collections were recovered from the surface of the site. All, however, are consistent with the assemblage from the Schmidt site and suggest that this occupation (or occupations, for Wright and

73

Fig. 26 Dustin points excavated at the Schmidt site (From Harrison: 1966)

Morlan feel that two stratigraphic levels can be discerned) is by a Dustin complex people or a group with a similar Late Archaic adaptation. The artifacts from the site consist of four narrow-bladed, expanding-stemmed projectile points and other point fragments and utilized flakes of local cherts and quartzite. The faunal assemblage is also small. Although 116 bones were recovered, the only species to be positively identified was drumfish. Bones of a "muskrat sized animal" are also present. Plant remains consist of a single raspberry or blackberry (*Rubus* sp.) seed.

The Feeheley site (Taggart 1967, n.d.) was excavated by a University of Michi-

gan field crew in the summer of 1960. It too is located on the shores of Shiawassee Bay. The site was once a major burial area; this will be discussed later. It is important to the study of the Late Archaic in the area, since not only cultural material but plant (Yarnell 1964: 22–29) and animal remains (Cleland 1966: 109–16) were recovered. There may be some problem with dealing with this site as representative of a single occupation (Fitting 1965f) but I believe like Schmidt, that it represents a fairly uniform Late Archaic adaptation.

Taggart places the Feeheley site in the Feeheley phase, which has been radiocarbon dated to 1980 B.C.±150 years (M-1139). The occupation debris consists of scattered fire-cracked rock, chert spalls, projectile points, end-scrapers, side-scrapers, composite scrapers, side-notched or hafted scrapers, small core tools or wedges, hammerstones, and other rough and polished stone tools. The basic elements of the assemblage are very similar to those from the Schmidt and Hart sites, so all three sites may date to approximately the same time period.

The diagnostic artifact of this phase is a short, broad bladed, ovate, corner-notched projectile point which Taggart calls the Feeheley point. I think that this is an artifact style which, like the Dustin point, is too widespread to be used as a horizon marker. Again, I restrict its use to the sites under consideration in this chapter.

Yarnell (1964: 22–29) has identified fourteen different kinds of charcoal from the site with red oak, white oak, pine, beech, and sycamore predominating. Plant food remains include walnut, butternut, hickory nut, acorn, and a grape seed. As at the Hart site, bone remains are sparse

Fig. 27 Projectile points from the Feeheley site (University of Michigan Museum of Anthropology)

and are represented by only 891 fragments (as opposed to the Schmidt site where 5774 fragments were recovered from approximately one fourth the area excavated at Feeheley). Fish bones identified as fresh-water drum, brown bullhead, and yellow perch, make up over sixty percent of the sample. The only mammals present were muskrat and one intrusive chipmunk.

Cleland (1966: 109–16) makes an interesting comparison of the fauna of these three sites. At all three sites people were exploiting the resources of this embayment. The Schmidt site is divergent from the others in the high frequency of mammal and bird remains. It perhaps served as a base camp while the other sites were shorter occupations directed toward more specific activities. The Feeheley site, for example, was used as a burial area. It is likely that fishing and gathering were the primary summer activities, while deer hunting and fowling were carried out during the fall and winter months. The Schmidt site might represent a fall and winter occupation of a people similar to those who spent their spring and summer months at the Feeheley and Hart sites.

Taggart (1967) carries this contrast even further with his study of the cultural material. He points out that the Feeheley site would have been located in a very exposed dune area on a small island or peninsula on the western side of Shiawassee Bay. It has a western exposure and would have been uncomfortable for winter occupation. In contrast, the Schmidt site, although still in the dune area, is located on the eastern exposure of what appears to have been a protected estuary of the mouth of the Cass River as it flowed into the bay. Taggart believes the lack of reported burials at the Schmidt site may have significance in that the

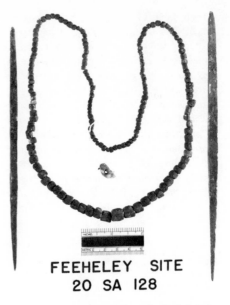

FEEHELEY SITE
20 SA 128

Fig. 28 Copper artifacts from the Feeheley site (University of Michigan Museum of Anthropology)

bodies may have been carried elsewhere for burial.

The form of midden accumulation at the two sites is also consistent with Taggart's theory. The Feeheley site midden consists of intermittent sheet and pit deposits scattered through several feet of depth. The occupational intensity, as measured by the number of fire-cracked rocks, chert spalls, and artifacts, is very low, particularly when compared with the Schmidt site midden. There are a number of pit types at the Feeheley site, including small fire pits, small basin-shaped cooking or storage pits, and large basin-shaped storage pits. The Schmidt site midden, in contrast, is about two feet thick and marked by a high density of fire-cracked rocks, chert spalls, and artifacts. Pits are rare, and those excavated were all shallow hearths. The occupation was intensive enough that midden development took place more rapidly than dune sand accumulation. Taggart suggests that these differences are attributable to an *extensive* outdoor summer occupation at Feeheley and an *intensive* winter occu-

pation centered in or near house structures at the Schmidt site.

At the Schmidt site the ratio of projectile points, bifacial tools in general, and small core wedges, · which had been interpreted as bone-splitting tools (Harrison

Fig. 29   Artifacts from the Warner School site (University of Michigan Museum of Anthropology)

1966: 63), to the total artifact assemblage is high. These are all tools associated with hunting and consistent with the interpretation derived from the faunal remains at the site. In contrast, the tools from the Feeheley site reflect fishing, gathering, and woodworking. There is a dominance of unifacial scrapers as well as concave scrapers and drills.

This interpretation of sites in terms of seasonal function is the key to our understanding of Great Lakes prehistory. These Saginaw Late Archaic occupations are the earliest occupations in the area where this technique has been applied, but I shall use it, whenever possible, throughout the rest of this volume. It also points to the dangers of basing a regional analysis on a single site. The full significance of these Late Archaic sites could only be understood when they could be compared with each other. Sites in any area are more meaningful as a part of a regional sequence.

The Butterfield site in Bay County to the north of the Saginaw Valley is another example of a Late, possibly terminal, Archaic occupation area. This site is in our eastern Michigan sub-area and located in the Pinconning River drainage. The Archaic occupation was later than that which we studied from Saginaw, and it was part of a different type of settlement system. As the Butterfield site was occupied by Archaic peoples, Early Woodland influence was coming into the Saginaw Valley just to the south.

The Butterfield site was excavated by Martin Wobst (1968) in 1965. Excavations were limited to 450 square feet but Wobst found a stratified sequence with evidence of intensive occupation. The lower of the two occupational levels was at an elevation of 588 to 590 feet above

sea level. Since the Algoma stage of Lake Huron dropped below 595 feet above sea level sometime around 1000 B.C., the occupation must date to after this time. Since there was an intensive Early Woodland occupation in the Saginaw Valley by the sixth century B.C., the Butterfield site, to escape its influence so completely, must have been occupied slightly before or during the very first part of this time. Wobst suggests 600 B.C. as the approximate time of the Archaic occupation. The upper occupation of the site is Late Woodland and will be covered in a later chapter.

The intensity of the occupation is marked by the occurrence of thirty-four features in only 450 square feet of area. Over 27,000 fragments of chipped stone were recovered along with 77,111 fragments of fire-cracked rock weighing over 1200 pounds from both occupations. The terminal Archaic debitage contrasts with the Late Woodland materials from the site in that more small flint nodules and blanks were used than in later times when there was a greater reliance on large cores.

Out of the 236 cores and tools on the site only sixty-four tools and five cores can be attributed to the Archaic occupation. The Archaic cores are primarily plano-convex. Side-scrapers, end-scrapers, blades, knives, drills, and projectile points are included in the assemblage. The projectile points include large side-notched and small corner-notched forms, as well as several narrow-bladed expanding-stemmed points that might be classified as Dustin points. The notched forms are also similar to some of the Schmidt site points and to those from the Feeheley and Andrews sites (Papworth 1967). There is a high frequency of blanks, which reinforces the idea that blanks, or preforms, rather than cores were used for knapping by the Archaic peoples at this site.

On the basis of the chippage and tool assemblage Wobst concludes that the site was continuously occupied by a people with a hunting and gathering economy, that is, it served as a base camp like the Schmidt site. He believes that game animals were not killed directly on the site but were skinned before they reached the site. In part, this is based on the relative scarcity of scraping and skinning tools within the Archaic component. The ratio of projectile points to tools, on the other hand, demonstrates the importance of hunting.

While 2354 bone fragments were found at the site, most were too small for positive identification. Three deer were found, only one of which was from the Late Archaic occupation. Mammal bone predominates in the rest of the sample with a very small amount of fish bone present. No bird or turtle remains were uncovered. This sample, while sparse, is consistent with the chipped stone assemblage. The only food plant remains were found in the plow zone but nineteen different kinds of trees are represented in the charcoal from the features. Spruce and pine are most common with lesser amounts of oak and other hardwoods.

This site represents a different type of Archaic adaptation than that in the Saginaw Valley. The geographical distance between the two areas is slight, but the environmental difference is great. Saginaw marks a northern extension of the Carolinian biotic province while the Butterfield site was in the mixed forest transitional area of the Canadian biotic province. If the charcoal does not represent an artificial selection of woods for fires, it indicates that the surrounding area leaned heavily

toward spruce and pine cover. At Butterfield, which I interpret as the seasonal equivalent of the Schmidt site, opportunities for fishing and fowling were rarer than in the Saginaw Valley. It was a rougher life based on hunting with a probably lower population density for the entire region.

This difference in site density between the northern and southern biotic provinces of the lower peninsula is reflected in mortuary practices too with the greatest concentrations of "Red Ocher" burials in the Carolinian biotic province.

Another settlement system found in the northern Lake Michigan area may also be Late Archaic, although this is based on a type of evidence—the lack of ceramics—that should be used with great caution. It is suggested by two sites with similar artifact styles and types of chippage but with different types of site location and artifact frequencies.

The first of these sites is the Bergquist site near Rapid River in Delta County. This site was visited long ago by Brown and Hulbert (1930) and also by Detroit collectors who left accounts of their visits in *The Totem Pole,* the journal of the Aboriginal Research Club of Detroit. Other than to note that these reports do not emphasize ceramics, I shall ignore earlier accounts and concentrate on an analysis of collections at the University of Michigan (Fitting 1968a).

The counterpart site is located in Sack Bay on the Garden Peninsula, also in Delta County. This site was surface collected in 1965 by a University of Michigan crew that recovered 388 chips and eight artifacts. No ceramics were found at this site. The Bergquist sample is slightly larger and consists of 909 chips and 39 artifacts. The Bergquist sample was collected in a shorter period of time than the Sack Bay sample and from a site which had repeatedly been collected before, so Bergquist represents a considerably larger site than Sack Bay. The sites have similar frequencies of flake types. At the Bergquist site, however, unifacial tools outnumber bifacial tools by a ratio of three to one, while at Sack Bay bifaces outnumbered unifaces by the same ratio. As I suggested before, in the Great Lakes, bifacial tools are characteristic of hunting activities while unifaces are more characteristic of fishing and gathering activities.

The locations of the sites also favor fishing at Bergquist, located on the river slightly back from the mouth, and hunting at Sack Bay where a shallow sandy bay provided a good canoe landing but poor fishing, while the hardwood forests of the southern Garden Peninsula would have been an excellent area for game. After looking at these and other sites in the northern Lake Michigan area (Fitting 1968a), I concluded that Bergquist was a base camp and Sack Bay a small hunting camp, each a part of the same settlement system.

Another site in Michigan that has been called Late Archaic but is subject to other interpretations as well is the Eastport site (Binford and Papworth 1963). Although it *may* be an Archaic quarry site, even Binford and Papworth suggest several occupations. I find several of their interpretations disturbing. One author, Binford, places a great deal of weight on the occurrence of block cores, which he considers diagnostic of Late Archaic sites (Binford and Quimby 1963: 305). These have since been found in Middle and, particularly, Late Woodland sites. I also doubt that the core illustrated by Binford and Papworth in Figure 2-A came from

the Eastport site; it has not been duplicated in any of the material I have seen from the site. The core illustrated in Figure 7-K is more typical. Also, Binford and Papworth feel that the associated artifacts are all Archaic types. Since they prepared their report, however, each artifact has been found in Woodland context. Even the "Pomranky Points" of Eastport chert are common on Late Woodland sites in the Straits of Mackinac sub-area.

When we deal with the Canadian biotic province, particularly in the edge area where it meets and blends with the Carolinian biotic province, we must consider potential types of settlement. In the historic period, the characteristic settlement pattern of this area was that of the Ottawa where males spent both summer and winter months on hunting trips away from the agricultural village, in the former season along the lakeshore and in the later season in the interior river valleys. The Hamlin Lake site (Fitting 1967) represents the type of site we would expect from such a male summer camp. The Eastport site has a very high ratio of bifaces to unifaces, almost five to one in the excavated areas and twelve to one for the total collection, indicating a male hunting camp. It also indicates participation in a settlement system typical of the Late Woodland period with the existence of an agricultural village somewhere in the area as a base camp.

The Eastport site does not fit in with the settlement pattern suggested by the Bergquist and Sack Bay sites. Here the dense and extensive cultural materials were at a fishing site, and the hunting site, which is what the Eastport artifact ratio suggests, contained only sparse cultural material. (This is in contrast to the apparently dense concentrations at Eastport.) I hope the work presently being carried out by Michigan State University on prehistoric settlement patterns in this part of Michigan will be able to place the Eastport site in a clearer perspective.

I also question the identification of an Archaic component on Summer Island in Delta County (Binford and Quimby 1963: 304–5). This was done on the basis of block cores that have since been found in other time horizons. Large-scale excavations on this site in 1967 demonstrated that there are several occupations on the Island but that the earliest is Middle Woodland.

Many of the surface collections mentioned earlier, those from the Welti, Stone School, and Warner School sites, contain many Late Archaic elements. These sites, however, contribute little additional material for our understanding of Late Archaic other than to fill in the distribution of this material throughout the lower part of the lower peninsula.

BURIAL CULTS AND "CULTURES"

The Late Archaic in the northeast is best known for its burial practices. Several "cultures" have been identified on the basis of burial modes alone, although such mortuary modes are a very small part of a total cultural adaptation. Such burial modes furnish little in the way of information about the economic lives of Late Archaic peoples, although they are an interesting study in themselves. They reflect patterns of trade and cultural contacts and a similarity of religious and ceremonial acitivity over a large area.

Ritchie (1955) noted a widespread burial cult on a Late Archaic to Early Woodland level. His Meadowwood Culture (1965: 198–99) represents such a

group near its eastern extreme. The Red Ocher burial groups of the western Great Lakes and upper Mississippi Valley (Ritzenthaler and Quimby 1962) represent the western extreme. In between are various related burial modes and practices. Many words have been spent on the relationship of Red Ocher to Glacial Kame. I believe that their differences are slight and that they are a part of the same type of cultural activity.

The same is true of the "old copper culture" (Ritzenthaler 1957, Quimby and Spaulding 1957). I cannot believe that the use of a locally available raw material, known again primarily from burial contexts, is evidence for a separate cultural unit. I will discuss the use of copper by peoples of the upper Great Lakes in more detail, but not as a separate "culture."

The Red Ocher burial complex is described by Ritzenthaler and Quimby (1962) who isolate it from other burial complexes on the basis of seven nuclear and eleven peripheral traits. Their nuclear traits include (1) the use of red ocher (hematite) to cover the grave, (2) burials in a flexed position in pits in sand (although cremations and bundle burials have also been reported), (3) the presence of large white flint ceremonial blades, ellipsoidal in shape which taper toward a truncated base, (4) turkey-tail blades of blue-gray Indiana hornstone, (5) small, unnotched ovate-triangular cache blades which may occur in large numbers, (6) the presence of worked copper beads, celts, awls, or points, and (7) tubular marine shell beads. Of these nuclear traits the large ceremonial blades, the cache blades, and the turkey-tails are considered to be diagnostic traits for Red Ocher.

Their peripheral traits are ones sometimes found in association with the nuclear traits. Some of these associations are more frequent than others. They include (1) interment in mounds, (2) use of cremation or bundle reburial as a method of interment, (3) the presence of unworked galena cubes, (4) circular or ovate shell gorgets, (5) birdstones, (6) bar amulets, (7) three-hole rectangular gorgets, (8) tube pipes, (9) grooved axes, (10) celts, and (11) Early Woodland pottery.

Ritzenthaler and Quimby include forty-four sites, five in Michigan, as a part of this complex. Since their publication appeared, several additional Michigan sites have been reported. Their summary report also stimulated additional work in Indiana (Faulkner 1960, 1964) and Illinois (Morse and Morse 1964), but these reports tend to substantiate the criteria used by Ritzenthaler and Quimby.

The Glacial Kame culture was defined by Wilbur Cunningham (1948) on the basis of burials in Michigan, Ohio, and Indiana but additional Glacial Kame material is known from Ontario and Vermont (Ritchie 1965: 131). The Burch site in Branch County, Michigan, furnished the type site for this complex. Five burials were uncovered at this site with grave goods consisting of copper artifacts and shell gorgets of a number of types. The shell gorget form which is now accepted as the diagnostic artifact of Glacial Kame is the sandal sole gorget of Gulf Coast marine shell. This appears to be the only item that would separate Glacial Kame from Red Ocher (Ritzenthaler and Quimby 1962: 255-56).

While there is some areal overlap, Glacial Kame burials seem to have a more southerly distribution than the main Red Ocher concentration (see Fogel 1963: Figure 2). Cunningham should be commended for his recognition of Glacial Kame as an early burial complex contemporary with Red Ocher. He maintained this position in spite of strong opposition from professional archaeologists (Griffin 1948) and was proven correct.

The Feeheley site, in spite of the lack of the diagnostic sandal sole gorgets, has been classed as a possible Glacial Kame burial site (Taggart n.d., Ritchie 1965: 199), which would place this complex at the beginning of the second millennium B.C. It might then be the mortuary complex for such groups as the peoples who lived at the Feeheley, Hart, and Schmidt sites.

Well over 1000 square feet were excavated in the burial area of the Feeheley site and fifteen individuals, four adults and the rest children and adolescents, were recovered. The bodies had been placed in tightly flexed positions, wrapped in bark or skin bags and put into shallow pits. Grave goods included both copper and shell beads, copper awls, celts, and a gouge. The conditions for shell preservation were very poor at the site, the reason suggested by Taggart for the absence of sandal sole gorgets, but a few fragments of worked shell were found in the burial area. Red ocher was also found with these burials. While not found in large groups, cache blades were located in the burial area along with the short, broad-bladed points that Taggart has called Feeheley points.

A single Late Archaic burial in Michigan was recovered from the Tomasco site in Washtenaw County (Cleland 1963). Here a young male was found with what Cleland interprets as a tool kit including stoneworking, woodworking, and hunting implements. The utilitarian nature of the grave goods suggests that the date for this site is earlier than the 1000 B.C. date

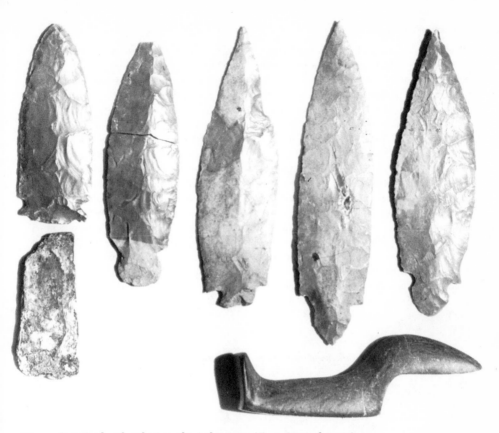

Fig. 30   Part of a burial cache from the Andrews site (From Papworth: 1967)

Fig. 31   Birdstone from the Andrews site (From Papworth: 1967)

mentioned by Cleland. Sites of this later date, as we shall see at Andrews and others, contain large quantities of ceremonial goods rather than utilitarian items.

The Andrews site in the Saginaw Valley is primarily a burial station. The main burial complex has been dated to 1220 B.C.±150 years (M-659) although there is at least one earlier burial dated to 3350 B.C.±150 years (M-941). A familiar site to archaeologists, Harlan I. Smith included it in a list of Saginaw Valley sites in the 1890s as did Fred Dustin in the 1920s. It was long a favorite ground for local collectors and Mark Papworth, who prepared the report on the site (Papworth 1967: 29–106), included an analysis of some of these earlier collections as well as the materials recovered by the

University of Michigan excavations at the site in 1957.

Burials at the Andrews site consist primarily of cremations with red ocher although at least two fragmentary uncremated burials were also recovered. Grave goods from the University of Michigan excavations include copper beads, abraders, some corner-notched points similar to those from the Feeheley site, and a number of birdstones—those delightfully carved little objects that delight relic collectors and make students of prehistory scratch their heads trying to figure out what they were used for. Other excavations produced large copper objects including celts and unilaterally barbed harpoons. Turkey-tails and at least one large group of cache blades were recovered. Surface collections

Fig. 32 Group of Late Archaic burial cache blades (University of Michigan Museum of Anthropology)

INCHES

Fig. 33 Turkey-tails from Michigan (University of Michigan Museum of Anthropology)

contained ceramics but none seem to have been found in the University excavations. Those in other collections include Early Woodland interior-exterior cord-marked pottery as well as Middle and Late Woodland pottery types.

In 1960 the University of Michigan conducted extensive excavations at the Stroebel site (Papworth 1967: 111–31). Although about 1600 square feet were excavated, relatively little cultural material was recovered. There were several cremation burials with red ocher. One of these contained sixty cache blades and several projectile points.

Two other burial sites in the Saginaw

Valley have been described in some detail. The Pomranky site (Binford 1963b) is located in Midland County and the burial group described was excavated in one day in May of 1966 by Mark Papworth and Malcomb Webb. A number of distinct cremation burials and several uncremated bone fragments were found in a single pit with several concentrations of red ocher. A group of 516 cache blades and fourteen turkey-tails were found with them.

The Hodges site (Binford 1963a) was excavated by James Hunt and Douglas Peacock of Saginaw who turned their collections over to the University of Mich-

85

igan for study. They uncovered the base of a burial pit, partially destroyed by a bulldozer, that contained cremations, red ocher, adze and gorget fragments, and notched and unnotched cache blades. Further excavations were conducted at this site in 1960 under the direction of William B. Roosa and in 1961 under the direction of Richard O. Keslin. This later work revealed a Late Woodland occupation but only one possible Late Archaic cremation which contained no grave goods and had been widely scattered by rodents.

Leaving the Saginaw Valley, we next turn to a series of Late Archaic burials from southwestern Michigan. The Kimmel site (Papworth 1958) was discovered in the back dirt of a construction operation, and both human bone and cultural material were recovered by screening this back dirt. The grave goods with the burials consist of a copper gorget, a copper cres-

cent, copper beads, fragments of turkey-tails and around 450 cache blades.

The Ueck cache (Ueck 1963) and the St. Joseph River Bluff cache (Green 1964) may both be part of the same cache. Green found that the artifacts in this cache were slightly larger than those from the Kimmel site. He also located and secured permission for a study of the Conrad cache (Green and Fitting 1964), a cache of 36 turkey-tails from Berrien County.

There are many other such caches from the lower part of the lower peninsula. Dustin reported several from the Saginaw Valley. Taggart (n.d.) collected information on one such cache of 116 from near Dimondale in Eaton County. Binford (1963c) presented metric data on another cache of sixty-three from the Huron Beach site north of Alpena, apparently the same cache which Ritzenthaler and Quimby

Fig. 34 Turkey-tails from the Pomranky site (University of Michigan Museum of Anthropology)

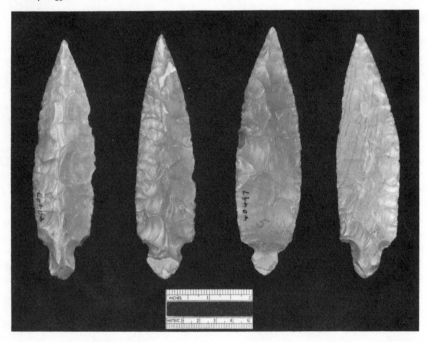

(1962: 265) referred to as the Haltiner cache. I think the most perplexing part of this cache is its northerly position, for all other such Late Archaic burial caches in the state have so far been reported to the south in areas in the Carolinian biotic province.

LATE ARCHAIC USE OF COPPER

Much of what has been written on copper utilization among prehistoric Indians of the Great Lakes is based on information from the state of Wisconsin. Many of the key papers from this area were collected in the single issue, Volume 38, Number 4, of *The Wisconsin Archeologist*. This collection, edited by Robert Ritzenthaler, contains reports on the Osceola, Oconto, and Reigh sites as well as a study of copper typology by Warren Wittry and a summary paper by Wittry and Ritzenthaler.

W. C. McKern first suggested that copper implements represent a separate cultural group in 1942 but the first site of this complex, the Osceola site, was not

Fig. 35 Aboriginal copper artifacts from Michigan (From Griffin: 1961a)

INCHES   2
CM 2 3 4 5

described until 1946. This was a burial site containing bundle burials with articles of copper and stone found throughout the burial area. Copper implements included awls, socketed spuds, socketed projectile points, and some ornamental pieces.

The Oconto site, originally reported in 1952, was primarily a burial site but the investigators did find some village debris and a possible oval house structure. Both primary and secondary burials were found and flint projectile points and copper awls were among the grave goods. Two radio-carbon dates, obtained by the solid carbon method, were 2700 B.C. and 5500 B.C. Both appear to be too old and beyond the

Fig. 36 Approximate range of Archaic copper complexes in North America (From Fogel: 1963)

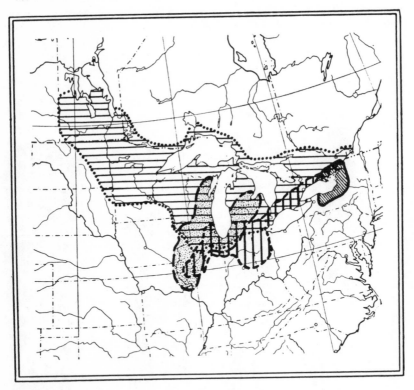

 Area of "Old Copper" (after Griffin, ed., 1961)

 Area of Glacial Kame (after Cunningham, 1948)

 Area of Red Ocher (after Ritzenthaler and Quimby, 1962)

Area of Brewerton and Point Peninsula I (after Ritchie, 1944)

usual range of radiocarbon dates for Great Lakes copper use in the Late Archaic (Mason and Mason 1961, Halsey 1966b). As an example, the dates for the Osceola and Reigh sites are respectively 1500 B.C. (M-643) and 1710 B.C. (M-644).

A similar burial complex was reported from the Reigh site in a series of papers in the early 1950s. The Reigh site did yield one sandal-sole gorget indicating a contemporaneity with Glacial Kame, if not an actual Glacial Kame burial.

In Michigan, elements of a Late Archaic copper complex have been reported from the Riverside Cemetery (Papworth 1967: 154–233) and from collections obtained in the Lake Superior area (Quimby and Spaulding 1957, Quimby and Griffin 1961). A great deal of work has been done on Isle Royale. Some of the earlier reports were prepared by such stalwarts of Michigan archaeology as George Fox (1911) and Fred Dustin (1932b, 1957). More recent work has been carried out by Griffin (1961), Roy Drier (1961), and Tyler Bastian (1963a, 1963b).

Bastian, who did the most thorough work in the area, concluded that copper working was quite incidental to the food quest and that groups did not deliberately seek out the island to extract copper. He, along with Quimby (1963b) and Griffin (1966), rightly pointed to extensive post-Archaic use of Lake Superior copper.

Another interesting paper, recently published by a geographer (Fogel 1963), goes a long way toward placing the Late Archaic use of copper in its proper perspective. While his models of dispersal and utilization may be somewhat altered by recent discoveries along the Ottawa River (Kennedy 1966) his general approach is excellent. He views the use of copper as a small part of the total Late Archaic way of life and believes that the avenues of its dispersal were also traveled by other materials, ideas, and concepts.

His map of Late Archaic complexes is interesting (Fogel 1963: 144) and I interpret it as indicating that Red Ocher and Glacial Kame burial complexes are limited to areas of broadleaf forests while the "copper complex" burials lacking specific Red Ocher and Glacial Kame traits are found within the Lake Forest formation. On the basis of this division I support Papworth's (1967: 234–53) suggestion of a Lake Forest Archaic but dispute the inclusion of the Andrews and Stroebel sites in this complex since they are found in the Carolinian biotic province.

I further suggest that the greater complexity of the southern Glacial Kame and Red Ocher burials has an economic basis. I see the southern area as supporting a greater population, allowing more population units to interact. With more groups there were more chances for intergroup contact and competition. Binford's (1963c) suggestion that cache blade variation in single grave lots represents the participation of several groups in the mortuary activities supports this interpretation.

Within the Lake Forest formation, where population density was probably lower, a single kin group could have prepared the burials, limiting grave goods to personal belongings. The inclusion of more copper could be a geographical rather than traditionally determined cultural feature since copper could be obtained more readily in these areas. On the other hand, the inclusion of copper in Red Ocher and Glacial Kame burials might indicate contacts over long distances, for copper was certainly more difficult to come by in the southern regions. The inclusion of such a valuable commodity in grave offerings is consistent with the generally greater burial, and possibly social, elaboration in this area.

EARLY WOODLAND

The Early Woodland cultural stage is marked by the initial appearance of pottery in the eastern parts of North America. I use the term stage rather than time horizon because pottery appears before 2000 B.C. in areas in the southeastern United States, while there are places in the northern parts of eastern North America where ceramics were not manufactured even at the time of European contact. Ceramics are a relatively small item in a cultural inventory and, by themselves, probably made little difference in the way of the peoples who made them. It is likely that many non-ceramic burials, which we have called Late Archaic, were made by people who lived in Early Woodland villages. Ritchie (1955, 1965: 178–99) includes even the non-ceramic elements of the northeastern burial cult in the Early Woodland stage, while other archaeologists talk of Archaic sites with pottery.

A new element in the subsistence pattern may also be introduced at this time. Several researchers have called attention to the occurrence of cultigens in Early Woodland sites (Black 1963, Yarnell 1964, 1965, Watson and Yarnell 1966). These include squash, gourd, sunflower, marsh elder, and *chenopodium*. In Michigan, one sixth century B.C. site, which is non-ceramic rather than pre-ceramic, has produced squash remains (Wright 1964). Although it is possible that the introduction of cultigens, as well as the initial appearance of ceramics, might be used to mark the Early Woodland period I do not believe that this is warranted. If we recall Cleland's observations about the diffuse nature of the Late Archaic economies, we can see that these cultigens were but another element in a broad spectrum of resources utilized by Early Woodland peoples. They were an addition to, not a substitute for, the existing Archaic economy. In Mesoamerica (MacNeish 1964) there was a long period of time between the introduction of cultigens and any alteration in the economic cycle and social organization. Although they may have made the existing economy more reliable and, therefore, more viable, this entailed only a small increase in efficiency rather than a major change in adaptive pattern.

Even the Middle Woodland cultural florescence in Michigan may have occurred without a true agricultural base. Groups with such an agricultural base did not exist until Late Woodland times. Perhaps this increase in efficiency was cumulative. Increases in the percentage of cultigens in the diet might have been gradual with no change in the pattern of exploiting these resources. When a point was reached where cultigens were a key resource, rather than just one of many, there may have been changes in the social pattern directed toward more efficiently exploiting this resource. This might be one reason why the Middle and Late Woodland settlement patterns are so drastically different from those of the Late Archaic. During the Early Woodland stage these new cultigens had little effect on a seasonal exploitative pattern that was essentially the same as that of the Late Archaic.

Let us now review the climatic milieu in which Late Archaic and Early Woodland cultural developments took place.

Griffin (1960) suggests that the period of 2300 to 1800 B.C. was warm, that of 1800 to 1300 B.C. cool, that of 1300 to 800 B.C. warm again with 800 to 300 B.C. cool. Note that two of our Saginaw Valley Late Archaic complexes, represented by the Feeheley site and the Andrews site, fall within two warm intervals. The 1800 to 1300 B.C. cool episode was noted by both Yarnell and Cleland and is marked by a resurgence of pine in some areas. While Cleland (1966: 27) thinks that the squash seeds from the Schultz site are evidence against a cool period for the development of Michigan Early Woodland, he points to two cool climate animal species, the martin and fisher, among the faunal remains from the same cultural level. It is possible that an increased reliance on cultigens was, in part, a response to a slightly cooler climate and less reliance on wild plants.

The Early Woodland is marked by the appearance of a thick, usually exterior and interior cord-marked pottery, which has been given a variety of names in different areas including Vinette I, Marion Thick, and Schultz Thick. It has been reported from a number of surface locations in Michigan (Flanders 1963), including Moccasin Bluff in Berrien County, the Spoonville Village site in Ottawa County, and a site near the Norton Mounds in Kent County. It was found in the fill of the Fort Wayne Mound (Halsey 1968) and has been found in the Saginaw Valley at the Schultz, Andrews, Mahoney, Bussinger, and Kantzler sites. The list of Michigan sites with such pottery is far from exhausted by these few examples.

Two sites in surrounding states furnish us with a reference for viewing the Early Woodland occupation of the Saginaw Valley where the best studied series of Early Woodland sites in the state are located. These are the Sheets site in Illinois (Munson 1966) and the Leimbach site in Ohio (Shane 1967). The Sheets site produced Marion Thick pottery, straight-stemmed projectile points, a few expanding-stemmed and side-notched points, ovate bifaces, and some end-scrapers. Munson and Hall (1966) have published a radiocarbon date of 560 B.C.±100 years (I-1652) for an oval pit containing Marion Thick pottery from the nearby Larson site, which Munson would accept as contemporary with the Sheets site.

At the Leimbach site (Shane 1967) a number of thick exterior-interior cord-marked and exterior cord-marked sherds were recovered. This site has been radiocarbon dated to 520 B.C.±310 years (OWU-185), which puts it at the same time level as Sheets and Larson in Illinois and the Schultz sites in the Saginaw Valley. Shane feels that because of the variety of surface treatment (interior-exterior cord-marked, exterior cord-marked and plain) the date is too early. I accept it since the same set of attributes occur at the Schultz site in Michigan. Lithic material is sparse but there is one straight-stemmed point (which looks like it was reworked) that is within the range of variation found among the stemmed points from the Sheets and Schultz sites.

An excellent example of this Early Woodland cultural adaptation comes from the Saginaw Valley, where we have not only a very large sample of cultural, faunal, and floral material, but several sites as well which give a picture of the seasonal round of these people. These include Schultz I (20 SA 2), which I shall refer to as the Schultz site, Schultz II

Fig. 37 Thick interior-exterior cord-marked rimsherds from the Early Woodland level at the Schultz site (University of Michigan Museum of Anthropology)

(20 SA 1), which I shall refer to by the site number; both are located inside the city limits of Saginaw and about one half mile from each other. A third key site is the Kantzler site located approximately twenty miles down the Saginaw River inside the city limits of Bay City.

Excavations were carried out at Schultz in 1960 under the direction of Mark Papworth, 1962 and 1963, under the direction of Richard O. Keslin and in 1964 and 1965 under my direction. Approximately 4000 square feet of Early Woodland living floor within a two-acre area were uncovered below the Middle and Late Woodland occupations represented in· the upper levels of the site. Surface indications suggest that the site was even more extensive.

During the Early Woodland period it was occupied by groups of nuclear families. Cultural material and fire-cracked rock cluster around groups of two to three oval pits and some of these clusters are marked by a single central postmold suggesting some type of structure.

As the Shiawassee Bay drained with the drop from the Nipissing through Algoma stages to near modern lake level, groups of people who had occupied its shores moved toward the center of the valley, following its diminishing shoreline. By the sixth century B.C., Early Woodland peoples were living in a high area in the swampy region along the Tittabawassee River in the center of the valley. Radiocarbon dates of 540 B.C. (M-1524) and 530 B.C. (M-1425) have been obtained for this occupation.

The ceramics from the site include thick

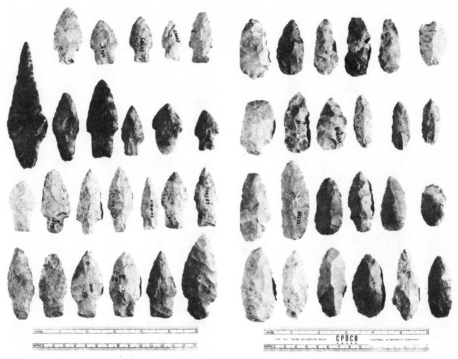

Fig. 38 Stemmed projectile points from the Early Woodland level at the Schultz site (University of Michigan Museum of Anthropology)

Fig. 39 Plano-convex ovate bifaces from the Early Woodland level at the Schultz site (University of Michigan Museum of Anthropology)

and thin, exterior-interior and exterior cord-marked and plane vessels that have been classified as Schultz Ware by Fred Fischer. Approximately 241 in situ sherds were recovered to adequately demonstrate the variability of an Early Woodland ceramic complex.

A sample of 186 chipped stone cores and artifacts were obtained from unquestionable Early Woodland levels. The points are primarily large straight-stemmed forms, many of which are reworked as drills. Plano-convex ovate bifaces are also characteristic of this occupation. Some small expanding stemmed points occur; drills are more frequent in this occupation

than in any later occupation at the site. The most common core type is a plano-convex form, which becomes less frequent in later occupations. Both block and bipolar cores are also found in this level. There are a number of unifacial tool types including sloping tip end-scrapers, retouched flakes, and a series of large Bayport chert blades.

Peter Murray, who analyzed the bone tools, found only eight such implements in the Early Woodland levels: a conical bone point, two splinter awls, a tine flaker, a percussion flaker, a beamer, and two ground teeth.

Cleland (1966: 117–44) identified eight

93

species of mammal, six of fish, and one of bird for a total of 148 individuals in the Early Woodland levels. He interprets the remains as representing that of a people primarily concerned with generalized hunting activities. Small mammals, as well as deer and elk, were hunted. Fishing, at Schultz, was relatively unimportant. Cleland thinks the small quantities of fish and the absence of reptiles indicates a winter occupation of the site.

April Allison identified walnut, butternut, and hickory nut as food species among the charcoal from the features. In contrast to later levels, charred nut shells make up almost ninety percent of the charcoal from these features. These are all fall nuts and, coupled with Cleland's observations, might have been stored for winter use.

Twenty SA 1 is located about one half mile to the east of Schultz at the junction of the Tittabawassee and Shiawassee rivers. The Early Woodland occupation is at a lower elevation which Speth (n.d.) feels would have been flooded during parts of the year. This site, as Wright (1964) describes it, was accidentally discovered seven feet below the surface in 1962. There were only limited excavations and five artifacts were recovered. One of these was a side-notched point similar to those from some of the Archaic burial sites in the area and from the surface, or levels of questionable cultural homogeneity, at the Schultz site. This led Wright to an Archaic placement of the site, but a radiocarbon date of 530 B.C. ±120 years (M-1432) indicates that it was contemporary with the Schultz site Early Woodland occupation.

In contrast to the Schultz Early Woodland occupation, faunal remains consist of bird, fish, turtle, muskrat, and beaver.

Plant remains consist of one acorn kernel, a beech or hazel nut, a grape seed, three seeds of either cherry or huckleberry, and two squash seeds. The overall interpretation is of a summer to fall occupation of short duration when food collecting was of primary importance.

The Kantzler site was excavated by a University of Michigan field crew in 1966 and additional material was recovered in 1967 in a joint project carried out by the University of Michigan and the Saginaw Valley Chapter of the Michigan Archaeological Society. As of this writing, the material has not been catalogued, let alone analyzed, but we can make some observations based on Carole Crumley's analysis of the first summer's work (1967) and on my own field observations.

The site is mixed with Early, Middle, and some Late Woodland cultural material at all levels. Diagnostic Early Woodland artifacts include the straight-stemmed points and plano-convex ovate bifaces similar to those from the Early Woodland levels at Schultz. No Schultz Ware was found in 1966 but a number of vessels were recovered, including one extensive ceramic feature, during the 1967 excavations.

In contrast to Schultz and 20 SA 1, over eighty percent of the animal bone in those features that Crumley thinks are Early Woodland is fish bone. Only about fifteen percent is mammal and, in contrast to Schultz, two percent of the 651 fragments is turtle. The fish are primarily channel cat and sturgeon. This, taken with the complete absence of nuts, would seem to indicate a spring or summer fishing camp.

The Early Woodland economic cycle is like that of the Late Archaic. Schultz represents a fairly large camp occupied by a number of families during the late fall and winter months when hunting of all available animals and stored nuts furnished the subsistence for the people. Because of the size and central location of the Schultz Early Woodland occupation, it might have been the base camp for most of the occupants of the valley.

In the spring, family units separated to fish and hunt. The Kantzler site is an example of this type of occupation. I suggest that the Early Woodland components at the Andrews and Mahoney sites represent a similar type of occupation. Food plants were collected during the summer and fall as people returned to the main camp area. Twenty SA 1 represents such an intermediate occupation. *If* burial sites such as Hodges and Andrews were cemetery areas for the Early Woodland peoples from Schultz, as Wright (1964) and Taggart (n.d.) suggest, it could be that cache blades were manufactured as a summer to fall activity.

The only other area with a concentration of excavated Early Woodland materials is in the Muskegon Valley near Croton Dam. A group of burial mounds was excavated here by University of Michigan field crews under the direction of Earl J. Prahl (1966) with the assistance of the Newaygo County Chapter of the Michigan Archaeological Society (Frantz 1967). The Croton Dam Mound A was excavated in 1965 and, while it contained no burials, a cache of heat-altered bifacial implements was found. This cache contained stemmed points and bifaces almost identical to those from the Early Woodland level at the Schultz site. A second mound in the group, Car-

rigan A, was excavated in the same season. It contained a burial with projectile points similar to those from the early Late Woodland Gibraltar and Bussinger sites and thin cord-marked sherds were found in the mound fill. Several artifacts that appeared to be Early Woodland forms were found in the mound fill. Charcoal with the burial in this mound was radiocarbon dated to A.D. 680±120 years (M-1759).

During the summer of 1966 Prahl directed further excavation in this group. Carrigan Mound B contained a burial pit with cremated human, deer, and turtle bone. This burial was dated to 590 B.C.±150 years (M-1849). Croton Dam Mounds B and C were also cremations of human and animal bone. Grave goods consisted of a rolled copper bead in the fill of Croton Dam C and the base of a stemmed projectile point, similar to those from the Early Woodland level at the Schultz site, in Croton Dam B. While neither of these cremations were dated, a second date on the primary mound construction, rather than the burial, at Carrigan A was 540 B.C.±150 years (M-1984).

All of these mounds appear to have been Early Woodland mounds that lacked the characteristic exterior-interior cord-marked ceramics of the period but contained chipped stone tools consistent with Early Woodland occupations elsewhere. Carrigan A was used, and probably rebuilt, during the Late Woodland period and it was the Late Woodland date on the burial from this mound which led Prahl (1966: 197) to suggest that the entire group was Late Woodland.

CHAPTER V

BURIALS AND FISHERMEN

MIDDLE WOODLAND
CULTURAL DEVELOPMENT

Time moves on and from generation to generation the lives and life ways of people change. While such change is inevitable, each new development must be based on past cultural achievements.

We have already discussed the problem of the Early Woodland and how ceramics have been used to define this unit, but the settlement and land use patterns are the same as in the preceding Late Archaic period. Early Woodland sites are marked by interior-exterior cord-marked ceramics in Michigan, which makes them easy for archaeologists to recognize. The identification of Middle Woodland sites is not such an easy matter and there is very little information available on the transition from Early to Middle Woodland in the state.

Even the definition of what is "Middle Woodland" is a problem. Griffin uses it synonymously with Hopewell (1964). To Griffin (1967: 9), "the term 'Middle Woodland' refers to the period when most of eastern North America was dominated by the Hopewellian culture, between 200 B.C. and A.D. 400." Evidence of this Hopewellian culture and contemporary cultural expressions is present, but the developmental sequence found in other areas of the eastern United States has, so far, not been identified in Michigan.

Perhaps the most spectacular of the Hopewellian antecedents in the eastern United States is the Adena Culture of the Ohio Valley. Recent studies of this cultural manifestation (Dragoo 1963, 1964) suggest that it is a development out of local Archaic burial cults. It is marked by mound burials and elaborate grave offerings that foreshadow later Hopewell developments in parts of the same area. The Adena cultural expression existed during the first millennium B.C. and was replaced in some areas by Hopewell. Adena traits with some Hopewell influence exist in a number of outlying areas on the same time horizon as Hopewell. This has been interpreted as a displacement of Adena groups by Hopewell peoples (Ritchie and Dragoo 1960).

Individual Adena traits have been found in several areas of Michigan but there is no site that I would consider Adena. Several sites with a strong Adena cast have been reported in Ontario. The most notable of these is the Killarney Bay #1 site in the Manitoulin district of Ontario (Greenman 1966). Many Adena traits were found there in association with each other, and the site has been radiocarbon dated to 230 B.C. ±150 years (M-194), 90 B.C. ±200 years (M-428), and A.D. 20±130 years (M-1482).

While Adena was spectacular, it was soon replaced over large areas by the Hopewell cultural expression which is used to mark the Middle Woodland period. However, transferring the burden of definition to Hopewell does not help us much. There is general agreement that certain similar stylistic elements, particularly in ceramics, and certain elaborate burial practices, are found in a large part of the eastern United States between 200 B.C. and A.D. 500. To some the definition of Hopewell stops there; others would expand it to include a religious cult, a massive exchange network, a new type of economic adaptation, or even an "interaction sphere."

Each of these associated concepts has some validity in certain areas and at certain times. As Struever (1965) indicates, Middle Woodland cultural developments must be studied in terms of local units before we can speak of the meaning of broader units with any accuracy. He holds that defining ceramic style zones is the beginning of the study of the meaning of Hopewell. I feel that studies of relatively closed environmental situations can be used to derive the same units. After this we can deal with local interpretations of burial cult practices, trade patterns, and local economies. It is only then that local adaptive patterns can be seen. Where this has been done the contrast between areas grouped under the very general rubric Hopewell becomes very apparent. The pattern seen in Ohio Hopewell (Prufer 1964a, 1964b, 1965) is drastically different from that in Illinois (Struever 1964, 1965, Brown 1964). Michigan is just as different but with more similarities to Illinois.

The Hopewell subsistence base is also a problem. Many feel that it must have had an agricultural base because of some of the very large and spectacular sites in Ohio. Prufer suggests that the Ohio ceremonial centers were surrounded by

farming hamlets such as the McGraw site. Griffin's (1967: 9) position is somewhat modified but is essentially the same: "the Hopewellian societies from Kansas City to Ohio are the first known growers of maize in the Midwest and it is assumed that this addition to the diet was partly responsible for the strong cultural growth during Hopewellian times." It should be pointed out that known Hopewell use of maize is rather late and it does not appear to be a major item in the diets of the people at those few sites where it has been found.

In Illinois, Struever (1964) has claimed that mud flats horticulture played an important part in the Hopewellian cultural adaptation. He documents this to the very late phases of the Havana Tradition, the local Hopewell expression in that area.

Specific evidence on the role of agriculture in Michigan Middle Woodland sites is slight. The only Hopewell Middle Woodland sites with clear evidence of the nature of the adaptive patterns are in the Saginaw Valley and there agriculture played no part in the local adaptation. In southwestern Michigan the animal bone refuse from both the Norton Mound and the Spoonville Village sites, in Cleland's words (1966: 66), reflects ". . . a similar cultural adaptation and subsistence economy, one which was based to a large extent upon agriculture." The Norton sample, however, was small and selective and the Spoonville assemblage may not be exclusively Middle Woodland.

The cultural expressions in Michigan most strongly influenced by, and included with, the southern Hopewell developments are all located in the Carolinian biotic province. As Quimby noted long ago (1952), their extension does not go to the north of the broadleaf forest zone (although they do not occupy the entire extent of this area). The Hopewell Middle Woodland sites follow the mud flats of the long and broad river valleys and are found in those drainages with intermediate amounts of impounded waters and near prairies. There are some exceptions, such as the Hardy Dam Mound and the Holtz site at the southern end of the Traverse Corridor, but neither of these are major sites.

To the north of the Carolinian Biotic Province in the Carolinian-Canadian transition area and in the entire Lake Forest Formation are a distinctive group of Middle Woodland sites that I call Lake Forest Middle Woodland. There is evidence that sites of this Middle Woodland tradition exist to the north of the Lake Forest formation but their occupational intensity is slight in comparison to those in the Lake Forest zone, and I would suspect that they are outlying camps for peoples who spent at least part of the year farther to the south.

If the main subsistence base for much of the Hopewell Middle Woodland adaptation was either agriculture or mud flats horticulture, then the corresponding Lake Forest Middle Woodland base was fishing. Almost all sites of the group are located in areas which would have been favorable for fishing and fish remains are plentiful at most of them. Even at sites where hunting was important, fish still played a major role in subsistence and are never entirely absent as at some Late Archaic and Late Woodland sites.

The cultural diversity of the Lake Forest Middle Woodland also matches that of the Hopewell Middle Woodland but I suspect a greater uniformity in the subsistence pattern. The best-known Lake Forest Middle Woodland expressions are the Laural culture in the west and the Middle Point Peninsula groups in the east. In recent years many similar cultural complexes have been described, including the North Bay complex (Mason 1966, 1967) and the Saugeen Focus (Wright and Anderson 1963), as well as a number of additional expressions within the Michigan area alone.

We have little evidence of the nature of the relationship between Hopewell Middle Woodland and Lake Forest Middle Woodland. In Michigan there are more Lake Forest Woodland village sites than Hopewell Middle Woodland village sites.

The logical interpretation for this would be a greater Lake Forest Middle Woodland population. This may be true for Michigan itself but we must also take the Hopewell centers farther to the south into consideration. The known Michigan Hopewell sites are impoverished Hopewell outlyers, perhaps the Middle Woodland equivalents of the trading posts and mission settlements of the historic period. Considering the great concentration of Hopewell Middle Woodland sites to the south, the total Hopewell Middle Woodland population would probably have been far larger than that of the Lake Forest Middle Woodland groups.

Evidence of trade connections between Hopewell Middle Woodland and Lake Forest Middle Woodland groups are chert, and a southern-looking Middle Woodland copper probably came from the Lake Superior region and there is evidence that goods moved back to the north. There is an obsidian core from a burial at the Riverside cemetery site in Menominee County which Griffin (1965a) believes to be Middle Woodland. His position has been supported by a number of recent radiocarbon dates between 500 B.C. and A.D. 1. There are several pieces of obsidian, some Saginaw Valley Bayport chert and a southern-looking Middle Woodland projectile point from the Naomikong Point site on Lake Superior. This obsidian, as with all known Hopewell obsidian, is from Obsidian Cliff in Wyoming (determined by Neutron Activation, G. A. Wright personal communication).

The Lake Forest Middle Woodland adaptive pattern was successful in Michigan. It is a pattern similar to that of the historic Chippewa, with large summer villages primarily dependent on fishing; and smaller winter camps, consisting of extended family units, that were primarily dependent on hunting. It represents a considerable increase in efficiency over the preceding Late Archaic pattern in this area with population concentrations in winter camps and dispersal to summer camps which were occupied by smaller groups. The Hopewell Middle Woodland in the Saginaw Valley adopted this pattern of land use at the same time as groups to the north but there is no evidence of a relative population increase; in fact, with the changing environmental situation there might have even been a population decline.

I believe that the Late Archaic pattern is of southern origin. Morse (1967) suggests winter population concentrations around rivers with population dispersal to outlying camps for hunting during the summer as the pattern for peoples of the Shell Mound Archaic in the middle south. This pattern was very effective in the Saginaw Valley around the Shiawassee Bay in Late Archaic times. Given a stable environment, the historic Chippewa pattern would only have been slightly more efficient than the Archaic pattern. However, with the drop in lake level and the draining of Shiawassee Bay, the site density of the Middle Woodland period appears to have been less, even with a more efficient adaptive pattern.

In the succeeding Late Woodland period the population density in the northern and southern areas again increased but the increase in the southern areas seems to be greater and, as in Late Archaic times, the site density in the southern parts of the state is higher than in the northern lower peninsula or upper peninsula.

The Middle Woodland cultural development took place against a fairly stable environmental background in comparison to preceding periods. There are a number of minor climatic changes that correlate with the expansion of Hopewell influence (Griffin 1960, 1961, Baerreis and Bryson 1965). Cleland (1966: 28) refers to this as the "Hopewell episode," which he suggests lasted from 300 B.C. to A.D. 300. Griffin attempts to correlate the Hopewell expansion with an expansion of the area potentially suitable for agriculture. Two things need to be taken into account when applying Griffin's model to the upper Great Lakes. First, it has not yet been demonstrated that agriculture played a major role, or any role for that matter, in the Hopewell Middle Woodland adaptation in this region. Second, as Baerreis and Bryson (1965) point out, factors other than temperature, including changes in circulation and rainfall patterns, may be the key factors in this climatic episode. In such places as the Saginaw Valley this might be a shift from fall to spring flooding which has been shown to have had a drastic effect even on the twentieth-century utilization of the area (G. A. Wright n.d.). In any event, there appear to be factors in the natural as well as the cultural environments which affected the development of the Middle Woodland cultural expressions in Michigan.

I will deal with the Hopewell Middle Woodland in western Michigan and in the Saginaw Valley separately since the types of evidence from the two areas is different and there is a suggestion of different adaptive patterns. This will be followed by a section on the problem of non-Hopewell Middle Woodland manifestations in the lower peninsula of Michigan. The final section will deal with the distinctive Middle Woodland adaptation within the Lake Forest formation.

HOPEWELL MIDDLE WOODLAND IN WESTERN MICHIGAN

Sites in western Michigan with Hopewell Middle Woodland materials have been excavated as far back as the mid-nineteenth century. Dr. W. B. Hinsdale, first curator of the Great Lakes Division of the University of Michigan Museum of Anthropology, recovered Hopewell artifacts from the Brooks Mound Group in 1928 (Hinsdale 1930). Later George Quimby restudied all of the older collections from the area (Quimby 1941a, 1941b, 1943, 1944) and included them within the Goodall Focus, a unit of the Midwestern Taxonomic System that became so popular in the 1930s.

A small amount of Hopewell material was recovered during the University of Michigan excavations at Moccasin Bluff in 1948 and Richard Flanders directed

University of Michigan excavations at the Spoonville Mounds and Village site in 1962 and at the Norton Mounds in 1963 and 1964 (Flanders 1965a, 1965b, Flanders and Cleland 1964, Halsey 1966a, Smith 1966). In 1966, while at Grand Valley State College, he did additional work at the Spoonville Village and salvaged material from one of the mounds that was being leveled by the owner (Flanders 1968).

In 1965 and 1966, Earl J. Prahl supervised University of Michigan field crews working on some Middle and Late Woodland sites in the Muskegon River Valley. A number of the mounds and the Jancarich village site were Middle Woodland (Prahl 1966, 1968). Timothy Losey (1967) excavated the Toft Lake Village site at the same time.

Quimby suggests that there was a time lag in western Michigan Hopewell running from the south to the north with sites along the St. Joseph River being early Hopewell, those along the Grand River middle Hopewell and those along the Muskegon River late Hopewell. This observation is based on the stylistic similarities of these materials to those from areas farther to the south. Some of the recent radiocarbon dates from the area, however, fail to support this hypothesis.

Quimby includes four components of the Goodall Focus in the St. Joseph River drainage: Goodall, Scott, Marantette, and Sumnerville. The type component, the Goodall site, consists of a group of twenty-two circular mounds which were excavated in the nineteenth century. There were a number of sub-floor oblong burial pits in these mounds, some possibly lined with logs. Artifacts recovered with the burials include celts, gorgets, cut wolf jaws, cut sheet mica, platform pipes, blades, corner-

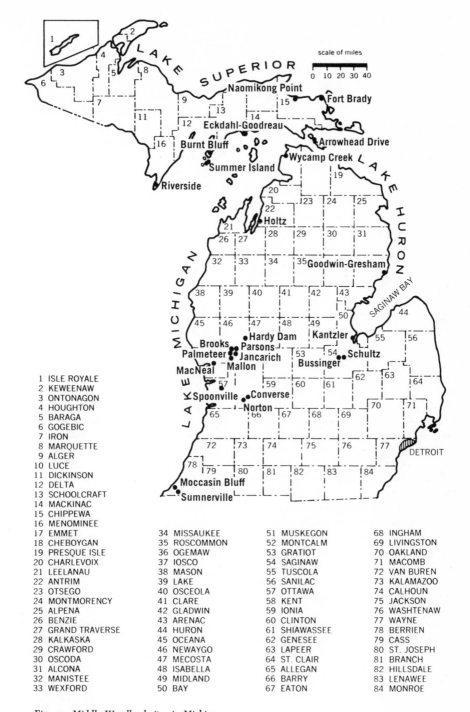

1 ISLE ROYALE
2 KEWEENAW
3 ONTONAGON
4 HOUGHTON
5 BARAGA
6 GOGEBIC
7 IRON
8 MARQUETTE
9 ALGER
10 LUCE
11 DICKINSON
12 DELTA
13 SCHOOLCRAFT
14 MACKINAC
15 CHIPPEWA
16 MENOMINEE
17 EMMET
18 CHEBOYGAN
19 PRESQUE ISLE
20 CHARLEVOIX
21 LEELANAU
22 ANTRIM
23 OTSEGO
24 MONTMORENCY
25 ALPENA
26 BENZIE
27 GRAND TRAVERSE
28 KALKASKA
29 CRAWFORD
30 OSCODA
31 ALCONA
32 MANISTEE
33 WEXFORD

34 MISSAUKEE
35 ROSCOMMON
36 OGEMAW
37 IOSCO
38 MASON
39 LAKE
40 OSCEOLA
41 CLARE
42 GLADWIN
43 ARENAC
44 HURON
45 OCEANA
46 NEWAYGO
47 MECOSTA
48 ISABELLA
49 MIDLAND
50 BAY

51 MUSKEGON
52 MONTCALM
53 GRATIOT
54 SAGINAW
55 TUSCOLA
56 SANILAC
57 OTTAWA
58 KENT
59 IONIA
60 CLINTON
61 SHIAWASSEE
62 GENESEE
63 LAPEER
64 ST. CLAIR
65 ALLEGAN
66 BARRY
67 EATON

68 INGHAM
69 LIVINGSTON
70 OAKLAND
71 MACOMB
72 VAN BUREN
73 KALAMAZOO
74 CALHOUN
75 JACKSON
76 WASHTENAW
77 WAYNE
78 BERRIEN
79 CASS
80 ST. JOSEPH
81 BRANCH
82 HILLSDALE
83 LENAWEE
84 MONROE

Fig. 40   *Middle Woodland sites in Michigan*

notched projectile points, and cache blades. The ceramics consist primarily of vessels with bands of zoned stamping and nodes along the rim. Zone-stamped bodies and zoned incising plus some rocker stamping was present.

James Brown (1964) has recently re-examined the collections from the Goodall site and reported on some new materials. He suggests there is a close stylistic similarity between the Goodall site and the Havana Tradition Middle Woodland in Illinois. The mounds and village sites in this area are built in relation to the marshes and Brown feels that the exploitation of marsh as well as prairie resources was important in the adaptation of the peoples living at these sites.

The Scott component consisted of a mound or group of mounds situated along an old glacial channel of the St. Joseph River near Colon in St. Joseph County. Quimby reported chipped stone implements, a shell gorget, an engraved turtle shell, and a small ceramic vessel with zoned rocker stamping on the body and a crosshatched rim set apart from the body by a row of punctates.

The Marantette component, located near Mendon in St. Joseph County, was also excavated in the nineteenth century. Artifacts included chipped stone implements, cut mica, cut wolf jaws, a bear canine, and a ceramic vessel similar to that from the Scott component.

The Sumnerville component consisted of a group of nine mounds located on Dowagiac Creek in the western part of Cass County. Artifacts recovered included a hafted copper awl, a copper celt, elk bone pins, an ivory effigy of a bear canine, gorgets, and corner-notched projectile points similar to those recovered from the Norton Mound group along the Grand River.

Fragments of fifteen ceramic vessels were in the collections from this mound group. Both grit and limestone tempering was found in these vessels. Several have smoothed bodies with zoned dentate or rocker stamping. Dentate stamping, rocker stamping, and horizontal fine-line incising were found on rims of vessels in this collection. One vessel had an unusual double body.

The Frantz-Green Mound is located just over the state line in Indiana and was excavated in 1919 by two stalwarts of Michigan archaeology, Amos Green and Harvey Frantz. Cut wolf jaws, corner-notched projectile points, and objects of copper were found with the burials in this mound.

A number of Hopewell Middle Woodland components have been reported in the Grand River Valley. All were excavated in the nineteenth century and several have been revisited in this century by University of Michigan field parties. The Gratten component was excavated by Wright L. Coffinberry, who explored this group of six mounds in Kent County in 1876. Several contained no artifacts while a copper implement, several fragments of mica, and part of a zoned stamped vessel with a crosshatched rim were found in the other mounds.

The Converse component consisted of a number of mounds once located within the present-day confines of the city of Grand Rapids. The artifacts reported from them included copper awls, beads and celts, corner-notched chipped stone projectile points, marine shell dippers, and platform pipes, including one effigy pipe. The one ceramic vessel from the site in the Grand Rapids Public Museum collection had horizontal bands of rocker stamping on the rim and two zoned bands of rocker stamping just below the rim.

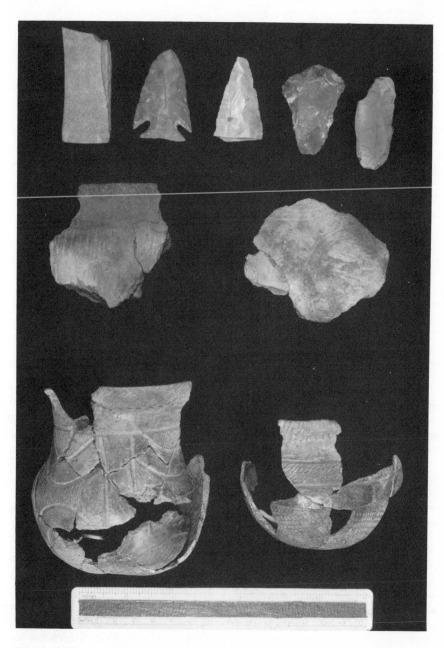

Fig. 41 Artifacts from the Spoonville Mound (From Flanders: 1965a)

Fig. 42 Rimsherds from the Spoonville Village site (University of Michigan Museum of Anthropology)

The Spoonville site was one of the sites reported by Quimby in his account of the Goodall Focus. The information that he had on the site came from accounts of the work of Abel Anderson in the nineteenth century and H. E. Sargent in the early twentieth century. The site is located at the junction of Crockery Creek and the Grand River in Ottawa County. Additional work was carried out there by Flanders in 1962 and 1966.

Quimby reported copper celts and awls, sheet mica, marine shell containers, and pipes as having been recovered from the mound. Flanders re-excavated one mound in 1962 and found a copper awl, a gorget fragment, a corner-notched projectile point, a blade, and some pottery fragments in the fill of the mound. The ceramics included a small restorable quadrilobate pot with zoned rocker stamping on the body and a crosshatched rim. Several other bodysherds were present with zoned stamping.

During salvage operations in 1966 Flanders recovered a complete small quadrilobate vessel with zoned decoration and a crosshatched rim. There was a cache of seven copper celts, a fragment of engraved turtle shell, and a complete blade core. One of the most interesting objects was a spoon or ladle of copper; perhaps this is the reason why the site was called Spoonville?

The village site was tested by Flanders in 1962 by means of thirty test pits which augmented material from the surface collections. There seemed to be a very sparse midden and a few occupational features.

The artifacts from the village site consisted by fifty-five projectile points, primarily expanding stemmed forms but also including small triangular forms, five drills, twenty-one scrapers, twelve small core "wedges," nine blades, twelve bifacially worked preforms, and several block cores. Celts, gorgets, hammerstones, and abraders were also present.

The ceramic sample consisted of 242 rimsherds and 3383 bodysherds. Some Early Woodland interior-exterior cordmarked sherds were found, but most of the ceramics were from later occupations. Middle Woodland ceramics included vessels with crosshatched and rocker stamped rims as well as other forms similar to those from the Norton and Sumnerville mound collections. The majority of the ceramics were described by Flanders as "Crockery Ware." Over seventy-five percent of the bodysherds of this ware were cord-marked and an additonal sixteen percent were cord-marked vessels which had been smoothed over. About four percent were plain and four percent fabric impressed. The rimsherds show great variation but most are cord-marked up to the lip. A smaller number of vessels have additional decorative elements, including several vessels with rocker stamping.

I am uncertain about the unity of Flanders' "Crockery Ware." Stylistically, some of the vessels included in this group are unquestionably of Middle Woodland origin. Some duplicate the Green Point Wares from the stratigraphically sealed levels at the Schultz site which have been radiocarbon dated to the fourth and fifth centuries of our era. However, most are simple cord-marked vessels that more closely approximate the Wayne Wares in southeastern Michigan, the Saginaw Thin ceramics from the Schultz site, and the Late Woodland ceramics from the Spring Creek site, in Muskegon County, than any of the positively Middle Woodland components in the state. I think this is a Late Woodland assemblage with some earlier Middle Woodland artifacts mixed in with the later materials.

Several radiocarbon dates have been run on charcoal from features at this site. These dates are A.D. 110±120 years (M-1428) and A.D. 215±110 years (M-1427). Both dates were earlier than even Flanders expected and surprising for a number of reasons. The ceramics are most similar to those from the Fort Wayne Mound, the latest occupation at the Schultz site, the West Twin Lake Mound, and the Spring Creek site—all Late Woodland sites dating within several centuries of A.D. 1000. The dates are even early for the Middle Woodland materials which are similar to forms dated to the fourth through fifth centuries in the Saginaw Valley.

Cleland's (1966: 64) faunal analysis from this site has not helped the situation. Approximately twenty-five individual animals were represented by ninety-five identifiable bone fragments. Over ninety-four percent of the meat represented by these bones came from deer, elk, and beaver. Small mammals were rare, bird and turtle absent, and fish represented by a single sturgeon. This faunal distribution is similar to that found on Late Woodland sites which presumably have an agricultural base. Cleland uses this to argue for an agricultural adaptation in western Michigan Hopewell Middle Woodland, accepting Flanders' interpretation of the ceramics. I feel that Cleland's evidence supports my interpretation that

THE NORTON MOUND GROUP
20 KT 1
KENT COUNTY, MICHIGAN

0 10 50 100
SCALE IN FEET
CONTOUR INTERVAL = TWO FEET

Spoonville is primarily a Late Woodland village site in spite of the radiocarbon dates.

In the summer of 1964 members of the Wright L. Coffinberry Chapter of the Michigan Archaeological Society were digging on the Spoonville site when they uncovered a feature that contained charred corn cobs. All concerned looked upon this as a chance to see if the presumed agricultural adaptation was Middle Woodland or Late Woodland. The resulting date of A.D. 1950±200 years (M-1649) did not help us.

Fig. 43 The Norton Mound group (From Flanders: 1965a)

Fig. 44 Central tomb area in Norton Mound M (University of Michigan Museum of Anthropology)

The best known of the western Michigan Hopewell Middle Woodland components is that represented at the Norton Mound group in Grand Rapids. Wright L. Coffinberry, Bela Hubbard, H. E. Sargent, and others have reported on materials from these mounds. Quimby reviewed these early excavations in the 1930s and E. P. Gibson did the same in the 1950s (Gibson 1959). While it was suspected that some of the mounds might still be untouched, the University of Michigan field crews, working under the supervison of Dr. Richard Flanders, did not anticipate the wealth of material they uncovered in the summers of 1963 and 1964.

Fig. 45   Ceramics from Norton Mound H (From Flanders: 1965a)

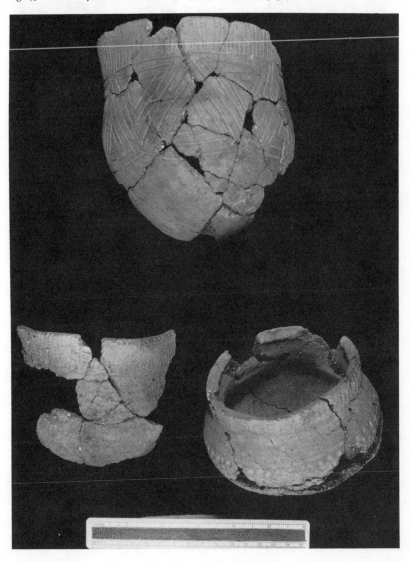

Fig. 46 Ceramics from the Norton Mound group (University of Michigan Museum of Anthropology)

In 1963, eleven of the seventeen mounds originally reported from the site could still be located. During that summer several of the smaller mounds, C, D, F, H, I, and J, were tested and only one was found to have been completely excavated before. A nineteenth-century shovel, reputed to have been the shovel of Wright L. Coffinberry himself, was found in this mound and presented to the Wright L. Coffinberry Chapter of the Michigan Archaeological Society.

In 1964, the largest mound in the group, Mound M, was opened, and it was found that Coffinberry's excavations had come down in the center of the tomb area, but all of the burials and most of the grave goods were clustered around the sides of the tomb and had been missed.

Flanders notes that many of these mounds had a prepared burial area. In some, this was a sub-floor pit covered by a dense level of mound fill. In Mound M there was a prepared floor, a burial chamber, and a very dense mound cap. This, in turn, was covered over with mound fill. Basket loading was clearly evident in many of the mounds and the University of Michigan field crew determined the average size of these basket loads of dirt and estimated that at least 500,000 of them went into the construction of Mound M.

The largest burial group was in Mound M where fourteen individuals, with fragments of several additional individuals, were buried. The remains of thirty-five individuals were found in the entire mound group. Flanders notes that in the smaller mounds there was a single extended burial surrounded by secondary bundle burials. He suggests that this was the individual for whom the mound was built and that older burials were exhumed and re-interred with the central high status burial.

There was a tremendous variety of grave goods with the burials. These included ceramic vessels, marine shell cups

Fig. 47 Cache of projectile points found with a burial in Norton Mound C (University of Michigan Museum of Anthropology)

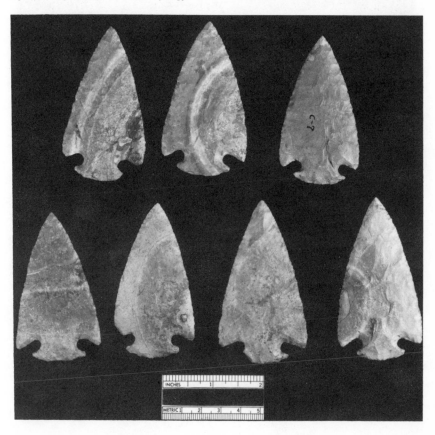

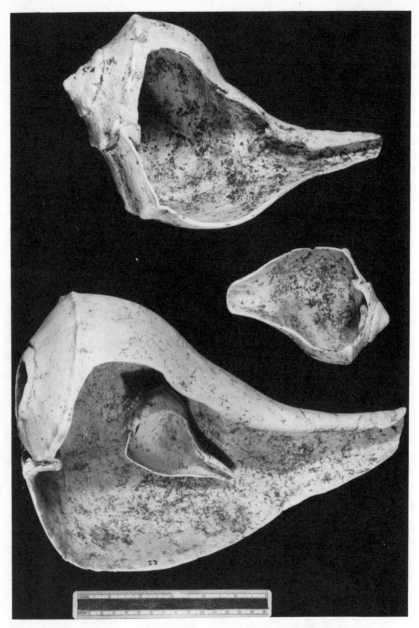

Fig. 48 Conches from the Norton Mound group (University of Michigan Museum of Anthropology)

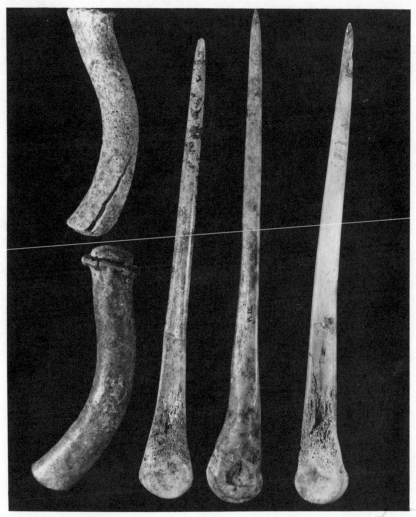

Fig. 49 *Bone implements from the Norton Mound group (University of Michigan Museum of Anthropology)*

and mussel shell and engraved turtle shell spoons, corner-notched projectile points, copper celts and awls, tools, and unworked mica and flint. Elk bone pins surrounded the burial pit, and Flanders suggests that these were used to hold skin coverings over the burial area.

The projectile points were of a corner-notched style common to many Hopewell Middle Woodland sites. Copper celts were found with traces of fabric adhering to them. Male burials were sometimes accompanied by tool kits with hammerstones, sandstone abraders, beaver tooth chisels, and worked antler sections which were probably flint knapping tools. The turtle shell spoons were engraved with geometric and zoomorphic designs.

Fig. 50 Vessel from the Brooks Mound group (University of Michigan Museum of Anthropology)

A number of ceramic vessels were recovered, including elongated and quadrilobate forms. Most were smooth with zoned decorations on the body areas. Rims were either dentate stamped or crosshatched and some vessels were marked by cord-wrapped stick impressions. Several platform pipes were recovered, including an elk effigy pipe and a turtle effigy pipe.

Cleland (1966: 65) believes that the bone recovered from the fill of some of the mounds is typical of that found on Late Woodland sites and has suggested that the Norton people were agriculturists. I am uncertain as to the meaning of food refuse found in such a situation. It might represent special activities associated directly with mound construction. Most

of the deer bone, which Cleland considers so important, was found in the fill of a single mound. If we use only the other mounds, the variety of resources would seem to indicate a generalized, rather than a specialized, hunting and fishing pattern.

There are a number of radiocarbon dates for the Norton Mound Group. Mound C has been dated to 10 B.C.±120 years (M-1493). There are two consistent radiocarbon dates from Mound H of A.D. 100±100 years (M-1490) and A.D. 160 ±120 years (M-1488). A third date on Mound H was A.D. 1000±100 years and has been rejected as inconsistent with the other dates from the site.

The best known of the Muskegon River

mound groups is the Brooks group. This mound group was tested by Hinsdale in 1928 (1930), retested in the 1950s by members of the Wright L. Coffinberry Chapter of the Michigan Archaeological Society, and the fill resifted by Prahl (1966) who has cross-correlated all of the previous excavations to give a coherent picture of the mound group. The mound group originally consisted of fourteen mounds, many of which had been partially destroyed by earlier excavations when Hinsdale was there. After sifting the fill, with the assistance of the Newaygo County Chapter of the Michigan Archaeological Society, Prahl restored the group to its original configurations.

The main group of burials in the large mound excavated by Hinsdale contained grave offerings, including ceramics, gorgets, and platform pipes. A small quadrilobate vessel with zoned stamped decoration was recovered, as well as a number of larger vessels. The larger vessels included very well-made forms with zoned stamped bodies and crosshatched rims (Prahl 1968).

Quimby (1941a) reported on the Mac-Neal component located in Muskegon County along the Muskegon River. This mound was excavated in 1931 by an amateur archaeologist from Muskegon who reported a single flexed burial in a rectangular sub-floor pit. A copper celt and copper beads and a number of exotic

Fig. 51 Vessel from the Brooks Mound group (University of Michigan Museum of Anthropology)

Fig. 52 Vessel from the Brooks Mound group (University of Michigan Museum of Anthropology)

flint blades were found with the burial. A very finely made limestone tempered quadrilobate vessel with a crosshatched rim and zoned stamped body decorations was attributed to this site, but Prahl (1968) has accumulated evidence indicating that this vessel was really from the Brooks group.

During the 1950s several members of the Wright L. Coffinberry Chapter of the Michigan Archaeological Society excavated a number of mounds along the Muskegon. These included the Parsons, Palmeteer, and Croton Bluff Mounds. Artifacts recovered from these small mounds included platform pipes, corner-notched projectile points, gorgets, and copper awls. The ceramics include some forms with characteristic Hopewell decorations as well as a number of plain vessels with both rounded and almost pointed bases. Material taken from below the floor of the Palmeteer Mound has been radiocarbon dated to 10 B.C.±140 years (M-1985). The mound was constructed after this date.

During the summer of 1965 Prahl directed a University of Michigan field crew in salvage work at a small mound above Hardy Dam. This mound had been badly pitted, and the burials removed years earlier. A projectile point, similar to those found at the Norton Mound group, and a small quadrilobate pot with a crosshatched rim and zoned punctate design on the body were found. This mound was of interest because it was the farthest upstream, almost to the border of Mecosta County, of any of the Hopewell Middle Woodland mounds along the Muskegon River.

In 1966 Prahl directed excavation at two additional Middle Woodland mounds in the area. The first of these, the Schumaker Mound, contained very little in the way

Fig. 53 Vessel from the Palmeteer Mound (University of Michigan Museum of Anthropology)

Fig. 54 Copper pan pipes from Mallon Mound F (University of Michigan Museum of Anthropology)

Fig. 55 Rimsherd section from the Jancarich Village site (University of Michigan Museum of Anthropology)

of grave offerings. The cache of flint chips and one biface were hardly diagnostic of a Hopewell Middle Woodland site, but the mound has been dated to 80 B.C.±140 years (M-1983).

The Mallon Mound F was the largest mound in the Mallon group. All of the other mounds (Prahl 1966, 1968, Losey 1968) were Late Woodland mounds. This mound, however, produced a group of eight burials with a small quadrilobate vessel marked by a crosshatched rim and zoned body decorations and a set of copper pan pipes.

Much of Prahl's field work during the 1966 season was done at the Jancarich Village site located on a low river terrace below the bluffs where the Brooks, Parsons, and Schumaker Mounds were located. About 1500 square feet of this site were excavated but features were rare and no house structures were located.

Smoothed bodysherds predominated over cord-marked bodysherds and a number of Middle Woodland decorative techniques, crosshatching and single cord-wrapped stick stamping, were found on the rims. Small expanding stemmed projectile points similar to those from the Middle Woodland levels at the Schultz site were recovered, as were a number of blades and blade core fragments of exotic chert of a type possibly derived from Illinois.

Prahl interprets this site as being similar, both in time and function, to the Late Middle Woodland McGraw site in Ohio (Prufer 1965). There is, however, no evidence that the Jancarich site, like the McGraw site, was agricultural. A radiocarbon date of 310 B.C. ±140 years (M-1982) does not support this interpretation either. This radiocarbon date seems much too early for the type of cultural material found at the site, but the entire series of "earlier than expected" Hopewell Middle Woodland dates from the Muskegon River Valley may be more than just a coincidence.

The Toft Lake Village site (Losey 1967) resembles the Jancarich Village site in some ceramic styles and in its low occupational intensity. Both plain and cord-marked ceramics were found. A number of rimsherds have been classified as Havana Hopewell forms by Losey. The projectile point forms very closely resemble those from the Schultz site Middle Woodland levels in the Saginaw Valley.

For a long while it had been assumed that the Muskegon River Valley represented the northernmost penetration of Hopewell Middle Woodland peoples in western Michigan. Recently, however, Hopewell Middle Woodland ceramics have been recovered by Michigan State University field parties from the Holtz site near the mouth of the Intermediate River in Antrim County (Cleland 1967). This site was excavated under the direction of Dr. Charles Cleland and is located in the Traverse Corridor, the rich coastal area between Traverse City and Mackinaw City.

HOPEWELL MIDDLE WOODLAND IN THE SAGINAW VALLEY

The Saginaw Valley contains a number of interesting sites which have contributed much to our understanding of the Middle Woodland cultural adaptation in the area. The region lacks the great number of Middle Woodland burial mounds found in western Michigan, so much of the excavation has been on village sites. Therefore, we know much more about the subsistence and settlement patterns of the people.

The key site for understanding the Middle Woodland adaptation in the Saginaw Valley is the Schultz site at Green Point. The importance of this site was recognized by Dustin long ago (see Dustin 1968) and University of Michigan field parties worked on the site during the summers of 1960, 1962, 1963, 1964, and 1965. The earlier excavations were carried out under the direction of Mark L. Papworth and Dr. Richard O. Keslin while the last two years' work was under my direction.

The following comments on the site are based on extensive reports, now in press as University of Michigan Museum of Anthropology Memoir No. 4, by myself and others: G. A. Wright and J. D. Speth on the geology, C. E. Cleland and B. Luxenberg on the faunal remains, A. Allison and F. V. Brunett on plant remains, D. S. Brose on molluscs, F. W. Fischer on ceramics, and Peter Murray on bone and shell implements. Additional information came from the work of Carole Crumley (1967) on the Kantzler site and

Fig. 56 *Excavations at the Schultz site at the end of the 1964 season* (*University of Michigan Museum of Anthropology*)

Fig. 57 *Map of the Schultz site* (*University of Michigan Museum of Anthropology*)

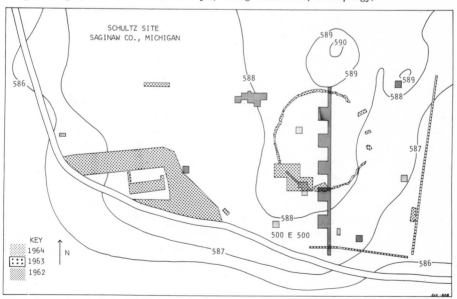

Fig. 58 Tittabawassee Ware from the Schultz site (University of Michigan Museum of Anthropology)

John R. Halsey on the Bussinger site, which is being prepared for publication.

The Schultz site is located on Green Point at the junction of the Tittabawassee and Shiawassee rivers where they form the Saginaw River. We have already discussed the Early Woodland occupation of the sixth century B.C. which took place when the site was emerging from the swamp that occupied the center of the basin of the Shiawassee Bay during the Lake Nipissing high water stage in the Great Lakes.

Speth's work on the geology of the site indicates a period of dropping water levels with only occasional flooding after the Early Woodland occupation until sometime around 10 B.C.; the site was then swampy during part of the year but, apparently, dry in the fall. The sparse occupation represented by what Fischer has called Shiawassee Ware ceramics and by a hunting tool assemblage which is found in these same levels dates to a period sometime between 500 B.C. and 10 B.C.

Starting about the time of Christ, there was a period of increased flooding which culminated in a high water level, apparently associated with a widespread high water level in the entire upper Great Lakes region, which occurred sometime

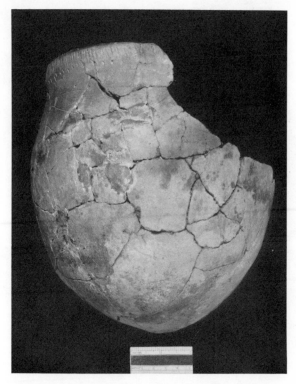

Fig. 59 Green Point Ware vessel from the Schultz site (University of Michigan Museum of Anthropology)

around A.D. 200. The earliest of the two main Middle Woodland occupations falls within this interval. Speth believes that this high lake level lasted less than a hundred and fifty years and the site was less swampy between A.D. 310±120 years (M-1646) and A.D. 450±200 years (M-1647), both representing the Late Middle Woodland occupations at the site. The site was again stabilized and by the later date a pattern of erosion was being established. The site was relatively dry with the exception of a period of flooding sometime prior to A.D. 1000. The Late Woodland occupation followed this period of flooding around A.D. 1000. The two

phases of Middle Woodland occupation, excluding the little known Shiawassee stage, can be dated to between 10 B.C. and A.D. 300 and A.D. 300 to A.D. 500.

The principal ceramic types of the Middle Woodland occupations consist of what Fischer has called Tittabawassee Ware and Green Point Ware. The first-named ware is very similar to, and perhaps a regional variant of the Havana Wares of the Illinois River Valley. The vessels tend to be large jars with little neck constriction, beveled rims which are often notched, thick walls, and rounded to subconoidal bases. Bodies were primarily smoothed or smoothed over cord-mark-

Fig. 60 *Green Point Ware from the Schultz site (University of Michigan Museum of Anthropology)*

ing. Tittabawassee Ware is represented by the types Tittabawassee Dentate Stamped, Tittabawassee Cord-wrapped Stick Impressed, and Tittabawassee Plain Noded, in order of decreasing frequency.

The second Middle Woodland Ware is Green Point Ware. It is similar to the Hopewell and Baehr wares of the Illinois drainage. The vessels are smaller with thinner walls, more constriction of the neck, and a tendency toward thickened rims. Bodies are plain and decoration is limited to the upper parts of the vessel. It is by far the more common of the two wares and is represented by over fourteen hundred identifiable sherds. It is represented by the following rim types: plain rocker stamped, dentate rocker stamped, cross-

hatched incised, brushed rims and plain rims, as well as a number of miscellaneous forms.

As expected, Tittabawassee Wares are most characteristic of the earlier phase of the Middle Woodland occupation and Green Point Wares are most characteristic of the later part of the Middle Woodland occupation. There is, however, a bimodal distribution of Tittabawassee Wares in some parts of the site. Fischer suggests that this is a result of erosion and that these wares were secondarily deposited on top of the Green Point occupation levels in the lower parts of the site during the dry period in the fifth and sixth centuries.

The lithic sample from the Middle Woodland levels consists of over ninety

Fig. 61 Expanding-stemmed projectile points from the Middle Woodland levels at the Schultz site (University of Michigan Museum of Anthropology)

Fig. 62 Triangular bifaces from the Middle Woodland levels at the Schultz site (University of Michigan Museum of Anthropology)

Fig. 63 Blades from the Schultz site (University of Michigan Museum of Anthropology)

thousand pieces of chipped stone, including over five hundred classifiable tools and cores. In both Middle Woodland levels unifacial tools outnumbered bifacial tools, a trait which I think reflects more emphasis on fishing and gathering and less emphasis on hunting. There are also fewer point tips and miscellaneous biface (knife?) fragments than at earlier and later levels. A new scraper type, the steep retouched end-scraper, appears for the first time in these levels but the percentage of drills and perforators is halved from that in the earlier level.

The most typical chipped stone artifacts are large thin triangular bifaces and large expanding-stemmed points. Small expanding-stemmed points are present in about the same frequency as the large expanding-stemmed forms and their relative frequency increases in later levels. Small triangular points and small narrow expanding-stemmed points, similar to Dustin points, are present in the Middle Woodland levels.

The Middle Woodland levels on the site produced over ninety percent of the shell and bone artifacts which could be assigned to specific levels. This includes a sample of 370 items. The most common artifact type is the turtle shell spoon with over two hundred *in situ* specimens, many engraved in a fashion reminiscent of those from western Michigan. Other common bone implements include projectile points and toggle head harpoons, awls, shuttles, tine flakers, ground teeth, many types of polished ornamental bone, and shell beads of several variants.

Cleland has identified eleven species of mammals, sixteen species of fish, seven birds, and two reptiles from the site. Approximately eighty-one percent of the animals identifiable as to species came from these levels. Cleland has noted two trends from the Middle Woodland occupations. One is an increasing emphasis on fewer game animals; that is, a concentration on hunting deer, elk, bear, and beaver. He feels that this is associated with increasing reliance on vegetable food plants. The second trend is for an increasing reliance on fish and birds during the Middle Woodland occupations and a decreasing utilization of mammals in comparison to the Early and Late Woodland levels. This is reflected in the tool ratios from the site. It also might indicate a slight change in the season of occupation, a position supported by the analysis of the plant remains.

Allison's examination of the plant remains from the site points to a trend that parallels Cleland's observations. The decreasing use of nuts as a food source seems to correlate with the increasing emphasis on a few game species among mammals. Allison also suggests that the later of the two Middle Woodland occupations is characterized by earlier ripening nuts and the only chenopodium seed recovered from the site. This might mean a shift from a summer-fall to a spring-summer occupation of the site.

Brose's examination of the remains of over sixteen thousand molluscs from the site yields information on both climate and diet. His environmental observations generally parallel those of Speth and others. He shows that thirteen food species were used on the site and that these were more common in the Middle Woodland levels than in the Early or Late Woodland occupations.

The picture that emerges from the Schultz site data is that of, first, an early Middle Woodland village site sporadically occupied during a period of general flooding and a high water lake stage sometime during the first two centuries of our era. These people occupied the site during the summer and fall and there was a great deal of emphasis on fishing and clamming in comparison to earlier and later occupations.

The later Middle Woodland occupation was more intensive and took place during a drier period after the water level had dropped at the site. It too was an occupation based on fishing and clamming, but there is more of a suggestion of spring activities than with the earlier occupation. The ceremonial activity at the site occurred during this second phase of Middle Woodland occupation, roughly A.D. 300 to A.D. 500, when more people were present.

One of the major occupational features at the site was a stockade about 150 feet in diameter marked by post molds approximately six inches in diameter and a yard apart. Where food refuse and living debris are scattered randomly over the site during the Early and Late Woodland occupations this is clearly not the case for the Middle Woodland occupation. During the Middle Woodland period debris is concentrated outside the stockade. Inside the stockade are a series of pits containing charcoal but very little other debris.

This feature could be interpreted as either a living area that was swept clean or a ceremonial area. I dismiss the former suggestion because the pits inside the stockade contain no food remains where pits in the same levels outside of the stockade contain large amounts of such debris. On the other hand, the stockade is nicely placed in relation to the main living area of the site, which is between the stockade and the river, and a group of at least three mounds that lie behind the stockade even farther away from the river than the village site.

The Green Point Mounds are a mysterious group. They were one of the first features noted in the Saginaw Valley by the early settlers, who arrived after the Indian treaty of 1819 opened the area for white settlement. There were three mounds, a large central mound directly in back of the stockade and bordering it, and two smaller mounds flanking it on either side. In the 1960s these were barely visible. An early pioneer account dating to 1834 tells how the big mound had been trenched and its contents removed by unknown parties at that time. Fred Dustin trenched it again in 1910 and found only one intrusive historic burial, which he interpreted to postdate even the disturbance

reported in 1834. By 1960 the mounds, which Dustin complained of having been plowed down sixty years ago, had been further leveled with a road grader in the 1940s to make cultivation easier. I attempted to relocate the former extent of the main mound in 1965 with electronic resistivity survey equipment but could find no regular pattern after 140 years of trenching, plowing, and grading, and could only define a large vague area where the mound might have been.

The easternmost mound had suffered the least destruction and we located it in 1964 and returned and almost totally excavated it in 1965. In spite of the clearly basket-loaded nature of this raised edifice no burials were found; the only cultural material was found in hearths below the clean sand level that marked the mound floor. This material clearly predated the construction of the mound.

We located and excavated burials from the westernmost mound but only with difficulty. In 1910, Dustin described how plowing had disturbed bones in this area of the site and suggested that it might represent a burial area which should be salvaged. In 1962, before actual excavations started on the site, a small test pit which the owner permitted us to open between a wheat and bean field came down on the burial but since we were not permitted to disturb any planted crops we could only leave it for a future year. We re-excavated the area in 1964 and found we were working in the bottom few inches of a burial chamber, the top of which had been totally destroyed by plowing and grading.

Remains of at least seven individuals were recovered although they were badly damaged. There were piles of skulls, long bones, and vertebrae and ribs indicating

Fig. 64 Tittabawassee Ware from the Bussinger site (University of Michigan Museum of Anthropology)

that they were secondary burials. In the plow zone above the burials, and along with them, were shell beads, cut wolf and bear teeth, a corner-notched projectile point similar to those recovered from the Norton Mound group and dissimilar to anything from the village refuse area, and fragments of a number of small ceramic vessels. Several of these were quadrilobate vessels with crosshatched rims and zoned dentate or rocker stamped bodies. Fragments of one vessel with red paint in the zoned area and another with small feet were recovered from the burial area of this mound.

The only other Hopewell Middle Woodland burials excavated in the Saginaw

Valley are from the Bussinger site on Swan Creek. Over 120 burials have been taken from this site; most, however, are Late Woodland which I will discuss in the next chapter.

The Middle Woodland occupation at this site is represented by some Shiawassee, Tittabawassee, and Green Point Wares in the general midden from the site and several specifically Hopewell Middle Woodland burials. These are single burials and are not associated with mounds of any sort. One such burial contained corner-notched projectile points similar to those from the Norton Mounds, copper celts and awls, and a marine shell dish. Still others contained small quadrilobate zoned incised

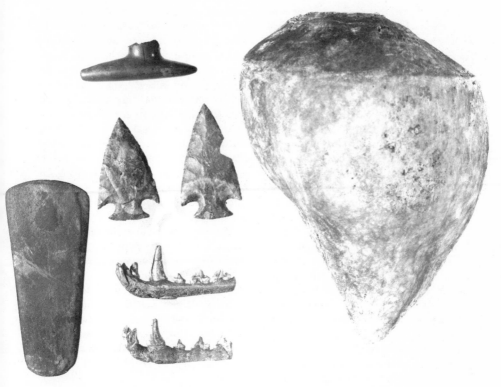

Fig. 65 Middle Woodland artifacts from the Bussinger site (University of Michigan Museum of Anthropology)

Fig. 66 Small Green Point Ware vessels from the Schultz and Bussinger sites (University of Michigan Museum of Anthropology)

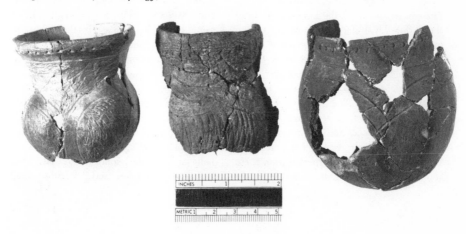

vessels with crosshatched rims, cut wolf jaws, columella beads, and engraved turtle shell spoons. One of the unquestionably Hopewell Middle Woodland features has been radiocarbon dated to A.D. 490±120 years (M-1756). This date may represent the very last of the Hopewell Middle Woodland influence in Michigan.

The multicomponent Kantzler site in Bay City was tested by a University of Michigan field crew under the supervision of Carole Crumley in 1966 (Crumley 1967) and was more extensively excavated under my direction, with assistance of members of the Saginaw Valley Chapter of the Michigan Archaeological Society, in 1967. This site produced a significant Middle Woodland component which corresponds most closely to the later of the two Middle Woodland components at the Schultz site so would probably date to some time between A.D. 300 and A.D. 500.

The ceramics consisted primarily of Green Point Wares although some Tittabawassee Wares and a sherd of Shiawassee Ware were found in the loose black sands of the poorly stratified midden. The lithic material also duplicated the range present at the Schultz site but, to date, comparable tool counts are not available.

While fish bone still accounts for almost fifty-seven percent of the bone refuse from the middle level of the site, mammal bone more than doubles from the lowest and, presumably, Early Woodland level. In the lower level it is only fifteen percent while in the middle level it increases to over thirty-six percent. The percentäge of the diet attributable to a few large mammal species, deer, bear, and beaver, would be considerably larger; eighty-five percent of the meat from identified species from these levels was from mammals. This is a greater reliance on mammals than is characteristic of the intermediate levels at the Schultz site. I believe this indicates a fall and winter occupation that balanced the spring and summer occupation of the comparable late Middle Woodland level at the Schultz site. Another factor that must be considered is the occupational intensity of the sites. The occupational intensity at Kantzler was much less than at the Schultz site. This is another factor that leads me to conclude that this is a small outlying fall and winter camp related to the larger and centrally located Schultz site farther up the river.

There are a number of sites in the Saginaw Valley which have produced Middle Woodland ceramics in surface collections. Quimby (1941a: 132) refers to, but does not identify, ten sites in the valley with such materials. I am personally familiar with Middle Woodland ceramics from the Andrews, Cook, Dead Creek, Mahoney, and Miller sites. In each case the Middle Woodland materials are sparse.

All of the Hopewell Middle Woodland materials from the Saginaw Valley are limited to the central part of the valley. This is an area marked by swamps, wet prairies, and broad flood plains which formed behind the moraines at Saginaw and Bay City during periods of heavy rainfall. The headwaters of the tributaries are devoid of such materials.

Within the central valley the center of the Middle Woodland occupation was at the Schultz site which appears to have served as a base camp. It also served as the ceremonial, if not mortuary, center of the valley, for the few other mounds excavated in the valley are Late Woodland. I believe that the sparse materials from Bussinger, Kantzler, and the other small sites in the valley represent the cold season outlying camps of the Schultz Middle Woodland peoples.

If the Schultz site represents a spring-summer-fall occupation while Kantzler represents a fall to winter occupation, then population concentration took place during the summer when fishing, clamming, and probably the collection of wild food plants could support such a population concentration. During the winter, population units broke up into smaller groups, probably extended family units.

This settlement pattern is exactly the reverse of that suggested for the Late Archaic and Early Woodland occupations when population concentration took place during the winter months and dispersal took place in the summer. It is a pattern which, as we shall see in later chapters, is a characteristic of the historic Chippewa of the Lake Forest formation. It is also a characteristic pattern of the contemporary Middle Woodland populations in the Lake Forest area.

The relationship between the more southern of the Hopewell Middle Woodland groups and those people in the center of the Saginaw Valley is perplexing. The adaptation in the Saginaw Valley is non-agricultural and certainly bears no resemblance to the pattern in Ohio, suggested by Prufer, with small farming villages surrounding vacant ceremonial centers. The Saginaw ceremonial center is not particularly impressive and is located at the largest village site in the valley.

I have the impression that the Middle Woodland settlements in the Illinois River Valley are a series of large villages along the major river valleys which are permanent occupations. The occupants variously turn to the river, the swamps, and the nearby, not the distant, uplands for food

during the course of the year. It would be interesting to see if the settlement pattern noted for the early historic agricultural groups in the area appears during the Middle Woodland period. This is a pattern with permanent village sites that are abandoned during the winter months as the entire group moves as a unit to distant hunting grounds.

In its pattern of settlement and subsistence, the cultural adaptation of the Saginaw Middle Woodland peoples resembles that of their non-Hopewellian neighbors to the north more than it does any of the patterns suggested by the Hopewellian Middle Woodland groups to the south. Their adoption of outward Hopewellian cultural forms is perplexing for they seem to be doing Hopewell things completely out of context.

They built mounds at their ceremonial center and buried their dead with all of the prescribed Hopewell trappings (forgetting the platform pipes), but they did not combine the traits of grave goods and mounds as is done in other Hopewell areas. The re-interment of several individuals near the edge of a low mound at Green Point seems almost like an afterthought.

In some respects they seem to overdo their role as Hopewell. In contrast to Ohio and Illinois, where the vast bulk of ceramics on Middle Woodland village sites are cord-marked and plain with decorated vessels in the minority, the exact opposite is true at the Schultz site. In the Middle Woodland levels there are over 1300 sherds clearly assignable to the Shiawassee, Tittabawassee and Green Point Ware groups, over 2500 plain bodysherds, and fewer than 350 cord-marked sherds. The design elements and decorative motifs which seem to be reserved for special vessels in other areas are used in a sloppily executed form on the utilitarian wares in this area. In the Schultz collection there is also a strong identification of types. Certain design elements and decorative techniques are usually found in association with certain vessel and rim forms. The "intermediate" vessels that do not fall easily into one type or another in other areas do not exist in any significant number here. It looks as if the Green Point potters were operating from mail order patterns or that someone had found a copy of an Illinois pottery type handbook such as Griffin's classic 1952 paper.

I suspect that in the Saginaw Valley a local Middle Woodland group adopted selected Hopewell characteristics. There are changes in settlement and land use patterns from earlier times but these are changes that more closely parallel those from non-Hopewellian areas to the north than they do the Hopewellian areas to the south.

These people maintained their own mortuary customs with single burials placed on sand ridges with grave goods as they had done in earlier times. The same burial patterns, and even the same cemeteries, with only changes in the styles of grave goods, were used throughout the entire Woodland sequence in the Saginaw Valley.

They never fully participated in Hopewell ceremonialism but the radiocarbon dates from both Schultz and Bussinger indicate that Hopewell traits continued to be a part of the cultural pattern in the area long after they ceased to be important in areas to the south—another indication that they were never completely involved in the full Hopewell ceremonial system.

Hopewell Middle Woodland culture traits seem to have persisted until at least A.D. 500 and perhaps later. I think their final disappearance correlates with the introduction of agriculture into the area and the development of a new adaptive pattern. Many groups moved in and out of the Saginaw Valley after the Middle Woodland period but I suspect that it was never again occupied on a year-round basis until the historic period.

A NON-HOPEWELL MIDDLE WOODLAND?

In the Carolinian biotic province in Michigan there are a number of Late Archaic village sites in the same areas where there are many Late Woodland village sites. In the same regions there is a wide distribution of interior-exterior cord-marked Early Woodland pottery so Early Woodland populations seem to have been fairly extensive. The same thing cannot be said for Hopewell Middle Woodland.

Materials of a Hopewell Middle Woodland form are restricted to the lower reaches of a few valleys. They do not seem to be found in the headwaters of these same river systems, concentrated around the immature drainage systems of the north, or located in the small river systems with few lakes or permanent swamps in the southeastern part of the state.

I find it difficult to believe that large areas in the richest part of Michigan, which were intensively occupied in earlier and later times, were empty during the Middle Woodland period. At first I thought that this might be a bias of the collections with which I had worked in some areas which, admittedly, were limited. One area, Monroe County in the southeastern part of the state, was intensively searched for Middle Woodland materials in a test of this hypothesis.

I had studied the Late Woodland collections, both public and private, from this area for many years and had the impression that Middle Woodland materials were rare; however, I was not looking for them. During the summer of 1966 I obtained a research grant to study this problem and David Brose made an intensive survey of the county, recording information on well over a hundred sites. His observations, looking specifically for Middle Woodland materials, paralleled my own peripheral impressions. No recognizable Hopewell or Lake Forest Middle Woodland cultural material was present.

An alternative explanation is that there is a Middle Woodland cultural manifestation in these "empty areas," and Monroe County is only one of them, that we are unable to recognize as Middle Woodland. Struever (1965: 216) suggests that these "less complex cultural systems" exist in the extensive areas outside the ribbon-like Hopewell distribution along the river valleys.

I suspect that these sites closely resemble the early Late Woodland sites described in the next chapter. It is possible that the Spoonville radiocarbon dates are associated with the Late Woodland-looking ceramics and that Greenman's identifications of some of the materials from the Gibraltar and Rivière au Vase sites as Hopewell are essentially correct. So far, however, the existence of a non-Hopewellian Middle Woodland tradition in the parts of the Carolinian biotic province in Michigan that were not occupied by Hopewellian Middle Woodland peoples is only a matter for speculation.

THE LAKE FOREST MIDDLE WOODLAND

In Chapter II, I noted that the northern part of the lower peninsula and the entire upper peninsula of Michigan fell within a mixed forest association which Weaver and Clements (1939) and later Potzger (1946) called the Lake Forest formation. Within this forest association there are a number of Middle Woodland cultural complexes which show a great deal of stylistic similarity and reflect a similar pattern of prehistoric cultural adaptation. These have been given a number of regional designations such as Laurel, North Bay, Saugeen, and Point Peninsula but I think that the widespread similarity permits a comprehensive term to be used for the entire group. Several years ago I suggested the term Lake Forest Middle Woodland (Fitting 1965a, 1965c) which has since been used by several others (Quimby 1965b, Mason 1967); I will continue to use it here.

In the eastern areas Ritchie (1965: 207) recognizes the distinctive environmental adaptation and exploitative pattern of the Lake Forest Middle Woodland quite clearly. He notes that the location of sites for these groups was in a region characterized ". . . by a heavy forest cover of hemlock, white pine and northern hardwoods, principally sugar maple, beach, basswood, and yellow birch." He observes that the major game animals reported in the refuse pits of these groups are Canadian forms including deer, black bear, moose, beaver, and raccoon but further notes that ". . . the general scarcity of such remains and the paucity of projectile points, as well as the situation of the sites themselves, argue that hunting was of less importance to the occupants of these sites than was fishing and collecting of fresh-water mussels, as judged from the relative abundance of fishing gear and the organic remnants of these aquatic animals."

Ritchie also writes that the sites that he has excavated are probably the summer camps of people whose ". . . winters may have been spent ranging the forest in small groups, as among the Algonkian bands of the Ottawa River area and their kinsmen to the west, the Chippewa; and the discovery and excavation of these winter camp sites might convey a different impression of the culture." Rather than a different impression, I suggest a more complete one.

At the opposite end of the Lake Forest extension is MacNeish's (1958) description of the environmental situation in which the Anderson and Nutimik Foci of southeastern Manitoba developed. It is a region of "poplar, burr oak, and elm" in the uplands and "box elder and maple" in the bottoms and valleys with "spruce, willow, and pine" covering part of the area. The historic fauna included black bear, elk, and deer. The Lake Forest Middle Woodland adaptation in this area was marked by fishing. When the fauna from these sites was compared with that of earlier horizons ". . . the most notable change is the numerous fish bones" and "one might guess that their life was now less nomadic and the groups were larger in size because of their heavy reliance on fishing, a more reliable food source in eastern Manitoba" (MacNeish 1958: 178).

Cleland (1966: 60–68) observes the same adaptive pattern in the central parts of the Lake Forest area. He believes that the development of summer fishing patterns, perhaps with the introduction of fish nets, allowed a greater Middle Woodland population in this area than had

existed during preceding periods. Like Ritchie, he feels that the large lakeshore sites are summer occupations. The overall settlement pattern was probably similar to that of the historic Chippewa (Fitting and Cleland 1969, Chapters VI and VII in this volume), a pattern that allowed the maximum possible concentration of population in this area. Greater population density occurred only when it was incorporated in larger economic networks during the Late Woodland and Historic periods.

A general observation on peripheral Lake Forest Middle Woodland sites is also necessary. Although J. V. Wright (1967) has demonstrated that Laurel sites are found in boreal forest areas, I am unimpressed with their size. More Laurel ceramics were found in a single excavation unit at the Naomikong Point site than were reported from all of the sites Wright worked with combined. His most productive site was Huron Bay which, located only a mile up the Pic River from Lake Superior, is in the Lake Forest formation in spite of the dotted line for the southern limits of the boreal forests that Wright includes on his distribution map (Wright 1967: xvi). I suspect that the sites located up the rivers and around the inland lakes in the boreal forests are either located at specialized fishing locations or are transient hunting camps.

The pattern of cultural contact to the south is more complex than to the north, where the Lake Forest borders the extremely low population density area of the boreal forest. To the south the population density and cultural influence was greater. Though the more northern Laurel Point Peninsula distribution shows a great deal of similarity, there is quite a bit of variation along the southern boundary, including such materials as those excavated

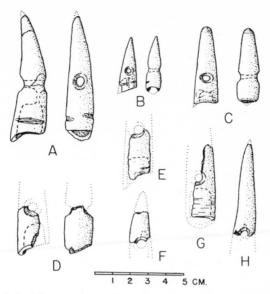

Fig. 67 Toggle head harpoons from the Porte des Morts site, Door County, Wisconsin (From Mason: 1965)

by Robert Salzer in northern Wisconsin, Ronald Mason's North Bay complex on the Door Peninsula (Mason 1966, 1967), and the Saugeen Focus in Ontario (Jury and Jury 1952, Kenyon 1959, Lee 1960, Wright and Anderson 1963). In addition to these, there is a strong Adena influence at the Killarney Bay site in Ontario (Greenman 1966) where a few classic Laurel sherds were found.

I am not disturbed by the stylistic syncretisms in these areas for it is exactly what would be expected along a cultural and ecological transition area. I am more impressed by the integrity of the adaptive pattern and, in spite of differences in the ceramics, I would group such sites as Mero and Summer Island together to examine the adaptive pattern in the area.

Mason's work on the Door Peninsula of Wisconsin is directly applicable to our study of Michigan archaeology, although the closest ceramic similarities in the state seem to be with the Goodwin-

Gresham site in eastern Michigan rather than the nearby Middle Woodland sites in Delta County, Michigan. Mason's North Bay complex is known from the Mero and Porte des Morts sites (Mason 1966, 1967).

The North Bay complex is divided into two components. The earlier North Bay I component is characterized by plain and cord-marked bodysherds and dentate stamped, corded stamped, and punctate rimsherds. North Bay II, which has been radiocarbon dated to A.D. 160 ± 100 years (I-888), is marked by plain and cord-marked bodysherds, corded stamped, dentate stamped, rocker stamped, pseudo-scallop shell stamped, and incised rimsherds. The North Bay I ceramic sample from the Mero site consists of 489 sherds, including 67 rimsherds representing 43 vessels. There are 462 North Bay II sherds from the Mero site with 18 rimsherds representing 16 vessels. The Porte des Morts sample is considerably larger and

131

more varied with 8284 bodysherds and 315 rimsherds representing at least 284 vessels.

The lithic industry was primarily a small tool industry with many small cores. Mason (1967: 302) writes of ". . . thousands of oddly fractured pieces of chert strewn about the Porte des Morts site, a situation earlier noted at the Mero site." Projectile points include stemmed and notched forms which are common at a number of sites in the Green Bay-Bay de Noc region (Cleland and Peske 1968, Janzen 1968). Other stone implements include bifacial cutting implements, preforms, chopping stools, end-scrapers, side-scrapers, and drills.

Copper artifacts include punches, awls, and fishhooks. There are a number of bone artifacts including awls, projectile points, and flaking tools. The most interesting of these bone tools is a group of toggle head harpoons that Mason (1965) feels is specifically Middle Woodland.

While the faunal remains from Porte des Morts have not been analyzed, Cleland (1966: 145–56) has worked with the collections from the Mero site. The Middle Woodland occupation at this site is marked by an absence of birds and a great deal of fishing activity. Even though eighty-two percent of the identified individuals of all species in the Middle Woodland levels are fish, mammals, because of their larger size, account for about seventy-five percent of the meat from the site. Cleland has characterized the Middle Woodland occupation as short-term, warm-weather camps and notes a heavier dependence on fishing than during

Fig. 68 The Summer Island Village site from Summer Harbor (Courtesy of David S. Brose)

later occupations at the Mero site and at the Heins Creek site.

A nearby Middle Woodland site located on Summer Island in Delta County, Michigan, shows a different type of occupation. This site was visited by Quimby (Binford and Quimby 1963) and University of Michigan survey parties for several years, but large-scale excavations were not possible until the summer of 1967. At that time David S. Brose supervised excavation by a University of Michigan field party, assisted by campers from Summer Science Incorporated, a science

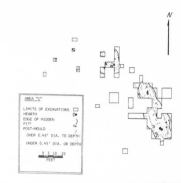

Fig. 69 The Middle Woodland level in Area C at the Summer Island Village site (Courtesy of David S. Brose)

Fig. 70 Vessel from the Middle Woodland level at the Summer Island Village site (Courtesy of David S. Brose)

camp that purchased the area of the site in 1966, and in 1967 allowed excavation.

Brose's analysis of the site formed the basis for his doctoral dissertation (n.d.). As Quimby noted earlier, this is a stratified site with Late Woodland, Upper Mississippian, and two historic components. The largest component, however, is a Lake Forest Middle Woodland occupation.

During eight weeks in 1967, approximately 2500 square feet of the site area was excavated. Three distinct Middle Woodland house patterns and many hearths and refuse pits were uncovered. The houses are elliptical structures marked by post mold patterns in the light sand of the site. Two are about twelve feet by twenty feet and the third was slightly smaller.

Ceramics from the site are numerous and there are about 3800 sherds representing approximately 150 vessels. Many of these were in close association with the lodges; there are some stylistic differences between areas of the site. A few of the ceramics resemble North Bay ceramics from the Door Peninsula but the majority are distinctive. There is virtually no cord-marking on the bodies of vessels in the Middle Woodland levels while this is common at the North Bay sites. The designs on Summer Island seem to be finer and executed with more care than on North Bay ceramics but with less care than more Northern Laurel variants. The radiocarbon date for this occupation is A.D. 250±140 years (M-1995). The spatially distant, but ceramically similar, Serpent Mound site in Ontario (Johnson 1968) has been radiocarbon dated to A.D. 290±75 years (M-1105) and A.D. 120±100 years (M-850).

Chipping debris from the site is ex-

tensive. Small pebble sources were used in the typical small core industry with some of these cores used as tools. There are many scrapers from the site and the corner-notched and stemmed projectile points are similar to those from the North Bay sites and the caves at Burnt Bluff on the Garden Peninsula across the Detour Strait.

Many copper implements, including awls and a fishhook, are associated with this occupation. Bone awls, flaking tools, and finished and unfinished toggle head harpoons are all present.

The analysis of faunal remains is not complete but about seventy percent is fish bone. This is understandable since the island is too small to have carried a large enough game population to have made hunting practical. The occupation would almost have to have been a summer occupation since the exposed location of the site, catching both the Bay de Noc and the Point Detour currents, would have made winter occupation most uncomfortable. A fairly large population could thus be supported during the summer season.

University of Michigan field parties worked in the caves of Burnt Bluff on the Garden Peninsula in Delta County in the summers of 1963 and 1965 (Fitting 1968b). Two caves in this area were used by Lake Forest Middle Woodland peoples; I suspect some of the people came from Summer Island.

"Used" rather than occupied is the correct word; the Spider Cave (Cleland and Peske 1968) was a shrine where stone-tipped projectiles were shot or thrown. The cultural material consists mainly of projectile points, many with tip fractures. The few faunal remains, bat skulls and bones and tiny fish bones, could

Fig. 71 Bone artifacts from the Summer Island Village site (Courtesy of David S. Brose)

points, only two points were found in cave B-95. One was a Middle Woodland form, the other was untypable.

The other cultural material from the cave consists of one ground stone object (perhaps a net sinker weight) and a number of items of the sort not normally found on Michigan sites including pointed wooden sticks, a polished bone awl, and fragments of cedar bark cordage. Remains of seven people were found in the cave, almost all of them sub-adults and several showing cut marks on the bones similar to the marks found on the long bones of butchered animals.

Janzen's detailed examination of the faunal remains from the site reported primarily bird and fish, although a single elk tooth would certainly skew the meat percentages toward mammal unjustly, for this tooth may have been a part of the ceremonial paraphernalia. While the food remains were extensive in comparison to Spider Cave, Janzen does not feel that they could have supported even a small group for more than a few weeks. Several hearths have been found in the cave in contrast to Spider Cave. Charcoal from one of these hearths has been dated to A.D. 375±130 years (M-1795), which would make it almost contemporary with the Middle Woodland occupation on Summer Island.

One of the attractions of Burnt Bluff was the cave paintings reported by Hinsdale over forty years ago (Hinsdale 1925) and by many others since then. Both their clarity and motif (Lugthart 1968) indicate a Late Woodland placement. However, almost all of the cultural material from the caves can be assigned with greater or lesser certainty to the Lake Forest Middle Woodland. Either these paintings were Middle Woodland

have been brought to the cave by agencies other than man. There were no hearths or other occupational features. All of the projectile point styles were found in Middle Woodland context at Mero, Porte des Morts, and Summer Island. A marine shell disk and several toggle head harpoons were also found in this cave.

Cave B-95 was excavated by a University of Michigan field crew working under the direction of Donald Janzen in the summer of 1965. It too is an unusual site; Janzen (1968b) interprets it as a ceremonial site. In contrast to the Spider Cave with over a hundred projectile

too or the caves and bluffs were used in later rituals by peoples whose material remains we have yet to locate; I favor the latter position.

In the summer of 1965, Earl J. Prahl undertook excavations for the University of Michigan at the Eckdahl-Goodreau site in Newton Harbor on Seul Choix Point in Schoolcraft County. This is another site that Quimby visited earlier (Binford and Quimby 1963). Prahl found a heavy Late Woodland occupation, stratified over an earlier occupation, which produced at least one vessel similar to some of the Middle Woodland vessels from Summer

Island. Prahl returned to the site with a field party from the University of Toledo in the summer of 1968 and located an extensive buried Middle Woodland midden.

University of Michigan field parties spent short periods of time in the summers of 1961 and 1962 at the Arrowhead Drive site, located near the Juntunen site on Bois Blanc Island in the Straits of Mackinac (Bettarel and Harrison 1962, Mac-Pherron 1967). Only one feature from this site was reported in detail but Mac-Pherron (1967: 123) notes a similarity in ceramics to ". . . the Laurel pottery

Fig. 72 Excavation of Unit A in 1966 at the Naomikong Point site (University of Michigan Museum of Anthropology)

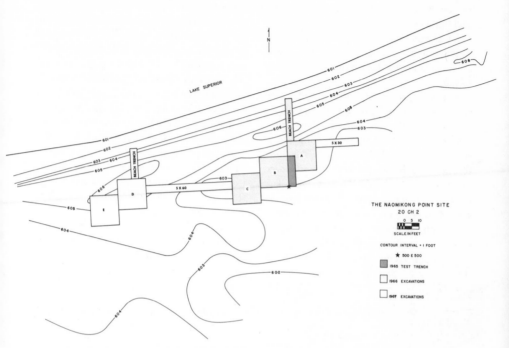

Fig. 73 Map of the Naomikong Point site (Courtesy of Donald Janzen)

Fig. 74 Rimsherd section from the Naomikong Point site (University of Michigan Museum of Anthropology)

of the Bruce Peninsula, Ontario (Wright and Anderson 1963), and to some of the Point Peninsula types of New York State (Ritchie and MacNeish 1949)." Brose sees a resemblance to the ceramics of Summer Island.

Feature #45 on the Arrowhead Drive site was excavated in 1962. It consists of a group of seven burials with some grave offerings, including a smooth-bodied vessel with a pointed base and crosshatching on the walls below the rim design. There are several rimsherds marked with fine dentate stamping. Other artifacts include a number of bifacial implements, an antler tine with a hafted beaver incisor, cut bear jaws, and a number of bone tools. This burial group has been radiocarbon dated to A.D. 50±120 years (M-1392).

Lake Forest Middle Woodland ceramics were recovered from two sites excavated by Michigan State University field parties in the summer of 1967. Dr. Charles Cleland uncovered a Laurel-like occupation at the Wycamp Creek site in Emmet County in the northern part of the lower peninsula. Some of the ceramics among the aboriginal materials recovered from the Fort Brady excavations at Sault Ste. Marie by Lyle Stone are unquestionably Lake Forest Middle Woodland forms and, as we would expect along the St. Marys River, they show a very close similarity to those from Naomikong Point.

One of the major Lake Forest Middle Woodland sites in the entire upper Great Lakes is located on Naomikong Point in Whitefish Bay in Chippewa County along

Fig. 75 Rimsherds from the Naomikong Point site (University of Michigan Museum of Anthropology)

the south shore of Lake Superior. While this site has been known for some time, intensive exploration did not start until 1965. At that time George Quimby and James Fitting, assisted by Donald Janzen, directed underwater exploration on the site (Fitting 1965a, Quimby 1965b) and Fitting returned to excavate approximately 120 square feet of the site later that summer after obtaining a special land use permit from the United States Department of Agriculture Forest Service. Fitting (1966d) directed excavations at the site in the summer of 1966 and opened 1420 square feet of site area. Donald Janzen

was in charge of the University of Michigan field party at the site in the summer of 1967 and excavated an additional 1420 square feet. The site served as the base for Janzen's doctoral dissertation (1968a).

A large quantity of ceramics was recovered from the site. Janzen's analysis so far indicates over 132,000 sherds and the rimsherds represent well over 1200 distinct vessels. All of the Middle Woodland ceramics have smooth bodies and, apparently, conical bases. The well-executed rim decorations, with some examples of crosshatching just below the several bands of the rim design, consist of drag

Fig. 76 Projectile points from the Naomikong Point site (University of Michigan Museum of Anthropology)

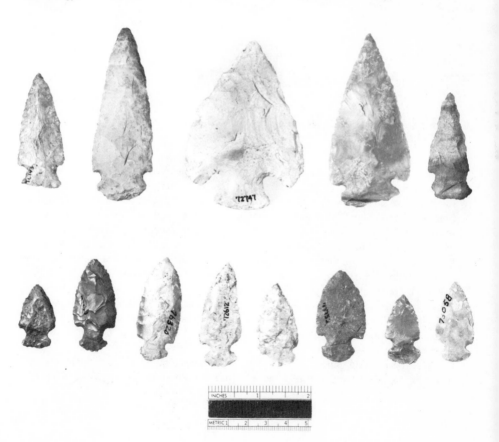

Fig. 77 *End-scrapers from the Naomikong Point site* (*University of Michigan Museum of Anthropology*)

and jab, dentate, and pseudo-scallop shell impressions. The ceramics from the site show a great deal of similarity to those from the north shore of Lake Superior (Wright 1967) and from the Laurel area of Minnesota (Stoltman 1962), where Laurel ceramics were first reported and named (Wilford 1941, 1950a, 1950b).

Flint is relatively rare at Naomikong Point and almost every fragment was retouched and used, which is in strong contrast to Summer Island and the North Bay sites where poor quality chert is readily available and unworked chipping debris is plentiful. Over twelve hundred

end-scrapers were found at the site. The few projectile points are small, thin side-notched forms. Large chipped stone tools are often made of exotic materials, including cherts, which have their closest equivalents in the lower peninsula. A few large tools are made of quartzite. One projectile point resembles the forms from the Goodall Mounds in Indiana in shape, size, and raw material. Several fragments of obsidian have been identified by neutron activation as coming from the area of Yellowstone National Park.

Copper fragments are numerous and several awls and beads of this material occur. Bone tools are rare. Several types of ground stone tools are present, including axes and adzes. Notched pebbles, possibly net sinkers or net weights, are common; our excavations have yielded over three hundred of them.

Because of the highly acid soil, preservation of faunal remains is poor. In the historic levels, fish bone and scales plus beaver bone are common. Most of the identified prehistoric bone, however, was preserved by charring in a single hearth area. Here mammal bone is more common than fish bone but I do not believe that this is generally true for the site. The site is located in an area that is traditionally important for fishing and poor for hunting. This, coupled with the tool types present, indicates a large summer fishing camp repeatedly occupied by Lake Forest Middle Woodland peoples.

Samples for radiocarbon dating have been submitted to the University of Michigan Phoenix Project Laboratory but the dates are not yet available. There are, however, a number of dated Laurel sites on the north shore of Lake Superior which furnish contributor dates. These include the Sand River site with a date of A.D. 320±100 years (M-1507) and the Heron Bay site with a date of about A.D. 1 (cited from Mason 1967).

I should mention the two Saugeen dates initially used by Wright to suggest an extremely early age for Laurel materials. There is a date of 530 B.C.±60 years (S-119) for the Donaldson site (Wright and Anderson 1963) and a date of 667 B.C.±220 years (C-192) on the Burley site (Jury and Jury 1952). These dates are entirely out of line with all of the other Lake Forest Middle Woodland dates from Wisconsin through Michigan and Ontario to New York. I second Mason's

Fig. 78 Rimsherd section from the Goodwin-Gresham site (Courtesy of David S. Brose)

(1967: 337) rejection of these dates as dating the Saugeen occupations of these sites. The majority of the other Lake Forest Middle Woodland dates fall in the first millennium A.D. The Saugeen material should date to this time period too.

Middle Woodland pottery has also been reported from Isle Royale (Bastian 1963a). It was found at the multicomponent Indian Point site and in a number of other areas. The sample from the whole island is small and consists of only 45 vessels, represented by 52 rimsherds and 188 decorated bodysherds. Decoration includes dentate stamping, pseudo-scallop shell stamping, some push-pull technique, incising, linear stamping, and some punctation. Like the later ceramics from the island, an extremely small sample is marked by a large variety of pottery styles.

The last Lake Forest Middle Woodland

site that I shall include here may be just that, the *last* Lake Forest Middle Woodland site. The Goodwin-Gresham site in Iosco County in eastern Michigan is located near the mouth of the Au Sable River in the town of Oscoda. It was excavated in the summer of 1964 by a University of Michigan field party under the supervision of Henry Wright, and several individuals have participated in the preparation of the report (Fitting, Brose, Wright, and Dinerstein 1969). Less than seven hundred square feet were excavated in the shifting sands of the site but a significant sample of cultural material was recovered. The site has been radiocarbon dated to A.D. 610±110 years (M-1625), but this date is from a feature that may be Late Woodland.

The ceramics from the site show some variation in paste and temper. Interior channeling occurs in sixteen out of the twenty-six vessels from the site. A majority of the bodysherds from the site are plain and a smaller number are cord-marked. A minority of the rimsherds are decorated with a cord-wrapped paddle and are similar to the Late Woodland forms which Fitting has called Wayne Cord-marked and Fischer, Saginaw Thin in areas to the south. Single cord impressions and cord-wrapped stick impressions are found but the most common, and most diagnostic, decorative technique seems to be rows of tool or fingernail impressions just below the lip along the rim of the vessel. These sherds are very similar to some North Bay types in Wisconsin. The execution of the decorative techniques on most of the sherds is very poor. While the stamped and tool impressed forms are clearly Middle Woodland, the cord-marked forms suggest a temporal placement in line with the radiocarbon date.

The lithic industry consists of projectile points and biface forms similar to those from more northern Lake Forest Middle Woodland sites. The triangular bifaces are duplicated at a number of the northern Lake Forest Middle Woodland sites and in the Middle Woodland levels of the Schultz site in the Saginaw Valley. There seems to have been a great deal of chipping activity but since the raw material was Bayport chert, the small core techniques used on many of the northern sites were not represented. Standardized scrapers are less frequent at this site than at more northern sites and the most common of unifacial tools are retouched flakes.

The preliminary faunal analysis of the feature contents suggests that some features represent the remains of hunting activities while most contain primarily fish remains. The distribution of lithic materials on the site supports the idea of mixed and isolable economic activities with a very high frequency of the bifaces concentrated in a single excavation unit. A very limited floral sample suggested a Lake Forest cover very similar to that in the area of the site today.

CHAPTER VI

CROPS AND COOPERATION

LATE WOODLAND
CULTURAL DEVELOPMENT

The term Late Woodland has been applied to certain late prehistoric cultural manifestations through default. Griffin's definition is typical: "if Middle Woodland Cultures of the northeast are identified by various forms of cultural behavior associated directly or indirectly with the dominant Hopewellian culture, the Late Woodland complexes are identified both by the disappearance of Hopewell traits and by the gradual development of different cultural forms" (1964: 245). Once we reach our Late Woodland cultures through the loss of Hopewellian characteristics, we further isolate them by not including them in the Mississippian (Griffin 1967) or Temple Mound (Willey 1966) climax of the eastern United States.

Although I cannot offer an alternative definition, I prefer to emphasize the new stylistic traditions and systems of settlement and land use that mark the development of the Late Woodland way of life. I object to terms like "Hopewell deterioration," particularly when it is used to imply a "cultural deterioration" or devolution. While certain distinctive land use patterns may have accompanied Hopewell, most of the so-called diagnostic traits function in the ideological sector of culture. Changes in burial practices and a diminution of energy expenditure on nontechnological items do not represent a dete-

rioration. Hopewell, as a functioning system, did not deteriorate. It was replaced by a system which functioned more efficiently (see Kaplan 1960). The Late Woodland adaptation had to be dominant over the Middle Woodland adaptation or it would never have succeeded in replacing it.

The Late Woodland period in Michigan was dynamic in nature. Hopewellian Middle Woodland sites are few and represent an adaptation that was not particularly efficient in Michigan. In contrast, Late Woodland sites are larger and more numerous than the Hopewell Middle Woodland village sites. The deterioration of material culture represents only small style shifts. The elbow pipes of the Late Woodland period in Michigan are more varied and more common than any pipe forms of the Middle Woodland period. Ceramics have less variation than was typical of the Middle Woodland period but they are more plentiful. It looks like a case of mass production of driving individual artistry underground or of utility replacing aesthetics as the criteria by which ceramics are judged.

Another important factor in the development and fluorescence of Late Woodland cultures was the introduction and efficient utilization of agriculture. Cultigens were present in Michigan as early as 600 B.C. However, from what we can tell from the food refuse and population distribution of the Early and Middle Woodland periods, agriculture played little part in the local economies. In the Late Woodland period, cultigens played an important role in the settlement systems and social organization of the entire area, *even in regions where agriculture was not practiced.*

There is a problem dating the Late Woodland period in Michigan to everyone's satisfaction. Like the Paleo-Indian and Archaic groups, it is possible that some groups were taking up a Late Woodland type of adaptation while others had a Middle Woodland way of life.

There is a noticeable separation of radiocarbon dates in Michigan, although this may not be true in other areas of the Midwest. The latest date for material that I call Middle Woodland in the state is A.D. 490±120 years (M-1756) for the Bussinger site. The earliest dates for Late Woodland materials, excluding the controversial Spoonville dates, are A.D. 610±110 years (M-1625) for the Goodwin-Gresham site, A.D. 650±200 years (M-772) for the Riverside Cemetery, A.D. 680±120 years (M-1759) for the Carrigan Mound A in Newaygo County, and A.D. 700±120 years (M-1519) for the Sissung site in Monroe County. The division between Middle and Late Woodland is the sixth century of our era.

If the Late Woodland adaptation was an agricultural adaptation, or an adaptation based on a nearby agricultural source, we must trace the introduction of this cultural trait in the upper Great Lakes. Yarnell (1964: 118) feels that corn first appeared east of the Mississippi before A.D. 100. Its distribution into the northeast, particularly into Michigan, is somewhat later, for all Michigan corn is Eastern Complex corn which was not developed

until around A.D. 1000 (Yarnell 1964: 107). Some attempts have been made to correlate the spread of agriculture into the attempts, arguing that climatic changes Baerreis and Bryson (1965) refute these attempts, aruging that climatic changes are not slow and gradual but "jump" from one region to another. "By contrast purely cultural events, such as the adoption of a farming economy, must be spread by diffusion from centers (or regions) of innovation" (Baerreis and Bryson 1965). Although the spread and establishment of the Late Woodland adaptive patterns in the area were not directly caused by climatic change, they must be viewed against the background of such change, for the climatic change altered the natural environments in which Late Woodland peoples lived. Such changes, however, were relatively minor and probably affected the *extent* rather than the *nature* of the Late Woodland adaptations. They prove of more interest for the study of Late Woodland culture history than for the study of Late Woodland cultural adaptations.

Griffin's interest in the correlation of climate and cultural development in the Midwest began with the study of Late Woodland culture history in the area (1961: 710). Baerreis and Bryson followed Griffin's lead and developed a refined climatic sequence for the Late Prehistoric period as they did for some of the earlier periods. Griffin (1960, 1961) suggested a mild climate for the period of 300 B.C. to A.D. 300, which Cleland (1966: 28) has called the "Hopewell Episode." Baerreis and Bryson refer to this as the Subatlantic episode. They view the Subatlantic as "more severe," recognizing that this is a term of limited application. More severe may mean only that it was more moist in some parts of the region and that precipitation patterns may have differed. For example some of the most accurate indicators of the extent of the Carolinian, Canadian, and transition regions in Michigan were the spring rainfall peaks, fall rainfall peaks, and bimodal rainfall peaks that mark these respective zones. A shift from spring to fall rainfall peaks would have had a considerable effect on the agricultural potential of an area.

The "Hopewell Episode" was followed by the Scandic period between A.D. 300 or 400 and A.D. 800 or 900. While it suggests an "amelioration of climate in Scandia" again this might have meant only a change in the precipitation regime in an area such as Michigan. Griffin (1961: 713) correlates this time with a generally colder period. In either case, the Scandic episode was different from the period which preceded it and must have placed stress on earlier patterns of cultural adaptation. Perhaps it was both colder and drier with rains concentrated in the months of August and September.

The period from A.D. 800 to A.D. 1300, which Baerreis and Bryson call the Neo-atlantic episode, was extremely favorable for groups with an agricultural adaptation. There was a cool, dry episode in the Midwest between A.D. 1300 and A.D. 1450 which Baerreis and Bryson refer to as the Pacific episode. This was followed by a return to the pattern of the Neo-atlantic episode around A.D. 1450 and another period of cooling between A.D. 1550 and A.D. 1880, the so-called "Little Ice Age." Baerreis and Bryson refer to this as the Neo-boreal episode and suggest that the poor conditions for agriculture in the early contact period would have made the aboriginal inhabitants of the area more amenable to the fur trade than they

otherwise would have been. Since 1880, we have enjoyed an episode of warm and favorable climate in the area.

According to the above sources a wetter, possibly warmer, period, the Sub-atlantic, lasted from approximately 300 B.C. to A.D. 400; it was followed by the possibly drier Scandic episode which lasted until some time around A.D. 900. The Neo-atlantic episode of A.D. 900 to A.D. 1300 favored an agricultural adaptation but was followed around A.D. 1300 by the less favorable Pacific episode. There was a brief return to Neo-atlantic conditions around A.D. 1450 and then a return to Neo-boreal conditions until the nineteenth century.

The Late Woodland Cultural adaptations in Michigan were either agriculturally based or strongly dependent on the presence of agriculturists (G. A. Wright 1967, Fitting and Cleland 1969). The increase in site density and size of the Late Woodland period is striking. The greater number of sites indicates a greater population density. This increased population density resulted from the efficiency of both the agricultural adaptation and the channels through which agricultural products were distributed to non-agricultural areas.

The Late Woodland period in Michigan was marked by the development of a regional symbiosis which allowed a more efficient use of the resources of the entire upper Great Lakes region. This symbiosis was dependent on the diversity of the region and the diversity of extractive patterns in these regions. In the Early Historic Period there were distinctive exploitative patterns in each of the two major biotic regions of Michigan and in the transitional area between them. In the Canadian zone the distinctive pattern associated with the early historic Chippewa can be projected back to the prehistoric period. The patterns characteristic of the historic Miami and Potawatomi have prehistoric precedent in the Carolinian province, while the Ottawa had an adaptive pattern specific to the transitional region.

The Miami pattern was most directly dependent on agriculture. It involved large, permanent villages occupied by the entire group during the summer months. During the winter months the entire group left the village to go out on winter hunts as a unit.

In sharp contrast, the Chippewa pattern involved little dependence on agriculture. It centered on hunting and fishing activities, with large summer villages and small winter hunting camps occupied by extended family units. In either case, entire family units were involved.

The Ottawa occupied the Carolinian-Canadian transition area in agricultural villages which they often relocated. Men left the villages to hunt and trade in the summer and to hunt in the winter. The very name Ottawa refers to their status as traders and, as Gary Wright (1967) has pointed out, it is primarily perishable goods that were exchanged during the Early Historic Period.

It has been argued that the exchange patterns of the seventeenth century were strongly influenced by the incorporation of the upper Great Lakes into the European exchange network. While this is true as far as the direction and emphasis of trade was concerned, these facets of European trade may also have been superimposed on already existing trade channels. If the settlement system of the seventeenth century existed before A.D. 1000, then the trade pattern on which it

was based may also have flourished at that time. At certain times perhistoric population densities were greater than they were during the Early Historic Period. I do not believe the conditions for agriculture in the Upper Great Lakes would have improved that much with relatively minor climatic changes. I suggest that the increased site densities and, presumably, population densities were, as in the Early Historic Period, a response to greater demands from an outside area —in this case an outside area, or areas, where climatic shifts might have had more influence on the extent of agriculture.

I am impressed by the spectacular Mississippian cultural development farther to the south at the same time as the Late Woodland adaptations which I have studied in Michigan. Griffin (1967) correctly refers to this development as the second major climax in eastern United States prehistory. The population size and density of some of these Mississippian occupations is very great. I suspect that in A.D. 1200 several times as many people lived in Cahokia in the American Bottoms around East St. Louis in Illinois as lived in the entire upper and lower peninsulas of Michigan combined. In addition to Cahokia there are many other large and spectacular sites in Illinois, Indiana, and Wisconsin and areas farther to the south.

The peoples of the upper lakes knew of these population centers and were probably influenced by them. These Mississippian sites served as centers of innovation. (I can picture a prehistoric pro-to-Chippewa from Michilimackinac speaking of Cahokia as a "nice place to visit but who would want to live there.") Archaeological evidence indicates a small movement of goods and ideas out of the

Mississippian centers into the upper lakes but does not show much movement in the opposite direction. This may only reflect the greater impact of trade on a less densely populated area than on a more heavily populated one.

Altruism did not motivate the Mississippian cultures. Mississippian influence in the upper lakes was not a one-way proposition; the peoples to the south were getting something in return, probably animal skins. The Europeans very likely entered into a ready-made exchange system.

I suspect a prehistoric trade pattern existed similar to that of the Early Historic Period. Instead of collecting furs for shipment to Paris or London, the prehistoric destinations were Mississippian centers such as Cahokia. In the same way that Early Historic exchanges were indirect, from Chippewa to Ottawa to Huron to French, so the prehistoric pattern was indirect. Items of local production were traded intermediately: furs from the upper peninsula for corn; corn for marine shell gorgets or shell tempered pottery. Such exchanges would continue until the furs reached their ultimate destination. Mississippian sherds occur in the Lake Superior basin, shell tempered ceramics in the Saginaw Valley, Ramey Incised pottery from Cahokia in the Straits of Mackinac, and several Gulf Coast shell gorgets with weeping eye motifs in western Michigan.

This trade pattern contrasts with that of the Middle Woodland period. In Middle Woodland trade more raw materials were exchanged for ceremonial use, apparently in much greater quantities than in later periods. On the other hand, Middle Woodland populated density was no greater than that of the preceding Archaic stage and site density was less. This could have been caused by the contrasting nature of the goods which were exchanged: solid objects of ceremonial significance in the Middle Woodland system in the Early Historic Period, in Late Woodland times. The avenues of exchange, which were traditional and hereditary trade partnerships between different families as in the Early Historic Period, were possibly opened in the Late Archaic or Middle Woodland periods. The late period is marked not by an abandonment of trade, but by a shift from solid ceremonial goods to perishable subsistence goods.

The Middle Woodland adaptation had no agricultural base in Michigan. While Middle Woodland groups to the south may have been agricultural, neither the few Michigan Hopewell village sites nor their Laurel and Laurel-like northern neighbors show evidence of agriculture.

The end of the Sub-atlantic climatic episode, however, may have had a considerable influence on the possibly agriculture-based populations in the Hopewell heartland. Griffin (1960) suggests this caused the Hopewell decline. Struever (1964), however, indicates that Illinois Hopewell had a collecting base rather than an agricultural base. Even if this was an agricultural adaptation, the Scandic episode may have been more favorable for it in some areas. In any event, the declining emphasis on ceremonial goods in the Hopewellian centers to the south would have meant less call for the goods of the outlying area. While Illinois Hopewell may have "deteriorated" to the point where, by A.D. 400, it is barely recognizable, the tradition lasted in outlying areas. Hopewellian mortuary articles were included in single graves in the Saginaw Valley up until the end of the fifth century A.D. The Green Point Wares in Saginaw lasted longer than their counterparts in Illinois. Some Middle Woodland decorative techniques, such as dentate stamping, continued well into the Late Woodland period in Ontario (Kidd 1954, Ridley 1958) and Michigan (Fitting 1965b).

The influence moving into Michigan was no longer ceremonial but economic. This agricultural adaptation may have existed during the later phases of more southern Hopewell sequences, but it entered Michigan at a later time. The single bean from the Goodwin-Gresham site might be an example of this movement.

The Sissung site yields corn at A.D. 700, and the type of settlement associated with agriculturists or people dependent on agriculturists is fully established between A.D. 800 and A.D. 1000. By this time corn is found at many sites and, throughout the entire area, there is a considerable increase in site size and density.

The full appearance of the Late Woodland settlement systems of the lakes also corresponds with the beginning of the Neo-atlantic climatic episode. It was an extremely favorable period for agriculture in Michigan. During the Neo-atlantic episode the northern Mississippian cultural variations had their greatest distribution. The extractive systems that developed in Michigan may have been invigorated by the demand for raw materials in other areas as much as by the favorable conditions for agriculture.

Within a century after the end of the Neo-atlantic episode, there was a settlement and population density decrease in Michigan. While conditions may have forced the abandonment of some areas in the state by agriculturists, they do not account for the population decline in such areas as southeastern Michigan and the Saginaw Valley.

A decline in the demand for goods produced in these areas rather than a climatic decline may have caused the population decrease. Better places for crops could easily have been found to the west, south, and east, and hunting within the boundaries of the state could have been so sporadic as to have left little trace. Even the early historic accounts refer to the lower peninsula, with the exception of the southwestern portions, as a buffer zone between groups, visited by hunting and fishing parties but serving as a homeland for no group.

The brief return to Neo-atlantic conditions around A.D. 1450 effected Michigan. The later phases of the Moccasin Bluff occupation, the Dumaw Creek site, and the earthworks of the northern lower peninsula were occupied then. The Mikado earthwork in the northern part of the Carolinian-Canadian transition area dates to the latter part of the fifteenth century and has produced corn and beans but little evidence of hunting. This earthwork, as well as the Boven and Reider earthworks, may represent a re-occupation of the transition zone by agriculturists.

In the northern areas, the groups with a Chippewa type of adaptation were dependent on large populations to the south. Between A.D. 1300 and 1400 there was a population decline in this area and not until the Early Historic Period, with the introduction of the European fur trade, was there extensive re-occupation.

In contrast to earlier time horizons, there are so many Late Woodland sites in the state that they do not lend themselves to analysis as a unit. Instead I will deal

Fig. 79 *Late Woodland sites in Michigan*

1 ISLE ROYALE
2 KEWEENAW
3 ONTONAGON
4 HOUGHTON
5 BARAGA
6 GOGEBIC
7 IRON
8 MARQUETTE
9 ALGER
10 LUCE
11 DICKINSON
12 DELTA
13 SCHOOLCRAFT
14 MACKINAC
15 CHIPPEWA
16 MENOMINEE
17 EMMET
18 CHEBOYGAN
19 PRESQUE ISLE
20 CHARLEVOIX
21 LEELANAU
22 ANTRIM
23 OTSEGO
24 MONTMORENCY
25 ALPENA
26 BENZIE
27 GRAND TRAVERSE
28 KALKASKA
29 CRAWFORD
30 OSCODA
31 ALCONA
32 MANISTEE
33 WEXFORD

34 MISSAUKEE
35 ROSCOMMON
36 OGEMAW
37 IOSCO
38 MASON
39 LAKE
40 OSCEOLA
41 CLARE
42 GLADWIN
43 ARENAC
44 HURON
45 OCEANA
46 NEWAYGO
47 MECOSTA
48 ISABELLA
49 MIDLAND
50 BAY

51 MUSKEGON
52 MONTCALM
53 GRATIOT
54 SAGINAW
55 TUSCOLA
56 SANILAC
57 OTTAWA
58 KENT
59 IONIA
60 CLINTON
61 SHIAWASSEE
62 GENESEE
63 LAPEER
64 ST. CLAIR
65 ALLEGAN
66 BARRY
67 EATON

68 INGHAM
69 LIVINGSTON
70 OAKLAND
71 MACOMB
72 VAN BUREN
73 KALAMAZOO
74 CALHOUN
75 JACKSON
76 WASHTENAW
77 WAYNE
78 BERRIEN
79 CASS
80 ST. JOSEPH
81 BRANCH
82 HILLSDALE
83 LENAWEE
84 MONROE

with them as they are represented in the several cultural and natural areas that I suggested earlier for the state: southeastern Michigan, southwestern Michigan, the Saginaw Valley, eastern Michigan, western Michigan, the Straits area, northern Lake Michigan, and southern Lake Superior.

SOUTHEASTERN MICHIGAN

Two major Late Woodland traditions have been recognized in this area, the Wayne Tradition and the Younge Tradition (Fitting 1965b, 1966c). These two traditions, based largely on differences in ceramics, overlap in time. The earlier Wayne Tradition may have been a continuation of a local non-Hopewellian Middle Woodland Tradition. It is represented at the Gibraltar site, the Sissung site (with early Younge influence), the Springwells site, and at the Rivière au Vase site as well as several smaller sites in Macomb and nearby counties.

The later Younge Tradition may have resulted from a cultural influence, or an actual movement of people, from southwestern Ontario into southeastern Michigan. There is some suggestion of continuity at Rivière au Vase and the Sissung site, where ceramics of both traditions are found in close proximity, often in the same refuse pits. Within a short time, however, the Younge Tradition became dominant and lasted until some time between A.D. 1300 and 1400. After it vanished, there were no large-scale later occupations until the historic period. Younge Tradition materials are represented at the Rivière au Vase, Springwells, and Wolf sites as well as the type site, the Younge site in Lapeer County. The Furton site is very distinct from these other sites and

may not be a Younge Tradition component.

The Gibraltar site is located in southern Wayne County near the town of Gibraltar at the mouth of the Detroit River. It was discovered in the early 1940s and much uncontrolled excavation took place. It was a rich burial site and many whole ceramic vessels and large caches of artifacts were recovered by collectors. Dr. Emerson F. Greenman attempted a survey of some of the private collections from the site and published a note on them in 1945. He was particularly impressed with some of the pipes which showed a similarity to some from Ohio Hopewell sites.

The ceramics from the site are small- to medium-sized globular vessels which I have described as Wayne Ware (Fitting 1965b: 158–59). All of the vessels have exterior cord-marking on the surface and there are a number of distinctive rim treatments. Rims are smoothed, marked with a cord-wrapped stick or paddle edge over the cord-marking, or incised or cross-hatched. This later variant is found at Springwells but not at Gibraltar.

With the burials at the Gibraltar sites, most of which were single to triple in-flesh interments, were large blades and caches of leaf-shaped cache blades of black chert similar to that called Upper Mercer chert in Ohio. Copper artifacts included beads and a copper awl with a bone handle. The two pipes that impressed Greenman were a simple platform pipe of Hopewellian style and a second platform pipe of an elaborate eagle effigy style. These pipes could indicate a Middle Woodland component at the site or they could indicate that material from earlier eras was included with early Late Woodland burials. In any event, the majority of the cultural material that I have ex-

Fig. 80 Vessel from the Fort Wayne Mound (University of Michigan Museum of Anthropology)

amined from the site falls into the period between A.D. 600 and 900.

One vessel recovered from the site is almost identical to vessels from the Krieger site in Ontario (Kidd 1954). I would use this to tentatively cross-date the sites. Another rimsherd from the general site collection is strongly reminiscent of the Ontario type Lalonde High Collared, a developmental Huron type in Ontario (Ridley 1952). This may be associated with the corn from the site which has been radiocarbon dated to A.D. 1600±200 years (M-288). The actual date for this material may be several centuries earlier because of the unreliability of dates on fast-growing plants like corn (Hall 1967).

The Sissung site on Stony Creek in Monroe County was tested by a University of Michigan field party in 1962 (Fitting 1966c). In one of the pits that was excavated at the site, we found cord-marked rimsherd and an early uncollared sherd

of Vase Dentate. Corn was also found in this feature which was radiocarbon dated to A.D. 700±120 years (M-1519). The date was on wood charcoal rather than corn so it is probably reliable. This is an acceptable date for the earliest overlap of the Wayne and Younge traditions and is the earliest corn date from Michigan. Since only one afternoon was spent on this site, no additional information on other aspects of the economy and settlement of these people is available.

The Springwells mound group was a burial place for the people of the Wayne Tradition. Accounts of the Springwells mound group can be traced back to 1817 and even then there are references to one of the mounds having been opened (Halsey 1968, Pilling 1961a, 1961b). John Blois undertook further excavations in the mound group in 1838. Henry Gillman trenched the single remaining mound on the parade ground of the military post of

Fig. 81 Vessel from the Fort Wayne Mound (University of Michigan Museum of Anthropology)

Fort Wayne in 1876 and left a fairly detailed account of his work. Gillman was assisted by Bela Hubbard, who also left an account of the work at Springwells as well as information on the Great Mound at the mouth of the Rouge River and the Carsten Mound, which had been excavated opposite Fort Wayne at Springwells in 1870.

In July 1944 Carl Holmquist, with the assistance of other members of the Aboriginal Research Club of Detroit, undertook excavation of the mound that Gillman had worked in the previous century (Holmquist 1946). Gillman's trenches were relocated and twenty-four additional burials associated with the mound were uncovered. There also were a number of intrusive pits containing material from later occupations.

Grave goods include Wayne Ware vessels of a number of variants, columella

beads, anculosa shell beads, sandstone abraders, Jack's Reef corner-notched points, cache blades, chipped slate disks, and other objects. A birdstone was found in the mound but may not have been associated with a burial. Halsey believes that this birdstone was related to the premound Early Woodland occupation of the site represented by interior-exterior cordmarked sherds in the fill. Halsey also noted that grave goods were only associated with females (Halsey 1968).

A number of other chipped and ground stone objects were found in the fill and in the pits. Out of the ninety-nine distinct vessels from the mound, thirty-one were Wayne Ware. A sample of human bone from Burial 14, which was associated with a Wayne Ware vessel with a crosshatched rim, has been radiocarbon dated to A.D. 750±120 years (M-1843).

A number of burials from the Rivière au

Fig. 82 Vessel from the Fort Wayne Mound (University of Michigan Museum of Anthropology)

Fig. 83 Wayne Ware vessel from the Rivière au Vase site (From Fitting: 1965b)

Vase site in the eastern part of Macomb County have also been associated with the Wayne Tradition and can be related to this general time period (Greenman 1945, DeVisscher 1957 cited in Fitting 1965b: 91–93). These also contained cache blades, Jack's Reef corner-notched points, slate gorgets, celts, copper beads, and a copper awl.

At a number of pits at Rivière au Vase, Wayne Wares and the later Rivière Wares of the Younge Tradition are found together. This could be accidental since the site is very disturbed. It could also represent the use of the site by groups with distinctive ceramic traditions or by one group in the process of adopting new ceramic traditions at some time around A.D. 1000.

In the past, I have noted a similarity of the form of Wayne Ware vessels to those from the Krieger site near Chatham, On-

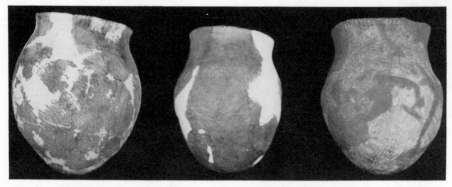

Fig. 84 Wayne Ware vessels from the Rivière au Vase site (From Fitting: 1965b)

tario (Kidd 1954). The decorative techniques and motifs on Krieger ceramics,
however, are more similar to late Rivière
Wares. These include dentate stamping,
oblique cord-wrapped stick and simple
tool impressions as well as zoned triangular
incising, and sometimes a zoned stamped
area below the rim on the shoulders of the
vessels.

In the 1950s the term Glen Meyer came
into use in Ontario to describe a Late
Woodland ceramic tradition and Lee
(1958a) includes the Krieger site in this
tradition. J. V. Wright (1966) made an
elaborate and detailed study of the development of Ontario ceramics and draws
a more rigid definition of Glen Meyer
which excludes the Krieger site.

Glen Meyer, along with Pickering, is an
early substage of the Ontario Iroquois
tradition which terminated before A.D.
1300. Wright speaks of the absorption of
the Glen Meyer branch by the Pickering
branch at that time. During the same
period, roughly A.D. 1000 to 1300, when
Pickering ceramics replaced Glen Meyer
ceramics in southwestern Ontario, Glen
Meyer-like motifs and vessel forms were
dominant in southeastern Michigan with
the Rivière Wares of the Younge Tradition.

While it cannot be demonstrated that
movements of ceramics represented movements of people, many archaeologists assume a correlation. I find it easy to accept
the Younge Tradition as being stimulated
by either strong influence from Glen
Meyer or by the actual movement of

*Fig. 85 Rivière Ware vessel from Rivière au Vase
(From Fitting: 1965b)*

Glen Meyer peoples into the area. This could account for the ceramics of both Wayne and Younge traditions in the same pits at the Rivière au Vase site. The people of the Wayne Tradition were either absorbed into the numerically greater Younge groups or moved to the north to join peoples with the same cultural tradition in the Saginaw Valley where the Younge Tradition exerted less influence. Some of the radiocarbon dates from the Saginaw Valley seem to indicate that Younge-influenced Wayne Tradition peoples survived until the twelfth century.

The largest of the Younge Tradition sites is the Rivière au Vase site (Greenman 1957, Fitting 1965b). During 1936 and 1937, approximately 10,200 square feet of the site were excavated. In this area there were 145 burial groupings representing at least 350 individuals. There were also 144 refuse pits. In spite of the intensive burial activity, the occupational density was very low. Only 407 rimsherds representing 371 vessels were found giving a density of only .035 ceramic vessels per square foot of excavated area, about one tenth of the density of such Late Woodland sites as Juntunen and Spring Creek.

The site produced ceramics, called Rivière Wares, characteristic of most of the Younge Tradition phases which indicates some time span for its use. These globular to elongated vessels exhibited a number of modes of surface treatment, including cord-marking, roughening, fabric impressing, simple stamping and smoothing. Smoothed shoulders with incised triangular designs were common as were collared rims with a tendency for the exterior rim design to be repeated on the lip and on the interior of the rim of the vessel.

The Younge Tradition differs from the Wayne Tradition in several aspects besides

Fig. 86 Triangular projectile points from Rivière au Vase (From Fitting: 1965b)

ceramics. Triangular projectile points replace corner-notched projectile points and elbow pipes become very common. Rivière au Vase is a major burial complex and many burials are of group or ossuary type. These burials are also marked by skull disk removal, perforation of skulls, femurs thrust into the pelvis, and the packing of clay into the faces of skulls. Most of the burials are re-articulated and much of the burial practice forshadows the feast of the dead ceremonies among historic Indian groups.

The earliest Younge Tradition phase dates to the later part of the first millennium A.D. and is marked by the transition from Wayne to Younge Tradition ceramics. A number of vessels include attributes of both wares. The Sissung site ceramics are transitional in some respects as are some vessels from Rivière au Vase. For example, uncollared Vase Dentate vessels are found with Wayne Wares while the collared variants occur later.

155

The first Younge Tradition phase marked exclusively by Rivière Wares was the Younge Phase itself. While this is represented at Rivière au Vase, it exists in an unmixed form at the Younge site (Greenman 1937b). This site, in Lapeer County, is in the extreme north of our southeastern Michigan sub-area. Located on Mill Creek, a branch of the Black River, it is less than a mile from Cedar Creek, a tributary of the Flint River in the Saginaw Valley.

The site was excavated under Dr. Greenman's direction in 1935. The excavations at this site were extensive and the most prominent features were post molds representing three longhouse patterns. One of these is 585 feet long by 30 feet wide; a second, 252 feet long by 30 feet wide; and the third, 40 feet long by 25 feet wide. Ash pits and fire hearths were found along the median line of these structures. Sixty-one pits were examined in Enclosure ⁄1 and twenty-seven were found in Enclosure ⁄2. These contained burnt and unburnt animal bone, primarily of smaller species, some mussel shell, corn, and some additional food plant remains.

A primary reason for excavating this site was to uncover burials, particularly of individuals with perforated crania. The 1935 excavations were undertaken because Dr. W. B. Hinsdale had found perforated crania at the site in 1934 (reported in Hinsdale and Greenman 1936). Remains of at least 102 individuals were recorded. Twenty-four of these were extended burials including four secondary burials with the femurs thrust into the pelvis. Four individuals were flexed and there were thirty-one bundle burials. Seven burials were represented by headless torsos, four by skulls and nineteen by other bone fragments. One cremation was reported.

As at Rivière au Vase, a number of individuals had perforated skulls, several had skull disks removed, and six had clay in their facial or nasal cavities.

Artifacts were rare at the site. Greenman reported fifteen hundred body sherds and only forty-eight rimsherds. In 1963, I studied the collection identifying only thirty-one distinct vessels among these sherds. The types include, in decreasing order of frequency, Vase Corded, Macomb Linear, Vase Dentate, and Vase Tool Impressed (Fitting 1965b: 138). In striking contrast to the sparsity of pottery, there were two complete elbow pipes and fragments of forty-seven other pipes. Only one scraper and eight projectile points were reported from the excavated areas of this site. Six of these points were triangular and two were notched.

The Younge site is a perplexing site. The dearth of artifacts and quantity of burials suggests a specific burial area. Yet the longhouse patterns and refuse pits indicate an economic purpose for the site. On most Michigan sites, deer accounts for seventy to ninety percent of the bone refuse, yet this food source does not appear to be well represented in the bone refuse and is not mentioned in Greenman's report. The fact that ceramic vessels outnumber flint artifacts by nearly three to one might indicate a primarily female occupation but pipes, usually associated with male manufacture and use, are twice as frequent as ceramic vessels.

The Younge site itself has not been radiocarbon dated but another Younge Phase site in southeastern Michigan, the Verchave II site, excavated in 1962 by a University of Michigan field party (Fitting 1965b), has been radiocarbon dated to A.D. 1095±100 years (M-1431). This date has been placed in sequence with other

Younge Tradition dates to indicate a range of A.D. 900 to 1100 for the Younge Phase (Fitting 1966c).

Bone refuse from Verchave II, as from the Younge site, consists of small mammals and quantities of fish. Plant remains from features on the site consists of quantities of hickory nuts with smaller amounts of walnut, hazelnut, acorn, hawthorn, and grape. Corn occurs in one of the features. Since excavation at this site was limited to 150 square feet, no evidence for prehistoric living structures, other than a few pieces of charred daub, were found. Excavation of the prehistoric material, however, was complicated by a dense level of historic material overlying the scattered prehistoric remains.

Cultural material from Verchave II, as well as Verchave I, III, and IV, is sparse. Ceramics are primarily Rivière Wares and there is one instance where a later Wolf Phase pit penetrated into a Younge Phase feature. Projectile points are predominantly triangular, tobacco pipes are not as common as at the Younge site, and scrapers and other small chipped stone tools are very rare, another characteristic similar to the Younge site.

The third phase of the Younge Tradition is the Springwells Phase. It has been most fully studied from the contents of a number of intrusive pits from the Fort Wayne Mound excavations (Fitting 1965b, Halsey 1968) but is also known from several other still unreported sites, including the Butler site in southern Wayne County and the Turkey Creek Ossuary across the Detroit River in Essex County, Ontario. It has been radiocarbon dated to A.D. 1150±75 years (M-741) at Springwells and I have suggested a time range of A.D. 1100 to 1250 for this phase (Fitting 1966c).

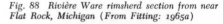

Fig. 87 Rivière Ware from the intrusive pits at the Fort Wayne Mound (From Fitting: 1965b)

Fig. 88 Rivière Ware rimsherd section from near Flat Rock, Michigan (From Fitting: 1965a)

Fig. 89 Younge Tradition pipe fragments (University of Michigan Museum of Anthropology)

Fitting's and Halsey's vessel counts and identifications for this site differ somewhat because of the large number of vessels which Halsey does not assign to any category. Vase Corded and Macomb Linear are important pottery types but Springwells Net Impressed is the marker type for this phase. Halsey notes the rare occurrence of projectile points in the mound and their complete absence from the later refuse pits. Other stone tools are also rare in these pits but several bone objects were found.

Halsey's analysis of faunal remains indicates that deer accounted for nearly eighty-one percent of the animal bone. Fish bones are next in frequency with small mammal and molluscs accounting for the remainder of the material. Un-

fortunately, no vegetable material was recovered.

The final phase of the Younge Tradition has been named the Wolf Phase after the Wolf site in eastern Macomb County. This site excavated by Dr. Emerson Greenman in 1936 (Greenman 1939), is located near the shore of Lake St. Clair. Several weeks of excavation uncovered four burials and twenty-five refuse pits. Deer bones were common but there were also large quantities of small mammal, fish, and, I suspect, birds and turtles. Corn was also recovered from one of the refuse pits.

Artifacts other than ceramics were rare. Only two chipped stone tools and one ground piece of sandstone were found. I was able to distinguish fifty-two distinct vessels among the ceramics. The most common pottery type was Parker Festooned, an elaborately decorated pottery type named for its occurrence at the Parker Earthwork across the St. Clair River near Corunna, Ontario (Lee 1958b). This type accounted for forty-two percent of the ceramics but lesser amounts of Macomb Linear, Springwells Net Impressed, Vase Corded, and Vase Tool Impressed ceramics were also found.

The temporal placement and cultural affiliations of the Wolf site are not fully understood. On the basis of a single shell tempered sherd and the Parker Festooned vessels, Greenman (1939) placed this site in the Mississippian Pattern. I think that this was because Parker Festooned sherds had been found at some northern Ohio sites which he had identified as Erie, an Iroquoian-speaking group (Greenman 1935a, 1935b, 1937a). Some of the earlier applications of the Midwest Taxonomic

System placed all Iroquoian materials in the Mississippian Pattern. Since then, the basic Woodland nature of the Iroquois cultural sequence has been reaffirmed. Furthermore, at the northern Ohio sites where Parker Festooned pottery does occur, it is extremely rare and can be considered an introduced foreign type (Fitting 1964b).

The Wolf site has not been radiocarbon dated but the Verchave I site (Fitting 1965b) has a ceramic assemblage that includes a considerable percentage of Parker Festooned vessels and a feature from this site has been radiocarbon dated to A.D. 1320±100 years (M-1520). I suggest a time range of between A.D. 1250 and 1450 for the Wolf Phase.

The Furton site in eastern Macomb County was also excavated by Greenman in the summer of 1936. This site is located directly on the shore of Lake St. Clair

Fig. 90   Parker festooned rimsherd section from the Wolf site (University of Michigan Museum of Anthropology)

and parts of the site had eroded out into the lake. Greenman has noted that the contents of the eight excavated refuse pits consisted primarily of large quantities of fish bone. A number of notched, stemmed, and triangular points were found and there seems to have been a fairly large quantity of chippage for a site in this area. Greenman was impressed by the very large number of raw materials which were not common to Michigan among the chipped stone assemblage.

The ceramics too are quite different from the typical Younge Tradition materials, a point made by Greenman in the 1930s. Many are uncollared but castellations are common. The most frequent decorations are massed and banked impressions of the tip of a cord-wrapped stick. The only site with which I am familiar which seems to be similar to the Furton site is the Fuller I site (Fitting 1965b) along the Salt River only a short distance away from the Furton site.

I suspect that these are both transient fishing stations. I cannot estimate the age of this material. The intensive Younge Tradition occupation for this area lasted through the fourteenth century and I would not expect an alien occupation until after that time. These sites might represent the remains of a more northern group fishing in the area after A.D. 1400 and before the European contact period.

Though much excavation has been carried out in southeastern Michigan we still cannot say too much about the cultural adaptation in this area. There are indications that corn was being grown by A.D. 700 but wild food plants continued to be used after that. Several of the sites, particularly Springwells, have produced some deer remains but deer are not as common as at Late Woodland sites in some other

parts of the state. Fish, water birds, small mammals, and turtles were common food sources. Molluscs are present at all of the Younge Tradition sites. This suggests a heavy dependence on aquatic resources but this is the part of the state where the river drainages have the least surface water cover. This is further complicated by such sites as the Younge site, which is located in an area which would have been excellent for hunting yet poor for fishing.

Village site debris, other than ceramics, are rare. This would indicate a low population density if it were not for the extremely high density of burials. At several sites there were more people than pots. Very likely the people had base villages somewhere else. From the ceramic styles I suspect these were somewhere to the east. Southeastern Michigan seems to have been a place where people went to die or were taken to be buried rather than a place where they lived. The emphasis on aquatic resources is reminiscent of the summer season burial occupation of the Archaic Feeheley site in Saginaw. The intensive use of this area, probably as a summer collecting and burial area, terminated long before the contact period. The time of most intensive use corresponded with the Neo-atlantic climatic episode and occupation diminished during the Pacific and later episodes.

SOUTHWESTERN MICHIGAN

The Spoonville village site along the Grand River in Ottawa County is perhaps the earliest reported Late Woodland site in this region (Flanders 1965a). The problems of dating this site including possible multiple occupations were mentioned in the preceding chapter. In spite of the radiocarbon dates, I think that most of the material is on a level with the sites of the Wayne Tradition and can be dated to the early part of the Late Woodland period. Cleland (1966: 66) found that the faunal remains at this site followed a pattern similar to Late Woodland sites with agricultural adaptations.

Excavations were undertaken at the Root site in Ingham County along the Grand River in 1958 by a field party from Michigan State University working under the direction of Dr. Moreau Maxwell. Further work was undertaken at the site by Leonard Griffin in 1961. Griffin (1962) prepared a report on his work that indicates a cultural assemblage similar to those reported from Wayne Tradition sites in southeastern Michigan and the Spoonville site farther down the Grand River.

Griffin's excavations revealed a circular post mold pattern that seems to represent a lodge about thirteen feet in diameter. Parts of what appears to be a stockade were also uncovered. Almost all of the bone material from the site was deer. Along with the general low density of cultural material and high ratio of chipped stone artifacts to ceramic vessels, this suggests that the site was used for hunting during the late fall or winter.

Another site with a low density of cultural material was the Whorely Earthwork (Speth 1966) located in Branch County in the upper reaches of the St. Joseph River drainage. This was a horseshoe-shaped earthwork enclosing 45,300 square feet and was on a low bluff overlooking Gilead Lake. Five rimsherds and 103 bodysherds, four triangular points and a minimal amount of chippage were all that was recovered from three weeks of excavation. Three of the five rims were collared and

Fig. 91 Rimsherds from the Moccasin Bluff site (University of Michigan Museum of Anthropology)

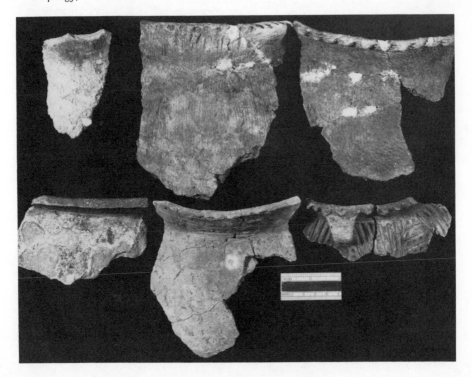

decorated by cord-marking, cord-wrapped stick impressions, and incising. The ceramics and lithic material were quite consistent with the radiocarbon date of A.D. 1080±100 years (M-1758).

The earthwork was topped with a palisade. Speth has noted that the density of ceramics from his limited excavations increased from the center to the outside of the stockaded area. This could mean either cleaning of the stockade and dumping of debris elsewhere, a trait noted for the historic Miami, or that the entire palisade was a ceremonial structure, a position which Speth seems to favor.

The most extensively excavated site in southwestern Michigan is the Moccasin Bluff site in Berrien County, which was excavated by the University of Michigan in 1948 under the supervision of Hale Smith. Approximately 4100 square feet were opened and ninety-six fire and refuse pits were uncovered.

The archaeological material from this site is being studied by Robert Bettarel, who has furnished information on the types of ceramics and their correlation with the radiocarbon dates. There were 530 rimsherds representing 429 vessels. This means an occupational intensity of about .105 ceramic vessels per square foot, only one third the density of the Spring Creek site. A small percentage of the vessels, about one percent, are Middle Woodland types.

The main Late Woodland occupation of the site began around A.D. 1000. This is marked by notched rims on cord-marked vessels and corded collared rims, which Bettarel feels are similar to those from the Spring Creek site. He believes that some of the shell tempered ceramics, those similar to Fischer Focus materials from Illinois, date to this time period. Two

radiocarbon dates of A.D. 1060±110 years (M-1937) and (M-1941) and one of A.D. 1090±110 years (M-1938) are related to this occupation.

There is a continuation of this type of ceramic material with the addition of vessels with higher collars and castellations similar to the Rivière Wares from southeastern Michigan. Radiocarbon dates of A.D. 1150±110 years (M-1940) and A.D. 1210±110 years (M-1939) attest to this occupation.

The final occupation of the site is marked by grit and shell tempered Oneota ceramics, vessels with globular shapes and outflaring rims, as well as shell and grit tempered vessels with notched appliqué strips added to the exterior surface near the rim. Bettarel relates the two dates of A.D. 1640±100 years (M-1935) and A.D. 1590±100 years (M-1936) to this occupation.

Although the analysis of lithic material is not yet complete, I thought at the time of sorting that the chipped stone artifacts other than points were not common and that chippage, in general, was rare. As expected, small triangular projectile points were the most common lithic material.

Corn was recovered from the site as well as the remains of walnut, plum, and acorn (Yarnell 1964). Cleland (1966: 211–23) notes a high occurrence of a few species of animals. Deer, elk, and beaver are most common as in most apparently agricultural villages. The Moccasin Bluff site represents the permanent agricultural village of a group with an adaptive pattern similar to that of the Miami and Potawatomi, the same groups that inhabited the area in the historic period. Quimby (1952) suggests that this site in its final stage represents an occupation by these groups.

THE SAGINAW VALLEY

The Schultz site at Green Point is the largest excavated Late Woodland site in the Saginaw Valley. Over five thousand square feet were excavated at this site by University of Michigan field parties between 1962 and 1965. Overlying the extensive Early and Middle Woodland occupations were scattered deposits of Late Woodland material which furnished us with a picture of the Late Woodland adaptation.

Speth, in his geological investigations of the site, notes an increase in flooding at the end of Middle Woodland times with a decrease in flooding and possible re-occupation of the site some time around A.D. 800. Brose suggests that the molluscs from the occupation indicate that water was seasonally ponded on parts of the site and that the climate may have been warmer than at present.

The Late Woodland occupation was not as intensive as the Middle Woodland occupation. Fisher found only eighty-six of the 816 vessels from the site were positive Late Woodland types. The most common of these is a type similar to Wayne Cord-marked, which he has called Saginaw Thin. This type is represented by thirty-four vessels. It is followed by thirty-two plain vessels with cord-wrapped stick decorations, seventeen vessels which were cord-marked and had cord-wrapped stick impressions on the lip, and three fabric-impressed vessels. One of the features at this site, which contained a castellated vessel with cord-marked surface treatment and a collared vessel with linear cord impressions along the rim, has been radiocarbon dated to A.D. 1180±100 years (M-1648).

Over 8600 flint chips and 92 cores and finished artifacts were found in the Late Woodland levels of the site. The most common projectile point forms from this level are small (thirty-nine) and large (twenty-six) expanding stemmed types. Small triangular and narrow expanding stemmed points each account for nine percent of the *in situ* Late Woodland projectile points. The vast majority of the small triangular projectile points from this site come from the plow zone. This, taken with other evidence such as the truncation of late features, indicates that much of the upper levels of the site has been destroyed by plowing and soil removal.

There was a decrease in industrial activity at the site in the Late Woodland period which is reflected in a much lower flake to artifact ratio than is typical of Middle Woodland levels. Cores are rare and most are small cores, which may have served as tools. The ratio of bifaces to unifaces is high, reflecting more hunting activity. There are many point tip fragments right on the site, which may indicate that hunting was done at Green Point itself.

Murray's study of bone tools from the site indicates both an absolute and a relative decrease in frequencies for these objects. Among the thirty-three bone and shell objects in the Late Woodland level, fifteen are turtle shell dishes and seven are beaver-tooth chisels. There are several shell beads, several bone projectile points, and a few other objects of bone and shell.

Brose found that molluscs declined in frequency as a food source in the Late Woodland levels and Allison noted a general decline in nut species. The single corn kernel from our excavations was found in a disturbed area; if it was related to an aboriginal occupation it would probably have been the directly underlying Late

Woodland level in the part of the site where it was found. Dustin (1968) reported quantities of corn from this site which Yarnell (1964: 117) has identified as Eastern Complex corn (which he feels is very late). Since Dustin's corn was found almost three quarters of a mile to the east of the main area of our excavations, it may be related to a component which we did not sample. Early nineteenth-century historic materials, which might represent the location of the farm of Judge Albert Miller, are located in the part of the site near where the corn was found.

Cleland's examination of the animal bone (1966: 117–44) indicates that big game hunting, with particular emphasis on deer, elk, and bear, was the most important activity of these people. There was a decrease in the utilization of small game and fish although their very presence indicates some spring and fall occupation.

I find it impossible to interpret the

Late Woodland occupation at the Schultz site as representative of a large Late Woodland village site as Cleland has suggested (1966: 144). Instead, I see a very low density occupation; there are less than .017 ceramic vessels per square foot of excavated area. Even this represents a time span of several hundred years. The lithic materials as well as the faunal and floral remains suggest that this was primarily a hunting camp occupied by a group which was based in an agricultural village located elsewhere.

The Kantzler site (Crumley 1967) farther down the Saginaw River in Bay City shows the same type of Late Woodland adaptation. Although the site was mixed, it is possible to separate out a ceramic series similar to the Late Woodland materials from the Schultz site. The same is true for the lithic assemblage, although the tool counts cannot be compared to those from the Schultz site.

The upper, presumably Late Woodland,

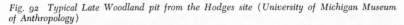

Fig. 92 Typical Late Woodland pit from the Hodges site (University of Michigan Museum of Anthropology)

levels on this site contained four times as much mammal bone as the Middle Woodland levels. Deer and beaver constituted the majority of identified animal species. Like the Schultz site, this served as a hunting camp in Late Woodland times.

Four other Late Woodland village sites have been tested in the Saginaw Valley by University of Michigan field parties in the last decade. The Hodges site (Fitting and Sassé 1969) was excavated in 1960 under the direction of Dr. William B. Roosa and in 1961 under the direction of Dr. Richard O. Keslin. This proved to

be another extensive Late Woodland site with few features, usually circular, straight-sided, flat-bottomed, and nearly empty pits. Chipped stone artifacts indicate a hunting complex and chipped stone tools far outnumber ceramic vessels from the site.

In the summer of 1965 John R. Halsey and David S. Brose supervised several weeks of excavation at the Mahoney site south of Saginaw along the Shiawassee River (Bigony n.d.). An area of 675 square feet was excavated and fourteen features were found. One of these was

Fig. 93 *Portions of a Late Woodland vessel from the Hodges site (University of Michigan Museum of Anthropology)*

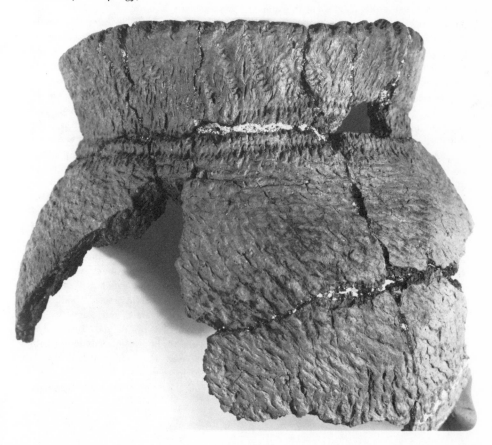

historic, one a living floor, and eight were circular, straight-sided, flat-bottomed storage pits similar to those found on the Hodges site.

The small ceramic sample consists of 456 bodysherds and 40 rimsherds representing only twenty-six vessels. The density of ceramic vessels per square foot of excavated area was .038. Even these few vessels represent a long time span. Chipped stone tools outnumber ceramic vessels four to one.

The Stadelmeyer site, located several miles up the Tittabawassee River from the Schultz site and just across the road from the Andrews site, was excavated by a University of Michigan field party under the supervision of Bea Bigony in the summer of 1967 (Bigony n.d.). Most of the thirty-seven features in the 1350 square feet of excavated area of the site were large, circular, straight-sided storage pits with very little cultural material.

The ceramic sample from the site consists of 1075 bodysherds and 63 rimsherds representing fifty vessels. The ceramics fall into two groups, one representing an immediate pre-A.D. 1000 occupation and the second group representing the period of A.D. 1200 to A.D. 1400. The index of occupational intensity, represented by ceramic vessels per square foot, is only .037 for several periods of occupation. Seven fragments of Late Woodland pipes were also recovered from the site. Lithic materials are slightly more numerous than ceramics but not to the extent that precludes a generally balanced sexual composition for the groups which occupied the site.

Quantities of fish bone were found in the lower levels of the site which might relate to a pre-ceramic occupation like that represented at the Andrews site across the road. The upper levels, where the ceramics were recovered, contained a greater percentage of deer bone. This was a large site which amateur archaeologists had been excavating for several years before the University of Michigan field crews got there in 1967. I suspect it represents a winter hunting camp of a group with a Miami type cultural adaptation.

Bea Bigony also spent several days in limited testing at the Foster site along the Flint River in Saginaw County during the summer of 1967 (Bigony n.d.). Only about 350 square feet of the site area, including seven features, was excavated. These included the same type of storage pits found at Hodges, Mahoney, and Stadelmeyer.

The artifact sample is extremely small. Only 228 bodysherds and 16 rimsherds representing twelve vessels were recovered. The index of occupational intensity, based on vessels per square foot, is .034 and compares with that of the other Late Woodland sites in the area. This site was similar to the Hodges site in that chipped stone tools outnumbered ceramics.

During the late summer of 1964, members of the Saginaw Valley chapter of the Michigan Archaeological Society undertook salvage excavations at the Valley Sweets site in the 900 block of North Hamilton Street in the city of Saginaw (Brose 1966b). A group of prehistoric materials falls into the early Late Woodland time range, about A.D. 600 to 1000. Brose notes a similarity of some vessels with fabric-impressed bodies to Wayne Ware vessels and suggests the type designation of Wayne Textile Impressed. Fabric impression was found with some frequency at a number of Late Woodland sites in the area.

Most of the burials from the Bussinger

Fig. 94 Late Woodland vessel from the Bussinger site (University of Michigan Museum of Anthropology)

Fig. 95 Late Woodland vessel from the Bussinger site (University of Michigan Museum of Anthropology)

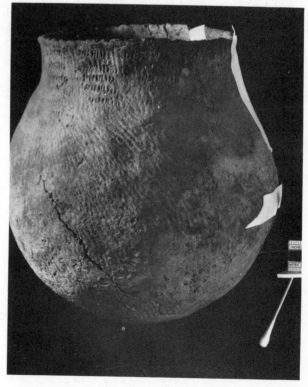

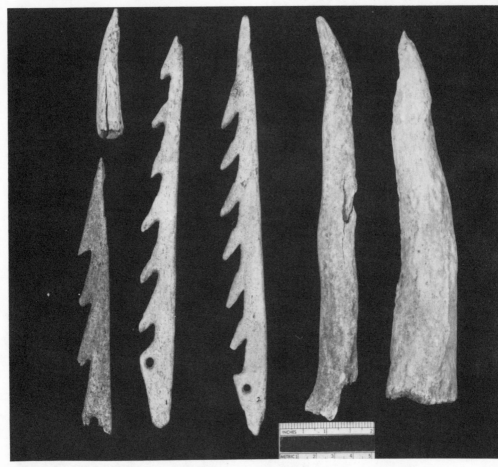

Fig. 96 *Bone harpoons and other bone artifacts from the Bussinger site (University of Michigan Museum of Anthropology)*

site along Swan Creek, a tributary of the Shiawassee River located just to the southwest of the city of Saginaw (Halsey 1967), are Late Woodland. While a University of Michigan field party worked at this site for several weeks under John Halsey in 1965, most of the burials have been excavated by Arthur Graves and several other members of the Saginaw Valley Chapter of the Michigan Archaeological Society. Over 38,000 square feet were excavated and, by summer of 1967, 120

burials were removed. Graves has continued his efforts at this site and has recovered several additional burials and associated cultural materials.

Several of the burials are Middle Woodland; most are Late Woodland burials with cultural materials similar to those from Gibraltar, Fort Wayne, and the Rivière au Vase sites in southeastern Michigan. The range of ceramics, copper objects, gorgets, celts, cache blades, corner-notched points, and bone harpoons are similar to materials from these sites or other sites of the same period in the Midwest.

Halsey believes the cultural materials from this site can be related on a broader level to materials from the Kipp Island Phase in New York (Ritchie 1965: 232–52) and what has been called the "Intrusive Mound" culture in Ohio.

This site offers an interesting dating problem. While similar cultural materials tend to date between A.D. 600 and 1000 elsewhere, two separate burials from the Bussinger site have been dated to A.D. 1220±100 years (M-1796) and A.D. 1290 ±100 years (M-1755). Both produced simple cord-marked globular ceramics which both Halsey and I would class as Wayne Ware, although one vessel has a somewhat less constricted neck than is usual for this ceramic style.

This part of the Saginaw Valley may have been affected to a lesser extent by eastern influences than those areas of southeastern Michigan or the Straits of Mackinac. While these outside influences were strong in some areas by A.D. 1000, local traditions may have persisted for several centuries in other areas. The Bussinger dates are not much later than those of the West Twin Lake Mound, the Spring Creek site, the earliest of the Late Woodland occupations at Moccasin Bluff, and, more important, the Late Woodland occupation of the Schultz site. They fall within the general range of the ,Neo-atlantic climate episode and, in lieu of contradictory dates for this area, should not be dismissed.

Many sites in the Saginaw Valley have produced ceramics (Dustin 1968). The University of Michigan has worked on other sites where at least a small quantity of ceramic material has been recovered. These include the Schmidt site (Harrison 1966), and the Andrews and the Stroebel sites (Papworth 1967). All of these sites impress me as being very similar to the Late Woodland sites where more detailed excavation and analysis have taken place.

In spite of nearly a decade of excavation at the most productive ceramic sites known to us from the Saginaw Valley, we have not found a permanent agricultural village site. I believe that there were no permanent agricultural villages in the valley, even during the favorable Neo-atlantic climatic episode. I interpret the sites that we have excavated as being hunting camps which were occupied seasonally by groups with both the Ottawa and Miami seasonal patterns. Such sites as Schultz, Stadelmeyer, and Mahoney represent sites of the Miami winter type while the Hodges and Foster sites were camps of people with an Ottawa adaptation. Following A.D. 1400, the valley seems to have been almost empty up until the Chippewa settled in the area in the early eighteenth century after the establishment of the French post in Detriot.

EASTERN MICHIGAN

While eastern Michigan was never intensively occupied during the prehistoric period (see G. A. Wright 1966 for a survey of this area) a number of sites have been excavated and reported that give us some very good information on this area. In 1927 and 1928 Dr. W. B. Hinsdale excavated a group of mounds near West Twin Lake in Montmorency County (Hinsdale 1929, 1930). Most of the mounds in this group contained no grave goods with the burials, a situation similar to that found by Halsey and Janzen in their excavations of the Birch Creek

Fig. 97 *Late Woodland cache blades and points from a burial at the Bussinger site (University of Michigan Museum of Anthropology)*

mound in the northern part of Arenac County in the summer of 1966.

One mound at West Twin Lake did produce grave goods, which include a globular, cord-marked Wayne Ware vessel, a ceramic elbow pipe with no decoration, several bone harpoons, both side-notched, and triangular cache blades and two antler fragments with hafted beaver incisors. A burial from this mound was radiocarbon dated to A.D. 950±100 years (M-1804), a date consistent with the cultural material from the site.

The Butterfield Village site on the Pinconning River in the northern part of Bay County (Wobst 1968) dates to the same time period as the West Twin Lake mound. Although only 450 square feet were excavated at this rich site, nine features could be attributed to the Late Woodland occupation. Over five thousand flint chips, fifty-two chipped stone artifacts, and one core were found in this stratigraphically isolated level. Twenty-one side-scrapers, twelve end-scrapers, and eleven projectile points account for the majority of the artifacts. Small triangular and large corner-notched projectile points are the most common forms.

The Late Woodland ceramic sample from the site consists of 6501 bodysherds and 77 rimsherds. Forty-six percent of the bodysherds are fabric impressed, twenty-three percent are cord-marked, twenty-two percent are plain and eight percent are marked with cord-wrapped stick impressions. Out of the seventy-seven rimsherds only fifty-eight can be used for vessel identification and these represent only twenty-four vessels. Most of these are "nondescript" and Wobst could type only fifteen of them. Out of this number eight are Wayne Cord-marked and seven are Mackinac Wares. In other words, the ceramic sample from the site, quite homogeneous in terms of manufacturing method and paste, contains both typically northern and typically southern ceramics forms in about equal numbers.

The ratio of ceramic vessels to chipped stone and cores is .45 which, while far from one to one, suggests a balanced sex ratio for the site (Fitting and Cleland 1969). Wobst notes that the Late Wood-land tool assemblage, in contrast to that of the Archaic occupation on the site, is characterized by a high percentage of scraping tools, by small thin knives and

perforators and a low percentage of pro-jectile points. Tools were made on the spot from preselected flakes and cores were rare. Wobst interprets this occupa-tion as a short-term hunting camp where butchering and meat preparation took place. The occupational intensity of the site was fairly high with .58 rimsherds per square foot of excavation or a ratio of .188 ceramic vessels to each square foot of excavated area.

As Wobst suggests, the site was prob-ably a winter hunting camp. Since it was probably a camp of balanced sexual com-position, it would fit either the Chippewa or Miami adaptive patterns. We could draw some conclusions about this if we knew the extent of the occupation, since a large homogeneous camp would fit the Miami pattern while a small camp would fit the Chippewa pattern. Unfortunately, this in-formation is not available and the balanced northern-southern distribution of ceramics makes it even more difficult to speculate.

One of the more mysterious archaeo-logical manifestations in eastern Michigan

Fig. 98   Late Woodland vessel from the West Twin Lake Mound group (University of Michigan Museum of Anthropology)

is a number of large earthwork enclosures with very little cultural material. The forts along the Rifle River in Ogemaw County have been described by M. L. Leach (1885), Cyrus Thomas (1894), W. B. Hinsdale (1924, 1925), Fred Dustin (1932a), Moll, Moll, and Cornelius (1958), and G. A. Wright (1966). The Walters-Linsenman Earthwork in Ogemaw County was excavated by Moll and his associates in the 1950s (Cornelius and Moll 1961) and the Mikado Earthwork by a University of Michigan field party under the supervision of Peter Carruthers in the summer of 1966.

The Rifle River Earthworks vary in size and shape. Three of the four reported by Dustin are oval. Number 1 is 208 feet long and 188 feet wide with walls two and one half feet high and an extreme depth of five feet for the ditch. Dustin's incidental digging produced three rimsherds and 125 bodysherds, representing only five vessels. The one illustrated rimsherd appears to be a Rivière Ware, either Vase Dentate or Vase Tool Impressed. He also recovered a few flint chips.

The second earthwork is the longest, 314 feet long and 280 feet wide. The walls vary between two and five feet high and the ditch surrounding it is between three and seven feet deep. Four gateways with causeways mark the entrances. Dustin's excavations in this massive structure produced three rimsherds representing three vessels, 130 bodysherds representing four additional vessels, 12 chert flakes, one roughed-out celt, and several additional objects brought to the site by man. The two illustrated rimsherds in Dustin's report are from Macomb Linear vessels.

Earthwork Number 3 is near the Rifle River and there is a path over the bank to a nearby spring. It is 180 feet long

and 139 feet wide. The walls average about three feet in height and the ditch is seven feet at its deepest point. This is the earthwork where Dustin found the most cultural material, including five rimsherds and 150 bodysherds representing six vessels, a cache of sandstone abraders, three projectile points, several scrapers, twenty-two chert chips, and some other materials. The illustrated rimsherds from this earthwork resemble more closely those from the Fox component at the Bell site in Wisconsin (Wittry 1963) than they do any Michigan pottery with which I am familiar.

The fourth earthwork reported by Dustin is horseshoe-shaped. It is 216 feet long at its maximum and arcs out about 120 feet. Both Hinsdale and Dustin felt that this structure was never finished. Excavations in this earthwork produced a single chert chip.

The Walters-Linsenman Earthwork in Ogemaw County was excavated by Eldon Cornelius and Harold Moll in 1956 and 1957 (Cornelius and Moll 1961). Much of the area was stripped in an attempt to find house patterns. Post molds were found below the surface which seemed to represent a stockade and the excavators also reported patterns of nineteen lodges inside of the stockade. While numerous refuse pits were uncovered, cultural material was very sparse. Only 1683 sherds were recovered which would probably have represented fewer than fifty different vessels. This site has been radiocarbon dated to A.D. 1350±75 years (M-779).

The Mikado Earthwork in Alcona County is located in the Huron National Forest and was excavated in 1966 under a Federal Government permit (Fitting 1966d). This earthwork is more than a thousand feet in circumference and encloses approximately 96,000 square feet within its walls. It is open on one end at a section overlooking a small bluff. In six weeks, 1825 feet were excavated. The top of the wall revealed a line of post molds indicative of a palisade and, in contrast to the Whorely Earthwork in Branch County, all cultural material was found within the walls in spite of testing along the walls and outside of the stockaded area.

Several refuse pits, two hearths, and part of a house pattern were uncovered within the stockaded area. The ceramics recovered from the site represent about ten vessels; some of these have oblique incisions and others have a notched appliqué rim strip. They are similar to very late prehistoric ceramics from a number of areas in the Midwest. Chipped stone artifacts consist of three very small triangular projectile points, one biface fragment, and very little chippage.

Corn, from earlier testing of this site, was described by Yarnell (1964: 118), and the 1966 excavations produced additional charred corn and corn cobs, beans, and other seeds. Animal bone was very rare at the site and most fragments found were small and calcined. An earlier radiocarbon assay of vegetable material from directly below the wall had yielded a date of A.D. 1450±100 years (M-777).

The settlement pattern suggested by the site is that of the Ottawa who inhabited the Carolinian-Canadian transition zone, where this site was found, in the Early Historic Period. Ceramics outnumber chipped stone artifacts by a ratio of at least two to one. The food remains recovered from the site are primarily agricultural products; hunting tools and bone remains are rare. This, as well as the other earthworks, appears to be a short-

term, low-density occupation by an agricultural group who left the women in the area by themselves for much of the time. The radiocarbon dates from these sites fall within the last century of the Pacific climatic episode just before the short return to Neo-atlantic conditions which occurred around A.D. 1500. These sites may represent attempts by people with an Ottawa type of adaptation to colonize a part of the transition region when the climatic conditions were so unfavorable as to drive them out within a very short period of time.

WESTERN MICHIGAN

Western Michigan is another part of the state where intensive archaeological investigations have been undertaken during the past few years. Earl J. Prahl (1966, 1968) has been particularly active in the Muskegon River Valley and Fel Brunett (1966) has undertaken work in the Manistee Valley.

Several of the sites, excavated by Prahl and University of Michigan field crews assisted by members of the Newaygo County Chapter of the Michigan Archaeological Society, are transitional from late Middle Woodland to Late Woodland. These include the Brunett Mound, several of the Mallon Mound Group, and the Carrigan A Mound (Prahl 1966, 1968, Losey 1968), although the Carrigan A Mound may initially have been built during an earlier time period. The Late Woodland burial at this mound has been radiocarbon dated to A.D. 680±120 years (M-1759) and contained cultural material similar to that from the Gibraltar and Bussinger sites.

The Crystal Lake Village site in Newaygo County was tested by Prahl in 1966

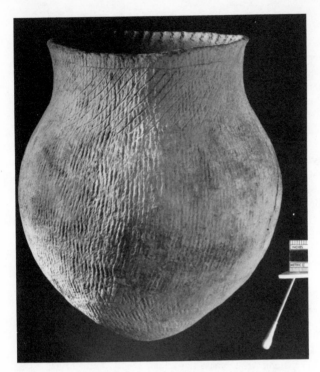

Fig. 99 Vessel from the Brunett Mound (University of Michigan Museum of Anthropology)

and belongs to this early Late Woodland time period as does the Spring Creek Village site farther down the Muskegon River in Muskegon County. This site was excavated in the 1950s by members of the Wright L. Coffinberry Chapter of the Michigan Archaeological Society and the collections were later loaned to the University of Michigan Museum of Anthropology for further study (Fitting 1968c).

Approximately three thousand square feet of the Spring Creek site were excavated and a great deal of cultural material was recovered. A number of post molds suggested circular lodges but, in general, the post molds were so dense that isolating individual lodges was impossible. Hearths and refuse pits were common and charcoal from one of these

pits gave a radiocarbon date of A.D. 960 ± 75 years (M-512).

Ceramics were particularly plentiful. A large mesh screen was used so only larger bodysherds were recovered. The 17,250 bodysherds and over 1100 rimsherds represent at least 966 separate vessels, giving a ceramic occupational intensity of .32 vessels per square foot. This is one of the most intensive occupations in Michigan.

With the exception of a few vessels, the ceramics belong in three categories: two Wayne Cord-marked variants and a low collared cord-marked form which is called Spring Creek Collared. The two Wayne Cord-marked variants are distinguished on the basis of plain rims and slightly thickened and everted rims. Fit-

0 10 20 30 40 50
MM.
IN.
0 1 2

Fig. 100 *Wayne Cord-marked rimsherds from the Spring Creek site (From Fitting: 1968c)*

ting and Halsey (1966) demonstrated a relationship between vessel size and rim diameter on Wayne Ware vessels. When this formula was applied to Wayne Cord-marked and Spring Creek Collared vessels from the Spring Creek site, it was found that the difference in rim form was directly related to vessel size. Smaller ves-

sels have plain rims, medium-sized vessels thickened rims, and the largest vessels collared rims. Furthermore, there is a differential distribution of vessels on the site with the collared forms occurring in largest numbers at greater distances from the creek, indicating a greater carrying capacity for vessels farther from the creek,

175

Fig. 101 *Spring Creek Collared rimsherds from the Spring Creek site* (*From Fitting:1968c*)

which would mean fewer trips to the creek for water.

In contrast to the quantities of ceramics from the site, chipped stone implements are comparatively rare and include only 1497 flakes, 253 artifacts, and 91 small cores, many of which were used as tools. The projectile point assemblage may be a continuation of trends noted at the Schultz site. If we exclude the material in the Late Woodland levels from Schultz, which was probably kicked or picked up from earlier occupations, and include the material from the plow zone,

the two assemblages are almost identical. Unifacial implements are rare at Spring Creek. The sparse assemblage indicates two things. First, little artifact manufacture was carried out at the site and, secondly, that which was carried out indicates hunting activities.

The faunal remains from the site were studied by Megan Biesele and indicate a great deal of emphasis on deer, bear, and beaver. If it were not for the dense ceramic occupation I would call this site a small seasonal hunting camp like those in the Saginaw Valley. It was, however,

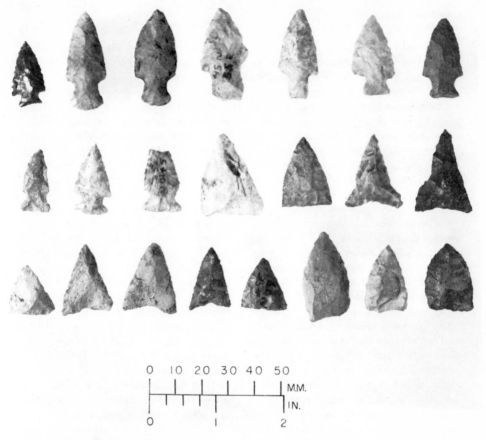

O I0 20 30 40 50
| | | | | | M.M.
| | | | | IN.
O I 2

Fig. 102 Projectile points from the Spring Creek site (From Fitting: 1968c)

a large, densely settled site, probably an agricultural village in which hunting played a small part in the activities of the people who lived there.

Fitting and Cleland (1969) have used this site as the classic example of a permanent village of a people with an Ottawa type of adaptation in the Carolinian-Canadian Transitional area. Several other sites in western Michigan along the Manistee and at the mouth of the Père Marquette continue the pattern.

Near the Spring Creek site is the South Flats Club Earthwork, a small earthwork excavated by George Quimby in 1937

(Quimby 1965a). Only a few cord-marked bodysherds were recovered from this site and no trace of internal structures were found. This site is probably related to the nearby Spring Creek site.

In the upper reaches of the Muskegon in Missaukee County are two additional earthworks. These were described by Dr. W. B. Hinsdale (1924, 1925) and Dr. Emerson Greenman undertook examinations in the area for the University of Michigan in 1925. One burial mound contained a copper celt (1927b) and has since been radiocarbon dated to A.D. 1200±75 years (M-790). Portions of both earthworks were tested by Greenman in 1925 (1927a) and these excavations were incorporated into his doctoral dissertation at the University of Michigan.

These earthworks were visited by Gibson and Herrick in 1957 (1957: 94–95), maps were drawn by Moll and his associates in 1959 (Moll, Moll, and Cornelius 1958), and Prahl relocated them during his first season of the Muskegon River Survey (Prahl 1966). Michigan State University again excavated areas in both earthworks in 1965 under the direction of Dr. Charles E. Cleland and Dr. Elizabeth Baldwin.

The collections from these earthworks in the University of Michigan Museum of Anthropology indicate a generalized Late Woodland style of cord-marked pottery. There is some tendency toward collars and castellations but the most common decoration is notching along the lip. One of these earthworks has been radiocarbon dated to A.D. 1470±100 years (M-100), making this occupation contemporary with that at the Mikado and Walters-Linsenman earthworks in eastern Michigan.

In the absence of the final Michigan State University report any conclusions are purely speculative. I would guess that the Missaukee County Earthworks represent the same type of agricultural villages of the Ottawa pattern as the eastern Michigan earthworks. They seem to have been occupied near the end of the first part of the Pacific episode, although the Boven Earthwork has been dated to the first part of the return to Neo-atlantic conditions. I suspect that they were temporarily occupied and abandoned because of the poor climate and unproductivity of the soils, factors which prevented an effective agricultural adaptation in this region even with the advanced technology and favorable climate of the twentieth century.

The second largest river system in the western Michigan sub-area is the Manistee. Recent work in this area includes a survey of the upper reaches by Peter Murray of Michigan State University (Stone 1967b), of the middle valley by Fel Brunett (1966, 1968), and some preliminary work in the lower valley by Fitting (1968a). To date, no large intensive occupations have been excavated.

Brunett (1966) excavated a Late Woodland burial mound at the Fife Lake I site which is similar to those dating to the second half of the first millennium A.D. in the Muskegon River Valley. The Fife Lake III site (Brunett 1968) is a village site of this same time period. The site was extensively rather than intensively occupied and the small ceramic sample contains both Wayne Cord-marked and Mackinac Ware rimsherds. It is a mixed lot and is stylistically reminiscent of the Butterfield site in eastern Michigan. Both sites are in the Carolinian-Canadian transition zone. I believe Fife Lake

Fig. 103 Clay pipes from Stony Lake Mound #3. Both obverse and reverse of the spotted salamander effigy are illustrated (From Quimby: 1964)

III was the winter camp of people with a Chippewa adaptive pattern and, because of ceramic and settlement similarities, think the Butterfield site is also a seasonal site of this type.

Another site sampled by Brunett is the Headquarters site, an extensive site with chipped stone tools very similar to those from the Spring Creek site, but no ceramics. It has been used as an example of the type of site which would be expected of the winter camp of a group with an Ottawa type of cultural adaptation (Fitting and Cleland 1969).

The Bear Creek site (Fitting 1968a) is a Late Woodland fishing station at the junction of Bear Creek and the Manistee River. Stone implements far outnumber ceramics and I suspect it represents a summer site occupied by a group with an Ottawa type of adaptive pattern.

Two other sites that represent summer sites of the Ottawa pattern are the Hamlin Lake site in Mason County (Fitting 1967) and the Silver Lake site in Oceana County (Cleland 1966: 79–80). The Hamlin Lake site has produced a sparse lithic industry with some Late Woodland artifact styles. It is an industry that suggests hunting activities. The faunal remains from the Silver Lake site have been studied, but the cultural material has not. Cleland found a high percentage of a few food species: deer, elk, and beaver. He concluded that these faunal remains were characteristic of a hunting site of a people with an agricultural base.

Quimby (1964) reported on a group of sites near Stony Lake in Oceana County, including a group of burial mounds. Some of these mounds were excavated by Dr. Carl Guthe of the University of Michigan in 1931 and one was excavated by Quimby for the Muskegon County Museum in

1942. These yielded cord-marked and fabric-impressed Late Woodland pottery with plain and slightly collared rims, a bone harpoon, and a number of elbow pipes. One of these pipes has the effigy of a spotted salamander on it, which Quimby thinks is a late style of decoration; he dates the site around A.D. 1200.

Quimby (1966a) prepared an extensive report on the finds from the Dumaw Creek site in Oceana County, which has been radiocarbon dated to A.D. 1680±75 years (M-1070). Since this places the burials in the Middle Historic Period (see Chapter VIII), Quimby does not accept it. He would prefer a date of A.D. 1605 to 1620, but I think the cultural material, particularly the pottery, is somewhat earlier.

The site was rediscovered by Quimby who traced mislabeled collections back through several sources and cross-correlated records in several different museums. The burials from the site had been excavated by Carl Schrumpf in 1915 and 1916, while later surface collections were made by a number of people, including Quimby.

The nineteen burials were obviously fairly recent with skin and hair still to be found on many. Several individuals were buried in robes made of beaver skin sewn together, as well as elk and raccoon skins. A belt of buffalo hair yarn was found with one burial. A number of copper hair pipes, copper beads, and marine and snail shell beads were found. A copper snake effigy and a marine shell gorget with a weeping eye design were among the more spectacular goods found with burials. There also were tinkling cones of native copper.

The pottery from Dumaw Creek consists of globular cord-marked and fab-

Fig. 104 *The Juntunen site before excavation* (*University of Michigan Museum of Anthropology*)

ric-impressed vessels which are similar to Wayne Wares. They have a slightly larger mouth and one of the most distinctive attributes is the crimping or pinching on the rims. Since the collections from the site were obtained over a fifty-year period by a number of individuals from several different areas of the site, it is impossible to compute the occupational intensity index for ceramics. Since the Seymour Rider collection alone has 491 rimsherds, the density must have been fairly high.

In addition to the 135 projectile points —many found in burial caches—there were chipped stone knives, drills, worked flakes, and scraping tools. Small cores were recovered from the site by Quimby. Bone awls, beaver incisor chisels, and one antler point were also found.

It was not possible to quantify the animal remains but bear, beaver, buffalo, deer, elk, raccoon, weasel, and hawk were represented. Plant remains included wild plant seeds and over a hundred pumpkin seeds.

While we cannot be too specific about the adaptive pattern of the people from Dumaw Creek, the site does furnish material for speculation on ethnic identification. The ceramics resemble those from the smaller of the two groups recovered from the Bell site, a Fox village site in Wisconsin (Wittry 1963). Quimby has variously identified this material as Sauk, Mascouten, Kickapoo, and Potawatomi (1966a, 1966b).

THE STRAITS OF MACKINAC

The most extensive excavations of prehistoric materials in the Straits of Mackinac sub-area were carried out by the University of Michigan under the direction of Alan McPherron, at the Juntunen site on Bois Blanc Island. McPherron (1967) assembled an extensive report on the site, including the observations of a number of specialists and his own interpretations of the cultural materials.

Excavations were undertaken at this site on the western end of Bois Blanc Island during the summers of 1960 and 1961 and for a brief period in the summer of 1962. The site was sporadically occupied during the warmer months of the year by peoples specialized in fishing between A.D. 800 and A.D. 1400. During the excavations a total of 4750 square feet were excavated, including several ossuary burials. The cultural material includes over 101,000 sherds representing 1616 vessels, 19,780 fragments of chipped stone with about 1900 cores and tools, 92 finished and 628 unfinished pieces of copper, and 120 bone tools.

The site was stratified and was divided into six main levels of occupation representing three phases: the Mackinac, Bois Blanc, and Juntunen phases. The Mackinac Phase has radiocarbon dates of

Fig. 105 *An early stage in the excavation of a Juntunen site ossuary (University of Michigan Museum of Anthropology)*

Fig. 106 *Mackinac Ware vessel from the Juntunen site (University of Michigan Museum of Anthropology)*

Fig. 107 *Mackinac Ware vessel from the Juntunen site (University of Michigan Museum of Anthropology)*

A.D. 835±75 years (M-1142), A.D. 1060 ±120 years (M-1816), and A.D. 1080± 120 years (M-1815); the Bois Blanc Phase to A.D. 900±75 years (M-1141), A.D. 1060±75 years (M-1140), and A.D. 1130 ±120 years (M-1817); while the Juntunen Phase has been dated to A.D. 1330 ±100 years (M-1391). One of the ossuaries on the site has been separately dated to A.D. 1320±75 years (M-1188) and relates these ossuaries to the final phase of occupation at the site.

The ceramics from the site belong to four major ware categories with several additional small categories important for cross-dating different occupations on the site. Mackinac Ware, including the types Mackinac Undecorated, Mackinac Punctate, Mackinac Cord Impressed, Mackinac Banded and Mackinac Zig-Zag Lip, is characteristic of the earliest of the Late Woodland occupations. It is a ware which lacks collars and castellations although some of the lips are undulating or wavy.

Rims are thickened and slightly outsloping, and surface decoration is by cordmarking or fabric impression.

Blackduck Wares, similar to types first defined in Minnesota and Manitoba, form a second important ceramic series. They are found throughout the deposits but reach a peak frequency some time between A.D. 900 and A.D. 1100. Two types, Blackduck Banded and Blackduck Punctate, are present.

Bois Blanc Ware, one of the major wares at the site, is marked by a thickened or folded-over rim, or the addition of a strip of clay along the rim, castellations, and cord-wrapped stick and cord decorations. It is represented by the types Bois Blanc Braced Rim, Bois Blanc Beaded, and Bois Blanc Castellated Corded.

Juntunen Ware is the fourth major ware group and is found in the latest phase of the occupation. It is characterized by true collars and decorations produced by

Fig. 108   Bois Blanc Ware vessel from the Juntunen site (University of Michigan Museum of Anthropology)

linear punctations and drag and jab techniques. The types present at the site include Juntunen Linear Punctate, Juntunen Collared, and Juntunen Drag and Jab.

The ratio of .34 ceramic vessels per square foot of excavated area indicates a high occupational intensity. However, since the site was occupied for perhaps six centuries the index for any major phase of occupation would be considerably less.

Chipped stone artifacts comprise a variety of projectile point styles, including several forms that are often attributed solely to Archaic occupations but belong with this Late Woodland material. The largest group of points, however, are small triangular forms. Scrapers, small cores, and small core tools are also present. The ratio of chips to tools and cores is only a little over ten to one so relatively little manufacturing activity took place on the site in comparison with

Fig. 109 Bois Blanc Ware rimsherd from the Juntunen site (University of Michigan Museum of Anthropology)

some sites where this ratio is as high as two hundred to one. The ratio of ceramics to cores and tools, about .90 to one, suggests of a balanced sexual composition for the groups inhabiting the site.

Copper materials from the site include awls, knives, beads, pendants, and two copper projectile points. Bone artifacts

Fig. 110 Juntunen Ware rim section from the Juntunen site (University of Michigan Museum of Anthropology)

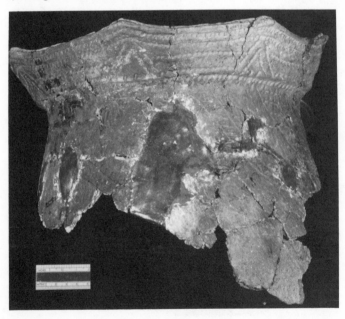

Fig. 111   Juntunen Ware vessel from the Juntunen site (University of Michigan Museum of Anthropology)

consist primarily of awls, harpoons, and polished bird bone tubes. About sixty-five pipe fragments, including an Iroquois trumpet pipe and a human effigy pipe, were found.

Remains of 153 different plants were identified from the site by Yarnell, including several wild food plants and nineteen kernels of corn. Corn is most frequent in the Juntunen Phase but occurs in Mackinac Phase levels. Cleland's faunal analysis (1966: 157–210) indicates the purpose of the occupation for over ninety percent of the bone refuse was fish bone. This must have been the summer site of a group of people with a Chippewa type of adaptation, possibly even a prehistoric Chippewa group.

McPherron notes a shift of stylistic influence in ceramic manufacture from the western areas to the eastern areas around A.D. 1000. I do not believe this represents any new introduction of peoples into the area, for groups that have been identified as prehistoric and early historic Chippewa (J. V. Wright 1965) show a wide range of ceramic variation and are influenced by a large number of outside sources.

While much is known about the Junt-

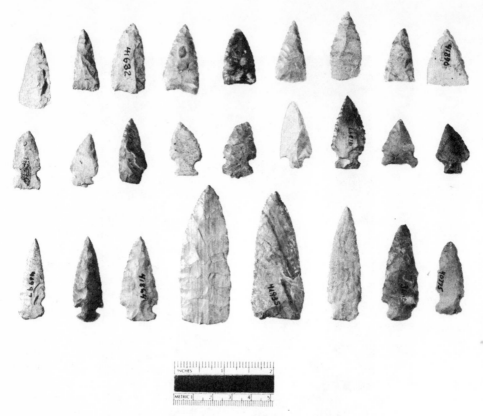

Fig. 112 Chipped stone artifacts from the Juntunen site (University of Michigan Museum of Anthropology)

unen site, little is yet known about other sites of the same time period in surrounding areas. The Point Scott site in Mackinaw County in the upper peninsula is a coastal occupation that may date to this time period. It is a site that has been tested by surface collection by University of Michigan field parties and others (Binford and Quimby 1963). There are great quantities of fish bone on the site but they may be associated with the nineteenth-century fishing camp also found there. We can only note the existence of this site until excavation is undertaken. This will be difficult, as the site consists of blown-out dunes; the parts of the cultural midden that are not blown out are under a great quantity of dune sand.

Brief excavations were undertaken at the Eisen site on Black Lake in Cheboygan County by members of the Clinton Valley Chapter of the Michigan Archaeological Society in October 1963 (Griffin 1963). Approximately 1000 square feet were excavated and over 1600 sherds, including 130 rimsherds (estimated 125 vessels), were recovered. The index of occupational intensity, with a ceramic sample representing a single phase of occupation, is .125 vessels per square foot, approximately equivalent to that of a single phase at the Juntunen site. Stone artifacts are scarce and only three projectile points were found. Parts of four clay pipes are present, including one with a human effigy face. No plant or animal remains are associated with the cultural levels, a factor which Griffin attributes to the very acid nature of the soil.

The ceramics from the site are Mackinac Wares. However, the site occupation pattern is entirely different from that suggested by the Juntunen site. This site looks like a village site of a group with an Ottawa type of adaptive pattern. Since these patterns are related to ecological adaptations rather than ethnic groups, in the Straits area there could have been genetically related groups with distinctive occupation patterns.

During the past four years, Michigan State University field parties, under the direction of Charles E. Cleland, have been engaged in an intensive study of the Traverse Corridor, a zone that runs from Traverse City along Grand Traverse Bay and Lake Michigan up to Mackinaw City. The environment within this zone was extremely favorable to man. In the early historic period the area was covered by extensive stands of hardwoods and the growing season was long enough for corn crops to ripen. The Carolinian biotic province extends along the lakeshore. During favorable climatic episodes agricultural groups lived in the area.

Although the recent Michigan State University work has been extensive, no published reports are yet available. I have seen some of the collections and Dr. Cleland has furnished me with data on the sites, so I can make a few preliminary comments.

One of the key sites excavated by Michigan State University was Skegemog Point on Skegemog Lake in Grand Traverse County. During the 1966 season over sixty thousand artifacts were re-covered. The distribution of cultural material on the site was in the form of a sheet midden; hundreds of hearth areas with food remains were excavated. The site has yielded radiocarbon dates of A.D. 900±120 years (M-1865), A.D. 1210 ±120 years (M-1863), and A.D. 1310± 120 years (M-1864) with the most intensive occupation occurring near the center of this time span.

The Schuler site on the north end of Skegemog Lake has produced a similar cultural assemblage and has been radiocarbon dated to A.D. 1040±120 years (M-1867). Ceramics from both the Schuler site and Skegemog Point are reminiscent of Mackinac Wares but still are a distinctive series with their own pattern of internal variation.

The Fauver site in southern Antrim County is located on Clam Lake at the point where it enters Torch Lake. It has produced pottery similar to that from Skegemog Point with the addition of some Blackduck materials. While the site has been radiocarbon dated to A.D. 1600±100 years (M-1866) it was probably occupied during an earlier time period.

Other sites in the general area from which Michigan State has obtained Late Woodland cultural material include the Henderson-Lamb site, the Holtz site, the Antrim Creek site, the Bass Lake site, the Mud Lake site, and two small sites on Lake Margarethe.

Late Woodland sites near the Straits that have been investigated by Michigan State University include the Halberg site in St. Ignace, one component of the Wycamp Creek site, and the Ponshewang site near Conway; the latter two sites are located in Emmet County. The cultural material from these sites is more similar to those from the Juntunen site than to sites from the southern part of the Traverse Corridor.

NORTHERN LAKE MICHIGAN

The north shore of Lake Michigan, the area from Point Scott west to Green Bay, shows strong cultural contacts with groups to the west. The largest excavations that have been carried out in this area are those on the Door Peninsula of Wisconsin, which have been undertaken by Ronald J. Mason (1966) of Lawrence University in Wisconsin. This area is included with our analysis of Michigan material because it is essential for an understanding of the archaeology of this region.

The early Late Woodland materials are represented by the Heins Creek site, which has been radiocarbon dated to A.D. 720±150 years (I–678). A typical Late Woodland cord-marked pottery was found at the site. Additional decorations over the cord-marking included cord-wrapped stick impression and punctations. There was a limited stone tool industry; only a few bone tools were recovered. The majority of the bone refuse was from fish, particularly sturgeon, but, in terms of meat weight, deer accounted for seventy-six percent of the food remains.

The Mero site, also on the Door Peninsula, was stratified with mixed Late Woodland and shell and grit tempered Oneota ceramics in the upper levels. Heins Creek ceramics were the most characteristic of the Late Woodland materials. The types and percentages of animal remains from these Late Woodland levels do not differ significantly from those of Heins Creek, or, for that matter, the earlier Middle Woodland levels at the Mero site itself. The general picture is of a hunting adaptation with utilization of some fish resources. These sites may represent the winter or fall occupations of groups who spent their summers fishing on nearby Washington and Summer islands.

Mason feels that, in spite of the mixing of ceramics of the Woodland and Mississippian traditions in the upper levels of the Mero site, there is a temporal separation. He sees ". . . replacement in the second of the two millennium A.D. of the resident Woodland cultures by others of Upper Mississippian (Oneota) affiliation" (Mason 1966: 193). While it is possible to find sites with pure Oneota assemblages farther to the west in Wisconsin, all of the northern Lake Michigan sites, even those with close stratigraphic control, show a mixture of ceramics. Oneota ceramics were found in the Juntunen Phase levels at the Juntunen site and along with Juntunen and Mackinac Wares in the surface collections from the Point Scott site as well as at several of the sites recently reported by David S. Brose.

Two small collections of Michigan materials relate to the Heins Creek occupation on the Door Peninsula. These include some sherds from the multicomponent Riverside Cemetery site in Menominee County (Papworth 1967: 176) and at the Port Bar site on the Garden Peninsula in Delta County (Fitting 1968a).

Collections of artifacts from the Eckdahl-Goodreau site on Seul Choix Point in Schoolcraft County made by Quimby (Binford and Quimby 1963) and later excavations there by Earl J. Prahl in the summer of 1965 show stronger correlations with the Mackinac area than with the Green Bay region in Late Woodland times.

In 1956, Albert C. Spaulding directed excavation on the Backlund Mound group in Menominee County (Brose

1968). This site has been radiocarbon dated to A.D. 1340±110 years (M-1891). Brose did not think that significant grave goods were included with any of the twenty-six burials. However, in the fill of the mound there were eight Upper Mississippian and four Late Woodland vessels. Brose views this as representative of ". . . the contact of emergent Oneota with northern Lake Woodland cultures . . ."

In the summer of 1967, excavations were carried out on Summer Island by a University of Michigan field crew under the direction of David S. Brose. In the upper levels of this site, there was a level with both Late Woodland and Oneota ceramics in association. Based on cross-dating with both Juntunen and Backlund, this level is estimated to date around A.D. 1300. The site was occupied during the summer months when the inhabitants lived primarily by fishing.

Brose also found another occupation above this associated with seventeenth-century trade materials. This level contained a very small sample of poorly made, thick, grit-tempered pottery with crude incising. So far, we have not been able to match this pottery with ceramics from other sites in Michigan. It also contained Dumaw Creek-like ceramics.

In view of the mixture of Late Woodland and Oneota ceramics on so many of these sites, I see no need to postulate separate peoples or separate cultures to account for the blending of ceramic traits. Groups with patrilocal postmarital residence patterns and marriage and trade contacts over long distances, such as the central Algonquin groups in this area, were not bound to single stylistic traditions. We should expect as much variation as among Chippewa sites in the Lake Superior drainage (J. V. Wright 1965).

SOUTHERN LAKE SUPERIOR

The largest unexplored area of Michigan lies along the southern shore of Lake Superior. Even today, this is an area of low population density and little agricultural activity. Sites which would be brought to light by plowing in the lower peninsula remain covered with dense sod and underbrush in this region. The river systems are either fast flowing or impounded in massive swamps, in either case difficult to traverse and of little value to the aboriginal inhabitants. The shores are either swampy or windswept and rocky; sites are found in bays or at the mouths of rivers. During one recent survey (Briggs 1968) not one aboriginal site was encountered along the entire Pictured Rocks National Lakeshore.

For example, the Naomikong Point site, primarily a Middle Woodland site, was known for years before its potential was realized. It was listed in the Hinsdale Atlas in 1931, and Emerson Greenman visited it in 1939 and collected a single sherd from the beach. In the 1950s, Charles S. Taylor of Newberry started to acquire a collection and took Quimby to the site; and he, in turn, told us of Taylor's collection. In 1965 our first field visit yielded less than a handful of water-worn sherds from the beach and we were ready to write the site off as a waste of time until scuba divers recovered more materials from under the water offshore from the site. Excavation of the densely sodded inland areas of the site, often covered by as much as four feet of dune sand, revealed a dense occupation with over 132,000 sherds recovered in about ten weeks of excavation.

Late Woodland materials at Naomikong Point usually found in the upper levels of the midden mixed with Middle Woodland sherds are sparse. They consist of

189

Blackduck sherds and Mackinac Wares although some Oneota with a grit temper and a concentration of Iroquoian ceramics were located. Taylor's collection also contains a number of Lalonde High Collared and Huron-Petun ceramics.

Stone (1967b) reports the recovery of some Late Woodland ceramics, apparently Mackinac Wares, during the excavation of Fort Brady at Sault Ste. Marie, but after that we must go far to the west to find another reported Late Woodland site. Griffin (1966) considers the "Calumet Ancient Pit," a cache of organic materials recovered from the upper levels of a copper mine, Late Woodland because of a radiocarbon date of A.D. 770±140 years (M-1776), although none of the material is particularly diagnostic. Aside from a mound in Gogebic County (Quimby 1952), we must go to Isle Royale to find excavated Lake Woodland materials.

A number of reports have appeared on Isle Royale, most concentrating on the copper mining activities. Quimby, while a student at the University of Michigan, prepared a statement on Woodland and Iroquoian pottery recovered from Isle Royale (1940a). More recently, Griffin (1961) described the cultural material from the Chippewa Harbor and Indian Point sites excavated by Drier in 1953. The Chippewa Harbor site has been radiocarbon dated to A.D. 890±100 years (M-1272). Tyler Bastian (1963a) prepared a large report on several seasons work carried out on Isle Royale for the National Park Service and described the ceramics from the sites on the island in great detail. Virtually every ceramic type from the Upper Great Lakes, from Wayne Ware to Oneota, from Dumaw Creek styles to Huron types, is found in small amounts on the island. I suspect these were left by peoples who came from

great distances to exploit the copper or else that the people who exploited the copper were traders and acquired materials in return for copper from over a wide area.

Cleland's (1968) report on animal bone from the Indian Point site identifies beaver, moose, caribou, sturgeon, and lynx as the major faunal forms. All are northern forms; moose, caribou, and beaver furnish the largest source of food. Cleland believes the site was a summer village with fishing more important than the bone refuse indicates.

ETHNIC IDENTIFICATION

One of the major tools of American archaeology over the past forty years has been the "direct historic approach." This approach enables the archaeologist to locate the European contact site and, through documentary sources, to identify the group that occupied it. The artifact styles are traced back to prehistoric sites and the movements of people as well as changes in the adaptive patterns through time are recorded. This approach has been used with success in the southwestern United States, the plains, and in the Iroquoian areas of the northeast. It has had less success in marginal areas or areas of great cultural and ecological overlap. It will therefore be of little use in Michigan.

Even sound identifications in other areas deteriorate when applied to similar cultural materials in Michigan. Ceramics that can be positively associated with historic Huron sites in Ontario are found on sites that are most likely Ottawa or Chippewa. At one time the most certain archaeological identification in the Midwest was Griffin's (1937) identification of the Oneota archaeological culture with

Chiwere Souian-speaking groups. The Winnebago in Wisconsin were linked directly to the Lake Winnebago Focus (McKern 1945). There are similar Oneota ceramics from the Door Peninsula on into Michigan. I cannot interpret this as a result of an intrusion of Souian speakers.

MacNeish (1958) identifies Blackduck materials with historic Assiniboine groups. Yet they are found on Chippewa sites (J. V. Wright 1965), are one of the major wares from the Juntunen site, and occur as far away as the southern part of the Traverse Corridor in the Michigan lower peninsula.

Since so little is known about the area in the Early Historic Period, lower Michigan peninsula sites are subject to even more controversy. Peske (1967) points out that Quimby (Quimby 1966a, 1966b) attributes two different identifications to the people who inhabited the Dumaw Creek site. It is impossible to apply the direct historic approach to most groups in the Upper Great Lakes and come up with anything but chaotic results. With this in mind, I will give a few identifications I believe are correct.

In Wisconsin, Warren Wittry (1963) excavated the Bell site, an historic Fox site that I will discuss in more detail later. The aboriginal ceramics from this site belong to two groups. One has plain outsloping rims with squared lips decorated with punctates. Wittry identifies this as seventeenth-century Fox pottery and I agree. There is a second ware marked by rims decorated with tool and finger impressions. He assumes this is either Sauk, Potawatomi, Kickapoo, Mascouten, or some group in close contact with the Fox.

Quimby relates the pottery from the Bell site to that from Dumaw Creek and suggests that the site is Potawatomi, Sauk, or Kickapoo. I prefer to group all of these people under a general heading, later giving them more specific names. As of A.D. 1600, and certainly as of A.D. 1500, it is difficult to call them anything more specific than "People of the Fire."

If, on the other hand, this pottery is characteristic of a central Algonquin group representing the ancestors of the historic Sauk, Kickapoo, Potawatomi, Mascouten, and Fox, granting some distinctness to the latter, then some very general identifications are valid. I have used these general ceramic similarities to trace the movement of "Fire People" from the Fairport Harbor site in northern Ohio (Fitting 1964b), which I feel represents an occupation of this generalized group before they were driven to the west by late prehistoric Iroquoian expansion.

I also think that a number of sites with strong Upper Mississippian elements are products of Algonquin speakers. Although the Blue Island culture around the Chicago area, particularly as represented at the Anker site (Bluhm and Liss 1961), may represent a Souian group as Quimby has suggested, I favor his alternative explanation of its being a Miami site. The mixed Woodland and Mississippian sites on the Door Peninsula, Summer Island, and along the Menominee River which are probably occupations of Algonquin speakers which might be Miami, Chippewa, or even Potawatomi, in spite of the Potawatomi use of rim-notched ceramics in other areas. Late Woodland and Upper Mississippian ceramics are both found at the Moccasin Bluff site, which was in an area where a mixed Miami and Potawatomi group was known to have lived in the historic period.

Huron sherds from the northern and eastern parts of Michigan and from the Straits of Mackinac could represent Huron, Ottawa, or Chippewa groups.

CHAPTER VII

THOSE WHO WERE THERE

HISTORIC INDIANS OF MICHIGAN

The five groups that spent some time in Michigan during the early historic period were the Chippewa, the Ottawa, the "People of the Fire," the Miami, and the Huron. These groups account for almost all of the Indians known in the state. I will consider the history of these groups only to the extent that it is necessary to place them in a particular environment at a particular time. The main emphasis will be on the economic base, settlement pattern, and type of social organization.

Quimby (1966b) has dealt with material acculturation but no one has described the social changes which must have followed. The distance and direction along the road of cultural change traveled by the people of the lakes between A.D. 1600 and 1900 is largely unmapped. It is too large a study to be dealt with here.

The records of Michigan Indians in the early historic period are the records of a changing way of life. The missionaries and traders who observed and recorded information on these groups altered their way of life just by being there. The arrival of the Europeans heralded the beginning of "pan-Indianism." When dealing with accounts of the native cultures, no matter how complete, we must remember that it is a changed culture.

I have long felt that many accounts of North American Indians have tried to impose structure on unstructured situations. European observers applied terms like "nation" to groups whose single tie may have been that several families fished in the same area regularly. Modern researchers have been dependent on early records and have attributed a structure to these people that existed primarily in the mind of the early observer.

There has been some reversal of this rigid position in the past few years as shown by J. V. Wright's (1965) use of the term Ojibway to refer to a wide range of Algonquin speakers; by Wakefield's (1966) linguistic analysis of the "Fire People" which shows the efficiency of a broader application of terms; and by Brose's (1969) illumination of the inconsistencies in the historic records.

THE CHIPPEWA

The Chippewa were the first group of Michigan Indians contacted by Europeans at Sault Ste. Marie in 1622. They were initially referred to as *Saulteur*, the "people of the falls," a French term for the description the Huron gave them. This is a geographical term used to describe several "clans" of Chippewa who regularly fished along the St. Marys River. These same groups were referred to by different terms when they moved to other locations within their seasonal cycle.

Chippewa is a generic term for the entire social and, possibly, linguistic group. It appears in early accounts as Outchibous, Otchipoy, Otchipwe, Ojibway, among others. Groups covered by this heading include the Noquet, Marameg, Nopeming, and Mississagi; Kinietz includes the Nipissing and Amikwa. Greenman suggests that these terms are clan designations. If some of them are areal rather than clan designations, the presence of a group with the same name in the same places over several years in an early account may not mean the presence of the same individuals. If these were clan designations, however, several clans might have lived in a single area and the early account might record simply the clan designation of the first person asked.

Prior to 1701, the Chippewa lived in the northern parts of the upper Great Lakes. After initial contact in the early seventeenth century, the Marameg were reported on the north side of Lake Superior in 1670, the Mississagi near Thessalon, Ontario, in 1634, and other groups in Chequamegon and Keweenaw bays prior to 1700. Kinietz notes a generally southern movement during the early contact period, and after the establishment of the French post at Detroit in 1701 they were often reported in the northern parts of the Michigan lower peninsula. I suspect that they were drawn to these areas by trade, for their particular adaptive pattern was more suited to the Canadian biotic province, which seems to have been their homeland. Even when they moved into areas where agriculture was possible, such as the Saginaw Valley, they held to their traditional pattern of seasonal hunting.

With a territory as vast as that of the Chippewa, from the western reaches of Lake Superior to the head of the St. Clair River, and with the degree of environmental variation within this area, we expect more variation in the cultural adaptation than actually occurred. This reflects the northern origin of these peoples and their late southerly movement. People who lived to the north of the Lake Superior region practiced no agriculture, living by hunting alone. Their diet was supplemented by agricultural products obtained by trade from the south. Groups living around the lakes practiced limited agriculture: planted corn in June, moved away from summer activities, and returned in the fall when the grain was nearly ripe. Several accounts stress that the corn was eaten while it was green because it would not ripen. I agree with Kinietz (1940: 322) that "from all of these accounts one gathers the impression that agriculture was not very important in the economy of the Chippewa . . ."

One of the best accounts of the seasonal activity of a Chippewa family is that contained in the diary of Alexander Henry. Henry was saved by the family of Wawatam after the massacre at Fort Michilimackinac in 1763 and spent the winter of 1763–64 with this family. Quimby (1962a, 1962b) placed Henry's account in the perspective of modern place names and reduced it to its essential pattern of seasonal activity.

The Wawatam family started its seasonal cycle with Henry in the Straits area during the summer months when fishing was the primary subsistence activity. In the fall the extended family group went west to Cross Village and obtained a supply of corn from the Ottawa agriculturists. They then proceeded to a shoreline camp along Lake Michigan. The family moved inland along a river that Quimby calls the Pere Marquette. They hunted over the winter, collecting furs for trade. In the spring the Wawatam family joined other families to make maple sugar. After sugaring they returned to the Straits for trading and summer fishing.

This activity takes place in 1763, nearly a century and a half after the Chippewa were first involved in the European trade network. While earlier accounts mention maize cultivation among some groups of Chippewa, it plays no part in the cycle of the Wawatam family. This could be caused either by the extreme involvement in trade (with both the Europeans and the Ottawa) or by the special circumstances of the year following the massacre. It is possible that the activities immediately following the massacre were not those of a normal year. The hunting range of the group is also farther to the south along the shore of Lake Michigan than would be expected from earlier accounts of Chippewa groups.

Nevertheless, I believe the general pattern is typical for Chippewa groups of the Early Historic Period. The Chippewa spent the summer months in a few key areas whose abundance of fish supported large populations. Limited agriculture, hunting, and wild food plant collection contributed to the subsistence base during the summer months. I suspect that in the summer they traded skins and meat to the Ottawa and Huron for corn, even in the prehistoric period. Seed corn was needed from the south almost every season.

In the winter, extended family units left the main group. The pattern of specialized hunting of fur-bearing animals *may* have existed in the late prehistoric period but it certainly received a new emphasis in the historic period. In any event, the pattern of winter fission into extended family groups has an adaptive value in an environment where the limited winter resources could not support large population units.

The spring sugaring activities led to a fusion of groups that had been separated over the winter. While sugaring cannot be demonstrated in the prehistoric period, some similar group consolidation must have taken place. The cycle ended where it had begun the year before with large groups fishing at places such as Bois Blanc Island, Big St. Martin Island, and the Sault.

The social structure was fluid. Some accounts record an exchange of women at marriage, indicating that some postmarital residence was virilocal and some natal residence was patrilocal. Earlier references to the existence of clans might mean that the Chippewa calculated descent patrilineally. They might also mean that the European observers calculated descent patrilineally and thought that groups which were not matrilineal had to be patrilineal.

I see a pattern of fluid macrogroup membership. Exchange of wives may have taken place between macrogroups but this might just be a characteristic of extended family groups. The extended family groups were free to join any summer macrogroup. They could have spent one summer as a Noquet and the next as a Saulteur or Marameg. They could even stop being Chippewa altogether without creating strain on the fabric of Chippewa society. The Mississagi did this and were even members of the Iroquois League between 1746 and 1756. The Amikwa might have shifted from being Chippewa to being Ottawa during the historic period in the same way that the Nassauaketon, apparently an Ottawa clan, continually associated with the Potawatomi. That the people grouped together under the general term

Chippewa were so loosely structured is the result of the economic adaptation required in the Canadian and Hudsonian biotic provinces north of the Carolinian-Canadian transition zone. This was an area that could not support a large population concentration in a single place on a year-round basis, or for more than several seasons in a row at any one place.

THE OTTAWA

The term Ottawa was almost as broad in application as that of Chippewa. While a broad usage, which would include virtually all of the groups in the upper Great Lakes (Kinietz 1940: 226), must be avoided, it cannot be too narrow. The first encounter of the Ottawa with Europeans was in 1615 when Champlain contacted three hundred members of them on the upper Ottawa River east of Lake Nipissing. Later accounts place them farther to the west and most ethnohistorians report a general westward movement during the historic period.

The term Ottawa means "traders" and early accounts refer to them as traveling about encumbered with goods. The Ottawa dwelt within the transition area between the Carolinian and Canadian biotic provinces. Their westward movement after the destruction of the Huron villages by the Iroquois League took place within this biotic zone. Gary Wright (1967) emphasizes their role as middlemen in the maintenance of trade networks across ecological boundaries. This interest and participation in exchange is one of their important, if not diagnostic, characteristics. To be an Ottawa was to participate in the Ottawa system, which centered more about trade than most other groups in the area.

Both Kinietz and Greenman recognize a number of bands or clans of the Ottawa. The Kiskakon, Sinago, Sable, Nassauaketon, Keinouche, Kinounchepirini, and Amikwa are all groups that have been classed as Ottawa. Greenman has traced the various spellings and meanings of the name Necariages which was applied to either one clan or the entire group of Ottawa located at Michilimackinac between 1710 and 1747. In 1710, the Negochendackirin were a clan of the Ottawa; in 1723, Neghkareage was the name for two villages at Michilimackinac; in the same year the names Denighariages and Negheariages were used to describe the Ottawa from Michilimackinac at Albany; in 1747, the name Necariages appeared on Cadwallader Colden's map as a group in the St. Ignace area.

During the first half of the seventeenth century, Ottawa groups were reported along the Ottawa River and in the eastern Lake Huron area, particularly on Manitoulin Island. After the Huron were driven from their villages in the mid-seventeenth century, the Ottawa were again reported on Manitoulin Island, around Saginaw, Thunder Bay, Michilimackinac, and "Huron Island" which some have interpreted as being Washington Island. The group which was reported on "Huron Island" is said to have gone farther west to an island on the Mississippi River, but by 1662 this same group is reported on Chequamegon Bay on Lake Superior. At the same time another group of Ottawa was reported on Keweenaw Bay on Lake Superior.

During the last half of the seventeenth century, the majority of the Ottawa groups again gathered at the Straits of Mackinac although many are reported hunting to the south and several groups moved to

Detroit at the invitation of Cadillac in 1701. During the first half of the eighteenth century the Ottawa again regrouped at Michilimackinac and in 1742 they established L'Abre Croche—Cross Village—as their principal village. This has served as their principal village since that time.

The economic activities of the Ottawa differed from those of the Chippewa as did their settlement pattern and social organization. Like other groups in the upper Great Lakes, the Ottawa depended on agriculture, hunting, and fishing for a livelihood, but they developed a unique pattern of exploiting these resources in the Carolinian-Canadian transition area. To quote Cleland (1966: 73–74), "their adaptation to this ecological zone was neither a simple one nor marginal to the more highly agricultural societies further to the south."

The Ottawa were semi-sedentary people who regularly moved their year-round villages to escape hostile tribes and secure more productive, fertile soil. Ottawa villages were clusters of bark-covered lodges. According to Cadillac, the Ottawa lived in long houses like those of the Huron, with villages similarly fortified with stockades.

Their principal agricultural crop was corn. Each family had its own fields and the women, assisted by older men no longer capable of hunting, cultivated the soil and sowed and harvested the crop. Cultivation was done with a digging stick; beans and squash were sown with the corn. Farming was successful, for there are accounts of surplus corn being traded to the Chippewa.

In contrast to the Chippewa hunting pattern, Ottawa parties consisted primarily, sometimes exclusively, of males who left the villages for long periods of time. In the summer, the men left most of their families in the villages and hunted at a distance of seventy-five to a hundred miles. Hinsdale (1932: 33–34) suggests that such summer hunting activity took place in the Lake Michigan dunes areas. These summer hunts were chiefly for meat. Trading activity took place during the summer months.

During the winter, groups of eight to ten related males would travel a considerable distance from the main village to establish a winter hunting camp. They hunted deer, bear, and beaver, and they dressed much of the meat and took it back to the village. Beaver meat and fur were valuable in the prehistoric period and became a prime trade objective in the Early Historic Period. Winter hunting territories shifted from year to year. For example, the Glen Lake region was hunted every third year, the Saginaw Valley every other year. I suspect that the region to be hunted each winter was chosen on the basis of the expert knowledge of a skilled hunter rather than by a traditional pattern.

Ottawa fishing activities were similar to those of the Chippewa. Although they fished extensively at the Straits of Mackinac, unlike the Chippewa, agricultural products rather than fish supported their population concentrations.

The Ottawa pattern was one of large villages occupied for several seasons. The inhabitants of such a village were primarily women since the men were away for much of the time on trading and hunting parties. This might account for the Ottawa habit of moving villages once their location became generally known.

I have mentioned groups that have, at times, been described as belonging to one or more of the major ethnic units of the upper Great Lakes. If such units were defined on settlement and subsistence activities, than a group could move freely between the ethnic units. To be an Ottawa was to trade and to follow a way of life similar to that which I have just described.

THE PEOPLE OF THE FIRE

The People of the Fire were an elusive group. Early in the seventeenth century Champlain was told by the Ottawa that they were at war with a group called the "Asistagueronon." This was a Huron term, translated as *Nation du Feu,* or Fire Nation, by the Jesuits. The Asistagueronon lived ten days' journey to the west of the south end of Georgian Bay, a distance of more than six hundred miles.

By the time that Europeans reached the land of the Fire People the Asistagueronon group was there. Kinietz notes that the term Potawatomi is derived from *Potowatamink,* which means "people of the place of fire" in Chippewa. Wakefield (1966), on the other hand, thinks that this is too simple an explanation. According to his interpretation, the name of the group was *mush-koon-dehns,* "people of the small prairies." The Huron interpreted this as *ish-koo-deh,* or Fire People, and translated it directly into Huron as Asistagueronon. Wakefield suggests that the term Mascouten was the major generic term for this central Algonquin group. He notes that the term Mascouten appears as a descriptive term for people in Wisconsin prior to 1779. After that time it is no longer as common, but the term Sauk is used more frequently. Wakefield indicates that this might be a specific reference to a group which was previously described by the more general term. He is impressed by the linguistic

and cultural similarity of the "Mascoutens, Sauks, Foxes, and Kickapoos."

Emerson Greenman (1961) agrees with J. N. B. Hewitt that the term Asistagueronon was a collective term for five Algonquin tribes: the Mascouten, Fox, Sauk, Potawatomi, and Nassauaketon (an Ottawa band?). Moreover, Greenman calls attention to the association of the Algonquin terms for "fire" and "small prairies" in current use. While the translation of the word Mascouten may be "people of the little prairies," the name of the site where the city of Flint stands today was called "Muscutawaingh" in the Chippewa treaty of 1819 which meant "open plain burnt over." This is essentially the same word that the Chippewa on Walpole Island use for the city of Flint today. He further notes that the Indians around Kalamazoo a century ago called Prairie Ronde, a prairie remnant area, "round fire-plain." Others have suggested that the many small prairies in Michigan survived because the Indians burned them over at regular intervals.

In light of the constant association of the Mascouten, Potawatomi, Sauk, Fox, and Kickapoo, and because of their linquistic similarities, I refer to them as People of the Fire. Perhaps their fires are also from burning over prairie areas. These were dynamic groups in the historic period, breaking up and re-forming at frequent intervals. Rigidity did not exist in the historic period and any designation other than "People of the Fire" would not do justice to the actual situation.

Even if we grant that the People of the Fire were a group of central Algonquin peoples in the Early Historic Period, we are still left with the problem of where they dwelled. By 1640, the Potawatomi, Nassauaketon, and Sauk were reported

197

living near the Winnebago along the shores of Green Bay. According to Allouez, the western shore of Lake Michigan in 1667 was the country of the Potawatomi; he later reported villages of Potawatomi, Sauk, Fox, and Winnebago around the shore of Green Bay. In 1679, LaSalle located a Potawatomi Village on an island near the mouth of Green Bay, which Quimby (1965c) identified as Summer Island. In 1695, a number of Potawatomi moved to the territory of the Miami, along the St. Joseph River in southwestern Michigan, and in 1701, another group settled near Detroit. They were the principal villages of this group.

A problem arises with the early location of the Sauk and Fox. There is a very strong traditional belief (Dustin 1968: 118) that the Saginaw Valley was the home of the Sauk and Fox who were driven out of the area by the Chippewa. Champlain's map of 1632, and many later maps, place the Asistagueronon in the lower peninsula of Michigan. This observation, coupled with the name "Saginaw," interpreted as "place of the Sauk," has been taken as proof of the location of the Sauk and Fox in the Saginaw Valley prior to 1640. Wakefield (1966) has reviewed the historical development of this idea and has pointed out a number of serious flaws. Among these is the observation that the distance from the south shore of Georgian Bay to Saginaw is only one hundred thirty miles instead of over six hundred. I find Wakefield's arguments for the original habitation of this area by groups other than the Sauk and Fox sound. The archaeological materials similar to those associated with known groups of People of the Fire after 1650 are almost completely absent from the Saginaw Valley. They, like the Potawatomi, were

located in areas other than the Saginaw Valley at the time of initial contact, probably during the late prehistoric period.

The economic aspects of the People of the Fire are as elusive as their location. The few references cited by Kinietz suggest that they were heavily dependent on agriculture "raising beans, peas, squashes, tobacco, melons, and an abundance of very fine corn." Like the Ottawa, the women were in charge of the fields. Their hunting activities, however, were different as were their social organization and settlement system. I mention this because Quimby (1960) groups the Ottawa with the Potawatomi and separates them from the Miami, which he puts with the Sauk and Fox. Quimby apparently based this on linguistic similarities but does not present his evidence in any detail. I view the type of adaptation as more important and group the People of the Fire with the Miami in opposition to the Ottawa. These groups were known by what they did and where they did it.

The Potawatomi pattern of hunting involved both winter and summer hunts. During the summer, the men hunted near the villages, presumably within a day's walk, and returned to the villages at night. This would be possible in the richer Carolinian province where game was more plentiful, particularly around the small prairies, than it was in areas farther to the north. Like most other groups in the upper Great Lakes, winter hunts were of greatest importance. In contrast to the Chippewa and Ottawa, the Potawatomi winter hunts, and those of the Sauk, Fox, Kickapoo, Mascouten, and any other People of the Fire, involved the removal of the entire village to hunt in a new territory during the winter as a unit. This too seems to be a characteristic of groups in the Carolinian biotic province and we shall see its occurrence again with the Miami.

THE MIAMI

The term Miami may have originated from the word *Omaumeg*, meaning "people who live on the Peninsula." It is found in the early literature as Oumamik, Oumamis, Oumami, and Miamiak and only after 1680 is it standardized to Miami. The Miami include the subdivisions of the Wea, Atchatchakangouen, Pepicokia, Nengakonkia, Piankashaw, and Kilatika. Some of these groups are spoken of as separate tribes or as the Miami of a given place.

They were first contacted in the 1650s in the Green Bay area. At that time most of the group was to the west of the southern end of Lake Michigan. There was a general movement of these people to the south and back to the east over the next century. In 1679, a Miami and Mascouten village was reported near the portage between the Kankakee and St. Joseph rivers. By the end of the seventeenth century, the St. Joseph River Valley was the favorite residence of these people and the river was often called the River of the Miami. They were joined in the area by groups of Potawatomi after 1718.

Groups are sporadically reported near Starved Rock in Illinois, near the sites of Vincennes and Lafayette in Indiana, and around Detroit after the establishment of Fort Pontchartrain. Later and more permanent settlements occurred near Fort Wayne, Indiana, along the Maumee and on Laramie Creek, a branch of the Big Miami River, in Ohio. Kinietz estimates that by this time their original number of

approximately five thousand individuals had been reduced to two thousand so the Miami were never a numerous or large group.

They are reported to have lived in "forts," presumably stockaded villages, and to have had a custom of sweeping out the villages and depositing debris at a distance from the village. The Miami villages were permanent and lived in by the entire group during the summer while people tended the fields. Agriculture was important. Crops included corn, beans, squashes, melons, pumpkins, and gourds. Agricultural products were preserved in storage pits dug in the ground and lined with bark while corn was also kept hanging inside of their lodges.

The women had primary responsibility for the fields as well as for gathering wild foods, fruits and roots, rushes and reeds for mats. During the summer, from April to October, the men hunted at short distances from the village. They returned to help the women with the harvest, a sign of the importance of agriculture.

The winter hunts were communal and women and children accompanied the men leaving only the older men and women in the villages. This was either to protect the women and children from attack in the absence of warriors, or to enable woman and children to assist the men in butchering the animals killed on the hunt and to help in processing the meat.

The principal game animal mentioned in most accounts of winter hunts was the buffalo, but there are also references to hunting elk, deer, bear, and beaver in both the prairies and woods. Animals were taken in drives with fire-surrounds and by stalking. A good hunter killed as many as a dozen animals in a day. Meat was smoked or cut into strips and either dried over a fire or in the sun. Fishing was unimportant.

The Miami pattern is one of large village agricultural adaptation. Women tended crops near the villages between April and October while men hunted in the area. After the harvest, the entire group packed up and went out hunting. Winter camps must have been temporary camps, perhaps changed several times during the winter, with storage and drying facilities but no stockades or permanent structures.

THE HURON

A large body of literature exists on the Huron. Kinietz (1940) has compiled almost as much information on the Iroquoian-speaking Huron as on *all* of the Algonquin-speaking peoples in the upper Great Lakes put together. The Huron have also been the subject of a recent and extensive monograph by Elisabeth Tooker (1964). However, the Huron had little direct influence on Michigan. The homeland of the Huron was in Ontario and by the time we find reference to them in Michigan all that are left are small refugee parties, often living among other groups.

The Huron were contacted by Cartier on the Island of Montreal in the St. Lawrence River in 1535. In the early seventeenth century, Champlain visited their villages in the Lake Simcoe area just to the south of Georgian Bay in the region known as Huronia. Here they lived in eighteen towns with a population of thirty thousand or more. During the following three decades, many priests and explorers lived with these groups, leaving us with detailed accounts of their life way.

The Huron warred with the league of the Iroquois to the south and east, particularly with the Seneca. But by the middle of the seventeenth century the Seneca acquired guns and destroyed the Huron villages. Groups of refugee Huron joined their Iroquoian-speaking neighbors, the Tionontati, in 1647, but they too were dispersed by the Seneca. Other Huron went to Christian Island in Georgian Bay while some Huron and Tionontati took refuge with the Ottawa on Manitoulin Island. During the 1650s they all fled to Michilimackinac and later the Green Bay region, where they were reported among the Potawatomi. Huron were among the Ottawa who moved to Chequamegon Bay on Lake Superior but, out of fear of the Sioux, they all moved back to the east: the Ottawa back to Manitoulin Island and the Huron to St. Ignace.

After the establishment of Fort Pontchartrain in 1701, Cadillac persuaded the remaining Huron to settle near Detroit. He reported that in 1703 only twenty-five Huron remained at Michilimackinac. The original Huron Village near Detroit was located on the west side of the Detroit River but it was relocated on the east side around 1733. The Huron term for themselves in this area was Wendat or Wyandot, meaning either "islanders" or "dwellers in a peninsula."

The economic activities of the Huron in Michigan varied as the group moved around the state. In Ontario, however, in the pre-1649 period, they had an agricultural adaptation in the northern extension of the Carolinian biotic province. Like the Ottawa, they played a strong role as traders across ecological boundaries but their adaptation was to the more reliable southern zone.

Accounts refer to large stockaded villages with as many as two hundred long houses, each containing many families. Corn, beans, squash, and sunflowers were grown by the Huron women during the summer. Most accounts emphasize the importance of corn in the diets of these people. Wild food plants, including cranberries, plums, grapes, and acorns, were collected to supplement and give taste to a corn diet.

Hunting and fishing were male activities and were carried out at some distance from the villages. Fishing was a fall activity and Tooker (1965: 63–64) relates Sagard's account of a group of men spending the month of October on an island in Lake Huron. They constructed a house "in the Algonquin fashion" and spent their days fishing with nets. The fish were sundried, smoked, and boiled to recover the fish oil.

Hunting was important in the spring and in the fall following the fishing season. Deer, bear, and beaver were the principal animals hunted. The larger animals were captured both by stalking and surrounds. Meat from such hunts was probably dried or smoked before being taken back to the villages.

Tooker (1964: 71–72) summarizes the seasonal cycle of the Huron. In the spring, the people left the villages to engage in various summer occupations such as trading, hunting, fishing, warfare, and agriculture. During the spring and summer the men traded while the women moved out of the village into houses in the fields. During the fall the men went first fishing and then hunting. They all returned to the villages in December and spent the winter "feasting, dancing, and playing games."

The Huron seasonal cycle has some similarities to that of the Ottawa, who shared the middleman role in trade. It was, however, a more efficient adaptation to a richer environment with a surplus that allowed winter leisure.

The efficient Huron economic adaptation also contributed to the destruction of the tribe, for the great population was maintained only by spending a large part of the time broken into smaller extractive units. The fewer Seneca could attack and destroy a village in the summer and fall when the men were away engaged in trading or other economic activities. When the absent parties returned to a destroyed village they had no option but to join other groups since the crops, on which they were so dependent, also would have been destroyed.

Since the Huron in Michigan were refugee groups, the type of adaptation described above does not apply to them while they were in the state. I suspect, however, that it is an apt description for some of the prehistoric groups in the southeastern part of the state which show a great deal of similarity in material culture to the developmental Iroquois groups to the east.

CHAPTER VIII

THE ARCHAEOLOGY OF HISTORY

HISTORICAL ARCHAEOLOGY

A dedicated group of individuals, unabashed by muttered snickering of many of their archaeological colleagues, met in Dallas, Texas, in January 1967 to found the Society for Historical Archaeology.

This group has gone far toward making historical archaeology respectable; toward removing it from the province of the bottle hunters and antique dealers and placing it on a firm footing in the American archaeological community. Michigan, located in an area of interesting sites, can point to many important contributions to this field. The excavations and restoration of Fort Michilimackinac has created a great deal of interest. This interest has been unified by the founding of the Society for Historical Archaeology and in the 1967 membership list more members came from Michigan than from any other single state.

One of the unresolved questions from the first organizational meeting of the Society was how to define historical archaeology. The Dallas meeting could not produce an answer and when the constitution for the group was adopted in Virginia in 1968 the question was wisely avoided. Two of the more recent attempts to define the subject have been by Walker (1967) and Fontana (1965). There are both strong similarities and differences in these two definitions. Walker has written a polemical but often beautiful statement on historical archaeology. He feels that "it is not too late to make it a field of distinction, independent of the confining bounds of anthropologically oriented theory." "To make a success," he added, "those who work in it must consider themselves not anthropologists, not archaeologists, but historical archaeologists."

Although Walker's article is well written and not without merit, I cannot accept his conclusion. Where Walker is a historian by background and training, I am an anthropologist. Historical archaeology is most valuable to me for the information that it can furnish on anthropological problems such as: ". . . questions involving rates, kinds, and amounts of cultural change, levels of sociocultural integration, and many more—all in terms of their relation to material culture—may best be examined in historic sites if they are to be examined at all" (Fontana 1965: 65).

Where Walker envisions historical sites archaeology as a separate field of study, Fontana defines it on the basis of the unit of analysis, the historical site. In his terms, which obviously apply to the New World, "historic sites archaeology may be defined as *archaeology carried out in sites which contain material evidence of non-Indian culture or concerning which there is contemporary non-Indian documentary record.* 'Indian,' in this definition, refers to the New World Aboriginal population" (Fontana 1965: 61).

More recently Cleland and Fitting (1968) have discussed the significance and extent of historical archaeology on a wider scale than either Walker or Fontana. They have suggested that the ends described by Walker are only part of the collection techniques from which historical, sociological, and anthropological studies must develop. Mere artifact description, and perhaps temporal ordering, will lead to the development of historical archaeology ". . . as an unimaginative hobby characterized by low level research undertaken by poorly trained technicians who are aided and abetted by hordes of specialists who are, in essence, academic antique collectors." Instead, historical archaeology has an obligation to move as rapidly as possible to higher levels of analysis involving social and cultural interpretations.

Historical archaeology in Michigan has been pursued with these ends in mind and most of its practitioners, Quimby, Maxwell, Pilling, Cleland, Brose, and Stone, have approached it as anthropologists trained in the techniques of archaeology. Perhaps this is the reason why interest runs so high in the state. It is not viewed as a separate field, aloof from other studies as Walker would have it, but as an integrated area where the techniques of archaeology and the data of history may be subjected to the wide spectrum of social science analysis.

Quimby (1966b) has summarized only one aspect of historical archaeology in the area. His concern is primarily with the acculturation of the Indians of the western Great Lakes as it is reflected in their material culture. At times he mentions the social change which trade goods

wrought but this is secondary to the study of the trade goods themselves. By the early nineteenth century, the majority of the population of the state was non-Indian and he ends his Late Historic Period in 1820. It could be argued that, in terms of historic archaeology, the real potential for this study is just beginning to develop at the time he would end it.

It is my intention here to review what is known and what we are in the process of learning. Of all the sections of this book, I am certain it is this one which will be obsolete first—a tribute to the dynamics of this area of archaeology.

AN OUTLINE OF MICHIGAN HISTORY

Before highlighting the archaeology of the historic period in Michigan, it is necessary to have some idea of the historical background of the state. The early visits of the French to the area, the rivalry between the French and British over the fur trade, and the role of the area in the Revolutionary War and the War of 1812 must be understood in order to deal with the archaeology of these times. The Indian land cessions during the territorial period, the nineteenth-century migrations to the rich agricultural land of the southern parts of the state, the exploitation of the natural resources of the north, and the rise of industrialism in the twentieth century are the main trends of Michigan history.

The literature on Michigan history is vast. The journal *Michigan History* has served the state for over fifty years and before it the Michigan Pioneer and Historical Collections go far back into the last century. The books on Michigan history number in the thousands. I have sometimes chided historians about devoting so much time and effort to the study of the last three hundred and fifty years when so very little is known about the previous twelve thousand years. Their reply, of course, is that this is my fault, not theirs. Still, their efforts are impressive, and their results are of great use. I am dependent for the outline presented here on two summaries sponsored by the Michigan Historical Commission: an extensive work prepared by F. Clever Bald (1954) and a recent brief review by George S. May (1964a).

Recorded history in Michigan can be traced back as far as in almost any state —back to the early seventeenth century. At the same time the pilgrims were settling in Massachusetts, the French were exploring the area around Sault Ste. Marie. In the upper peninsula the French established outposts at Sault Ste. Marie in 1668 and at St. Ignace in 1671. In the lower peninsula there were posts near the present-day cities of St. Joseph, Port Huron, and Niles before Cadillac established the settlement around Fort Pontchartrain at Detroit in 1701.

The French who came to the region were of two minds. The priests, including Recollects, Sulpicians, and Jesuits, came with the idea of exploration and conversion. The mission was one of the principal buildings in a French settlement. The second group, however, valued the area because of the lucrative fur trade. Michilimackinac, St. Joseph, and Detroit were all at key locations for the fur trade.

The French and the British were bitter rivals in the fur trade. While no battles took place in Michigan, the French supplied and led bands of Michigan Indians on raids to the east during the French and Indian War. In 1760 and 1761, the control of Michigan passed from the French to the British. British rule was not really accepted and in 1763 Pontiac, an Ottawa leader, led an uprising against the British. Detroit was besieged for several months and Fort St. Joseph at Niles and Fort Michilimackinac in the Straits of Mackinac were captured but not held. Within a year this uprising was suppressed but thereafter the British paid more attention to their relations with the Indians of the area.

The British prohibited further white settlement in Michigan and won the allegiance of the Indians who raided American settlements during the American Revolution. The British strengthened their defensive positions in Detroit and moved the Fort at the Straits from the area near Mackinaw City out to Mackinac Island in 1781. After the Treaty of Paris in 1783 the region became a part of the new United States of America but the British did not relinquish control of their posts in Michigan until 1796.

Michigan was a part of the Northwest Territory, established in 1787. In 1803, when Ohio became a state, Michigan was part of the Indiana Territory. The Michigan Territory, including the lower peninsula and the eastern portion of the upper peninsula, was established in 1805 with William Hull as governor. At that time the capital of the Territory in Detroit consisted of a few hundred people and there were only four other non-Indian settlements. The several thousand residents were mostly French-speaking Indians.

Both Detroit and Mackinac fell to the British in the War of 1812. While Detroit was retaken in 1813 the British held Fort Mackinac until the treaty of 1814 returned all of Michigan to the United

States. It was 1822, however, before an American garrison was stationed at Sault Ste. Marie. The period after the War of 1812 saw the rapid settlement of Michigan as the second territorial governor, Lewis Cass, arranged several major land cessions from the Indians. Between 1805 and 1835 the population of Michigan jumped from around four thousand to over eighty-five thousand people. In 1835, the people of Michigan drafted a state constitution, elected Stevens T. Mason governor, and applied for admission to the Union. Because of a dispute over state boundaries, admission was delayed until 1837. This conflict over the boundary with Ohio led to the "Toledo War." Michigan gave up its claim to Toledo in exchange for the western part of the upper peninsula. The capital of the state was moved from Detroit to its present location in Lansing .in 1847.

Michigan was primarily an agricultural state in the pre-Civil War period, although America's first major mining boom started in the upper peninsula in the 1840s with the exploitation of the iron and copper resources of that part of the state. In the second half of the nineteenth century, the lumber industry became a prime factor in the economy of Michigan. Saginaw, Muskegon, and Menominee were all leading lumbering centers. Lumbering altered much of the landscape, as all of the timber of the northern lower peninsula and much from the upper peninsula was removed between 1860 and 1910. Around the turn of the century the economic activity of the state began to focus to an even greater extent on Detroit.

In reviewing the archaeology of the historic period in Michigan, we are no longer dealing with small hunting and gathering units but with an area which is participating in a worldwide pattern of economic and political development. The archaeology of history can only be seen through the framework of history.

THE EARLY HISTORIC PERIOD

Quimby (1966b) defines the Early Historic Period as that of 1610 to 1670. Europeans were sparse in the area during this time; so few, in fact, that we can name them individually. The personal effects of these men contributed nothing to the archaeological record of this period. Their influence is reflected primarily in those Indian sites that contain trade goods.

Unfortunately, no site in Michigan has yet yielded evidence of trade material from this period so we must turn elsewhere for examples of traces of early European influence. In Ontario, Dr. J. N. Emerson has spent a number of years excavating a site which he believes is Cahiague, the largest town in Huronia, which was visited by Champlain in 1615. The site is reported to have contained two hundred long houses. The average long house so far excavated is approximately 30 feet by 120 feet and is assumed to have housed twenty-five to thirty-five people. Most of the archaeological assemblage is indistinguishable from that of the immediate prehistoric period but French trade items are found, including woolen blankets, brass kettles, iron axes, knives, awls, and needles.

Other Ontario sites which contain pre-1670 material include an ossuary, which Kidd (1953) has identified as the Huron ossuary near Ossossane described by the Jesuit priest Bréfeut in 1636, and the upper levels of the Frank Bay site on Lake Nipissing (Ridley 1954). In addi-

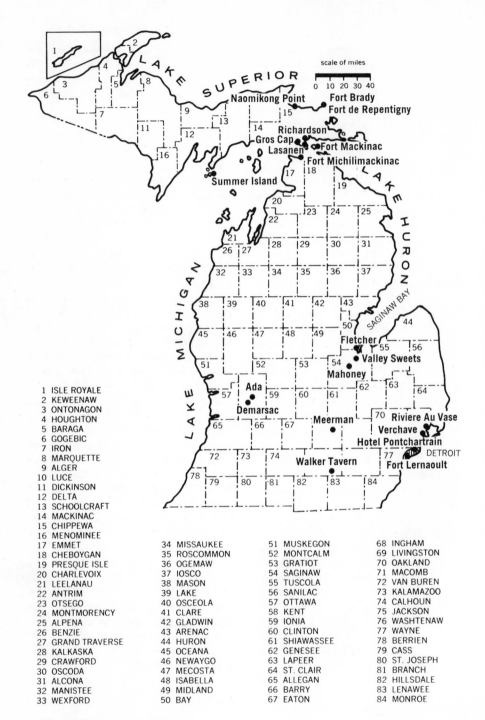

Fig. 113 *Historic sites in Michigan*

1 ISLE ROYALE
2 KEWEENAW
3 ONTONAGON
4 HOUGHTON
5 BARAGA
6 GOGEBIC
7 IRON
8 MARQUETTE
9 ALGER
10 LUCE
11 DICKINSON
12 DELTA
13 SCHOOLCRAFT
14 MACKINAC
15 CHIPPEWA
16 MENOMINEE
17 EMMET
18 CHEBOYGAN
19 PRESQUE ISLE
20 CHARLEVOIX
21 LEELANAU
22 ANTRIM
23 OTSEGO
24 MONTMORENCY
25 ALPENA
26 BENZIE
27 GRAND TRAVERSE
28 KALKASKA
29 CRAWFORD
30 OSCODA
31 ALCONA
32 MANISTEE
33 WEXFORD

34 MISSAUKEE
35 ROSCOMMON
36 OGEMAW
37 IOSCO
38 MASON
39 LAKE
40 OSCEOLA
41 CLARE
42 GLADWIN
43 ARENAC
44 HURON
45 OCEANA
46 NEWAYGO
47 MECOSTA
48 ISABELLA
49 MIDLAND
50 BAY

51 MUSKEGON
52 MONTCALM
53 GRATIOT
54 SAGINAW
55 TUSCOLA
56 SANILAC
57 OTTAWA
58 KENT
59 IONIA
60 CLINTON
61 SHIAWASSEE
62 GENESEE
63 LAPEER
64 ST. CLAIR
65 ALLEGAN
66 BARRY
67 EATON

68 INGHAM
69 LIVINGSTON
70 OAKLAND
71 MACOMB
72 VAN BUREN
73 KALAMAZOO
74 CALHOUN
75 JACKSON
76 WASHTENAW
77 WAYNE
78 BERRIEN
79 CASS
80 ST. JOSEPH
81 BRANCH
82 HILLSDALE
83 LENAWEE
84 MONROE

tion to Huron-like ceramics, Ridley recovered iron and bronze swords and dagger guards, iron fishhooks and fish spears, bayonet fragments, iron awls and knives, Jesuit rings engraved with crosses and the letters "IHS" and a brass kettle with large rivets on the bracket section, fragments of other brass kettles, tinklers and bangles made of kettle brass, and some glass beads.

Another area occupied during this period has been reported by Quimby on Madeline Island at the mouth of Chequamegon Bay on Lake Superior. The bulk of the pottery recovered in this area suggests Huron styles with some Oneota materials. Associated European trade materials include arrowheads of iron, French clasp knife blades, fragments of brass kettles, and long tubular beads of blue and brick red glass. It is possible that sites of this time period will be located in Michigan, for they must have existed around Sault Ste. Marie and the Straits of Mackinac.

THE MIDDLE HISTORIC PERIOD

I will also use Quimby's (1966b) definition for the Middle Historic Period of 1670 to 1760. There are three types of sites in Michigan and close surrounding areas that we need to deal with separately since they represent different types of activity or different groups of people. These are historic Indian villages, historic Indian cemeteries, and European sites; all European sites are forts. The Indian village sites are: the Bell site in Wisconsin, identified as a Fox site; the historic Indian occupation at Summer Island which may have been Potawatomi; the pre-fort or early fort occupation at Michilimackinac

which may be either Huron or Ottawa; and the upper levels of the Shebishikong, Michipicoten, and Pic River sites, all in Ontario, which were probably occupied by the Chippewa. The reported Indian cemeteries of this period include the Richardson or St. Ignace Ossuary, the Lasanen site in St. Ignace, and the Gros Cap cemetery just west of St. Ignace. Fort Michilimackinac is the most important, and most completely excavated, of the European forts of this period but work has recently been done at Fort de Repentigny at Sault Ste. Marie.

The Bell site is located on the south shore of Big Lake Butte des Morts, five miles west of Oshkosh, in Winnebago County, Wisconsin. It was excavated in 1959 as a salvage project under the direction of Dr. Warren Wittry (Wittry 1963). It was found to be a palisaded village with internal evidence of rectangular wall trench houses and circular post mold patterns indicating less substantial lodges.

The aboriginal pottery was mentioned in an earlier chapter. The items of European manufacture are numerous. Brass artifacts include beads, bells, Jesuit rings, kettle lugs, projectile points, tinklers, a thimble, a bracelet, a button, and some scraps of wire. Iron artifacts include awls, axes, firesteels, grenades similar to those excavated from Fort Michilimackinac, knives, musket parts, a hoe, a jew's-harp, and a key. Seven fragments of glass and about 120 glass beads also occur. The artifacts, as well as the historic accounts of the area which were examined by Wittry, indicate this was a Fox Indian village, occupied between 1680 and 1730.

Parmalee's (1963) account of the bone refuse and Blake and Cutler's (1963) notes on the plant remains give a good picture of the economic activities of these people.

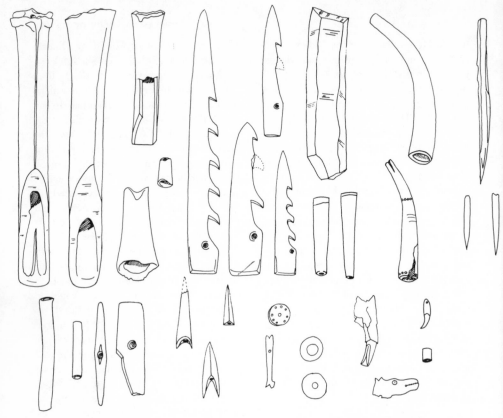

Fig. 114 *Indian artifacts from the Fort Michilimackinac excavations* (*From Maxwell: 1964*)

Several fragments of charred corn cobs and fragments of charred squash indicate that the people were either agricultural or in contact with an agricultural group. The distribution of animal remains reveals a great deal of emphasis on a few species, deer, beaver, and black bear in particular. Fish was an important food source. In spite of the use of European goods and evidence of direct European contact, the way of life of the people at the Bell site was similar to that of peoples of the Late Woodland period.

There is less evidence of contact in the Middle Historic level of the site on Summer Island, excavated by David Brose

for the University of Michigan in the summer of 1967. It consists of beads and a few metal objects. This is one of the latest occupations of the site and is poorly represented in a few areas overlying richer and earlier occupation levels. It has also been radiocarbon dated to A.D. 1620± 100 years (M-2014), which, if taken at face value, would make it Early Historic. The analysis of this site is not yet complete and we have no information on the economic activities of these people. However, since the island is too small to have carried a large enough game population to make hunting worth while, and since earlier occupations seem to be summer

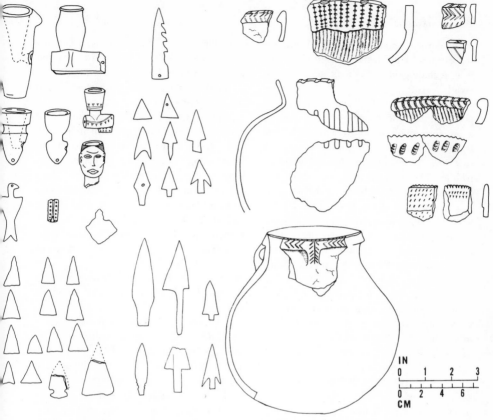

Fig. 114 *continued*

occupations which are dependent on fishing, it is likely that this occupation too is that of a summer fishing station. Summer Island is the island that Quimby (1965a) believes to be the Island of the Potawatomi visited by LaSalle.

There are some problems involved in interpreting the aboriginal cultural materials from Fort Michilimackinac (Maxwell 1964). In comparison to the European materials from this site, the aboriginal materials are sparse. Maxwell decided that most of this aboriginal material was probably deposited on the site during the period immediately prior to the construction of the original French stockade. The sample of artifacts consists of 750 sherds of Indian pottery and 78 other objects clearly of Indian manufacture. Any trade goods which these people might have had cannot be distinguished from the materials left by the French who later built the fort. The historic Indian goods consist of bone harpoons, bone hide dressers, and bird bone tubes as well as other bone implements and ornaments. There are twenty-two small triangular chipped stone projectile points as well as two points chipped from green bottle glass. A large brass projectile point is a copy of one of the elk antler harpoons. There are sixteen small brass points, including triangular and shouldered forms. There are stone pipes of local and foreign manufacture, including both Calumet and Micmac styles.

Maxwell sorted the small sample of pottery into four categories. The first is a jar form with a constricted neck and squared lip which is completely covered with the impressions of a cord-wrapped paddle. The second form is apparently similar to the Bois Blanc and Juntunen Wares recovered from Bois Blanc Island, while the third is a grit tempered Oneota Ware similar to that from so many sites of the prehistoric period in the area. While these sherds may be late, as Maxwell believes, the evidence from other sites indicates that his second and third variants were more common three hundred years before the establishment of the fort rather than fifty years before as he suggests. Maxwell thinks the fourth style, the most common rim style on the site, is characteristic of the local Indians. This is a smooth-walled, slightly collared style with sharply incised chevron designs being the most common rim decoration. From the description and published line drawings, I am impressed with the similarity to Huron styles from farther to the east. While refugee Huron groups were definitely present in the Straits region during the Middle Historic Period this does not preclude Maxwell's identification of this pottery with the Ottawa. Many sites in the upper Great Lakes that were probably occupied by Algonquin-speaking peoples have produced Huron-like ceramics. These include the possible Nipissing occupation at the Frank Bay site (Ridley 1954), the Mississagi site at the mouth of the Mississagi River (cited from Quimby 1966b), and a number of possible Chippewa sites along the north shore of Lake Superior (J. V. Wright 1965). Quimby 1966b: 138) suggests that Maxwell's hypothesis can be tested by comparing this material to the ceramics recovered from the Chequamegon Bay area.

Artifacts from Fort Michilimackinac that could have been trade goods include hawk bells, Jesuit rings, C-shaped bracelets of brass wire, brass tinkling cones, brass braid, iron spear points, French clasp knives, iron awls, butcher knives, iron strike-a-lights, brass buttons with holes drilled in the shanks, brass kettles with riveted lugs, religious medals, and blond gun flints. There is also a wide range of glass trade beads which may be placed in fairly tight chronological sequence when the final Fort Michilimackinac report is available.

J. V. Wright (1965) has reported on a series of sites which he believes to be Middle Historic Period Chippewa sites. Two, Michipicoten and Pic River, are located on the north shore of Lake Superior, while the third, Shebishikong, is located on Georgian Bay. The contact level at Shebishikong yielded sixty-one items of European manufacture with trade beads, kettle fragments, gun flints, and iron knife fragments heading the list of probable late seventeenth- or early eighteenth-century manufacture. Half of the fourteen aboriginal rimsherds are of the Huron-Petun styles with the next most frequent category of the Blackduck style. Scrapers predominated among the thirty-four other items of Indian manufactures in the contact level.

The Michipicoten site yielded more aboriginal ceramics but fewer trade goods. The most common European artifact classes are trade kettle beads and trade beads, but two gun flints, a kettle fragment, a metal triangle, a metal pendant, and an iron knife were also recovered. Again, the most common type of ceramics are those of the Huron-Petun style with "Peninsular Woodland," a style apparently similar to Bell site Type II ceramics and the ceramics from Dumaw Creek, almost as common. Wedges or utilized small cores, scrapers, and abraders are most common among the forty-four other aboriginal items.

Trade items, particularly beads, represented by 1156 out of a total of 1335 specimens, are plentiful in the historic level of the Pic River site. After beads, lead shot, kettle fragments, metal bangles, and gun flints are most common with twenty-five other classes of European objects represented by one to six occurrences.

The majority of the fourteen aboriginal rimsherds are of a style related to Juntunen Ware with Blackduck rims next in frequency. Wedges, or utilized small core fragments, and scrapers account for two thirds of the sixty-five other stone items of aboriginal manufacture. Only the Pic River site has historic bone artifacts, including awls and other fragments of worked bone.

These sites are characteristic of the type of contact sites that occur along the St. Marys River and along the south shore of Lake Superior in Michigan. They also furnish us with a very good picture of Indian values. In contrast to some of the burial sites which we will discuss later there are high percentages of economic

Fig. 115 Burial pit at the Lasanen site (Courtesy of Charles E. Cleland)

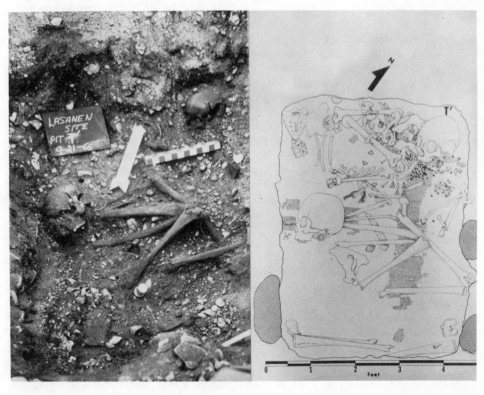

goods in the adopted tool kits. Beads are common on village sites but not as common as in burial sites. Kettles, knives, guns, and metal projectile points played the greatest role in the developing European trade system. Items of aboriginal manufacture have not disappeared at this time. Potsherds and chipped stone tools on these sites are similar to prehistoric forms and, on many sites, just as frequent. If anything, the European goods of the Middle Historic Period led to a craft elaboration for some of the bone carving, and certainly the stone carving is more elaborate than during the prehistoric period.

A second group of Middle Historic Period sites are burial sites.

The earliest of these is the Richardson Ossuary site located on the corner of Airport and State roads in St. Ignace. The site was visited and reported on in 1958 by Emerson Greenman (1958). The artifacts recovered with the ossuary include twenty-two brass bangles, three hawk bells, three brass coils, a shell runtee or disk-shaped pendant decorated with engraving, and, according to Quimby (1966b: 135) two brass kettles.

In 1679, LaSalle's ship the "Griffin" reported two villages at Michilimackinac, one Huron and one Ottawa. Since it is known that the Ottawa adopted the feast of the dead in the historic period and that prehistoric Algonquin peoples buried their dead in ossuaries, this site could have been either Ottawa or Huron although ossuaries are more characteristic in the Huron.

The Lasanen site is also in St. Ignace and was excavated by field parties from Michigan State University in 1966 and 1967. Charles Cleland directed these excavations and has kindly furnished me

with a summary of the results of his work through the 1967 season. Burials of an undetermined number of individuals were found in the twenty-seven pits. The ossuary type of burial, like that reported from the Richardson site, is representative of an earlier period. The Lasanen site represents a transitional stage between an ossuary burial and individual burials. Several individuals were found in almost every pit. The practice of the feast of the dead, of collecting bodies for several years and reburying them together with great ceremony, a characteristic of ossuary burials, is continued in a minor way at Lasanen. It is apparently the grave goods rather than the body that represents a burial. Cleland found individuals represented by as few as three finger bones.

The grave goods recovered from the site include an incredible range of materials. Most are of French manufacture but there are also items of native manufacture using both native and European raw materials. For example, there are European-made projectile points of both iron and brass, aboriginal chipped stone projectile points, and projectile points of native manufacture from European brass.

Glass beads by the thousand were recovered as were wampum, shell gorgets, runtees, and tubular shell pipes. Catlinite zoomorphic effigies include otters, beavers, owls, fish, and a porpoise. Iron artifacts include clasp knives, sheath knives, scissors, harpoons, awls, compacts, and snuff boxes. Other European items are brass kettles, buttons, Jesuit rings, wire bracelets, coiled rings, and tinkling cones. There are textiles of flax, cotton, and wool, wooden spoons and dishes, and bone combs.

The artifacts can all be placed in the time range of 1680 to 1750 but the burials

Fig. 116 Artifacts from the Gros Cap Cemetery (From Quimby: 1963a)

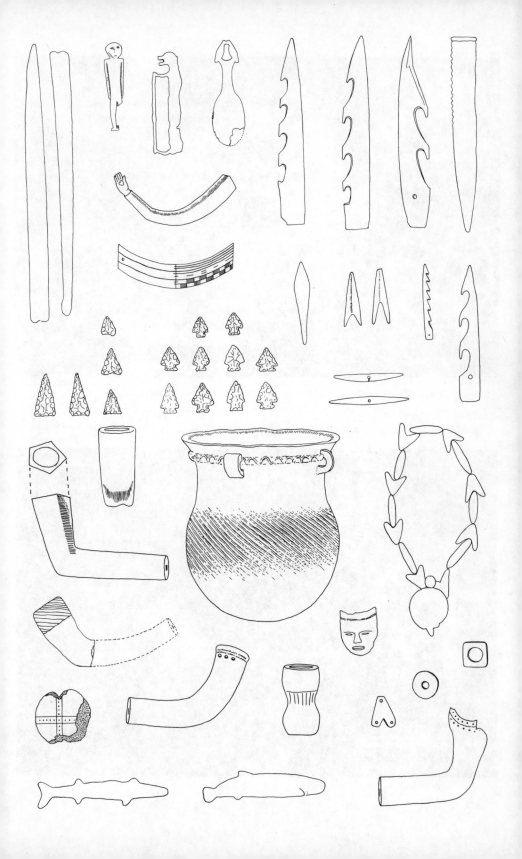

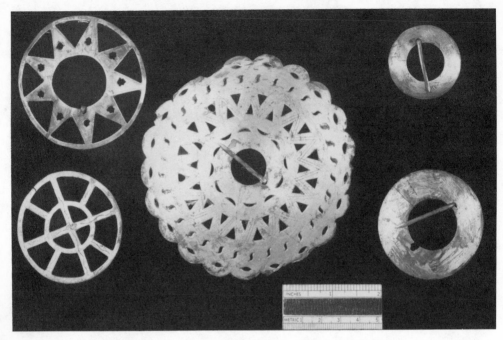

Fig. 117 Trade silver from Michigan (University of Michigan Museum of Anthropology)

Fig. 118 Trade silver from Michigan (University of Michigan Museum of Anthropology)

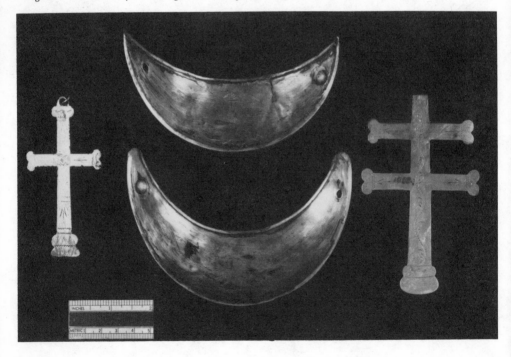

probably date to some time between 1690 and 1710. Cadillac left a description of the type of burials at the Lasanen site in a report dealing with St. Ignace in 1697. Cleland identifies the people buried at the Lasanen site as Ottawa but holds that by 1700 the population at Michilimackinac was a very mixed group.

The Gros Cap cemetery (Quimby 1963a, 1966b: 125–37), located five miles to the west of St. Ignace on West Moran Bay, represents a burial site which is younger than the Lasanen and Richardson sites. On the basis of trade beads Maxwell (1964: 27) narrows Quimby's suggested time range of 1710 to 1760 down to 1730 to 1750. Quimby was working with collections obtained from private excavations which had taken place over a number of years and did not have any control over grave lot associations. From what information he could gather, the burials were single extended burials, on their backs with hands crossed on their chests. Cremations were also found.

Trade materials from the site include the usual iron awls, clasp knives, butcher knives, strike-a-lights, and barbed arrowheads. There are fragments of brass kettles, Jesuit rings, brass hair coils, hawk bells, and tinkling cones. One religious medal is brass or bronze. The glass beads from the site are especially important in dating the site.

Artifacts of aboriginal manufacture include many objects of carved bone: mat needles, a human effigy, a polished bone tube, several bone awls, chipping tools, unilaterally barbed harpoons, and bone arrowheads. Items of catlinite consist of an effigy pipe, beaver effigy pendants, and beads. There are tubular pipes of shell, a shell pendant, and a shell fish effigy. A number of trumpet pipes reminiscent of the Huron style occur. Chipped stone arrowheads are both corner-notched and triangular.

Only a few aboriginal sherds have been recovered from the site and they represent a great deal of variation. Much of the material is tempered with both shell and grit. Sherds with notched lips, plain rims, and notched appliqué strips and lugs are present. The range of ceramics represents everything from what has tentatively been identified as historic Erie to historic Fox. Either because of the specific mortuary nature of the site with emphasis on exotic ceramics, or because of the accelerated pace of cultural contact and homogenation following the establishment of Fort Michilimackinac, no single ceramic tradition is dominant. Quimby notes that Ottawa were the principal native residents of the Straits around 1700 and, because of the absence of specific styles of Huron ceramics, would favor the Ottawa as the group buried at Gros Cap. Maxwell questions this because he thinks he has Ottawa material which is different at Fort Michilimackinac at a slightly earlier period. Recalling the amalgamation of materials found at J. V. Wright's contact sites, I suggest it is a wise potsherd that can tell the ethnic identification of its user in the year 1700.

The largest archaeological project ever undertaken in Michigan was the excavation of Fort Michilimackinac at Mackinaw City. It was started in 1959 under the direction of Moreau Maxwell of Michigan State University and has been under the direction of Charles Cleland since 1964. Work has continued up to the present under the field supervision of Maxwell, Lewis Binford, Ronald Vanderwal, Lyle Stone, and James Brown. Only the first season's work has been reported in detail

(Maxwell and Binford 1961) but a number of summary reports on the archaeology have been prepared (Vanderwal 1966, Stone 1965, 1966, 1967a) and there are a large number of secondary reports which include archaeological data (Peterson 1963a, 1963b, 1964, May 1964b, 1964c, Campbell 1965).

The Straits of Mackinac had long been strategic for trade in the upper lakes, a fact the French readily recognized. Prior to 1701 the French maintained Fort Dubois, as yet unlocated by archaeologists, in the St. Ignace area. Cadillac officially moved the French center in the upper lakes south to Detroit in 1701 but, many

Jesuits and *coureurs-de-bois* remained at Michilimackinac. There was agitation for the establishment of a French fort in the area and this was finally done in connection with the expedition against the Fox Indians in Wisconsin in the second decade of the eighteenth century. Accounts were left from this expedition of the Fox village with which the Bell site is associated. Initially, the French garrison occupied the St. Ignace area but between 1715 and 1720 they established a new fort on the south side of the Straits at the site of Fort Michilimackinac.

Between 1720 and 1760, the Fort was expanded to at least three times its original

Fig. 119 Michigan State University excavations at Fort Michilimackinac (Courtesy of Lyle M. Stone)

size, incorporating much private property. A church was built and a significant French settlement collected on the site. In September 1760, the French governor surrendered the Fort to the British General Amherst and the British occupation of the Fort began. Although the British occupation of the Fort, by definition, falls within Quimby's Late Historic Period it might be worth following the final fate of the Fort at this time. The British occupation was filled with trouble. Since much of the land inside the stockade was privately owned and this ownership had been recognized in the treaty of surrender, the British had to pay rent on most of the area of the Fort while they were there. Maintaining a garrison also proved to be a problem. In 1763, as a part of the Pontiac uprising, Chippewas camped outside the Fort and by trickery managed to massacre or capture most of the British garrison. The Fort was under the supervision of one of the French inhabitants for the next year until the British regarrisoned it in 1764. For the next fifteen years the command of the Fort was frequently changed and in 1779 the commandant, Patrick Sinclair, razed the Fort, moving "bricks, boards, and planks" from the mainland out to Mackinac Island. By 1781 the last vestige of military occupation had disappeared.

In contrast to the previous sites that have been discussed, Michilimackinac excavations are not easily summarized, for excavation is still in progress. Artifacts have been recovered at a rate of around twenty thousand a year for eight summers, and the features, many of which are entire buildings, number in the hundreds. The artifact categories listed in the first season's report alone include: awls, axes, bailing seals, barrel hoops, beads, bells, buckles, buttons, ceramics, combs, cuff links, fishhooks, games and toys, glassware, grenades, gun flints, gun flint patches, gun parts, files, saws, chisels, screwdrivers, locks, keys, door hooks, latches, pintles, hinges, ice creepers, jewelry, jew's-harps, knives, razors, lancets, musket balls, lead shot, needles, pins, pipes, metal projectile points, scissors, spigots, spoons, forks, strike-a-lights, sword fragments, thimbles, and tinkling cones. The best record published so far on the range of materials is Petersen's (1964) picture book of Michilimackinac artifacts *Gentlemen on the Frontier*. As one reviewer described it, it gives you the feeling of looking through drawer after drawer of artifacts in the storage cabinets of a museum. While not furnishing any provenience record or definitive analysis, it hints that such analysis will be forthcoming.

The same thing may be said of Petersen's study of pipes (1963a, 1963b) and Campbell's study of buttons (1965). These studies also tend toward utilization of documentation for interpretation rather than dealing with the important cultural associations that were present in the Fort Michilimackinac excavations. They show the promise of Fort Michilimackinac as one of the best and most extensive historic site projects in North America.

During the summer of 1967, Lyle Stone directed a Michigan State University field party in the excavation of the Fort Brady site at Sault Ste. Marie (Stone 1967b). While this work was in progress, two walls of the French Fort de Repentigny were uncovered. This Fort, apparently 110 feet on a side, was occupied between 1754 and 1762 or near the end of the Middle Historic Period. The analysis of the 1967 season's work is not complete but French artifacts do not seem to be frequent.

THE LATE HISTORIC PERIOD

Quimby (1966b) defines the Late Historic Period as 1760 to 1820. This creates some problems in placing sites. He is concerned primarily with Indian archaeology and it is true that materials manufactured specifically for and by Indians disappears around this time, but the process is gradual. Some of the Indian burial lots described by Quimby quite probably postdate 1820.

Quimby's end date of 1820 coincides roughly with the Cass Treaty of 1819 which opened large areas of the lower peninsula for settlement. It marks the first period of major agricultural settlement of the area. It also marks the beginning of the intensive historic occupation of the state so the term Late Historic is somewhat misleading.

Most of the archaeological attention for this period has been paid to burials. No Indian village sites of this period have been excavated and reported in the state. Herrick (1958) has reported some evidence for an Indian village at the Ada site. Little is known about the village occupation since historic and prehistoric materials are mixed on the surfaces and the area is disturbed ". . . due in all likelihood to sharp-eyed collectors' previous efforts."

If a village site of this period were found and excavated it would probably be similar to the Fox village in Illinois of the late eighteenth century excavated by Elaine Bluhm (cited from Quimby 1966b: 141). It contained a row of rectangular houses with verticle pole walls all running along a sand ridge. Numerous storage pits, fire pits, and refuse pits were uncovered, including some which contained charred corn.

Conservativism was reflected in the native manufacture of stone pipes, bone knife handles, weaving implements, and hair ornaments. The greatest quantity of artifacts were of European manufacture. They included parts and accessories of flintlock guns, iron knives, brass kettle fragments, iron axes, kaolin pipes, glass beads, and silver ornaments. It is these silver ornaments which are, as Quimby pointed out long ago (1937, 1938, 1939b), the marker of the Late Historic Period.

Almost all we know of the Indian archaeology of the Late Historic Period in Michigan is from burial sites, including a number of small sites reported by Quimby (1938), and more recent reports on the Ada, Herron, Meerman, Valley Sweets, and Fletcher sites. Sites of European occupation of this time which have been excavated include the British levels of Fort Michilimackinac, dated from 1761 to 1780, and the recent work of Wayne State University at Fort Lernoult in Detroit.

Burial sites with trade goods have been reported from many parts of the state. In the 1930s Quimby excavated a burial site near Niles in the southwestern part of the state which contained two graves. One contained an adult in a semiflexed position with a brass kettle and a polished stone tobacco pipe of native manufacture but patterned after European kaolin pipes. Nearby was a child's grave with hawk bells, an iron spoon, and a number of small silver brooches.

Another burial near Niles was excavated by Arthur Jelinek in 1958 (Jelinek 1958) This was a coffin burial of a young woman. She was clothed in trade cloth ornamented with silver brooches; her hair was in braids. With the burial were glass beads, silver brooches, crosses, and pendants.

CENTIMETERS

CENTIMETERS

Fig. 120   Trade artifacts from the Valley Sweets site (From Brose: 1966b)

Jelinek dates the burial to the first half of the nineteenth century.

To the north there are several historic burial sites along the Grand River. Quimby (1966b: 149–50) has described some of the material recovered from the Battle Point site near Grand Rapids, probably an Ottawa cemetery of the 1830 through 1850 period. Artifacts of native manufacture include wooden ladles, fragments of animal skin robes, and strips of trade silver with native engraving. Artifacts of European manufacture consist of many styles of silver brooches and crosses and a hair pipe of silver. There are a large variety of glass beads, iron tools, and brass tools and ornaments.

Farther up the Grand River, Herrick (1958) has reported several burial groups from the Ada site located at the junction

THE ARCHAEOLOGY OF MICHIGAN

of the Grand and Thornapple rivers. This was a salvage excavation and in only one case could the burial positions ·and associations be determined. The artifacts from the site are both historic and prehistoric. Some of the ceramics and chipped stone tools might have been made by historic Indian groups but, because of lack of association, this could not be demonstrated. Trade goods include iron knives, a tomahawk pipe of iron, strike-a-lights, gun flints, brass cooking pots, brass thimbles, glass bottles, and trade silver all described in detail in Herrick's report. The historic burials appear to date to the early part of the nineteenth century.

Quimby (1938) has described a single female burial from the Thornapple River Valley. Artifacts include beads, a brass kettle, iron scissors, a strike-a-light, a silver cross, a bone matting needle, and an iron awl with a bone handle. Like the Ada and Battle Point sites, Quimby believes that this too is an Ottawa site.

Several burials were salvaged from the Meerman site in Ingham County in 1958 by members of the Central Michigan (now Upper Grand Valley) Chapter of the Michigan Archaeological Society (Hogg and Darling 1959). This site is on the Red Cedar River, a tributary of the Grand. Parts of two burials were recovered from back dirt piles and the walls of a basement excavation. There is one chipped stone artifact, several trade brooches and a fragment of a "Henderson" pipe stem, a mid-nineteenth century type. Like the other Grand River burials these are early to mid-nineteenth century associations.

In the Saginaw Valley the Valley Sweets site in the city of Saginaw (Brose 1966b, Jones 1966) has yielded a number of burials which seem to represent several phases of the Late Historic Period. This

site was also excavated as a salvage project by members of the Saginaw Valley Chapter of the Michigan Archaeological Society. By working with the grave associations and descriptions, Brose identified a group of 1760s burials in bark coffins with many beads, early silver artifacts, and artifacts of iron and brass. A later nineteenth-century group of Indian burials in wooden plank coffins with later trade silver and other artifacts was also present.

A number of historic burials have been excavated at the Fletcher site in the Saginaw Valley in Bay City. Trade goods have been recovered from this site in the past along with aboriginal materials, and a University of Michigan field crew, while working at the nearby Kantzler site in 1966, put in several test pits. These excavations suggested that there was little chance of stratigraphically isolating prehistoric and historic components which seemed to be thoroughly mixed near the river bank with a strong suggestion of secondary deposition. In 1967, a number of historic burials were discovered in a different part of the site and a field crew from Michigan State University, assisted by members of the Saginaw Valley Chapter of the Michigan Archaeological Society, were able to halt local looting and recover information on many burials. These Michigan State University excavations were carried out under the direction of Moreau Maxwell and the collections are now housed at the Michigan State University Museum.

About thirty burials were recovered, mostly single burials in coffins. The grave goods indicate a time range of 1780 through 1820. There are quantities of silver brooches, crosses, bracelets, and baubles. Other metal artifacts include kettles, a complete gun, a big iron pike point, clasp knives, and sheath knives. Most of the beads are small seed beads, and the larger beads, common in earlier and later Indian sites and even in sites of the same time period in other areas, are very rare. A number of fragments of fabric were found and a catlinite tomahawk pipe was reportedly found but disappeared, along with many other items, in the general looting that took place before archaeologists arrived at the site.

As in the Middle Historic Period, the best excavated fort site in Michigan is Fort Michilimackinac, occupied by the British between 1761 and 1781 or during the first part of the Late Historic Period. The French and British features and artifacts have been reported in the same sources mentioned earlier and will not be repeated. The occupational intensity of the British period was greater than during the French occupation and communications with the outside world were better. Larger numbers of non-Indians were in the area and greater quantities of goods, to supply both Indian and European demands, can be assigned to this time period.

Cleland (n.d.) has made a comparative study of the food remains represented in the refuse pits from the French and British occupations at Fort Michilimackinac and has contrasted the diet of these European groups to the diet of the aboriginal inhabitants on nearby Bois Blanc Island. As mentioned in Chapter VI, the diet of the Late Woodland inhabitants of the Straits, an area occupied by them during the summer months, was primarily based on fish, including whitefish, sturgeon, and trout. Hunting contributed deer, beaver, and a few other animals while corn apparently had little place in their diets—at least it is poorly represented in the refuse pits.

The French were ready to adopt the diet of the Indians and fish and game species found in the Indian refuse pits are also present in the French refuse pits. Several new food sources appear: pigs, chickens, and a few horses. Several old resources, water birds and upland game birds in particular, were exploited to a greater extent than in the precontact period. This was probably a result of the use of firearms in hunting. The French attempted agriculture but with little success because of the short and unpredictable growing season, the same factors which limited the prehistoric development of agriculture in the area. This was one of the reasons for the move from the Straits down to Detroit. In 1741, even the Ottawa gave up trying to farm in this area and moved to L'Abre Croche where the soils and climate were a bit better for agriculture. The French were forced to import foodstuffs from Detroit and even farther to keep the post in operation.

The British, faced with an even larger population and greater logistics problems, had to import even more food. This parallels the British disinclination to utilize local resources. In contrast to the French and Indian refuse pits, fish and wild game of all sorts are drastically diminished in British refuse pits. In their place are the bones of chickens, pigs, and cattle, for cattle were being raised at Fort Michilimackinac and salt beef, as well as salt pork, was imported from great distances. Tradition as well as necessity played a role in the British dietary pattern and made an already difficult logistics problem worse.

Little work has been done in Fort Mackinac on Mackinac Island. Brose

(1966a) spent a few days in test excavation in the southeast bastion in 1965 and located several cultural features and some small amount of cultural material from the late eighteenth century. This material dates to both the immediate preconstruction period and to the period of initial occupation. Hopefully further work will be done inside the Fort on Mackinac Island, for this site is significant to both eighteenth- and nineteenth-century history and archaeology.

Salvage excavations have been undertaken at the site of Fort Lernoult, later known as Fort Shelby, in downtown Detroit (Mason 1964, Pilling 1965, 1966). Fort Lernoult was built by the British during the American Revolution and was completed in 1779. It was built in haste, for it was feared that the Americans would attack Detroit. The attack never came but Fort Lernoult served as a center for the

British campaigns in the west. According to the Treaty of Paris in 1783 the British were to have surrendered the Fort but they did not yield it to the Americans until 1796. At that time they built a new post at Amherstburg across the Detroit River. The Fort was captured by the British in the War of 1812, held for a year, and abandoned in 1813. When reoccupied by the Americans it was renamed Fort Shelby. It was held until 1826 when the military garrison was removed to Green Bay. The Fort was given to the city of Detroit which leveled it in 1827 and the area was surveyed for building lots.

Pilling and field crews from Wayne State University were able to do salvage work in the area when construction was undertaken on the new Detroit Bank and Trust building in 1962, 1963, and 1964. It

Fig. 121 Michigan State University excavations at Fort Brady (Courtesy of Lyle M. Stone)

was possible to define many stages in the construction and rebuilding of the Fort, and many artifacts were recovered. When building activities prevented further excavation, Pilling arranged for the truckloads of dirt removed from the Fort area to be placed where it could be later sorted by archaeologists and artifacts recovered. The soil types adhering to the artifacts were checked against the stratigraphic pattern noted in the excavations and many additional associations were possible. Therefore, the "excavation" of Fort Lernoult continued long after the archaeologists were unable to work at the site. The final report on this excavation will increase our understanding of late eighteenth- and early nineteenth-century archaeology and complement the activities at Fort Michilimackinac.

THE PRE-CIVIL WAR PERIOD

Further classification is needed for the archaeology of the period following Quimby's Late Historic Period. Following the British precedent of referring to recent historical sites archaeology as "Post-Medieval Archaeology" I could speak of "Post-Late Historic Archaeology," but this would be confusing. Brose (1967: 81–82) notes that the Upper Great Lakes supply systems and, therefore, cultural associations differ greatly between the pre-Civil War and post-Civil War periods. This is based on the observation that the later combination of railroad and water transportation was more efficient than the pre-Civil War system based primarily on water transportation. The burgeoning industrial development in the twentieth century also suggests a distinctive archaeological subdivision.

While the first professional excavation of a site of this period was Greenman's excavation of the historic cabin site at Rivière au Vase in Macomb County in 1936 and 1937 (Greenman 1957, Fitting 1965b), the material from this excavation was not described until the early 1960s and then only in light of work done by Wayne State University in the late 1950s and early 1960s. Arnold Pilling has taken the lead in the study of nineteenth-century archaeology in the state and many other studies are in debt to his pioneer work (see Pilling 1965, 1966, 1967a, 1967b).

Pilling has developed a ceramic chronology for the area based partly on his work elsewhere and partly on the excavations in Detroit which include the upper levels encountered in the Fort Lernoult excavation discussed above, the Michigan Consolidated Gas Company site (Pilling 1960c), the Hotel Pontchartrain ceramic importers dump (Pilling 1965, 1966), and a number of other sites. The University of Michigan data from the Rivière au Vase site and the Verchave II site (Fitting 1965b) in Macomb County have also been added to this sequence.

Members of the Wright L. Coffinberry Chapter of the Michigan Archaeological Society have furnished some additional information on this period from the De-Marsac Trading Post near Grand Rapids (Gibson, Peru, and Herrick 1960) which was occupied in the second quarter of the nineteenth century. They have located the fireplace, old cabin foundation, and many artifacts from this site.

While the analysis is not yet complete, the Naomikong Point site on Whitefish Bay has produced considerable cultural material of this pre-Civil War Period. This is related to a mission known to have

Fig. 122 *Bottles from the Custer Road Dump site (From Brose: 1967)*

been on the site in the 1840s and 1850s. The Naomikong collections show a great deal of similarity to those from the Hudson Bay company post near the mouth of the Pic River in Ontario. This occupation, dated to between 1831 and 1865, has recently been described by Gall (1967).

Brose's work on Summer Island in northern Lake Michigan in the summer of 1967 included some work on a fishing camp known to have been abandoned some time around 1870. Bea Bigony directed additional excavations of this component in the summer of 1968. George

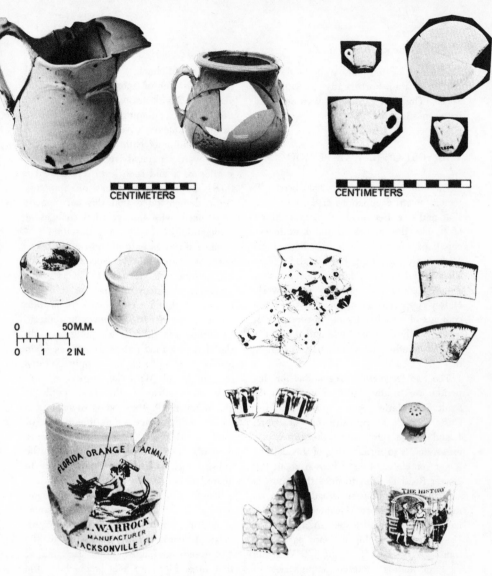

Fig. 123 Ceramics from the Custer Road Dump site (From Brose: 1967)

Miller (1967), from Wayne State University, excavated at the Walker Tavern site in the summer of 1967, a pre-Civil War tavern site near Brooklyn, Michigan. Gordon Grossup, also from Wayne State, directed additional excavations in 1968.

Two forts that were occupied during this period have been excavated. Brose (1966a) spent a short time in Fort Mackinac on Mackinac Island and recovered traces of pre-Civil War material as well as eighteenth-century artifacts and post-Civil War materials. In the summer of 1967, Lyle Stone (1967b) from Michigan State

225

University located the walls and some buildings from Fort Brady at Sault Ste. Marie. This American fort was occupied between 1822 and 1892.

THE POST-CIVIL WAR PERIOD

Very little archaeology has been directed toward occupations of the post-Civil War and twentieth-century periods. Much of it, like the studies of the historic occupations of sites in the northern Lake Michigan area (Rupp n.d.) and Saginaw Valley (Halsey n.d.), consists of reports on data collected incidently to other work. Halsey's report contains an analysis of the contents of an early twentieth-century refuse pit at the Mahoney site and this is the only twentieth-century site analysis I know of.

The two large-scale excavations for this period are military sites, Fort Brady at Sault Ste. Marie (Stone 1967b) and the Custer Road Dump site on Mackinac Island (Brose 1967). Since the Fort Brady excavation is so recent, little of the analysis is yet complete. More is known about the Custer Road Dump site since the report is available. The Custer Road Dump is located behind Fort Mackinac on Mackinac Island. It was tested in 1963 by a University of Michigan field party and found to be clearly stratified. With the hope of finding material dating back to the initial occupation of the Fort, a Uni-

versity of Michigan field party returned in the summer of 1965 under the supervision of David Brose. It was a stratified site but the dumping levels recorded a cultural sequence covering only the final third of the nineteenth century. The dump levels were separated from each other by sterile layers and each level represented a three- or four-year period of dumping. Brose demonstrated that this corresponds very nicely with the recorded changes of commanding officers during this time.

Since this was entirely refuse, no occupational features were encountered but Brose was able to use the very tight artifact associations of three- or four-year intervals to build a chronology for historic artifacts of the late nineteenth century. In addition to this, he was able to study the changing food habits and, to a certain extent, the logistical and supply patterns of that period. With the decreasing military importance of the Fort until its abandonment in the 1890s, there was a corresponding decrease in the quality of food served to the garrison until, as Brose observes, one would imagine that the enlisted men at least were quite ready to abandon the post by 1895.

The field of nineteenth-century archaeology is one of the fastest growing areas of endeavor in Michigan archaeology. Almost all work can be attributed to the last decade and most to the last half of that time. More work is planned for the future.

CHAPTER IX
PATTERNS OF THE PAST

Can *the* archaeology of an area ever be written? I think not. The "definitive" statement of the moment is the progress report of yesterday for the archaeologist of tomorrow. By the following day it becomes a straw man. However complete a report we prepare, we are still dealing with our own interests and our own bias. Even a site report, and particularly a synopsis of regional archaeology, reveals more of the author than of the peoples he purports to describe.

This volume is concerned with the relationship of past peoples to their natural environment. It is a chronicle of changing adaptive patterns for the inhabitants of Michigan over nearly twelve thousand years. In some cases specific relationships are clear, in others they are vague and our current understanding disappointing. My goal has been, on one hand, to study the land, the lakes, the rivers, and the plants and animals which lived in Michigan. On the other hand, I have tried to present what is known of the way people lived in this land. The results of this two-pronged approach are summarized in the following paragraphs.

Michigan has a long geological history. Although some pre-Cambrian rocks are present most of the rocks underlying the state were formed during Paleozoic times. Because of uplift and erosion Michigan lacks Mesozoic and early Cenozoic deposits. The surface of the state is, today, largely covered by glacial features. The most prominent of these features are moraines which can be used to interpret patterns of glacial advance and retreat. Other glacial features include till plains, outwash plains, lake plains, kames, and eskers.

The Great Lakes are another prominent feature of the area. Four of these lakes border Michigan: Superior, Michigan, Huron, and Erie. In the past the lakes have had different sizes, shapes, and drainage patterns than they do today. Gravel ridges, old beach lines, wave-cut notches and terraces have been studied to interpret the history of the lakes.

The rivers of Michigan are also a prominent feature of the state. Michigan has thirty-four rivers with drainage areas over 250 square miles. Eight of these have been considered as first-class rivers: the St. Joseph, Kalamazoo, Grand, Muskegon, Manistee, Menominee, Au Sable, and the Saginaw. Six of these drain into Lake Michigan while two, the Au Sable and Saginaw, drain into Lake Huron.

Michigan has a temperate, humid climate. Over most of the state, temperatures average below 27° Fahrenheit in the winter and below 72° Fahrenheit in the summer. Some areas in the southern parts of the state have either warmer summers or winters or both. Rainfall varies between 28 and 36 inches per year with a mean of 31 inches. The lakes have a modifying influence on the temperatures in the state, which is neither as cold in the winter nor as warm in the summer as states farther to the west.

Despite a great deal of variation in local soil types it is possible to divide Michigan into an area of podzols in the north and an area of gray-brown podzolic soils in the south. A similar north-south split occurs in vegetation with oak-hickory and maple, basswood, and beech forests in the southern half of the lower peninsula and the mixed Lake Forest in the rest of the state. The distribution of animals follows a similar pattern with distinctive southern and northern species. The division between a southern Carolinian biotic province and a northern Canadian biotic province, which is transitional to the Hudsonian biotic province, has proven significant for the study of the past several thousand years of Michigan prehistory. In addition to these major divisions, nine smaller natural areas were defined for convenience of description and to make smaller study units. These include southeastern Michigan, southwestern Michigan, the Saginaw Valley, eastern Michigan, western Michigan, the Straits of Mackinac, the south shore of the upper peninsula and the eastern and western portions of the north shore of the upper peninsula. It is against this environmental background that we must view the archaeological record of Michigan.

Before man entered Michigan he had to reach the New World. He might have entered the New World prior to the advance of the last phase of the Wisconsin glaciation but much of the evidence for this is equivocal and many who hold this position do so more on faith than on fact. The first well-dated archaeological horizon in North America is that characterized by fluted points. A vast body of evidence points to the period of 10,000 to 9000 B.C. as the time of a major and dramatic spread of this cultural tradition. While many of these Paleo-Indian peoples were big game hunters, it would be unreasonable to suppose that they were not aware of, and did not utilize, other food resources where they were available.

The Paleo-Indian settlement and utilization of eastern North America can best be viewed within the framework provided by the post-glacial environmental diversity of the area. The environments included a peri-glacial forest-tundra edge or spruce parkland area with a relatively high carrying capacity for these early hunters, a boreal forest environment with a decidedly lower carrying capacity and a deciduous forest environment which, although it lacked the rich hunting potential of the tundra-forest edge, held many resources available to man. The deciduous forest environment was expanding in size and richness while that of the tundra-forest was decreasing.

The early peri-glacial Paleo-Indian hunters in the north either moved farther to the north with the retreat of the ice sheet or remained to carry on an extended Late Paleo-Indian cultural tradition in special environmental situations in the boreal forest zone. In the deciduous forest areas to the south, many local cultural traditions rapidly developed with a denser population and with more restricted group territories than in the north. Here there was a gradual development from the Paleo-Indian into the Archaic tradition. These peoples were in a more varied environment and exploited more diverse resources. As broadleaf forest spread to the north and contemporary drainage patterns were established, people with this Archaic cultural tradition also moved to the north. In terms of cultural tradition, we can talk of a gradual transition from Paleo-Indian to Meso-Indian or Early Archaic in the south. If we use the term "Archaic" as a cultural adaptation, then even the people who made fluted points in the broadleaf forests had an "Archaic," or foraging, economy as opposed to a "Paleo-Indian," or primarily large game hunting, economy.

In Michigan, the Paleo-Indian occupation is readily distinguished from the Archaic occupations. The Paleo-Indian occupation can be divided into two phases using Mason's typological criteria with some refinements for our particular area. The earlier Paleo-Indian occupation is marked by unstemmed lanceolate projectile points, the majority of which are fluted. It represents an occupation by periglacial hunters or by people hunting in an environment similar to peri-glacial conditions because of differences in drainage patterns. The Late Paleo-Indian occupation is marked primarily by stemmed lanceolate projectile points as a key artifact. These people seem to have lived in a rich lakeshore environment which existed between the high and low water stages of 9000 to 7000 B.C.

Evidence from the distribution of Early Paleo-Indian cultural materials suggests that these people were in Michigan in some number between 11,000 and 9000 B.C. Careful studies of fluting techniques indicate diversity among cultural groups with distinctive artifact styles even within this time range. The Barnes site in Midland County is an example of a short-term camp site of these people. The Holcombe beach contains a number of sites dating to the final stage of the Early Paleo-Indian occupation. Here we were able to deal in more detail with environment, type of adaptation, and the nature of the social units.

Our understanding of the Late Paleo-Indian occupation is complicated by the history of the Great Lakes themselves. The shorelines that furnished the home for these peoples, who were apparently more forest oriented than their predecessors, were in areas now as much as four hundred feet below modern lake levels. Many of their sites are today under hundreds of feet of water. We have only scattered artifacts found in what then would have been forested interior areas, perhaps left during seasonal hunting forays into these areas. In the northern parts of the Great Lakes the post-glacial uplift has been much greater than the rise in lake levels following the Chippewa-Stanley low stage. Because of this a number of sites that would otherwise have been flooded have been preserved. These sites include the George Lake and Sheguiandah sites in the Manitoulin district of Ontario; plus the Renier site in Wisconsin. These northern sites are marked by a widespread use of quartzite which may be the complement of a widespread use of argillite in the lower peninsula. It may be that Archaic peoples occupied the southwestern part of Michigan at this time. Archaic influence on Late Paleo-Indian people is suggested by the notched projectile points found in many of these assemblages.

The concept of the Archaic has been increasingly useful in eastern North America over the past thirty-five years. Definitions of the Archaic center on temporal, subsistence, and technological factors. Problems are encountered with every set of definitions but I favor a set of technological definitions separating Paleo-Indian from Archaic assemblages on the basis of projectile point types and from Woodland assemblages by a lack of ceramics. Time overlaps at both the beginning and end of the Archaic with first, Paleo-Indian. and, later, Woodland groups. Definitions based on subsistence are ambiguous since many Paleo-Indian groups could have been gathers and hunters as well as big game hunters.

The Early and Middle Archaic are poorly represented in Michigan as they are throughout much of northeastern North America. This is primarily because of the post-glacial environments in this area which were much more boreal in nature than they are today and had a lower frequency of plant and animal foods useful to man. What information we have on the sparse Early and Middle Archaic occupation comes from interior river valleys, particularly high areas, which would first have been colonized by hardwoods, in the southern part of the state. If lakeshore occupations occurred, they would have been covered during the subsequent rise in lake levels. Early and Middle Archaic materials in Michigan are represented by scattered surface finds and by minor components at mixed sites.

The intensive Late Archaic occupation of Michigan coincides with the establishment of near modern environmental conditions and the return of high water levels in the Great Lakes. The economy of these people, as known from the Feeheley, Schmidt, Butterfield, and other sites, was a diffuse economy making use of a number of resources. It probably involved seasonal movements within a restricted territory.

There is a great deal of similarity in material culture as well as cultural adaptations during the Late Archaic. One aspect of this is an elaboration of burial practices which takes several forms. In the southern broadleaf forests, the Carolinian biotic province, the Red Ocher and Glacial Kame "Cultures" are found. It is here that we have the greatest elaboration of burial practices, perhaps involving a number of social units in a common ceremonial activity. This burial activity takes a simpler form in the Canadian biotic province with the Lake Forest Archaic where simpler burials still contain grave goods, many of copper. During Late Archaic times there was a widespread use of copper indicating wide trade networks. This use of copper, however, is just one trait in an otherwise complex Late Archaic adaptation. It is best studied as one factor of Late Archaic culture rather than as a culture in itself.

Some time in the sixth century B.C. the introduction of ceramics marks the appearance of Early Woodland in the southern parts of Michigan. It is possible that the use of cultivated plants was introduced at this time as well as ceramics. Such cultigens, however, were just added to the total economic inventory of these people although they might have made Early Woodland cultures more viable under environmental stress. There is evidence from the Schultz and Kantzler sites that these people pursued a seasonal pattern of hunting, fishing, and gathering activities similar to that of Late Archaic peoples.

During the Middle Woodland period we can see both a florescence and extension of cultural traits evident in earlier times as well as the development of new patterns of land use in some areas. The traditional method of defining the Middle Woodland period is based on the beginning and the end of the Hopewell cultural development in the central and southern parts of the eastern United States and comparable non-Hopewell developments in northeastern North America.

The most obvious expression of the Hopewellian "interaction sphere," as Caldwell (1964) has called it, is in mortuary activities involving elaborate burials in mounds. Such burial practices have a precedent in the Adena burial mounds of the Ohio River Valley which have been radiocarbon dated to the first millennium B.C. The earliest Hopewell materials are from the Illinois River Valley and Hopewell materials are later than Adena in the Ohio drainage. It may be that Adena survived in outlying areas to the north, south, and east of the area where it originally developed.

The Hopewell culture, cult, or interaction sphere is marked by certain types of burial practices, usually in mounds, which include elaborate grave offerings. Items typically associated with Hopewell, and sometimes considered diagnostic of it, include platform pipes, bear teeth, cut animal jaws, true blades, corner-notched projectile points, and a variety of other goods. Ceramics tend to be decorated with dentate stamping, rocker stamping, and incising. There is some variation in rim form and vessel shape. Small quadrilobate vessels with crosshatched rims separated from the bodies by a small row of punctates and zoned stamping or incising on the bodies seem to be very common in Michigan burial sites.

There is much variation in the settlement and subsistence patterns of groups that have been called Hopewell. In Ohio there are a number of massive earthworks. It has been postulated that these ceremonial centers were supported by many small agricultural hamlets spread out along the river bottoms. The McGraw site, where corn was found, along the Scioto

has been used as an example of one of these hamlets. In the Illinois River Valley the earthworks are less elaborate and the mounds smaller. There are a number of large village sites. It has been suggested that use or perhaps cultivation of seed plants, as well as the intensive utilization of a variety of other resources, was responsible for this cultural development.

In Michigan, Hopewell Middle Woodland materials have been found in the southwestern and western parts of the state and in the Saginaw Valley. Much of what is known from western Michigan is known from the numerous burial mounds in the area which have been subject to excavations for over a century. Most of the material recovered seems to be related to the assemblages from Illinois mounds.

Quimby studied collections from a number of these sites in the 1930s and included them in the Goodall Focus. More recent work has been undertaken along the Grand River at the Spoonville and Norton Mounds by Flanders and in the Muskegon River Valley by Prahl and members of the Wright L. Coffinberry and Newaygo County chapters of the Michigan Archaeological Society.

Village sites that have been tested in western Michigan include the Spoonville site on the Grand River and the Toft Lake and Jancarich sites along the Muskegon and more recently the Holtz site in Antrim County. Spoonville has produced some early radiocarbon dates but the ceramic assemblage seems to contain much that is Late Woodland. Cleland's analysis of the fauna suggests that it is typical of that found in Late Woodland agricultural villages. I feel that the faunal remains and the majority of artifacts on this admittedly mixed site are Late Woodland while the radiocarbon dates and some of the ceramics are Middle Woodland. The exact season or reason for the occupation of the Jancarich and Toft Lake sites is not yet known but Prahl has suggested that Jancarich is a McGraw-like occupation which would imply an agricultural base.

The Saginaw Valley, in contrast to western Michigan, is known primarily from village sites, particularly the large, stratified Schultz site at Green Point. There are a series of Middle Woodland occupations dating from the centuries preceding the birth of Christ up through the fifth century A.D.

The overall Middle Woodland occupation of the valley can be interpreted from the Schultz site and other Middle Woodland sites such as Kantzler and Bussinger. It looks as though a resident population developed an exploitative pattern similar to that of peoples to the north with summer camps containing population concentrations and winter camps with small dispersed groups. This is in contrast to the Late Archaic and Early Woodland pattern with winter concentration camps and summer dispersal camps. At the same time, a number of material traits from the Hopewell areas to the south were adopted, many of them not in the context in which they originated.

Either because of the cultural conservativism of the area or the lack of understanding of the cultural context in which the Hopewell traits functioned, some Hopewell expressions last until the fifth century A.D. in the Saginaw Valley, apparently long after they have been abandoned in the Hopewell heartland to the south. In the southern parts of the lower Michigan peninsula the only positively Middle Woodland materials are Hopewell and these have a very restricted distribution. In some parts of the midwest it has

been suggested that there is a "generalized Middle Woodland" which co-exists with the Hopewell Middle Woodland in areas away from the large river valleys. There may be such a Middle Woodland occupation in Michigan but it has not yet been positively identified.

To the north in the Lake Forest formation there is a distinctive Middle Woodland adaptation which has an historic Chippewa type of settlement system: summer population concentrations in areas of good fishing and winter dispersal for hunting. This Lake Forest Middle Woodland pattern exists from Manitoba to New York and there is a great deal of stylistic similarity in items of material culture throughout the region. The Lake Forest Middle Woodland is represented in our area by the North Bay complex of the Door Peninsula in Wisconsin and a number of sites in Michigan including Summer Island, the Burnt Bluff Caves, the Eckdahl-Goodreau site, Arrowhead Drive, Wycamp Creek, Fort Brady, Naomikong Point, Isle Royale, and the Goodwin-Gresham site.

The transition between Middle and Late Woodland can be seen in the Spoonville, Root, Gibraltar, Rivière au Vase, and Fort Wayne Mound sites in the southern parts of the Michigan lower peninsula. The ceramics for this transitional stage are globular cord-marked vessels and other artifacts found with them are corner-notched projectile points, gorgets, celts, and copper ornaments. Maize agriculture may have played a part in the subsistence base as indicated at the Sissung site. Several sites of this transitional stage have been radiocarbon dated to the latter half of the first millennium of our era.

Both southeastern and southwestern Michigan were responsive to cultural developments in surrounding areas, particularly around A.D. 1000. Southwestern Michigan was first influenced by developmental Mississippian from the south and later by extensive Oneota or upper Mississippian influence. This later style horizon had a distribution around the western and southern shores of Lake Michigan and is reported in southwestern Michigan at the Moccasin Bluff site, which appears to have been a permanent agricultural village.

At the same time, southeastern Michigan seems to be acting more in harmony with southwestern Ontario. The Younge Tradition in Michigan is strongly influenced by, and probably related to, the Glen Meyer stage of the lower Ontario Iroquois Tradition. Many traits associated with Iroquoian groups, such as long houses and ossuary burials and the feast of the dead, are represented at Younge Tradition sites. Younge Tradition materials have been excavated at Springwells, Rivière au Vase, the Wolf site, and the Younge site. Both ceramic seriation and radiocarbon dating suggest a developmental sequence which starts slightly before A.D. 1000 and lasts until some time around A.D. 1400. After that time there seems to have been little permanent use of this area until the eighteenth century.

The site patterning and land use pattern in this area are perplexing. Plant remains suggest that these people were agricultural, yet bone refuse is not typical of that found on agricultural village sites. The bone refuse is more characteristic of that found on Late Archaic summer occupations. Ceramics vastly outnumber lithic materials and chipping detritus is almost nonexistent. There are fewer ceramic vessels on many Younge Tradition sites than there are burials, a strange demographic situation where there are more people than pots. From the distribution and ratios of archaeological materials, it has been argued that the Younge Tradition people lived somewhere else, or pursued their major economic activities elsewhere, and spent only a few months during the summer in southeastern Michigan and then primarily for mortuary activities.

The Saginaw Valley Late Woodland sequence starts with an archaeological cultural expression very similar to that found in the more southern parts of the state during the same time period. The same type of cultural materials persist to the eleventh and twelfth centuries in the Saginaw Valley, while they disappear around A.D. 1000 in other areas. The Bussinger site contains some living debris but is primarily a Late Woodland burial site. Over 120 burials have been recovered from the site. We have also excavated a number of Late Woodland living sites including the upper levels of the Schultz and Kantzler sites and the Mahoney, Hodges, Stadelmeyer, and Foster sites.

All of these Late Woodland sites are low density occupations where chipping is common and chipped stone tools are equal to, or outnumber, ceramic vessels. The most common feature at these sites is large, circular, straight-sided and flat-bottomed pits in which there is little or no cultural material. They appear to be emptied storage pits. Animal bone refuse from these sites as well as the types of stone tools present indicate that hunting of a few large animal species was the primary subsistence activity. While the pattern of hunting is characteristic of a people with an agricultural village base, we find no evidence of the practice of agriculture by these Late Woodland peoples.

I believe the Late Woodland sites in the Saginaw Valley are the winter and spring hunting camps of people who do have an agricultural adaptation but whose main villages are located elsewhere. The division of Late Woodland sites between those which have approximately equal amounts of ceramics and stone tools and those where stone tools outnumber ceramics may mean that groups with both Ottawa and Miami and Potawatomi patterns hunted in the valley at various times but did not have their permanent camps there. This was the historic pattern for the first use of the valley recorded in the early historic period before the Chippewa groups moved in during the eighteenth century.

The eastern Michigan sub-area is located in the Carolinian-Canadian transition zone and the few sites in this area seem to reflect both northern and southern influences. The first of these occupations suggests the same early Late Woodland culture as much of the rest of the state. The West Twin Lake burial mound, for example, has been radiocarbon dated to A.D. 950. The Butterfield site has ceramics which date to this time period but they include both the southern Wayne Wares and the northern Mackinac Wares. The Butterfield site is apparently a Late Woodland hunting camp with balanced sexual composition. The Late Woodland occupation of this site is of intermediate density and I would guess that it is the winter hunting camp of a group with a Chippewa pattern of subsistence and settlement. A later occupation is marked by the sites located in a number of earthworks which date to the period of A.D. 1350 to 1450. These are large structures with palisades along the walls. They include the Rifle River Earthworks, the Walters-Linsenman Earthwork, and the Mikado Earthwork. The artifact densities are very low, which I would interpret as meaning a short-term occupation. Chipping debris and stone artifacts are rare and are outnumbered by even the few ceramics which are found. The ceramics seem to be a mixed lot with indications of stylistic influences from many directions.

I believe these were villages of a people with an Ottawa type of cultural adaptation. The large fortified villages were occupied primarily by women while the men spent a great deal of time elsewhere in hunting and trading activities. Meat was probably brought to the earthwork villages from the hunting camps in a processed form, as indicated by the contents of the Mikado earthwork refuse pits. The occupation took place during the Pacific climatic episode which, along with the poor soils of the areas where the earthworks are located, could have forced their rapid abandonment. Like the Saginaw Valley and southeastern Michigan, there was no very late prehistoric occupation and the areas were visited only sporadically in the Early Historic Period.

In western Michigan there are a number of burial and village sites which relate to a wider early Late Woodland horizon such as I have noted elsewhere. In the Muskegon River Valley stylistic influence came from a southern source but by the time we get as far north as the Manistee River Valley northern stylistic influences are also found. Early Late Woodland mounds include the Brunett, Carrigan A and some of the Mallon Mounds in the Muskegon River Valley and the Fife Lake Mound in the Manistee drainage. The largest excavated village site is the Spring Creek site along the Muskegon River which has been radiocarbon dated to the tenth century A.D. Spring Creek represents one of the densest ceramic occupations so far known in the state. The ceramics are of a fairly homogeneous Late Woodland style. Chipping debris and stone tools are not at all common and reflect hunting activities. The bone refuse from the site is indicative of specialized hunting activities. This site is the model site for a permanent village of the Ottawa type and suggests that this type of adaptation can be traced back to the early Late Woodland period.

The Hamlin Lake, Bear Creek, and Silver Lake sites could represent the summer sites of an Ottawa-like group while the Headquarters site might represent the winter occupation of a group of male hunters of this pattern. This would form a complete Ottawa settlement system within the western Michigan area. A number of earthworks have been reported in the Muskegon River drainage. The South Flats Club Earthwork may be related to the Spring Creek Village site but those earthworks in Missaukee County are certainly later. The Boven Earthwork, excavated by both University of Michigan and Michigan State University, has been radiocarbon dated to the fifteenth century. While the final reports are not yet out on these sites, I suspect they represent an occupational pattern similar to those from eastern Michigan: agricultural villages occupied for a short time by people with an Ottawa settlement pattern.

The Dumaw Creek site is a very late prehistoric or proto-historic village and burial site in Oceana County. Quimby's analysis of this site indicates a possible agricultural occupation by a group with a southern orientation. This site might be tied in with such historic groups as the Potawatomi, Sauk, or Kickapoo.

The Late Woodland sequence in the Straits of Mackinac sub-area is best represented at the Juntunen site on Bois Blanc Island. This stratified site was oc-

cupied during the summer season by peoples with a Chippewa adaptive pattern between A.D. 800 and 1400. The principle subsistence activity was fishing. McPherron has suggested three phases of occupation: the Mackinac, Bois Blanc, and Juntunen. The earlier occupations received major cultural stimulus from the west while the later occupations interacted more closely with peoples to the east. Long houses and ossuary burials are present in the Juntunen Phase. As is true for so much of Michigan, it is difficult to find any occupation which postdates A.D. 1400 in this area until the historic period. In the Early Historic Period the Straits area was again occupied.

Few other reports are yet out on sites in the area. Point Scott represents a summer fishing station occupied at the same time as Juntunen itself. The Eisen site near Black Lake, on the other hand, represents the year-round village of a group with an Ottawa adaptive pattern.

One of the key features of this sub-area is the Traverse Corridor, where Michigan State University field parties have been working for the past few years. The occupational sequence in the area, dated to between A.D. 800 and 1600, will add much to our understanding of this region.

Earlier Late Woodland sites along the north shore of Lake Michigan show similarities to both the earlier occupations at the Juntunen site and the Heins Creek site in Door County, Wisconsin. The sites in this area, such as Eckdahl-Goodreau and Summer Island, fit into a Chippewa settlement pattern but were not necessarily occupied by the Chippewa.

After A.D. 1000 there is a mixing of Woodland and upper Mississippian ceramics influences at such sites at Mero, Backlund, and Summer Island. I do not believe that this represents any new ethnic element in the area. The settlement patterns seem to say the same. Again, there seems to have been an occupational hiatus between A.D. 1400 and the historic period.

Nothing is known about the Late Woodland occupation along the south shore of Lake Superior. Late Woodland ceramics were found during the Fort Brady excavations and at Naomikong Point but in both instances they were minor components. Late Woodland materials have been excavated on Isle Royale but copper mining activities here seem to have been highly specialized. Bone refuse indicates both the hunting of Hudsonian species and some fishing during a summer occupation. The ceramics indicate extensive trade contacts or visits to the island by peoples from a number of different areas.

The key to understanding the Late Woodland period in Michigan is the regional symbiosis which can be observed closely in the Early Historic Period. The development and distribution of the Miami-Potawatomi, Ottawa, and Chippewa adaptive patterns must be viewed against the background of climatic change. The two factors necessary for this symbiosis were agriculture and a demand for goods from the upper Great Lakes region in areas outside the region. This demand led to a cultural florescence which took place during the Neo-atlantic climatic episode and again during the Early Historic Period.

The task of identifying the Indian groups in Michigan as of A.D. 1600 is almost impossible. Either the accounts place them elsewhere or the group terminology is so loose and fluctuating that the names used in 1600 would be as different by 1650 as they were by 1700. The Chippewa were probably the paramount group in the

Michigan upper peninsula. At the beginning of the historic period, however, many of the Indian groups usually associated with the state were found elsewhere. The Ottawa were in Ontario and on Manitoulin Island while the People of the Fire and the Miami were in the Green Bay area. It is only later that these groups move into Michigan and there appears to have been no major Indian population in the lower peninsula until later.

Greenman (1961: 24–25) has called attention to the fact that there are no accounts of Indians in Michigan south of Michilimackinac until 1675, when a few Nipissings, Hurons, and others are reported on a winter hunting trip near Midland. The lower peninsula was a no-man's-land during the late prehistoric and Early Historic periods. It was a buffer zone, empty except for sporadic hunting activities, separating the Iroquoian tribes of the east from the Algonquin groups to the west. Though there are numerous legends that Algonquin groups inhabited this area before 1650 there are no direct accounts of their presence there until after 1670.

Historic sites archaeology in Michigan takes us back about three hundred years. While there are sites which show European contact material of an earlier date in other areas of the upper Great Lakes, none has yet been located in Michigan. This Early Historic Period of 1610 to 1670 is not represented in the state but there are many sites of the Middle Historic Period of 1670 to 1760 in Michigan and nearby areas.

An excellent example of an Indian village site of the Middle Historic Period is the Bell site, a Fox village site in Wisconsin. An occupation of the same time period has been found on Summer Island. There are several cemetery sites in the

Straits area of Michigan which seem to date to this period starting with the Richardson Ossuary, possibly the earliest, with the Lasanen site and the Gros Cap Cemetery following later in time. Excavations at the European fort at Michilimackinac have been extensive and are still under way. More recent work has also been done at the site of Fort de Repentigny located at Sault Ste. Marie.

The Late Historic Period, in Quimby's terminology, lasts from 1760 until 1820. No Indian village sites have been excavated in Michigan from this period but one in Illinois associated with a historic Indian group gives us a good idea of what they must have been like. Indian burial sites dating to this period are frequent, including several near Niles and along the Grand River as well as the Valley Sweets and Fletcher sites in the Saginaw Valley. The Battle Point and Ada sites may fall toward the end or slightly after Quimby's Late Historic Period. The British occupation at Fort Michilimackinac in Mackinaw City and Fort Lernoult in Detroit date to this time period.

After 1820, there was a tremendous population increase in Michigan, caused by the movement of peoples of European origin into the state. The archaeology of this time is a new field of study. Pre-Civil War sites where some work has been done include a number of salvaged sites in and around Detroit, a site on Big Summer Island, and a Mission site at Naomikong Point. Some work has also been done at Fort Mackinac on Mackinac Island and at Fort Brady at Sault Ste. Marie. The most extensive excavations of sites of the post-Civil War period are those undertaken at Fort Brady and at the Custer Road Dump site on Mackinac Island.

Historical sites archaeology is a relatively new area of study in this country and there are many archaeologists who have yet to be convinced of its value. Once convinced, however, its techniques and results are more satisfying than prehistoric work where chronology often remains a mystery and social patterns rarely become clearer than broad conjecture will allow. The contribution to archaeological theory that has and can be made by historical sites work is impressive. It is perhaps because of this ability to constantly cross-check archaeological and historical hypothesis and to make past peoples so real to the present that has made historical sites archaeology so popular. Our knowledge of Michigan's past is much greater today than it was a century or even a decade ago. We have reached a point of understanding where we can begin to comprehend how much we do not know about it. I hope that our efforts will serve as a base for the increased understanding of others as those of the past have served as a base for our knowledge of today.

APPENDIX:

MICHIGAN RADIOCARBON CHRONOLOGY

A list of radiocarbon dates from sites in Michigan and surrounding areas is presented below. All dates have been converted to the Christian calendar system and are followed by the one sigma deviation. The Roman numeral in parenthesis following the laboratory number refers to the group of University of Michigan Radiocarbon Dates with which the particular date was published. Full references to the University of Michigan Radiocarbon Dates series are listed in the References under H. R. Crane and H. R. Crane and James B. Griffin.

DATE	SITE	LAB. NO.
3350 B.C.±150	Andrews Site, Saginaw County (Date on charcoal with skull but no cultural material)	M-941 (V)
2470 B.C.±150	Minong Site, Isle Royale (Copper mine)	M-1384 (X)
2450 B.C.±150	Minong Site, Isle Royale (Copper mine)	M-1390 (X)
2160 B.C.±130	Lookout Site, Isle Royale (Copper mine)	M-1275, d, e, f, g, (IX)
1980 B.C.±150	Feeheley Site, Saginaw County (Dates Burial complex at site)	M-1139 (VII)
1850 B.C.±250	Minong Site, Isle Royale (Copper mine)	M-371c (I)
1710 B.C.±125	Reigh Site, Wisconsin (Old Copper Complex Date)	M-644 (IV)
1510 B.C.±130	Minong Site, Isle Royale (Copper mine)	M-1388 (X)
1500 B.C.±125	Osceola Site, Wisconsin (Old Copper Complex Date)	M-643 (IV)
1420 B.C.±130	Siskiwit Site, Isle Royale (Copper mine)	M-1386 (IX)

1410 B.C.±130	Minong Site, Isle Royale (Copper mine)	M-1385 (X)
1370 B.C.±130	Minong Site, Isle Royale (Copper mine)	M-1387 (X)
1360 B.C.±130	Minong Site, Isle Royale (Copper mine)	M-1389 (X)
1220 B.C.±150	Andrews Site, Saginaw County (Date for Late Archaic Burial Complex at the site)	M-659 (V)
1100 B.C.±130	Finn Point Site, Isle Royale (Date is too early, this is a Late Woodland site)	M-1274 (X)
1090 B.C.±150	Riverside Cemetery, Menominee County (Dates Archaic burial)	M-658 (III)
1050 B.C.±175	Minong Site, Isle Royale (Copper mine)	M-320 (I)
850 B.C.±120	Lookout Site, Isle Royale (Copper mine)	M-1275c (IX)
590 B.C.±150	Carrigan Mound B, Newaygo County (Dates Early Woodland mound construction)	M-1849 (XII)
540 B.C.±150	Carrigan Mound A, Newaygo County (Dates first or Early Woodland use of this mound)	M-1984 (XIII)
540 B.C.±130	Schultz Site, Saginaw County (Dates Early Woodland occupation)	M-1524 (XI)
530 B.C.±150	Schultz Site, Saginaw County (Dates Early Woodland occupation)	M-1525 (XI)
530 B.C.±120	Schultz Site, Saginaw County (Dates Early Woodland occupation)	M-1432 (IX)
510 B.C.±140	Riverside Cemetery, Menominee County	M-1719 (XII)

310 B.C.±140	Jancarich Site, Newaygo County (This date seems too early for this apparently Late Middle Woodland village site)	M-1882 (XIII)
240 B.C.±140	Riverside Cemetery, Menominee County	M-1717 (XII)
230 B.C.±150	Killarney Bay I Site, Ontario (Date on mixed Adena-like and Laurel occupation)	M-194 (I)
130 B.C.±140	Riverside Cemetery, Menominee County	M-1718 (XII)
100 B.C.±140	Riverside Cemetery, Menominee County	M-1716 (XII)
90 B.C.±100	Killarney Bay, Ontario (Date on an Adena-like and Laurel site)	M-428 (IV)
80 B.C.±140	Schumaker Mound, Newaygo County	M-1983 (XIII)
10 B.C.±120	Norton Mound C, Kent County	M-1493 (XI)
10 B.C.±140	Palmeteer Mound, Newaygo County	M-1985 (XIII)
A.D. 1±130	Riverside Cemetery, Menominee County	M-1715 (XII)
A.D. 20±130	Killarney Bay I Site, Ontario (Dates mixed Adena-like and Laurel occupation)	M-1482 (XI)
A.D. 50±120	Juntunen Site, Mackinaw County (Feature #45, Lake Forest Middle Woodland burial)	M-1392 (IX)
A.D. 70±140	Spring Creek Site, Muskegon County (This date seems much too early for this apparently single component Late Woodland site)	M-1808 (XII)
A.D. 100±100	Norton Mound H, Kent County	M-1490 (XI)
A.D. 110±120	Spoonville Site, Ottawa County (Dates Middle Woodland occupation)	M-1428 (IX)

A.D. 120±100   Serpent Mound, Ontario   M-850 (IV)
(Middle Point Peninsula)

A.D. 160±120   Norton Mound H, Kent   M-1488 (XI)
County

A.D. 215±110   Spoonville Site, Ottawa   M-1427 (IX)
County
(Dates Middle Woodland
occupation)

A.D. 250±140   Summer Island, Delta County   M-1995 (XIII)
(Middle Woodland
component)

A.D. 255±120   Feeheley Site, Saginaw   M-1435 (X)
County
(This date is too late, it
should have been Late
Archaic. Taggart noted that
roots contaminated the
sample)

A.D. 290±75   Serpent Mound, Ontario   M-1105 (VIII)
(Middle Point Peninsula
mound)

A.D. 310±120   Schultz Site, Saginaw County   M-1646 (XII)
(Early part of the late
Middle Woodland occupa-
tion)

A.D. 320±100   Site CiIe-1, Ontario   M-1507 (X)
(Date on Laurel site on
north shore of Lake
Superior)

A.D. 375±130   Cave B-95, Delta County   M-1795 (XII)
(Dates Lake Forest Middle
Woodland occupation at this
cave on Burnt Bluff)

A.D. 380±120   Schultz Site, Saginaw   M-1644 (XII)
County
(Date is too late for the early
Middle Woodland feature. It
appears to have been
contaminated by rodent
burrows)

A.D. 450±200   Schultz Site, Saginaw   M-1647 (XII)
County
(Late part of the late
Middle Woodland occupa-
tion)

A.D. 490±120   Bussinger Site, Saginaw   M-1756 (XII)
County
(Dates late Middle
Woodland refuse pit)

A.D. 610±110   Goodwin-Gresham Site, Iosco   M-1625 (XI)
County
(Late Woodland date)

A.D. 650±200   Riverside Cemetery,   M-772 (IX)
Menominee County
(Dates Late Woodland
component)

A.D. 680±120   Carrigan Mound A,   M-1759 (XII)
Newaygo County
(Dates early Late Woodland
burial)

A.D. 700±120   Sissung Farm Site, Monroe   M-1519 (XI)
County
(Dates Rivière au Vase
Phase of the Younge
Tradition. Overlaps with
Wayne Tradition)

A.D. 750±120   Fort Wayne Mound, Wayne   M-1843 (XII)
County
(Dates early Late Woodland
burials)

A.D. 770±140   Calumet Ancient Pit,   M-1776 (XII)
Houghton County

A.D. 825±75   Juntunen Site, Mackinaw   M-1142 (VI)
County
(Dates Mackinac Phase)

A.D. 890±100   Chippewa Harbor I Site,   M-1272 (X)
Isle Royale
(Late Woodland village
site)

A.D. 900±75   Juntunen Site, Mackinaw   M-1141 (VI)
County
(Bois Blanc Phase)

A.D. 900±120   Skegemog Point, Grand   M-1865 (XII)
Traverse County

A.D. 950±100   West Twin Lake Mounds,   M-1084 (XII)
Montmorency County
(Dates an early Late
Woodland burial)

A.D. 960±75   Spring Creek Site, Muskegon   M-512 (III)
County
(This appears to be a good
date for the Late Woodland
occupation of this site)

A.D. 1000±100   Norton Mound H, Kent   M-1489 (XI)
County
(Date is much too late and
does not agree with other
dates in Norton Mound
series)

A.D. 1040±120   Schuler Site, Antrim County   M-1867 (XII)

A.D. 1060±120   Juntunen Site, Mackinaw   M-1816 (XII)
County
(Mackinac Phase)

A.D. 1060±75   Juntunen Site, Mackinaw   M-1140 (VI)
County
(Date on Bois Blanc Phase)

A.D. 1060±110   Moccasin Bluff, Berrien   M-1937 (XIII)
County

A.D. 1080±120   Juntunen Site, Mackinaw   M-1815 (XII)
County
(Mackinac Phase)

A.D. 1080±100   Whorley Earthwork, Branch   M-1758 (XII)
County
(Dates Late Woodland
earthwork)

A.D. 1090±110   Moccasin Bluff, Berrien   M-1938 (XIII)
County

A.D. 1095±100   Verchave II Site, Macomb   M-1431 (IX)
County
(Dates Younge Phase of
Younge Tradition)

A.D. 1130±120   Juntunen Site, Mackinaw   M-1817 (XII)
County
(Bois Blanc Phase)

A.D. 1150±75   Fort Wayne Mound, Wayne   M-741 (V)
County
(Dates Springwells Phase,
Younge Tradition)

A.D. 1150±110   Moccasin Bluff, Berrien   M-1940 (XIII)
County

A.D. 1180±100   Schultz Site, Saginaw County   M-1648 (XII)
(Dates Late Woodland
Occupation to its final phase)

A.D. 1200±75   Missaukee Mound ⚹2,   M-790 (VI)
Missaukee County

A.D. 1210±120   Skegemog Point, Grand   M-1863 (XII)
Traverse County

A.D. 1210±110   Moccasin Bluff, Berrien   M-1939 (XIII)
County

A.D. 1220±100   Bussinger Site, Saginaw   M-1796 (XII)
County
(Dates Late Woodland
burial)

A.D. 1290±100   Bussinger Site, Saginaw   M-1755 (XII)
County
(Dates Late Woodland
burial)

A.D. 1310±110   Skegemog Point, Grand   M-1864 (XII)
Traverse County

A.D. 1320±100   Verchave I Site, Macomb   M-1520 (XI)
County
(Probably dates Wolf Phase
of Younge Tradition)

A.D. 1320±75   Juntunen Site, Mackinaw   M-1188 (VIII)
County
(Ossuary ⚹2, Juntunen
Phase)

A.D. 1330±100   Juntunen Site, Mackinaw   M-1391 (IX)
County
(Juntunen Phase)

A.D. 1340±110   Backlund Site, Menominee   M-1891 (XIII)
County

A.D. 1350±75   Walters-Linsenman Earth-   M-779 (V)
work, Alcona County
(Date for Late Woodland
Earthwork in Carolinian-
Canadian Transition area
in Michigan)

A.D. 1450±100   Mikado Earthwork, Alcona   M-777 (V)
County
(Date for Late Woodland
Earthwork in Carolinian-
Canadian Transition area in
Michigan)

A.D. 1470±100   Boven Earthwork, Missaukee   M-1768 (XII)
County
(Dates Late Woodland

earthwork in the Carolinian-
Canadian transition area in
Michigan)

A.D. 1510±100	Lookout Site, Isle Royale (Copper mine)	M-1640 (XI)
A.D. 1540±100	Lookout Site, Isle Royale (Copper mine)	M-1276b (IX)
A.D. 1590±100	Moccasin Bluff, Berrien County	M-1936 (XIII)
A.D. 1600±100	Gibralter Site, Wayne County (Corn cobs from feature with no cultural material)	M-228 (I)
A.D. 1600±100	Fauver Site, Antrim County	M-1866 (XII)
A.D. 1620±100	Summer Island, Delta County (Protohistoric level)	M-2014 (XIII)
A.D. 1625±100	Lookout Site, Isle Royale (Copper mine)	M-1276a (IX)
A.D. 1675±75	Cedar Lake Dugout Canoe (Canoe manufactured with steel axe)	M-905 (V)
A.D. 1640±100	Moccasin Bluff, Berrien County	M-1935 (XIII)
A.D. 1680±75	Dumaw Creek Site, Oceana County (Quimby feels that this date should be older but within the standard deviation)	M-1070 (VI)
A.D. 1725 ±100	Fort Michilimackinac, Emmet County (Dates French occupation of the Fort)	M-1556 (X)
A.D. 1750±75	"The Griffin" (Date on ship at bottom of Mississagi Strait. Iron pin also recovered is pre-eighteenth century. Date is within one standard deviation of A.D. 1679 when the Griffin sank)	M-1145b (VIII)
A.D. 1950±200	Spoonville Site, Ottawa County (Corn cobs from feature)	M-1649 (XII)

REFERENCES

ANDERSON, SVEND TH.

1954 "A Late-Glacial Pollen Diagram from Southern Michigan, U.S.A." *Danmarks Geologiske Undersøgelse*, Vol. 2, No. 80, pp. 140–55. Copenhagen, Denmark.

ALLISON, APRIL L.

1966 "Analysis of Plant Remains from the Schmidt Site." *Michigan Archaeologist*, Vol. 12, No. 2, pp. 76–80. Ann Arbor.

BALD, F. CLEVER

1954 *Michigan in Four Centuries*. Harper and Brothers. New York.

BAERREIS, DAVID A. and REID A. BRYSON

1965 "Climatic Episodes and the Dating of the Mississippian Cultures." *The Wisconsin Archeologist*, Vol. 46, No. 4, pp. 203–20. Lake Mills.

BAERREIS, DAVID A., HIROSHI DAIFUKU, and JAMES E. LUNDSTED

1957 "The Burial Complex of the Reigh Site." *The Wisconsin Archeologist*, Vol. 38, No. 4, pp. 244–77. Lake Mills.

BASTIAN, TYLER J.

1963a "Archaeological Survey of Isle Royale National Park, Michigan, 1960–1962." Manuscript on file with the National Park Service.

1963b "Prehistoric Copper Mining in Isle Royale National Park, Michigan." M.A. dissertation, the University of Utah.

BENNINGHOFF, WILLIAM S.

1964 "The Prairie Peninsula as a Filter Barrier to Postglacial Plant Migration." *Proceedings of the Indiana Academy of Science*, Vol. 72, pp. 116–24. Bloomington.

BETTAREL, ROBERT and SIDNEY HARRISON

1962 "An Early Ossuary in Michigan." *Michigan Archaeologist*, Vol. 8, No. 4, pp. 37–42. Ann Arbor.

BIGONY, BEA

n.d. "Late Woodland Occupations of the Saginaw Valley." Unpublished manuscript in possession of the author.

BINFORD, LEWIS R.

1963a "The Hodges Site: A Late Archaic Burial Station." *Anthropological Papers, Museum of Anthropology, The University of Michigan*, No. 19, pp. 124–48. Ann Arbor.

1963b "The Pomranky Site: A Late Archaic Burial Station." *Anthropological Papers, Museum of Anthropology, The University of Michigan*, No. 19, pp. 149–92. Ann Arbor.

1963c "Red Ocher Caches from the Michigan Area: A Possible Case of Cultural Drift." *Southwestern Journal of Anthropology*, Vol. 19, No. 1, pp. 89–108. Albuquerque.

BINFORD, LEWIS R. and MARK L. PAPWORTH

1963 "The Eastport Site, Antrim County, Michigan." *Anthropological Pa-*

pers, *Museum of Anthropology, The University of Michigan,* No. 19, pp. 71–123. Ann Arbor.

BINFORD, LEWIS R. and GEORGE I. QUIMBY
1963 "Indian Sites and Chipped Stone Materials in the Northern Lake Michigan Area." *Fieldiana: Anthropology,* Vol. 36, No. 12, pp. 277–307. Chicago.

BLACK, M. J.
1963 "The Distribution and Archaeological Significance of the Marsh Elder, *Iva annua*." *Papers of the Michigan Academy of Science, Arts and Letters,* Vol. 48, pp. 541–47. Ann Arbor.

BLAKE, LEONARD and HUGH C. CUTLER
1963 "Plant Materials from the Bell Site, WN 9, Wisconsin." *The Wisconsin Archeologist,* Vol. 44, No. 1, pp. 70–71. Lake Mills.

BLUHM, ELAINE A. and ALLEN LISS
1961 "The Anker Site." *Illinois Archaeological Survey Bulletin* No. 3, pp. 138–61. Urbana.

BRIGGS, JEFFREY P.
1968 "An Archaeological Survey of the Pictured Rocks National Lakeshore." Manuscript on file with the National Park Service.

BROSE, DAVID S.
1966a "Excavations in Fort Mackinac, 1965." *Michigan Archaeologist,* Vol. 12, No. 2, pp. 88–101. Ann Arbor.

1966b "The Valley Sweets Site, 20 SA 24, Saginaw County, Michigan."

Michigan Archaeologist, Vol. 12, No. 1, pp. 1–21. Ann Arbor.

1967 "The Custer Road Dump Site: An Exercise in Victorian Archaeology." *Michigan Archaeologist,* Vol. 13, No. 2, pp. 37–128. Ann Arbor.

1968 "The Backlund Mound Group." *The Wisconsin Archeologist,* Vol. 49, No. 1, pp. 34–52. Lake Mills.

1969 "The Direct Historic Approach and Early Ethnic Groups in Michigan." *Ethnohistory.* In press.

n.d "The Archaeology of Summer Island: Changing Settlement. Systems in Northern Lake Michigan." *Anthropological Papers, Museum of Anthropology, The University of Michigan,* No. 41. In press.

BROSE, DAVID S. and JAMES E. FITTING
n.d. "An Archaeological Survey of Monroe County, Michigan." Unpublished manuscript in possession of the authors.

BROWN, CHARLES E. and M. F. HULBURT
1930 "Some Village and Camp Sites in Northern Michigan." *The Wisconsin Archeologist,* Vol. 9, No. 4, pp. 180–84. Milwaukee.

BROWN, JAMES A.
1964 "The Northeastern Extension of the Havana Tradition." *Illinois State Museum Scientific Papers,* Vol. 12, pp. 107–22. Springfield.

BROYLES, BETTYE
1966 "Excavations at the St. Albans Archaic Site, 1964–1965." *Eastern States Archeological Federation Bulletin,* No. 25. Berwyn.

REFERENCES

BRUNETT, FEL V.

1966 "An Archaeological Survey of the Manistee River Basin: Sharon, Michigan to Sherman, Michigan." *Michigan Archaeologist*, Vol. 12 No. 4, pp. 169–82. Ann Arbor.

1968 "The Fife Lake III Site: A Contribution to Paleoecology." Paper presented at the 72nd annual meeting at the Michigan Academy of Science, Arts and Letters.

BRUNNSCHWEILER, DIETER

1962 "Precipitation Regime in the Lower Peninsula of Michigan." *Papers of the Michigan Academy of Science, Arts and Letters*, Vol. 47, pp. 367–82. Ann Arbor.

BURT, WILLIAM H.

1957 *Mammals of the Great Lakes Region*. The University of Michigan Press. Ann Arbor.

BURT, WILLIAM H. and RICHARD P. GROSSENHEIDER

1964 *A Field Guide to the Mammals*. Houghton Mifflin Company. Boston.

BUTZER, KARL W.

1964 *Environment and Archaeology*. Aldine Publishing Company. Chicago.

BYERS, DOUGLAS S.

1959 "The Eastern Archaic: Some Problems and Hypotheses." *American Antiquity*, Vol. 24, No. 3, pp. 233–56. Salt Lake City.

CALDWELL, JOSEPH R.

1958 "Trend and Tradition in the Prehistory of the Eastern United States." *American Anthropological Association*, Memoirs No. 88. Menasha.

1964 "Interaction Spheres in Prehistory." *Illinois State Museum Scientific Papers*, Vol. 12, pp. 133–43. Springfield.

1966 *New Roads to Yesterday*. Basic Books. New York.

CAMPBELL, J. DUNCAN

1965 "Military Buttons: Long-lost Heralds of Fort Mackinac's Past." *Mackinac History*, Leaflet No. 7. Mackinac Island State Park Commission. Mackinac Island.

CHANG, K. C.

1967 *Rethinking Archaeology*. Random House. New York.

CLELAND, CHARLES E.

1963 "A Late Archaic Burial from Washtenaw County, Michigan." *Michigan Archaeologist*, Vol. 9, No. 3, pp. 41–44. Ann Arbor.

1965 "Barren Ground Caribou *Rangifer Arcticus* From an Early Man Site in Southeastern Michigan." *American Antiquity*, Vol. 30, No. 3, pp. 350–51. Salt Lake City.

1966 "The Prehistoric Animal Ecology and Ethnozoology of the Upper Great Lakes Region." *Anthropological Papers, Museum of Anthropology, University of Michigan*, No. 29. Ann Arbor.

1967 "Progress Report on National Science Foundation Grants Nos. GS-1026 and GS-1669." Report on file with the National Science Foundation and Michigan State University Museum.

1968 "The Food Remains of the Indian Point Site, Isle Royale, Michigan." *Michigan Archaeologist*, Vol. 14, No. 3–4, pp. 143–46. Ann Arbor.

n.d. "A Comparison of Faunal Remains From Refuse Pits of the French and British Occupations of Fort Michilimackinac, Emmet County, Michigan." In press.

CLELAND, CHARLES E. and JAMES E. FITTING
1968 "The Crisis of Identity: Theory in Historic Sites Archaeology." *The Conference on Historic Site Archaeology, Papers*, Vol. 2, Part 2, pp. 124–38.

CLELAND, CHARLES E. and JOAN KEARNEY
1966 "An Analysis of Animal Remains From the Schmidt Site." *Michigan Archaeologist*, Vol. 12, No. 2, pp. 81–83. Ann Arbor.

CLELAND, CHARLES E. and G. RICHARD PESKE
1968 "The Spider Cave." *Anthropological Papers, Museum of Anthropology, University of Michigan*, No. 34, pp. 20–60. Ann Arbor.

CORNELIUS, ELDON and HAROLD W. MOLL
1961 "The Walters-Linsenman Earthwork Site." *The Totem Pole*, Vol. 44, No. 9, pp. 1–9. Detroit.

CRANE, H. R.
1956 "Univeristy of Michigan Radiocarbon Dates I." *Science*, Vol. 124, No. 3224, pp. 664–72. Lancaster.

CRANE, H. R. and JAMES B. GRIFFIN
1958 "University of Michigan Radiocarbon Dates III." *Science*, Vol. 128, No. 332, pp. 1117–23. Lancaster.

1959 "University of Michigan Radiocarbon Dates IV." *American Journal of Science, Radiocarbon Supplement*, Vol. 1, pp. 173–99. New Haven.

1960 University of Michigan Radiocarbon Dates V. *American Journal of Science, Radiocarbon Supplement*, Vol. 2, pp. 31–48. New Haven.

1961 "University of Michigan Radiocarbon Dates VI." *Radiocarbon*, Vol. 3, pp. 105–25. New Haven.

1962 "University of Michigan Radiocarbon Dates VII." *Radiocarbon*. Vol. 4, pp. 183–203. New Haven.

1963 "University of Michigan Radiocarbon Dates VIII." *Radiocarbon*, Vol. 5, pp. 228–53. New Haven.

1964 "University of Michigan Radiocarbon Dates IX." *Radiocarbon*, Vol. 6, pp. 1–24. New Haven.

1965 "University of Michigan Radiocarbon Dates X." *Radiocarbon*, Vol. 7, pp. 123–52. New Haven.

1966 "University of Michigan Radiocarbon Dates XI." *Radiocarbon*, Vol. 8, pp. 256–85. New Haven.

1968 "University of Michigan Radiocarbon Dates XII." *Radiocarbon*, Vol. 10. In press.

1969 "University of Michigan Radiocarbon Dates XIII." *Radiocarbon*, Vol. 11. In press.

CRUMLEY, CAROLE L.
1966 "Field Geology of the Schmidt Site." *Michigan Archaeologist*, Vol. 12, No. 2, pp. 71–75. Ann Arbor.

1967 "The Kantzler Site: A Multi-component Manifestation of the Woodland Pattern." M.A. dissertation, The University of Calgary.

CUNNINGHAM, WILBUR M.
1948 "A Study of the Glacial Kame Culture in Michigan, Ohio, and Indiana." *Occasional Contribution from the Museum of Anthropology of the University of Michigan*, No. 12. Ann Arbor.

CUSHING, EDWARD J.
1965 "Problems in the Quaternary Phytogeography of the Great Lakes Region." In: *The Quaternary of the United States* edited by H. E. Wright, Jr., and David G. Frey. Princeton University Press. Princeton.

DAVIS, CHARLES M.
1936 "The High Plains of Michigan." *Papers of the Michigan Academy of Science, Arts and Letters*, Vol. 21, pp. 303–41. Ann Arbor.

1964 *Readings in the Geography of Michigan.* Ann Arbor Publishers. Ann Arbor.

DEETZ, JAMES
1967 *Invitation to Archaeology.* The Natural History Press. New York.

DEKIN, ALBERT A., JR.
1966 "A Fluted Point from Grand Traverse County." *Michigan Archaeologist*, Vol. 12, No. 1, pp. 35–36. Ann Arbor.

DEVISSCHER, JERRY
1957 "Three Macomb County 'Copper and Mica' Burials." *The Totem Pole*, Vol. 40, No. 4, unpaged. Detroit.

DRAGOO, DON W.
1959 "Archaic Hunters of the Upper Ohio Valley." *Carnegie Museum, Anthropological Series* No. 3, pp. 139–246. Pittsburgh.

1963 "Mounds for the Dead: An Analysis of the Adena Culture." *Annals of Carnegie Museum*, Vol. 37. Pittsburgh.

1964 "The Development of Adena Culture and Its Role in the Formation of Ohio Hopewell." *Illinois State Museum Scientific Papers*, Vol. 12, pp. 1–34. Springfield.

DRIER, ROY
1961 "The Michigan College of Mining and Technology Isle Royale Excavations, 1953, 1954." *Anthropological Papers, Museum of Anthropology, University of Michigan*, No. 17, pp. 1–7. Ann Arbor.

DUSTIN, FRED
1932a "Report on the Indian Earthworks in Ogemaw County, Michigan." *Cranbrook Institute of Science, Scientific Publications* No. 1. Bloomfield Hills.

1932b "A Summary of the Archaeology of Isle Royale, Michigan." *Papers of the Michigan Academy of Science, Arts and Letters*, Vol. 16, pp. 1–16. Ann Arbor.

1935 "A Study of the Bayport Chert." *Papers of the Michigan Academy of Science, Arts and Letters*, Vol. 20, pp. 465–75. Ann Arbor.

1957 "An Archaeological Reconnaissance of Isle Royale." *Michigan History*, Vol. 41, No. 1, pp. 1–34. Lansing.

1958 "Saginaw Valley Archaeology." *Michigan Archaeologist*, Vol. 14, Nos. 1–2. Ann Arbor.

EICHMEIER, A. H.

1964 "Climate of Michigan." In *Readings in the Geography of Michigan* edited by C. M. Davis, pp. 41–47. Ann Arbor Publishers. Ann Arbor.

FAULKNER, CHARLES H.

1960 "The Red Ocher Culture: An Early Burial Complex in Northern Indiana." *The Wisconsin Archeologist*, Vol. 41, No. 2, pp. 35–49. Lake Mills.

1964 "The Morrow Site: A Red Ocher Workship Site in the Kankakee Valley, Indiana." *The Wisconsin Archeologist*, Vol. 45, No. 4. pp. 151–56. Lake Mills.

FITTING, JAMES E.

1963 "An Early Post Fluted Point Tradition in Michigan: A Distributional Analysis." *Michigan Archaeologist*, Vol. 9, No. 2, pp. 21–24. Ann Arbor.

1963b "The Hi-Lo Site: A Late Paleo-Indian Site in Western Michigan." *The Wisconsin Archeologist*, Vol. 44, No. 2 pp. 87–96. Lake Mills.

1963c "The Welti Site: A Multi-component Site in Southeastern Michigan." *Michigan Archaeologist*, Vol. 9, No. 3, pp. 34–40. Ann Arbor.

1964a "Bifurcate-Stemmed Projectile Points in the Eastern United States." *American Antiquity*, Vol. 30, No. 1, pp. 92–94. Salt Lake City.

1964b "Ceramic Relationships of Four Late Woodland Sites in Northern Ohio." *The Wisconsin Archeologist*, Vol. 45, No. 4, pp. 160–75. Lake Mills.

1965a "The Archaeological Potential of Naomikong Point, 20 CH 2, Chippewa County, Michigan." Manuscript on file at the University of Michigan Museum of Anthropology.

1965b "Late Woodland Cultures of Southeastern Michigan." *Anthropological Papers, Museum of Anthropology, University of Michigan*, No. 24. Ann Arbor.

1965c "Middle Woodland Manifestations in Eastern Michigan." Paper presented at the 30th Annual Meeting of the Society for American Archaeology in Urbana, Illinois.

1965d "Observations on Paleo-Indian Adaptive and Settlement Patterns." *Michigan Archaeologist*, Vol. 11, Nos. 3–4, pp. 103–9. Ann Arbor.

1965e "A Quantitative Examination of Paleo-Indian Projectile Points in the Eastern United States." *Papers of the Michigan Academy of Science, Arts and Letters*, Vol. 50, pp. 365–71. Ann Arbor.

1965f "Report on the Radiometric Analysis of Animal and Fish Bones from the Feeheley Site (28 SA 128), Saginaw County, Michigan."

Anthropological Papers, Museum of Anthropology, University of Michigan, No. 25, pp. 45–52. Ann Arbor.

1966a "Archaeological Investigation of the Carolinian-Canadian Edge Area in Central Michigan." *Michigan Archaeologist,* Vol. 12, No. 4, pp. 143–50. Ann Arbor.

1966b "The Archaeology Explosion in Michigan." *Michigan History,* Vol. 50, No. 3, pp. 219–27. Lansing.

1966c "Radiocarbon Dating the Younge Tradition." *American Antiquity,* Vol. 31, No. 5, p. 738. Salt Lake City.

1966d "Report of Archaeological Field Work Carried Out on Lands Under the Supervision of the United States Department of Agriculture, Forest Service, Summer 1966." Unpublished manuscript on file with the United States Department of Agriculture Forest Service.

1967 "The Camp of the Careful Indian: An Upper Great Lakes Chipping Station." *Papers of the Michigan Academy of Science, Arts and Letters,* Vol. 52, pp. 237–42. Ann Arbor.

1968a "Northern Lake Michigan Lithic Industries." *Anthropological Papers, Museum of Anthropology, University of Michigan,* No. 33, pp. 116–33. Ann Arbor.

1968b "The Prehistory of Burnt Bluff." *Anthropological Papers, Museum of Anthropology, University of Michigan,* No. 34. Ann Arbor.

1968c "The Spring Creek Site, 20 MU 3, Muskegon County, Michigan." *Anthropological Papers, Museum of Anthropology, University of Michigan,* No. 32, pp. 1–78. Ann Arbor.

FITTING, JAMES E., DAVID S. BROSE, HENRY T. WRIGHT, and JAMES DINERSTEIN
1969 "The Goodwin-Gresham Site, 20 IA 8, Iosco County, Michigan." *The Wisconsin Archeologist,* Vol. 50. In press.

FITTING, JAMES E. and CHARLES E. CLELAND
1969 "Late Prehistoric Settlement Patterns in the Upper Great Lakes." *Ethnohistory,* Vol. 16. In press.

FITTING, JAMES E., JERRY DEVISSCHER, and EDWARD J. WAHLA
1966 "The Paleo-Indian Occupation of the Holcombe Beach." *Anthropological Papers, Museum of Anthropology, University of Michigan,* No. 27. Ann Arbor.

FITTING, JAMES E. and JOHN R. HALSEY
1966 "Rim Diameter and Vessel Size in Wayne Ware Vessels." *The Wisconsin Archeologist* Vol. 47, No. 4, pp. 208–11. Lake Mills.

FITTING, JAMES E. and SUSAN SASSÉ
1969 "The Hodges Site, 20 SA 130, Saginaw County, Michigan. *Michigan Archaeologist,* Vol. 15. In press.

FLANDERS, RICHARD E.
1963 "Marion Thick Pottery in Michigan." *The Coffinberry News Bulletin,* Vol. 10, No. 5, pp. 47–48. Grand Rapids.

1965a "A Comparison of Some Middle Woodland Materials from Illinois and Michigan." Ph.D. dissertation, The University of Michigan. University Microfilms. Ann Arbor.

1965b "Engraved Turtle Shells from the Norton Mounds." *Papers of the Michigan Academy of Science, Arts and Letters,* Vol. 50, pp. 361–64. Ann Arbor.

1968 "The Spoonville Mound Salvage." *The Coffinberry News Bulletin,* Vol. 15, No. 1, pp. 3–7. Grand Rapids.

FLANDERS, RICHARD E. and CHARLES E. CLELAND

1964 "The Use of Animal Remains in Hopewell Burial Mounds, Kent County, Michigan." *The Jack-Pine Warbler,* Vol. 42, No. 4, pp. 302–9. Kalamazoo.

FLANNERY, KENT V.

1967 Review of: *An Introduction to American Archaeology,* Vol. I, by Gordon R. Willey. *Scientific American,* Vol. 217, No. 2, pp. 119–21.

FOGEL, IRA L.

1963 "The Dispersal of Copper Artifacts in the Late Archaic Period of Prehistoric North America." *The Wisconsin Archeologist,* Vol. 44, No. 3, pp. 129–80. Lake Mills.

FONTANA, BERNARD L.

1965 "On the Meaning of Historic Sites Archaeology." *American Antiquity,* Vol. 31, No. 1, pp. 61–65. Salt Lake City.

FOWLER, MELVIN L.

1959 "Summary Report of Modoc Rock Shelter, 1952, 1953, 1955, 1956." *Illinois State Museum, Report of Investigations,* No. 8, Springfield.

FOX, GEORGE R.

1911 "The Ancient Copper Workings on Isle Royale." *The Wisconsin Archeologist,* Vol. 10 (old series), No. 2, pp. 73–100. Milwaukee.

FRANTZ, CHARLES

1967 "Excavation of Croton Dam Mound B (20 NE 112)." *Michigan Archaeologist,* Vol. 13, No. 1, pp. 11–12. Ann Arbor.

FUNK, ROBERT

1965 "The Sylvan Lake Rock Shelter (Clo 2) and Its Contribution to Knowledge of the Archaic Stage in Eastern New York: A Brief Report." *New York State Archaeological Association,* Bulletin 33, pp. 2–12. Buffalo.

GALL, PATRICIA L.

1967 "Excavation of Fort Pic, Ontario." *Ontario Archaeology,* No. 10, pp. 34–63. Guelph.

GIBSON, EDMOND P.

1959 "The Norton Mounds in Wyoming Township, Kent County, Michigan." *Michigan Archaeologist,* Vol. 5, No. 2, pp. 19–38. Ann Arbor.

GIBSON, E. P. and RUTH HERRICK

1957 "Spot Hunting in Missaukee County, Michigan." *Michigan Archaeologist,* Vol. 3, No. 4, pp. 94–96. Ann Arbor.

GIBSON, EDMOND P., DONALD PERU, and
RUTH HERRICK
1960 "The DeMarsac Trading Post."
Michigan Archaeologist, Vol. 6,
No. 3, pp. 42–53. Ann Arbor.

GOODRICH, CALVIN
1932 "The Mollusca of Michigan."
Michigan Handbook Series No. 5.
The University of Michigan Press.
Ann Arbor.

GREEN, AMOS R.
1964 "A Red Ocher Cache in Berrien
County, Michigan." *Michigan Archaeologist,* Vol. 10, No. 1, pp. 1–4.
Ann Arbor.

GREEN, AMOS R. and JAMES E. FITTING
1964 "A Turkey Tail Cache from
Southwestern Michigan." *Michigan
Archaeologist,* Vol. 10, No. 4, pp.
83–88. Ann Arbor.

GREENMAN, EMERSON F.
1927a "Michigan Mounds with Special
Reference to Two in Missaukee
County." *Papers of the Michigan
Academy of Science, Arts and
Letters,* Vol. 7, pp. 1–9. Ann Arbor.

1927b "The Earthwork Enclosures of
Michigan." Ph.D. dissertation, The
University of Michigan. Ann Arbor.

1935a "Excavation of the Reeve Village
Site, Lake County, Ohio." *The
Ohio State Archaeological and
Historical Quarterly,* Vol. 44, No.
1, pp. 2–64. Columbus.

1935b "Seven Prehistoric Sites in Northern Ohio." *The Ohio State Archaeological and Historical Quar-*

terly, Vol. 44, No. 2, pp. 220–37.
Columbus.

1937a "Two Prehistoric Villages Near
Cleveland, Ohio." *The Ohio State
Archaeological and Historical
Quarterly,* Vol. 46, No. 4, pp.
305–66. Columbus.

1937b "The Younge Site: An Archaeological Record from Michigan." *Ocsional Contributions (from the
Museum of Anthropology of the
University of Michigan, No. 6.*
Ann Arbor.

1939 "The Wolf and Furton Sites, Macomb County, Michigan." *Occasional Contributions from the
Museum of Anthropology of the
University of Michigan, No. 8.*
Ann Arbor.

1945 "The Hopewellian in the Detroit-Windsor Area." *Papers of the
Michigan Academy of Science,
Arts and Letters,* Vol. 30, pp.
457–64. Ann Arbor.

1948 "The Killarney Sequence and Its
Old World Connections." *Papers
of the Michigan Academy of
Science, Arts and Letters,* Vol.
32, pp. 313–32. Ann Arbor.

1957 "Rivière Au Vase Site." *Michigan Archaeologist,* Vol. 3, No. 1,
pp. 9–11. Ann Arbor.

1958 "An Early Historic Cemetery at
St. Ignace." *Michigan Archaeologist,* Vol. 4, No. 2, pp. 28–35.
Ann Arbor.

1961 "The Indians of Michigan." *John
M. Munson Michigan History
Fund Pamphlet Number 5.* Michigan Historical Commission. Lansing.

1966 "Chronology of Sites at Killarney, Canada." *American Antiquity*, Vol. 31, No. 4, pp. 540–51. Salt Lake City.

GREENMAN, E. F. and GEORGE M. STANLEY
1940 "A Geologically Dated Camp Site, Georgian Bay, Ontario." *American Antiquity*, Vol. 5, No. 3, pp. 194–99. Menasha.

1943 "An Early Industry on a Raised Beach near Killarney, Ontario." *American Antiquity*, Vol. 8, No. 3, pp. 260–65. Menasha.

GRIFFIN, JAMES B.
1937 "The Archaeological Remains of the Chiwere Sioux." *American Antiquity*, Vol. 2, No. 3, pp. 180–81. Menasha.

1948 "An Interpretation of the Glacial Kame Culture." *Occasional Contributions from the Museum of Anthropology of the University of Michigan*, No. 12, pp. 46–51. Ann Arbor.

1952 "Some Early and Middle Woodland Pottery Types in Illinois." *Illinois State Museum, Scientific Papers*, Vol. 5, pp. 93–129. Springfield.

1960 "Climatic Change: A Contributary Cause of the Growth and Decline of Northern Hopewellian Culture." *The Wisconsin Archeologist*, Vol. 41, No. 1, pp. 21–33. Lake Mills.

1961a "Lake Superior Copper and the Indians: Miscellaneous Studies of Great Lakes Prehistory." *Anthropological Papers, Museum of Anthropology, University of Michigan*, No. 17. Ann Arbor.

1961b "Some Correlations of Climatic and Culture Change in Eastern North American Prehistory." *Annals of the New York Academy of Sciences*, Vol. 95, pp. 710–17. New York.

1964 "The Northeastern Woodland Area." In: *Prehistoric Man in the New World*. Edited by Jesse D. Jennings and Edward Norbeck. The University of Chicago Press. Chicago.

1965a "Hopewell and the Dark Black Glass." *Michigan Archaeologist*, Vol. 11, Nos. 3–4, pp. 115–55. Ann Arbor.

1965b "Late Quaternary Prehistory in the Northeastern Woodlands." In: *The Quaternary of the United States* edited by H. E. Wright, Jr., and David G. Frey. Princeton University Press. Princeton, New Jersey.

1966 "The Calumet Ancient Pit." *Michigan Archaeologist*, Vol. 12, No. 3, pp. 130–33. Ann Arbor.

1967 "Eastern North American Archeology: A Summary." *Science*, Vol. 156, No. 3772, pp. 175–91. Lancaster.

GRIFFIN, LEONARD
1962 "An Interim Report on the Root Site." *Michigan Archaeologist*, Vol. 8, No. 2, pp. 10–15. Ann Arbor.

1963 "The Eisen Site: A New Concept in Amateur Archaeological Endeavor." *Michigan Archaeologist*, Vol. 9, No. 4, pp. 73–78. Ann Arbor.

REFERENCES

GUTHE, ALFRED
1967 "The Paleo-Indian of Tennessee."
*Eastern States Archaeological
Federation Bulletin*, No. 26. Berwyn.

HALL, ROBERT L.
1967 "Those Late Corn Dates: Isotopic
Fractionation as a Source of Error
in Carbon-14 Dates." *Michigan
Archaeologist*, Vol. 13, No. 4, pp.
171–80. Ann Arbor.

HALSEY, JOHN R.
1966a "Additional Hopewell Engraved
Turtle Shells from Michigan."
*Papers of the Michigan Academy
of Science, Arts and Letters*, Vol.
51, pp. 389–98. Ann Arbor.

1966b "Radiocarbon Dates From Archaeological Sites of Old Copper
and Related Cultures in the Great
Lakes Area." *Artifacts*, Vol. 4, No.
4, pp. 1–11. Northville.

1967 "The Bussinger Site." *Saginaw
Valley Archaeologist*, Vol. 4, No.
2, unpaged. Saginaw.

1968 "The Springwells Mound Group
of Wayne County, Michigan."
*Anthropological Papers, Museum
of Anthropology, University of
Michigan*, No. 32, pp. 79–159.
Ann Arbor.

n.d. "The Historic Occupation of Two
Sites in the Saginaw Valley."
Manuscript in possession of the
author.

HARRISON, SIDNEY
1966 "The Schmidt Site (20 SA 192),
Saginaw County, Michigan."
Michigan Archaeologist, Vol. 12,
No. 2, pp. 49–70. Ann Arbor.

HAYNES, C. VANCE, JR.
1964 "Fluted Projectile Points: Their
Age and Dispersion." *Science*,
Vol. 145, No. 3639, pp. 1408–13.
Washington, D.C.

1966 "Elephant-hunting in North America." *Scientific American*, Vol.
214, No. 6, pp. 104–12. New York.

HEIZER, ROBERT F. (editor)
1962 *A Guide to Archaeological Field
Methods*. The National Press.
Palo Alto.

HERRICK, RUTH
1958 "A Report on the Ada Site, Kent
County, Michigan." *Michigan Archaeologist*, Vol. 4, No. 1, pp.
1–27. Ann Arbor.

HIMMLER, FRANK and GEORGE C. DELONG
1963 "The Mesothermal Climates of
Michigan. 1951–1960." *Papers of
the Michigan Academy of Science,
Arts and Letters*, Vol. 48, pp.
413–17. Ann Arbor.

HINSDALE, W. B.
1924 "The Missaukee Preserve and
Rifle River Forts." *Papers of the
Michigan Academy of Science,
Arts and Letters*, Vol. 4, pp. 1–14.
Ann Arbor.

1925 "Primitive Man in Michigan."
Michigan Handbook Series, No. 1.
Ann Arbor.

1929 "Indian Mounds, West Twin Lake,
Montmorency County, Michigan."
*Papers of the Michigan Academy
of Science, Arts and Letters*, Vol.
10, pp. 91–100. Ann Arbor.

1930 "Reports of Archaeological Field
Work in the Summer of 1928 in

Montmorency, Newaygo, and Lake Counties, Michigan." *Papers of the Michigan Academy of Science, Arts and Letters,* Vol. 12, pp. 127–35. Ann Arbor.

1932 "Distribution of the Aboriginal Population of Michigan." *Occasional Contributions from the Museum of Anthropology of the University of Michigan,* No. 2. Ann Arbor.

HINSDALE, W. B. and EMERSON F. GREENMAN

1936 "Perforated Indian Crania in Michigan." *Occasional Contributions from the Museum of Anthropology of the University of Michigan,* No. 5. Ann Arbor.

HOGG, VICTOR and BIRT DARLING

1959 "An Indian Burial of the Historic Period." *Michigan Archaeologist,* Vol. 5, No. 1, pp. 3–7. Ann Arbor.

HOLMQUIST, CARL E.

1946 "The Fort Wayne Mound." *Aboriginal Research Club Bulletin.* Detroit.

HOUGH, JACK L.

1958 *Geology of the Great Lakes.* University of Illinois Press. Urbana.

1963 "The Prehistoric Great Lakes of North America." *American Scientist,* Vol. 51, No. 1, pp. 84–109. Easton.

HUBBS, CARL L. and KARL F. LAGER

1947 "Fishes of the Great Lakes Region." *Cranbrook Institute of Science Bulletin* No. 26. Bloomfield Hills.

JANZEN, DONALD R.

1968a "The Naomikong Point Site and the Dimensions of Laurel in the Lake Superior Region." *Anthropological Papers, Museum of Anthropology, University of Michigan,* No. 36. Ann Arbor.

1968b "Survey and Excavations at Burnt Bluff in 1965." *Anthropological Papers, Museum of Anthropology, University of Michigan,* No. 34, pp. 61–94. Ann Arbor.

JELINEK, ARTHUR J.

1958 "A Late Historic Burial from Berrien County." *Michigan Archaeologist,* Vol. 4, No. 3, pp. 48–51. Ann Arbor.

1965 "The Upper Paleolithic Revolution and the Peopling of the New World." *Michigan Archaeologist,* Vol. 11, Nos. 3–4, pp. 85–88. Ann Arbor.

n.d. "Man's Role in the Extinction of Pleistocene Faunas." Paper presented at the 1965 INQUA Symposium on Pleistocene Extinction. Boulder, Colorado.

JOHNSON, RICHARD B.

1968 "The Archaeology of the Serpent Mound Site." *Royal Ontario Museum, Division of Art and Archaeology, Occasional Paper* No. 10. Toronto.

JONES, VOLNEY

1966 "Two Textiles from the Valley Sweet Site." *Michigan Archaeologist,* Vol. 12, No. 1, pp. 22–24. Ann Arbor.

257

REFERENCES

JURY, WILFRID and ELSIE JURY
1952 "The Burley Site." *University of Western Ontario, Museum of Archaeology and Pioneer Life, Bulletin* No. 9. London.

KAPLAN, DAVID
1960 "The Law of Cultural Dominance." In: *Evolution and Culture* edited by Marshall D. Sahlins and Elman R. Service, pp. 69–92. The University of Michigan Press. Ann Arbor.

KELLEY, R. W. and W. R. FARRAND
1967 "The Glacial Lakes Around Michigan." *Michigan Geological Survey, Bulletin* No. 4. Lansing.

KENNEDY, CLYDE C.
1966 "Preliminary Report on the Morrison's Island-6 Site." *National Museum of Canada, Bulletin* No. 206, pp. 100–24. Ottawa.

KENYON, WALTER A.
1959 "The Inverhuron Site." *Royal Ontario Museum, Art and Archaeology Division, Occasional Paper* No. 1. Toronto.

KIDD, KENNETH E.
1953 "Excavation and Identification of a Huron Ossuary." *American Antiquity*, Vol. 18, No. 4, pp. 359–79. Salt Lake City.

1954 "A Woodland Site near Chatham, Ontario." *Transactions of the Royal Canadian Institute*, Vol. 30, Pt. 2, pp. 141–78. Ottawa.

KINIETZ, W. VERNON
1940 "The Indians of the Western Great Lakes: 1615–1760." *Occa-*

sional Contributions from The Museum of Anthropology of the University of Michigan, No. 10. Ann Arbor.

KRIEGER, ALEX D.
1964 "Early Man in the New World." In: *Prehistoric Man in the New World* edited by Jesse D. Jennings and Edward Norbeck. The University of Chicago Press. Chicago.

LEACH, M. L.
1885 "Ancient Forts in Ogemaw County, Michigan." *Annual Report, Smithsonian Institution,* 1884. Washington, D.C.

LEE, THOMAS E.
1953 "A Preliminary Report on the Sheguiandah Site." *National Museum of Canada, Bulletin* No. 128, pp. 58–67. Ottawa.

1954 "The First Sheguiandah Expedition, Manitoulin Island, Ontario." *American Antiquity*, Vol. 20, No. 2, pp. 101–11. Salt Lake City.

1955 "The Second Sheguiandah Expedition, Manitoulin Island, Ontario." *American Antiquity*, Vol. 21, No. 1, pp. 63–71. Salt Lake City.

1956 "The Position and Meaning of a Radiocarbon Sample from the Sheguiandah Site, Ontario." *American Antiquity*, Vol. 22, No. 1, p. 79. Salt Lake City.

1957 "The Antiquity of the Sheguiandah Site." *Canadian Field Naturalist*, Vol. 71, No. 3, pp. 117–37. Ottawa.

1958a "Appendix to the Boys and Barrie Sites." *Ontario Archaeological*

Society Publication No. 4, pp. 40–41. Toronto.

1958b "The Parker Earthwork, Corunna, Ontario." *Pennsylvania Archaeologist*, Vol. 28, No. 1, pp. 3–30. Honesdale.

1960 "The Lucas Site, Inverhuron, Ontario." *National Museum of Canada, Bulletin* No. 167, pp. 29–65. Ottawa.

1964 "Sheguiandah: Workshop or Habitation?" *Anthropological Journal of Canada*, Vol. 2, No. 3, pp. 16–24. Ottawa.

1965 "A Point Peninsula Site, Manitoulin Island, Lake Huron." *Bulletin of the Massachusetts Archaeological Society*, Vol. 26, No. 2, pp. 19–30. Attleboro.

LEONARDY, FRANK C. (editor)
1966 *Domebo: A Paleo-Indian Mammoth Kill in the Prairie-Plains.* Great Plains Historical Association. Lawton.

LEWIS, T. M. N. and M. K. LEWIS
1961 *Eva, An Archaic Site.* University of Tennessee Press. Knoxville.

LOSEY, TIMOTHY C.
1967 "Toft Lake Village Site." *Michigan Archaeologist*, Vol. 13, No. 3, pp. 129–34. Ann Arbor.

1968 "Excavation of the Mallon Mound B (20 NE 31)." *Michigan Archaeologist*, Vol. 14, Nos. 3–4, pp. 135–42. Ann Arbor.

LUGTHART, DOUGLAS
1968 "The Burnt Bluff Rock Paintings." *Anthropological Papers, Museum of Anthropology, University of Michigan*, No. 34, pp. 98–115. Ann Arbor.

MACDONALD, GEORGE F.
1966 "Excavations at Debert, Nova Scotia; A Study of Lithic Technology and Settlement Patterns at Fluted Point Site." Ph.D. dissertation, Yale University. New Haven.

1967 Review of *The Paleo-Indian Occupation of the Holcombe Beach* by James E. Fitting, Jerry DeVisscher, and Edward J. Wahla. *American Antiquity*, Vol. 32, No. 3, pp. 407–8. Salt Lake City.

MCKERN, W. C.
1945 "Preliminary Report on the Upper Mississippi Phase in Wisconsin." *Milwaukee Public Museum Bulletin*, Vol. 16, No. 3, pp. 109–285. Milwaukee.

MCNAMEE, ROBERT L.
1930 "The Surface Waters of Michigan's Hydrology and Qualitative Characteristics and Purification for Public Use." *Engineering Research Bulletin* No. 16. Department of Engineering Research, The University of Michigan. Ann Arbor.

MACNEISH, RICHARD S.
1952 "A Possible Early Site in the Thunder Bay District, Ontario." *National Museum of Canada, Bulletin* No. 126, pp. 23–47. Ottawa.

1958 "An Introduction to the Archaeology of Southeast Manitoba."

National Museum of Canada, Bulletin No. 157. Ottawa.

1964 "Ancient Mesoamerican Civilization." *Science,* Vol. 143, No. 3606, pp. 531–37. Lancaster.

MCPHERRON, ALAN
1967 "The Juntunen Site and the Late Woodland Prehistory of the Upper Great Lakes Area." *Anthropological Papers, Museum of Anthropology, University of Michigan,* No. 30. Ann Arbor.

MARTIN, HELEN M.
1964 "The First Four Billion Years." In: *Readings in Michigan Geography,* edited by Charles M. Davis, pp. 7–27. Ann Arbor.

MARTIN, PAUL S.
1958 "Pleistocene Ecology and Biogeography of North America." In: *Zoogeography,* edited by C. D. Hubbs. American Association for the Advancement of Science.

MASON, CAROL IRWIN and RONALD J. MASON
1961 "The Age of the Old Copper Culture." *The Wisconsin Archeologist,* Vol. 42, No. 4, pp. 143–55. Lake Mills.

MASON, PHILIP P.
1964 *Detroit, Fort Lernoult, and the American Revolution.* Wayne State University Press. Detroit.

MASON, RONALD J.
1958 "Late Pleistocene Geochronology and the Paleo-Indian Penetration of the Lower Michigan Peninsula." *Anthropological Papers, Mu-*

seum of Anthropology, University of Michigan, No. 11. Ann Arbor.

1962 "The Paleo-Indian Tradition in Eastern North America." *Current Anthropology,* Vol. 3, No. 3, pp. 227–78. Chicago.

1963 "Two Late Paleo-Indian Complexes in Wisconsin." *The Wisconsin Archeologist,* Vol. 44, No. 4, pp. 199–211. Lake Mills.

1965 "Wisconsin Middle Woodland Toggle Head Harpoons." *Michigan Archaeologist,* Vol. 11, Nos. 3–4, pp. 156–64. Ann Arbor.

1966 "Two Stratified Sites on the Door Peninsula." *Anthropological Papers, Museum of Anthropology, University of Michigan,* No. 26. Ann Arbor.

1967 "The North Bay Component at the Porte Des Morts Site, Door County." *The Wisconsin Archeologist,* Vol. 48, No. 4, pp. 267–344. Lake Mills.

MASON, RONALD J. and CAROL IRWIN
1960 "An Eden-Scottsbluff Burial in Northeastern Wisconsin." *American Antiquity,* Vol. 26, No. 1, pp. 43–57. Salt Lake City.

MAXWELL, MOREAU S.
1964 "Indian Artifacts at Fort Michilimackinac, Mackinac City, Michigan." *Michigan Archaeologist,* Vol. 10, No. 2, pp. 23–30. Ann Arbor.

MAXWELL, MOREAU S. and LEWIS H. BINFORD
1961 "Excavations at Fort Michilimackinac, Mackinac City, Michigan, 1959 Season." *Michigan State Uni-*

versity Museum, Cultural Series,
Vol. 1, No. 1. East Lansing.

MAY, GEORGE S.
1964a "A Brief History of Michigan."
Chronicle, Vol. 1, No. 4, pp. 2–8.
Lansing.

1964b "The Mess at Mackinac or, No
more Sagamity for me, thank you!"
Mackinac History, Leaflet No. 5,
Mackinac Island State Park Commission. Mackinac Island.

1964c "The Reconstruction of the
Church of Ste. Anne de Michili-
mackinac." *Mackinac History,*
Leaflet No. 6, Mackinac Island
State Park Commission. Mackinac
Island.

MEIGHAN, CLEMENT W.
1966 *Archaeology: An Introduction.*
Chandler Publishing Company.
San Francisco.

MILLER, GEORGE L.
1967 "Activities in Historical Archaeology in 1967: Michigan." *Historical
Archaeology in 1967,* p. 84. Philadelphia.

MOLL, HAROLD W., NORMAN G. MOLL, and
ELDON S. CORNELIUS
1958 "Earthwork Enclosures in Ogemaw, Missaukee, and Alcona
Counties." *The Totem Pole,* Vol.
41, No. 3. Detroit.

MORSE, DAN F.
1967 "The Robinson Site and the Shell
Mound Archaic Culture in the
Middle South." Ph.D. dissertation,
The University of Michigan. Uni-
versity Microfilms. Ann Arbor.

MORSE, DAN F. and PHYLLIS A. MORSE
1964 "1962 Excavations at the Morse
Site: A Red Ocher Cemetery in
the Illinois Valley." *The Wisconsin Archeologist,* Vol. 45, No. 2,
pp. 79–98. Lake Mills.

MUNSON, PATRICK J.
1966 "The Sheets Site: A Late Archaic-
Early Woodland Occupation in
West-Central Illinois." *Michigan
Archaeologist,* Vol. 12, No. 3, pp.
111–20. Ann Arbor.

MUNSON, PATRICK J. and ROBERT L. HALL
1966 "An Early Woodland Radiocarbon
Date from Illinois." *Michigan Archaeologist,* Vol. 12, No. 2, pp. 85–
87. Ann Arbor.

PAPWORTH, MARK L.
1958 "Artifacts from the Kimmel Site,
Berrien Springs." *Michigan Archaeologist,* Vol. 4, No. 3, pp.
51–56. Ann Arbor.

1967 "Cultural Tradition in the Lake
Forest Region During the Late
High-Water Stages of the Post
Glacial Great Lakes." Ph.D. dis-
sertation, The University of Mich-
igan. University Microfilms. Ann
Arbor.

PAPWORTH, MARK L. and L. R. BINFORD
1962 "A Guide to Archaeological Excavations." *Southwestern Lore,*
Vol. 28, No. 1, pp. 1–24. Boulder.

PARMALEE, PAUL W.
1963 "Vertebrate Remains from the Bell
Site, Winnebago County, Wiscon-
sin." *The Wisconsin Archeologist,*
Vol. 44, No. 1, pp. 58–69. Lake
Mills.

REFERENCES

PERU, DONALD V.

1965 "The Distribution of Fluted Points in the Counties of Kent and Allegan, Michigan." *Michigan Archaeologist*, Vol. 11, No. 1, pp. 1–8. Ann Arbor.

1967 "The Distribution of Fluted Points in Cass County, Michigan." *Michigan Archaeologist*, Vol. 13, No. 3, pp. 137–46. Ann Arbor.

PESKE, G. RICHARD

1963 "Argillite of Michigan: A Preliminary Projectile Point Classification and Temporal Placement from Surface Materials." *Papers of the Michigan Academy of Science, Arts and Letters*, Vol. 48, pp. 557–66. Ann Arbor.

1967 "Review of the Dumaw Creek Site by George I. Quimby." *Michigan Archaeologist*, Vol. 13, No. 4, pp. 208–9. Ann Arbor.

PETERSEN, EUGENE T.

1963a "Clay Pipes: A Footnote to Mackinac History." *Mackinac History*, Leaflet No. 1, Mackinac Island State Park Commission. Mackinac Island.

1963b "Some 18th Century Clay Pipes found at Mackinac." *Michigan Archaeologist*, Vol. 9, No. 1, pp. 1–6. Ann Arbor.

1964 *Gentlemen on the Frontier: A Pictorial Record of the Culture of Michilimackinac*. Mackinac Island State Park Commission. Mackinac Island.

PILLING, ARNOLD R.

1960 "Wayne State University, Museum of Anthropology, Report to Dean Victor A. Rapport for the Period between May 1, 1959, and May 1, 1960." Mimeograph Manuscript, Wayne State University Museum of Anthropology. Detroit.

1961a "Six Archaeological Sites in the Detroit Area. Part I." *Michigan Archaeologist*, Vol. 7, No. 3, pp. 13–30. Ann Arbor.

1961b "Six Archaeological Sites in the Detroit Area. Part II." *Michigan Archaeologist*, Vol. 7, No. 4, pp. 33–54. Ann Arbor.

1961c "Wayne State University, Museum of Anthropology, Report to Acting Dean J. Russell Bright for the Period between May 1, 1960, and April 30, 1961." Mimeographed Manuscript, Wayne State University Museum of Anthropology. Detroit.

1965 "Wayne State University, Museum of Anthropology, Report to Dean Martin Stearns for the Period between May 1, 1962, and April 30, 1963." Mimeographed Manuscript, Wayne State University Museum of Anthropology. Detroit.

1966 "Wayne State University, Museum of Anthropology, Report to Dean Martin Stearns for the Period between May 1, 1963, and April 30, 1964." Mimeographed Manuscript, Wayne State University Museum of Anthropology. Detroit.

1967a "Nineteenth Century Glazed Ceramics in Michigan and Elsewhere: Part I: Rationale." *The Coffinberry News Bulletin*, Vol. 14, No. 5, pp. 49–55. Grand Rapids.

1967b "Nineteenth Century Glazed Ceramics in Michigan and Elsewhere: Part II: Archaeological Evidence." *The Coffinberry News Bulletin*, Vol. 14, No. 6, pp. 60–71. Grand Rapids.

POTZGER, J. E.

1946 "Phytosociology of the Primeval Forest in Central-Northern Wisconsin and Upper Michigan, and a Brief Post-Glacial History of the Lake Forest Formation." *Ecological Monographs*, Vol. 16, No. 3, pp. 211–50. Durham.

PRAHL, EARL J.

1966 "The Muskegon River Survey: 1965 and 1966." *Michigan Archaeologist*, Vol. 12, No. 4, pp. 183–212. Ann Arbor.

1968 "Archaeological Investigations in the Muskegon River Valley." Unpublished manuscript in possession of the author.

PRUFER, OLAF H.

1963 "The McConnell Site: A Late Paleo-Indian Workshop in Coshocton County, Ohio." *Cleveland Museum of Natural History, Scientific Publications*, Vol. 2, No. 1. Cleveland.

1964a "The Hopewell Complex of Ohio." *Illinois State Museum Scientific Papers*, Vol. 12, pp. 35–84. Springfield.

1964b "The Hopewell Cult." *Scientific American*, Vol. 211, No. 6, pp. 90–102. Washington, D.C.

1965 "The McGraw Site: A Study in Hopewellian Dynamics." *The Cleveland Museum of Natural History, Scientific Publications*, Vol. 4, No. 1. Cleveland.

QUIMBY, GEORGE I.

1937 "Notes on Indian Trade Silver Ornaments in Michigan." *Papers of the Michigan Academy of Science, Arts and Letters*, Vol. 22, pp. 15–24. Ann Arbor.

1938 "Dated Indian Burials in Michigan." *Papers of the Michigan Academy of Science, Arts and Letters*, Vol. 23, pp. 63–72. Ann Arbor.

1939a "Aboriginal Camp Sites on Isle Royale, Michigan." *American Antiquity*, Vol. 4, No. 3, pp. 215–23. Menasha.

1939b "European Trade Articles as Chronological Indicators for the Archaeology of the Historic Period in Michigan." *Papers of the Michigan Academy of Science, Arts and Letters*, Vol. 24, pp. 25–31. Ann Arbor.

1941a "The Goodall Focus: An Analysis of Ten Hopewellian Components in Michigan and Indiana." *Indiana Historical Society Prehistory Research Series*, Vol. 2, No. 2, 63–161. Indianapolis.

1941b "Hopewellian Pottery Types in Michigan." *Papers of the Michigan Academy of Science, Arts and Letters*, Vol. 26, pp. 489–95. Ann Arbor.

1943 "The Ceramic Sequence Within the Goodall Focus." *Papers of the Michigan Academy of Science, Arts and Letters*, Vol. 28, pp. 543–48. Ann Arbor.

1944 "Some New Data on the Goodall Focus." *Papers of the Michigan Academy of Science, Arts and Letters,* Vol. 29, pp. 419–23. Ann Arbor.

1952 "Archeology of the Upper Great Lakes Area." In: *Archeology of Eastern United States* edited by James B. Griffin. The University of Chicago Press. Chicago.

1954 "Culture Areas Before Kroeber." *American Antiquity,* Vol. 19, No. 4, pp. 317–31. Salt Lake City.

1958 "Fluted Points and Geochronology of the Lake Michigan Basin." *American Antiquity,* Vol. 23, No. 3, pp. 247–54. Salt Lake City.

1959 "Lanceolate Points and Fossil Beaches in the Upper Great Lakes Region." *American Antiquity,* Vol. 24, No. 4, pp. 424–26. Salt Lake City.

1960 *Indian Life in the Upper Great Lakes.* The University of Chicago Press. Chicago.

1962a "Alexander Henry in Central Michigan, 1763–1764." *Michigan History,* Vol. 46, No. 3, pp. 193–200. Lansing.

1962b "A Year with a Chippewa Family, 1763–1764." *Ethnohistory,* Vol. 9, No. 3, pp. 217–39. Bloomington.

1963a "The Gros Cap Cemetery Site in Mackinaw County, Michigan." *Michigan Archaeologist,* Vol. 9, No. 4, pp. 50–57. Ann Arbor.

1963b "Late Period Copper Artifacts in the Upper Great Lakes Region." *The Wisconsin Archeologist,* Vol. 44, No. 4, pp. 193–98. Lake Mills.

1964 "The Stony Lake Mounds, Oceana County, Michigan." *Michigan Archaeologist,* Vol. 10, No. 1, pp. 11–16. Ann Arbor.

1965a "An Indian Earthwork in Muskegon County, Michigan." *Michigan Archaeologist,* Vol. 11, Nos. 3–4, pp. 165–69. Ann Arbor.

1965b "Exploring an Underwater Indian Site." *Chicago Natural History Museum Bulletin,* Vol. 36, No. 8, pp. 2–4. Chicago.

1965c "The Voyage of the Griffin: 1679." *Michigan History,* Vol. 49, No. 2, pp. 97–107. Lansing.

1966a "The Dumaw Creek Site: A Seventeenth Century Prehistoric Indian Village and Cemetery in Oceana County, Michigan." *Fieldiana: Anthropology,* Vol. 56, No. 1, pp. 1–91. Chicago.

1966b *Indian Culture and European Trade Goods.* The University of Wisconsin Press. Madison.

QUIMBY, GEORGE I. and JAMES B. GRIFFIN
1961 "Various Finds of Copper and Stone Artifacts in the Lake Superior Basin." *Anthropological Papers, Museum of Anthropology, University of Michigan,* No. 17, pp. 103–17. Ann Arbor.

QUIMBY, GEORGE I. and ALBERT C. SPAULDING
1957 "The Old Copper Culture and the Keweenaw Waterway." *Fieldiana: Anthropology,* Vol. 36, No. 8, pp. 189–201. Chicago.

RIDLEY, FRANK

1952 "Huron and Lalonde Occupations of Ontario." *American Antiquity*, Vol. 17, No. 3, pp. 197–210. Salt Lake City.

1954 "The Frank Bay Site, Lake Nipissing, Ontario." *American Antiquity*, Vol. 20, No. 1, pp. 40–50. Salt Lake City.

1958 "The Boys and Barrie Sites." *Ontario Archaeological Society Publication* No. 4, pp. 18–42. Toronto.

RITCHIE, WILLIAM A.

1932 "The Lamoka Lake Site." *Researches and Transactions of the New York State Archaeological Association*, Vol. 7, No. 2. Rochester.

1955 "Recent Discoveries Suggesting an Early Woodland Burial Cult in the Northeast." *New York State Museum and Science Service*, Circular No. 40. Albany.

1961 "Typology and Nomenclature of New York Projectile Points." *New York State Museum and Science Service Bulletin* No. 384. Albany.

1965 *The Archaeology of New York State*. The Natural History Press. New York.

RITCHIE, WILLIAM A. and DON W. DRAGOO

1960 "The Eastern Dispersal of Adena." *New York State Museum and Science Service Bulletin* No. 379. Albany.

RITCHIE, WILLIAM A. and RICHARD S. MACNEISH

1949 "The Pre-Iroquoian Pottery of New York State." *American Antiquity*, Vol. 15, No. 2, pp. 97–124. Menasha.

RITZENTHALER, ROBERT E.

1957 "The Osceola Site, an 'Old Copper' Site Near Potosi, Wisconsin." *The Wisconsin Archeologist*, Vol. 38, No. 4, pp. 186–203. Lake Mills.

1957 "The Old Copper Culture of Wisconsin." *The Wisconsin Archeologist*, Vol. 38, No. 4, pp. 183–332. Lake Mills.

RITZENTHALER, ROBERT E., NEIL OSTBERG, KIRK WHALEY, MARTIN GREENWALD, PENNY FOUST, ERNEST SCHUG, WARREN L. WITTRY, HEINZ MEYER, and EDWARD LUNDSTED.

1957 "Reigh Site Report—Number 3." *The Wisconsin Archeologist*, Vol. 38, No. 4, pp. 278–310. Lake Mills.

RITZENTHALER, ROBERT E. and GEORGE I. QUIMBY

1962 "The Red Ocher Culture of the Upper Great Lakes and Adjacent Areas." *Fieldiana: Anthropology*, Vol. 36, No. 11, pp. 243–75. Chicago.

RITZENTHALER, ROBERT E. and WARREN L. WITTRY

1957 "The Oconto Site—An Old Copper Manifestation." *The Wisconsin Archeologist*, Vol. 38, No. 4, pp. 222–43. Lake Mills.

ROBERTS, FRANK H. H., JR.

1935 "A Folsom Complex: Preliminary Report on the Lindenmeier Site in Northern Colorado." *Smithsonian Miscellaneous Collections*, Vol. 94, No. 4. Washington.

REFERENCES

ROLINGSON, MARTHA ANN and DOUGLAS W. SCHWARTZ

1966 "Late Paleo-Indian and Early Archaic Manifestations in Western Kentucky." *University of Kentucky Studies in Anthropology*, No. 3, University of Kentucky Press. Lexington.

ROOSA, WILLIAM B.

1963 "Some Michigan Fluted Point Sites and Types." *Michigan Archaeologist*, Vol. 9, No. 3, pp. 44–48. Ann Arbor.

1965 "Some Great Lakes Fluted Point Types." *Michigan Archaeologist*, Vol. 11, Nos. 3-4, pp. 89–102. Ann Arbor.

1966 "The Warner School Site." *Michigan Archaeologist*, Vol. 12, No. 1, pp. 25–34. Ann Arbor.

RUPP, DAVID W.

n.d. "Four Historic Sites From the North Shore of Lake Michigan." Manuscript in possession of the author.

SERVICE, ELMAN R.

1966 *The Hunters*. Prentice-Hall. Englewood Cliffs.

SHANE, ORRIN C. III

1967 "The Leimbach Site: An Early Woodland Village in Lorain County, Ohio." In: *Studies in Ohio Archaeology* edited by Olaf H. Prufer and Douglas H. McKenzie, pp. 98–120. Western Reserve Press. Cleveland.

SHAY, CREIGHTON T.

1963 "A Preliminary Report on the Itasca Bison Site." *The Minnesota Academy of Science*, Vol. 31, No. 1, pp. 24–27. Minneapolis.

SMITH, HARLAN I.

1901 "The Saginaw Valley Collection." *American Museum of Natural History, Supplement to American Museum Journal*, Vol. 1, No. 12, pp. 1–24. New York.

SMITH, ROBERT

1966 "Excavating the Hopewell Burial Mounds at Grand Rapids." *Research News*, Vol. 16, No. 8, pp. 1–12. Ann Arbor.

SPETH, JOHN D.

1966 "The Whorely Earthwork." *Michigan Archaeologist*. Vol. 12, No. 4, pp. 211–27. Ann Arbor.

n.d. "Geology of the Schultz Site." Manuscript on file at the University of Michigan, Museum of Anthropology.

STRUEVER, STUART

1964 "The Hopewell Interaction Sphere in Riverine-Western Great Lakes Culture History." *Illinois State Museum Scientific Papers*, Vol. 12, 85–106. Springfield.

1965 "Middle Woodland Culture History in the Great Lakes Riverine Area." *American Antiquity*, Vol. 31, No. 2 pp. 211–23. Salt Lake City.

STOLTMAN, JAMES B.

1962 "A Proposed Method for Systematizing the Modal Analysis of Pottery and Its Application to the Laurel Focus." Unpublished M.A. thesis, University of Minnesota.

1966 Review of *The Paleo-Indian Occupation of the Holcombe Beach* by James E. Fitting, Jerry DeVisscher, and Edward J. Wahla. *The Wisconsin Archeologist*, Vol. 47, No. 4, pp. 214–18. Lake Mills.

STONE, LYLE M.

1965 "Preliminary Report—1965, Archaeological Investigation of Fort Michilimackinac, Mackinac City, Michigan." Mimeograph manuscript, Michigan State University Museum. East Lansing.

1966 "Preliminary Report—1966, Archaeological Investigation of Fort Michilimackinac, Mackinac City, Michigan." Mimeograph manuscript, Michigan State University Museum. East Lansing.

1967a "Archaeology at Fort Michilimackinac." *Mackinac History*, Leaflet No. 9. Mackinac Island State Park Commission. Mackinac Island.

1967b "Michigan State University Museum Field Activities, Summer 1967." *Michigan Archaeological Society Newsletter*, No. 674, pp. 27–28. Northville.

TAGGART, DAVID W.

1967 "Seasonal Patterns in Settlement, Subsistence, and Industries in the Saginaw Late Archaic." *Michigan Archaeologist*, Vol. 13, No. 4, pp. 153–70. Ann Arbor.

n.d. "The Feeheley Site: A Late Archaic Site in the Saginaw Valley." Manuscript on file at the Museum of Anthropology, the University of Michigan. Ann Arbor.

TAYLOR, WALTER W.

1948 "A Study of Archaeology." *American Anthropological Association Memoir Number 69*. Menasha.

THOMAS, CYRUS

1894 "Report on the Mound Explorations of the Bureau of American Ethnology." *12th Annual Report of the Bureau of American Ethnology, 1890–91*. Washington, D.C.

TOOKER, ELISABETH

1964 "An Ethnography of the Huron Indians, 1615–1649." *Bureau of American Ethnology Bulletin* No. 190. Washington, D.C.

UECK, LOUIS P.

1963 "A Report of a Discovery of Cache Blades in Berrien County, Michigan." *Michigan Archaeologist*, Vol. 9, No. 2, p. 20. Ann Arbor

VANDERWAL, RONALD L.

1966 "Fort Michilimackinac: Dating Techniques." *Michigan Archaeologist*, Vol. 12, No. 3, pp. 121–29. Ann Arbor.

WAKEFIELD, FRANCIS

1966 "The Elusive Mascoutens." *Michigan History*, Vol. 50, No. 3, pp. 228–34. Lansing.

WALKER, IAIN C.

1967 "Historic Archaeology—Methods and Principles." *Historical Archaeology 1967*, pp. 23–33. Philadelphia.

WATSON, PATTY JO and
RICHARD A. YARNELL

1966 "Archaeological and Paleoethnobotanical Investigations in Salts Cave, Mammoth Cave National Park, Kentucky." *American Antiquity*, Vol. 31, No. 6, pp. 842–49. Salt Lake City.

WAYNE, WILLIAM J. and
JAMES H. ZUMBERGE
1965 "Pleistocene Geology of Indiana and Michigan." In: *The Quaternary of the United States* edited by H. E. Wright, Jr., and David G. Frey. Princeton University Press. Princeton.

WEAVER, JOHN E. and
FREDERIC CLEMENTS
1938 *Plant Ecology.* McGraw-Hill. New York.

WHITE, LESLIE A.
1959 *The Evolution of Culture.* McGraw-Hill. New York.

WHITEHEAD, DONALD R.
1965 "Palynology and Pleistocene Phytogeography of Eastern North America." In: *The Quaternary of the United States* edited by H. E. Wright, Jr., and David G. Frey. Princeton University Press. Princeton.

WHITESIDE, E. P., I. F. SCHNEIDER, and
R. L. COOK.
1956 "Soils of Michigan." *Agricultural Experiment Station, Michigan State University, Special Bulletin* 402. East Lansing.

WILFORD, LLOYD A.
1941 "A Tentative Classification of the Pre-historic Cultures of Minnesota." *American Antiquity*, Vol. 6, No. 3, pp. 231–49. Menasha.

1950a "The Prehistoric Indians of Minnesota: Some Mounds of the Rainy River Aspect." *Minnesota History*, Vol. 31, No. 3, pp. 163–71. Minneapolis.

1950b "The Prehistoric Indians of Minnesota: The McKinstry Mounds of the Rainy River Aspect." *Minnesota History*, Vol. 31, No. 4, pp. 231–37. Minneapolis.

WILLEY, GORDON R.
1966 *An Introduction to American Archaeology:* Vol. 1. Prentice-Hall. Englewood Cliffs.

WILLEY, GORDON R. and PHILLIP PHILLIPS
1958 *Method and Theory in American Archaeology.* The University of Chicago Press. Chicago.

WILLIAMS, STEPHEN and
JAMES E. STOLTMAN
1965 "An Outline of Southeastern United States Prehistory with Particular Emphasis on the Paleo-Indian Era." In: *The Quaternary of the United States* edited by H. E. Wright, Jr., and David G. Frey. Princeton University Press. Princeton.

WINSLOW, M. L.
1926 "Revised Checklist of Michigan Mollusca." *Occasional Papers, Museum of Zoology, University of Michigan*, No. 181. Ann Arbor.

WINTERS, HOWARD D.
1963 "An Archaeological Survey of the Wabash Valley in Illinois." *Illinois State Museum, Report of Investigations*, No. 10. Springfield.

WISSLER, CLARK

1917 "The New Archaeology." *The American Museum Journal,* Vol. 17, No. 2, pp. 100–1. New York.

WITTHOFT, JOHN

1952 "A Paleo-Indian Site in Eastern Pennsylvania: An Early Hunting Culture." *Proceedings of the American Philosophical Society,* Vol. 96, No. 4, pp. 464–95. Philadelphia.

WITTRY, WARREN

1959 "The Raddatz Rockshelter, SK5, Wisconsin." *The Wisconsin Archeologist,* Vol. 40, No. 2, pp. 33–69. Lake Mills.

1963 "The Bell Site, WN9, An Early Historic Fox Village." *The Wisconsin Archeologist,* Vol. 44, No. 1, pp. 1–57. Lake Mills.

WITTRY, WARREN L. and
ROBERT E. RITZENTHALER

1957 "The Old Copper Complex: An Archaic Manifestation in Wisconsin." *The Wisconsin Archeologist,* Vol. 38, No. 4, pp. 311–20. Lake Mills.

WOBST, MARTIN H.

1965 "The Stone School Site: A Discussion of a Large Surface Collection from Washtenaw County, Michigan." *Michigan Archaeologist,* Vol. 11, No. 2, pp. 59–70. Ann Arbor.

1968 "The Butterfield Site, 20 BY 29, Bay County, Michigan." *Anthropological Papers, Museum of Anthropology, University of Michigan,* No. 32, pp. 173–275. Ann Arbor.

WORMINGTON, H. M.

1957 "Ancient Man in North America." *Denver Museum of Natural History, Popular Series,* No. 4. Denver.

WRIGHT, GARY A.

1966 "Eastern Edge Survey: 1965 Season." *Michigan Archaeologist,* Vol. 12, No. 4, pp. 151–68. Ann Arbor.

1967 "Some Aspects of Early and Mid-seventeenth Century Exchange Networks in the Western Great Lakes." *Michigan Archaeologist,* Vol. 13, No. 4, pp. 181–97. Ann Arbor.

n.d. "Historic Floods of the Saginaw Valley." Manuscript on file at the University of Michigan Museum of Anthropology.

WRIGHT, HENRY T.

1964 "A Transitional Archaic Campsite at Green Point (20 SA 1)." *Michigan Archaeologist,* Vol. 10, No. 1, pp. 17–22. Ann Arbor.

WRIGHT, HENRY T. and
RICHARD E. MORLAN

1964 "The Hart Site: A Dustin Fishing Camp on the Shiawassee Embayment." *Michigan Archaeologist,* Vol. 10, No. 3, pp. 49–53. Ann Arbor.

WRIGHT, HENRY T. and
WILLIAM B. ROOSA

1966 "The Barnes Site: A Fluted Point Assemblage From the Great

Lakes Region." *American Antiquity,* Vol. 31, No. 6, pp. 850–60. Salt Lake City.

WRIGHT, J. V.
- 1965 "A Regional Examination of Ojibway Culture History." *Anthropologica,* Vol. 7, No. 2, 189–227. Montreal.

1966 "The Ontario Iroquois Tradition." *National Museum of Canada, Bulletin* No. 210. Ottawa.

1967 "The Laurel Tradition and the Middle Woodland Period." *National Museum of Canada, Bulletin* No. 217. Ottawa.

WRIGHT, J. V. and J. E. ANDERSON
1963 "The Donaldson Site." *National Museum of Canada, Bulletin* No. 184. Ottawa.

YARNELL, RICHARD ASA
1964 "Aboriginal Relationship Between Culture and Plant Life in the Upper Great Lakes Region." *Anthropological Papers, Museum of Anthropology, University of Michigan,* No. 23. Ann Arbor.

1965 "Early Woodland Plant Remains and the Question of Cultivation." *Florida Anthropologist,* Vol. 18, No. 2, pp. 77–82. Gainsville.

ZIM, HERBERT S. and
ALEXANDER C. MARTIN
1965 *Trees: A Guide to Familiar American Trees.* Golden Press. New York.

ZIM, HERBERT S. and HOBART M. SMITH
1964 *Reptiles and Amphibians: A Guide to Familiar American Species.* Golden Press. New York.

ZIMMERMAN, DALE A. and
JOSSELYN VAN TYNE
1959 "A Distributional Check List of Birds of Michigan." *Occasional Papers of the Museum of Zoology, University of Michigan,* No. 608. Ann Arbor.

INDEX